# SOURCES

## Notable Selections in *American Government*

### SECOND EDITION

S0-AXJ-118

*About
the
Editor*

**MITCHEL GERBER** is a professor of political science at Southeast Missouri State University, where he has been teaching American government and political theory courses for many years. As an undergraduate, he attended Brooklyn College, where he earned his B.A. in political science in 1973. He received his M.A. in political science from Columbia University in 1975 and his Ph.D. in political science from New York University in 1982. He is the coauthor of several teaching publications for American government courses, including *State and Local Government Supplement* (HarperCollins, 1991), as well as the accompanying instructional and test bank materials. He has published several instructor-module articles in *Tocqueville in the Classroom: An Educator's Resource* (C-SPAN, 1997). He has published many scholarly articles in political philosophy and American foreign policy for Salem Press. In addition, he has published numerous articles in English political theory in *Hanoverian Britain: An Encyclopedia* (Garland Press, 1997). He has served as Faculty Consultant and Reader to the College Board's Advanced Placement Reading in Government and Politics and as National Governing Board Member of the National Social Science Association. He has published numerous scholarly articles and papers in the *National Social Science Journal* and other journals. He has presented numerous scholarly papers at various professional national and regional annual meetings, including the Northeastern Political Science Association, the Southern Political Science Association, the Missouri Political Science Association, and the Illinois Political Studies Conference. He has been awarded many National Endowment for the Humanities Fellowships, several Southeast Missouri State University research grants, and several C-SPAN in the Classroom Seminar for Professors grants. In addition to American government, he teaches American political thought, modern political thought, contemporary political theory, the Holocaust, ancient Greek and Roman political thought, and American foreign policy. As a participant in the Missouri-London program, he was a visiting professor at Imperial College in London, England, in spring 1996. In recognition of his exemplary scholarly performance, Dr. Gerber received the Outstanding Scholarship Honors Award of the College of Liberal Arts, Southeast Missouri State University. In recognition of his exemplary teaching performance, Dr. Gerber received both the *Exempli Gratia,* the Most Exemplary Honors Faculty, and the Outstanding Teaching Honors Award of the College of Liberal Arts, Southeast Missouri State University. He was also selected for membership in the Southeast Missouri State University chapter of the Honor Society of Phi Kappa Phi. He was nominated and selected for inclusion in the fourth and fifth editions of *Who's Who Among America's Teachers: The Best Teachers in America Selected by the Best Students* and the 26th edition of *Who's Who in the Midwest.* His current scholarly research interests include French Jewish resistance in the Holocaust, American interest group theory, the American executive branch as an articulator of common interests, and classical Greek political thought. He is a member of many professional organizations, including the American Political Science Association, the Academy of Political Science, the Midwest Political Science Association, the National Social Science Association, the North American Conference on British Studies, and the Association of Integrative Studies. He is also the founder and faculty adviser to the Political Theory Club, a Southeast Missouri State University student organization.

# SOURCES

## Notable Selections in
## *American Government*

### SECOND EDITION

**Edited by**
**MITCHEL GERBER**
*Southeast Missouri State University*

*Dushkin/McGraw-Hill*

*A Division of The McGraw-Hill Companies*

This book is dedicated to the loving memory of my grandparents, Morris and Yetta Slossman; my nurturing parents, Stanley and Jeanette Gerber; my loving wife, Barbara; and my exceptional son, Yale Philip, my future.

Manufactured in the United States of America

Second Edition

123456789FGRFGR32109

**Library of Congress Cataloging-in-Publication Data**
    Main entry under title:
    Sources: notable selections in American government/edited by Mitchel Gerber.—2nd ed.
    Includes bibliographical references and index.
    1. United States—Politics and government. I. Gerber, Mitchel, *comp.*

973
95-83883

0-07-303185-2

 Printed on Recycled Paper

# Preface

$P$olitics is dynamic! The study of American government entails a critical analysis of human political behavior within the context of diverse institutions and processes. The fundamental objective of political scientists who study American government is to acquire a broad understanding of American politics through descriptions, explanations, and evaluations of often complex political phenomena. Political scientists systematically attempt to make intelligible those governmental activities that often seem remote, obscure, inaccessible, complicated, and unintelligible to most citizens. Observations, explanations, and analyses of American politics also offer ample opportunities for evaluative critiques of how the government ought to function.

American government has been explored through a rich diversity of perspectives, approaches, and interpretations. Political scientists who focus on the American government do not conform to one particular mode of inquiry; they follow different paths of investigation and use distinct tools, techniques, and methods of analysis. *Sources: Notable Selections in American Government* brings together 41 selections from classic primary sources that have dramatically impacted upon the ways in which people think about American government and politics. Many of these selections have not only influenced contemporary understanding of complex institutions, processes, and behavior, but they have directly shaped and altered the critical political decisions and acts of a multitude of policymakers and political practitioners (e.g., voters, lobbyists, legislators, judges, presidents, bureaucrats, and political party leaders). The literature included here reflects the efforts of numerous American government scholars to intertwine insights and interpretations of the political system with invaluable predictions and suggestions for reform.

The selections chosen for this book cover a wide range of substantive topics and incorporate an extensive variation of the most notable perspectives found within the study of American government. For example, the selections in Part 1 provide exposure to the distinct world views and interpretative analyses of the classical liberal theoretical tradition (founded by John Locke in the seventeenth century), the democratic-egalitarian tradition (represented by Alexis de Tocqueville), and the communitarian school of American political thought (articulated by Robert N. Bellah and Amitai Etzioni) in reference to the cultural, ideological, and intellectual context of the American political system. This format is consistent throughout this book, as alternative scholarly views and explanatory models are offered to the critically active reader for her or his interpretation and assessment.

I consistently focused on several criteria as I engaged in the design of this volume of readings. I wanted students to become enthusiastic in their discovery of topics that have been of profound significance to the evolution of the American government. In order to fulfill this objective, I initially collected over 100 potential sources for inclusion in this book. I subsequently weeded out those selections that replicated other sources as well as those that were not as readable as others. Second, I chose selections that would inspire the reader to seriously think about key issues, topics, themes, theories, concepts, problems, and solutions pertinent to the literature on American government. A good number of selections provide examples of how concrete political behavior or policies are linked to abstract political concepts and political theories. Third, I incorporated sources that were rich in their depth and scope of coverage of the American political system. The selections range from a source that was written in the seventeenth century to many sources from the twentieth century; from English and French theorists to many American analysts; and from sources that are highly laudatory of the American government to sources that suggest major political, social, and economic reforms. Although most of the sources were written by traditional political scientists who primarily study American government, several of the selections were authored by nonpolitical scientists (e.g., sociologists, historians, and mass media communication experts). Fourth, I wanted the selections to articulate as lucidly as possible the multiple tensions endemic to the American political system and the continuous struggle of ethnic and racial minorities and women to fully achieve their democratic rights. Finally, and perhaps most important, a fundamental objective of this book is to enable students to develop some proficiency in their critical thinking, critical reading, reasoning, and analysis skills, in addition to acquiring general information on the American government. I firmly believe that the selections chosen are provocative, challenging, and readable.

*Organization of the book.*     The selections are organized topically around the major areas of study within American government. Part 1 includes selections on the intellectual and ideological context of American government; Part 2, the constitutional framework and the Federalist system; Part 3, civil liberties and civil rights; Part 4, democratic participatory organizations; Part 5, democratic participatory processes; Part 6, institutions of national government; and Part 7, dimensions of public policy. The selections are further organized into 15 chapters that correspond to most introductory American government textbooks and therefore offer ample opportunities for students to read and analyze the original sources of topics as they are presented throughout the course. Selections can be assigned as independent entities or in sets of readings, depending upon the preference of the instructor. Each selection is introduced by a brief headnote that establishes the selection's significance to the literature and offers pertinent biographical information on the author.

*On the Internet.*     Each part in this book is preceded by an *On the Internet* page. This page provides a list of relevant Internet site addresses from which students can begin further research on the topics presented in this volume.

*Suggestions for reading the selections.* I strongly recommend that students first read the introductory headnotes before reading the selections, as they provide substantial commentary on significant issues in American government and elaborate on the general context from which the text is derived. The reader should be sensitive to the direct impact and influence of context (e.g., conventional and scholarly language usage of the period and the cultural, intellectual, social, economic, demographic, and political forces) upon the content of each particular selection. In this regard, the reader should remember the evolutionary nature of language. Each selection is culturally and socially derived and consequently reflects the language used in the period. For example, many of the older selections use the masculine pronouns *he* and *him* to refer to all humans regardless of gender. Contemporary authors are much more sensitive to such gender-biased language.

Be aggressive in your reading, analysis, and interpretation of each selection. Do not hesitate to raise both explanatory and evaluative questions. For example, when reading a selection on interest groups or political parties, ask yourself what factors might help to explain their behavior and whether or not such behavior is legitimate.

*A word to the instructor.* An *Instructor's Manual With Test Questions* (multiple-choice and essay) is available through the publisher for instructors using *Sources: Notable Selections in American Government* in the classroom.

*Sources: Notable Selections in American Government* is only one title in the Sources series. If you are interested in seeing the table of contents for any of the other titles, please visit the Sources Web site at `http://www.dushkin.com/sources/`.

*Acknowledgments.* I was very enthusiastic when Mimi Egan, former publisher for the Sources series, communicated with me about developing the first edition of *Sources: Notable Selections in American Government.* For many years I have strongly desired to be able to offer my students the opportunity to read original sources in American government that have had a profound impact upon the dialogue over the objectives of the American government and the actual shaping of the political system. Mimi provided endless encouragement, outstanding counsel, and enthusiastic support to me during the entire publication process.

My colleagues in the political science department offered many helpful insights on this project. In particular, I want to thank Theresa Haug, graduate assistant of the political science department, for her feedback and constructive commentary on the URL sites of this edition. And the Southeast Missouri State University library staff was very helpful in locating many resources. I also want to take this opportunity to thank David Dean, former list manager, and Ted Knight, current list manager of the Sources series, for their support and assistance, and David Brackley, senior developmental editor, for his work on this project. My wife, Barbara, proofread the original manuscript and provided enthusiastic support and encouragement throughout the process of completing this book. And my son, Yale Philip, was always patient in my delays to play catch with him as I worked on *Sources: Notable Selections in American Government,* 2d ed.

Special thanks go to those who reviewed the first edition of *Sources* and responded with specific suggestions for the second edition:

Scott McLean
Quinnipiac College

Scott Waalkes
Calvin College

Forrest Nielsen
University of Wyoming

Geoff Wells
Wayland Baptist University

Valerie Simms
Northeastern Illinois University

I would greatly appreciate any commentary from readers about this book or suggested sources for consideration for future revisions. I encourage you to write to me in care of Sources, Dushkin/McGraw-Hill, Sluice Dock, Guilford, CT 06437.

Mitchel Gerber
Southeast Missouri State University

# Contents

"A first step is to reexamine that peculiarly American institution, federalism. The current confusion of responsibilities between federal and state government is undermining confidence in government and impeding the implementation of policies needed to restore a healthy economy. Sorting out the roles more clearly could break the logjam, help both levels function more effectively, and improve both domestic and foreign policy."

"If all mankind minus one were of one opinion, and only one person were of the contrary opinion, mankind would be no more justified in silencing that one person, than he, if he had the power, would be justified in silencing mankind."

"Not only these precedents but also reason and reflection require us to recognize that in our adversary system of criminal justice, any person haled into court, who is too poor to hire a lawyer, cannot be assured a fair trial unless counsel is provided for him. This seems to us to be an obvious truth."

"In this atmosphere the state-imposed character of an invocation and benediction by clergy selected by the school combine to make the prayer a state-sanctioned religious exercise in which the student was left with no alternative but to submit."

"This right of privacy, whether it be founded in the Fourteenth Amendment's concept of personal liberty and restrictions upon state action, as we feel it is, or, as the District Court determined, in the Ninth Amendment's reservation of rights to the people, is broad enough to encompass a woman's decision whether or not to terminate her pregnancy."

# The Intellectual and Ideological Context of American Government

# On the Internet . . .

## Sites appropriate to Part One

This site provides links to a wealth of Internet resources for research in American studies, including agriculture and rural development, government, and race and ethnicity.

http://www.georgetown.edu/crossroads/asw/

This C-SPAN tribute to Alexis de Tocqueville offers links to biographical information on Tocqueville, modern references to Tocqueville, some passages from his book *Democracy in America,* other sources of information on Tocqueville, and highlights of the tour that the C-SPAN School Bus took in 1997–1998, in which Tocqueville's 1831 visit to America with his friend Gustave de Beaumont was traced.

http://www.c-span.org/alexis/

The Communitarian Network is a coalition of individuals and organizations who have come together to shore up the moral, social, and political environment. A nonsectarian, nonpartisan, international association, this group believes that individual liberties depend upon the bolstering of the foundations of civil society: families, schools, and neighborhoods.

http://www.gwu.edu/~ccps/

# CHAPTER 1 American Political Culture and Ideology

*(handwritten note: 1787 Constitution)*

## 1.1 JOHN LOCKE

# *The Second Treatise*

John Locke (1632–1704), the English political philosopher and the founder of classical liberalism, articulated a political theory of natural rights, individualism, private property ownership, constitutionalism, and limited government that greatly influenced the framers' design of the U.S. Constitution. Classical liberalism emphasizes human rationality, the legitimacy of a constitutional limited government, the central significance of natural rights (particularly property rights), the freedom of the individual, and the critical need of privacy. In particular, the idea of legitimate government based upon a social contract and the consent of individuals inspired James Madison and the other framers.

In the following selection, excerpted from his classic work *Two Treatises of Government* (1690), Locke expounds on his political theory, which was derived from his interpretation of human nature in the context of a state of nature. He depicts the state of nature as a primitive society without government, in which individuals are relatively equal, free, independent, rational agents primarily motivated by the pursuit to acquire private property. The law of nature is defined as an objective moral principle obliging individuals to preserve their own lives and property and not to harm the lives and property of others. The universal applicability of this normative principle of natural rights directly influenced Thomas Jefferson's writing of the Declaration of Independence.

3

Locke's classical republican justification of citizen rebellion against a tyrannical government also influenced the development of the American political system. Locke's radical political theory has remained a dominant element of American political ideology.

**Key Concept:** the political ideology of classical liberalism

# OF THE STATE OF NATURE

To understand Political Power right, and derive it from its Original, we must consider what State all Men are naturally in, and that is, a *State of the perfect Freedom* to order their Actions, and dispose of their Possessions, and Persons as they think fit, within the bounds of the Law of Nature, without asking leave, or depending upon the Will of any other Man.

A *State* also *of Equality*, wherein all the Power and Jurisdiction is reciprocal, no one having more than another: there being nothing more evident, than that Creatures of the same species and rank promiscuously born to all the same advantages of Nature, and the use of the same faculties, should also be equal one amongst another with Subordination or Subjection, unless the Lord and Master of them all, should by any manifest Declaration of his Will set one above another, and confer on him by an evident and clear appointment an undoubted Right to Dominion and Sovereignty....

But though this be a *State of Liberty*, yet it is *not a State of Licence*, though Man in that State have an uncontroleable Liberty, to dispose of his Person or Possessions, yet he has not Liberty to destroy himself, or so much as any Creature in his Possession, but where some nobler use, than its bare Preservation calls for it. The *State of Nature* has a Law of Nature to govern it, which obliges every one: And Reason, which is that Law, teaches all Mankind, who will but consult it, that being all equal and independent, no one ought to harm another in his Life, Health, Liberty, or Possessions.... And being furnished with like Faculties, sharing all in one Community of Nature, there cannot be supposed any such *Subordination* among us, that may Authorize us to destroy one another, as if we were made for one another's uses, as the inferior ranks of Creatures are for ours. Every one as he is *bound to preserve himself*, and not to quit his Station wilfully; so by the like reason when his own Preservation comes not in competition, ought he, as much as he can, *to preserve the rest of Mankind*, and may not unless it be to do Justice on an Offender, take away, or impair the life, or what tends to the Preservation of the Life, the Liberty, Health, Limb or Goods of another.

And that all Men may be restrained from invading others Rights, and from doing hurt to one another, and the Law of Nature be observed, which willeth the Peace and *Preservation of all Mankind*, the *Execution* of the Law of Nature is in that State, put into every Mans hands, whereby every one has a right to punish the transgressors of that Law to such a Degree, as may hinder its Violation. For the *Law of Nature* would, as all other Laws that concern Men in this World, be in vain, if there were no body that in the State of Nature, had a *Power to Execute* that Law, and thereby preserve the innocent and restrain offenders, and if any one in the State of Nature may punish another, for any evil he has done, every one may do so. For in that *State of perfect Equality,* where naturally there is no superiority or jurisdiction of one, over another, what any may do in Prosecution of that Law, every one must needs have a Right to do.

And thus in the State of Nature, *one Man comes by a Power over another;* but yet no Absolute or Arbitrary Power, to use a Criminal when he has got him in his hands, according to the passionate heats, or boundless extravagancy of his own Will, but only to retribute to him, so far as calm reason and conscience dictates, what is proportionate to his Transgression, which is so much as may serve for *Reparation* and *Restraint....*

Every Offence that can be committed in the State of Nature, may in the State of Nature be also punished, equally, and as far forth as it may, in a Common-wealth; for though it would be besides my present purpose, to enter here into the particulars of the Law of Nature, or its *measures of punishment;* yet, it is certain there is such a Law, and that too, as intelligible and plain to a rational Creature, and a Studier of that Law, as the positive Laws of Common-wealths, nay possibly plainer....

# OF THE ENDS OF POLITICAL SOCIETY AND GOVERNMENT

If Man in the State of Nature be so free, as has been said; If he be absolute Lord of his own Person and Possessions, equal to the greatest, and subject to no Body, why will he part with his Freedom? Why will he give up this Empire, and subject himself to the Dominion and Controul of any other Power? To which 'tis obvious to Answer, that though in the state of Nature he hath such a right, yet the Enjoyment of it is very uncertain, and constantly exposed to the Invasion of others. For all being Kings as much as he, every Man his Equal, and the greater part no strict Observers of Equity and Justice, the enjoyment of the property he has in this state is very unsafe, very unsecure. This makes him willing to quit this Condition, which however free, is full of fears and continual dangers: And 'tis not without reason, that he seeks out, and is willing to joyn in Society with others who are already united, or have a mind to unite for the mutual *Preservation* of their Lives, Liberties and Estates, which I call by the general Name, *Property.*

The great and *chief end* therefore, of Mens uniting into Common-wealths, and putting themselves under Government, *is the Preservation of their Property.* To which in the state of Nature there are many things wanting.

*First,* There wants an *establish'd,* settled, known *Law,* received and allowed by common consent to be the Standard of Right and Wrong, and the common measure to decide all Controversies between them. For though the Law of Nature be plain and intelligible to all rational Creatures; yet Men being biassed by their Interest, as well as ignorant for want of study of it, are not apt to allow of it as a Law binding to them in the application of it to their particular Cases.

*[handwritten: - Men do what they want to do]*

*Men
can not judge
their peers*

*In society
you do whatever
it takes to make you
happy*

*Secondly,* In the State of Nature there wants *a known and indifferent Judge,* with Authority to determine all differences according to the established Law. For every one in that state being both Judge and Executioner of the Law of Nature, Men being partial to themselves, Passion and Revenge is very apt to carry them too far, and with too much heat, in their own Cases; as well as negligence, and unconcernedness, to make them too remiss, in other Mens.

*Thirdly,* In the State of Nature there often wants *Power* to back and support the Sentence when right, and to *give* it due *Execution.* They who by any Injustice offended, will seldom fail, where they are able, by force to make good their Injustice: such resistance many times makes the punishment dangerous, and frequently destructive, to those who attempt it.

Thus Mankind, notwithstanding all the Priviledges of the State of Nature, being but in an ill condition, while they remain in it, are quickly driven into Society. Hence it comes to pass, that we seldom find any number of Men live any time together in this State. The inconveniencies, that they are therein exposed to, by the irregular and uncertain exercise of the Power every Man has of punishing the transgressions of others, make them take Sanctuary under the establish'd Laws of Government, and therein seek *the preservation of their Property.* 'Tis this makes them so willingly give up every one his single power of punishing to be exercised by such alone as shall be appointed to it amongst them; and by such Rules as the Community, or those authorised by them to that purpose, shall agree on. And in this we have the original *right and rise* of both *the Legislative and Executive Power,* as well as of the Governments and Societies themselves.

For in the State of Nature, to omit the liberty he has of innocent Delights, a Man has two Powers.

The first is to do whatsoever he thinks fit for the preservation of himself and others within the permission of the *Law of Nature:* by which Law common to them all, he and all the rest of *Mankind are one Community,* make up one Society distinct from all other Creatures. And were it not for the corruption, and vitiousness of degenerate Men, there would be no need of any other; no necessity that Men should separate from this great and natural Community, and by positive agreements combine into smaller and divided associations.

The other power a Man has in the State of Nature, is the *power to punish the Crimes* committed against that Law. Both these he gives up, when he joyns in a private, if I may so call it, or particular Political Society, and incorporates into any Common-wealth, separate from the rest of Mankind.

The first *Power, viz. of doing whatsoever he thought fit for the Preservation of himself,* and the rest of Mankind, *he gives up* to be regulated by Laws made by the Society, so far forth as the preservation of himself, and the rest of that Society shall require; which Laws of the Society in many things confine the liberty he had by the Law of Nature.

*Secondly,* the *Power of punishing* he wholly *gives up,* and engages his natural force, (which he might before imploy in the Execution of the Law of Nature, by his own single Authority, as he thought fit) to assist the Executive Power of the Society, as the Law thereof shall require. For being now in a new State, wherein he is to enjoy many Conveniencies, from the labour, assistance, and society of others in the same Community, as well as protection from its whole strength; he is to part also with as much of his natural liberty in providing for himself, as the good, prosperity, and safety of the Society shall require: which is not only necessary, but just; since the other Members of the Society do the like.

But though Men when they enter into Society, give up the Equality, Liberty, and Executive Power they had in the State of Nature, into the hands of the Society, to be so far disposed of by the Legislative, as the good of the Society shall require; yet it being only with an intention in every one the better to preserve himself his Liberty and Property; (For no rational Creature can be supposed to change his condition with an intention to be worse) the power of the Society, or *Legislative* constituted by them, *can never be suppos'd to extend farther than the common good;* but is obliged to secure every ones Property by providing against those three defects above-mentioned, that made the State of Nature so unsafe and uneasie. And so whoever has the Legislative or Supream Power of any Common-wealth, is bound to govern by establish'd *standing Laws,* promulgated and known to the People, and not by Extemporary Decrees; by *indifferent* and upright *Judges,* who are to decide Controversies by those Laws; And to imploy the force of the Community at home, *only in the Execution of such Laws,* or abroad to prevent or redress Foreign Injuries, and secure the Community from Inroads and Invasion. And all this to be directed to no other *end,* but the *Peace, Safety,* and *publick good* of the People....

## OF THE EXTENT OF THE LEGISLATIVE POWER

The great end of Mens entering into Society, being the enjoyment of their Properties in Peace and Safety, and the great instrument and means of that being the Laws establish'd in that Society; the *first and fundamental positive Law* of all Common-wealths, *is the establishing of the Legislative* Power; as the *first and fundamental natural Law,* which is to govern even the Legislative it self, is *the preservation of the Society,* and (as far as will consist with the publick good) of every person in it. This *Legislative* is not only *the supream power* of the Commonwealth, but sacred and unalterable in the hands where the Community have once placed it; nor can any Edict of any Body else, in what Form soever conceived, or by what Power soever backed, have the force and obligation of a *Law,* which has not its *Sanction from* that *Legislative,* which the publick has chosen and appointed. For without this the Law could not have that, which is absolutely necessary to its being a *Law, the consent of the Society,* over whom no Body can have a power to make Laws, but by their own consent, and by Authority received from them....

These are the *Bounds* which the trust that is put in them by the Society, and the Law of God and Nature, have *set to the Legislative* Power of every Commonwealth, in all Forms of Government.

First, they are to govern by *promulgated establish'd Laws,* not to be varied in particular Cases, but to have one Rule for Rich and Poor, for the Favourite at Court, and the Country Man at Plough.   – TRUE

Secondly, these *Laws* also ought to be designed *for* no other end ultimately but *the good of the People.*

Thirdly, they must *not raise Taxes* on the Property of the People, *without the Consent of the People,* given by themselves, or their Deputies. And this properly concerns only such Governments where the *Legislative* is always in being, or at least where the People have not reserv'd any part of the Legislative to Deputies, to be from time to time chosen by themselves.

Fourthly, the *Legislative* neither must *nor can transfer the Power of making Laws* to any Body else, or place it any where but where the People have....

Whosoever uses *force without Right,* as every one does in Society, who does it without Law, puts himself into a *state of War* with those, against whom he so uses it, and in that state all former Ties are cancelled, all other Rights cease, and every one has a *Right* to defend himself, and *to resist the Aggressor....*

[T]he common Question will be made, *Who shall be Judge* whether the Prince or Legislative act contrary to their Trust? This, perhaps, ill affected and factious Men may spread amongst the People, when the Prince only makes use of his due Prerogative. To this I reply, *The People shall be Judge;* for who shall be *Judge* whether his Trustee or Deputy acts well, and according to the Trust reposed in him, but he who deputes him, and must, by having deputed him have still a Power to discard him, when he fails in his Trust? If this be reasonable in particular Cases of private Men, why should it be otherwise in that of the greatest moment; where the Welfare of Millions is concerned, and also where the evil, if not prevented, is greater, and the Redress very difficult, dear, and dangerous?...

To conclude, The *Power that every individual gave the Society,* when he entered into it, can never revert to the Individuals again, as long as the Society lasts, but will always remain in the Community; because without this, there can be no Community, no Common-wealth, which is contrary to the original Agreement: So also when the Society hath placed the Legislative in any Assembly of Men, to continue in them and their Successors, with Direction and Authority for providing such Successors, *the Legislative can never revert to the People* whilst that Government lasts: Because having provided a Legislative with Power to continue for ever, they have given up their Political Power to the Legislative, and cannot resume it. But if they have set Limits to the Duration of their Legislative, and made this Supreme Power in any Person, or Assembly, only temporary: Or else when by the Miscarriages of those in Authority, it is forfeited; upon the Forfeiture of their Rulers, or at the Determination of the Time set, *it reverts to the Society,* and the People have a Right to act as Supreme, and continue the Legislative in themselves, or erect a new Form, or under the old form place it in new hands, as they think good.

# Democracy in America

The first comprehensive social and political analysis of the early American republic was written by Alexis de Tocqueville (1805–1859), a young French aristocrat. His observations of American society and political culture were documented during his nine-month visit to the United States in 1831 and led to the publication of the two-volume classic *Democracy in America* (1835), from which the following selection has been taken. *Democracy in America* was a scholarly political philosophical and sociological work intended to provide an objective understanding of the unique American experiment in democracy.

American social scientists have focused on issues of political behavior and governmental institutions emphasized in the first volume of *Democracy in America*. The general theme of democracy and the particular issues of social, political, and economic equality and freedom examined in Tocqueville's treatise have been continuously debated and reexamined by American political scientists. Both American and European commentators have studied Tocqueville's argumentation on the political and sociological implications of popular democratic institutions.

In the following selection, Tocqueville articulates a causal linkage between the great number of diverse voluntary associations and autonomous local communities and the rapid development of political equality, opportunity, and freedom in the American context. However, Tocqueville expresses serious concerns about the potential tyranny of the majority, in which individuals and minorities are open to the coercion of mass conformity and dominant public opinion.

**Key Concept:** American democratic beliefs and practices

# SOCIAL CONDITION OF THE ANGLO-AMERICANS

Social condition is commonly the result of circumstances, sometimes of laws, oftener still of these two causes united; but when once established, it may justly be considered as itself the source of almost all the laws, the usages, and the ideas which regulate the conduction of nations: whatever it does not produce, it modifies.

If we would become acquainted with the legislation and the manners of a nation, therefore, we must begin by the study of its social condition....

Many important observations suggest themselves upon the social condition of the Anglo-Americans; but there is one that takes precedence of all the rest. The social condition of the Americans is eminently democratic; this was its character at the foundation of the colonies, and it is still more strongly marked at the present day.

I have stated... that great equality existed among the immigrants who settled on the shores of New England. Even the germs of aristocracy were never planted in that part of the Union. The only influence which obtained there was that of intellect; the people became accustomed to revere certain names as representatives of knowledge and virtue. Some of their fellow citizens acquired a power over the others that might truly have been called aristocratic if it had been capable of transmission from father to son....

At this period society was shaken to its center. The people, in whose name the struggle had taken place, conceived the desire of exercising the authority that it had acquired; its democratic tendencies were awakened; and having thrown off the yoke of the mother country, it aspired to independence of every kind. The influence of individuals gradually ceased to be felt, and custom and law united to produce the same result.

But the law of inheritance was the last step to equality. I am surprised that ancient and modern jurists have not attributed to this law a greater influence on human affairs....

In the United States it has nearly completed its work of destruction, and there we can best study its results. The English laws concerning the transmission of property were abolished in almost all the states at the time of the Revolution. The law of entail was so modified as not materially to interrupt the free circulation of property. The first generation having passed away, estates began to be parceled out; and the change became more and more rapid with the progress of time. And now, after a lapse of a little more than sixty years, the aspect of society is totally altered; the families of the great landed proprietors are almost all commingled with the general mass. In the state of New York, which formerly contained many of these, there are but two who still keep their heads above the stream; and they must shortly disappear. The sons of these opulent citizens have become merchants, lawyers, or physicians. Most of them have lapsed into obscurity. The last trace of hereditary ranks and distinctions is destroyed; the law of partition has reduced all to one level.

I do not mean that there is any lack of wealthy individuals in the United States; I know of no country, indeed, where the love of money has taken stronger hold on the affections of men and where a profounder contempt is expressed for the theory of the permanent equality of property. But wealth circulates with inconceivable rapidity, and experience shows that it is rare to find two succeeding generations in the full enjoyment of it.

This picture, which may, perhaps, be thought to be overcharged, still gives a very imperfect idea of what is taking place in the new states of the West and Southwest. At the end of the last century a few bold adventurers began to penetrate into the valley of the Mississippi, and the mass of the population very soon began to move in that direction: communities unheard of till then suddenly appeared in the desert. States whose names were not in existence a few years before, claimed their place in the American Union; and in the Western settlements we may behold democracy arrived at its utmost limits. In these states, founded offhand and as it were by chance, the inhabitants are but of yesterday. Scarcely known to one another, the nearest neighbors are ignorant of each other's history. In this part of the American continent, therefore, the population has escaped the influence not only of great names and great wealth, but even of the natural aristocracy of knowledge and virtue. None is there able to wield that respectable power which men willingly grant to the remembrance of a life spent in doing good before their eyes. The new states of the West are already inhabited, but society has no existence among them.

It is not only the fortunes of men that are equal in America; even their acquirements partake in some degree of the same uniformity. I do not believe that there is a country in the world where, in proportion to the population, there are so few ignorant and at the same time so few learned individuals. Primary instruction is within the reach of everybody; superior instruction is scarcely to be obtained by any. This is not surprising; it is, in fact, the necessary consequence of what I have advanced above. Almost all the Americans are in easy circumstances and can therefore obtain the first elements of human knowledge.

In America there are but few wealthy persons; nearly all Americans have to take a profession. Now, every profession requires an apprenticeship. The Americans can devote to general education only the early years of life. At fifteen they enter upon their calling, and thus their education generally ends at the age when ours begins. If it is continued beyond that point, it aims only towards a particular specialized and profitable purpose; one studies science as one takes up a business; and one takes up only those applications whose immediate practicality is recognized.

In America most of the rich men were formerly poor; most of those who now enjoy leisure were absorbed in business during their youth; the consequence of this is that when they might have had a taste for study, they had no time for it, and when the time is at their disposal, they have no longer the inclination.

There is no class, then, in America, in which the taste for intellectual pleasures is transmitted with hereditary fortune and leisure and by which the labors of the intellect are held in honor. Accordingly, there is an equal want of the desire and the power of application to these objects.

A middling standard is fixed in America for human knowledge. All approach as near to it as they can; some as they rise, others as they descend. Of course, a multitude of persons are to be found who entertain the same number of ideas on religion, history, science, political economy, legislation, and government. The gifts of intellect proceed directly from God, and man cannot prevent their unequal distribution. But it is at least a consequence of what I have just said that although the capacities of men are different, as the Creator intended they should be, the means that Americans find for putting them to use are equal.

In America the aristocratic element has always been feeble from its birth; and if at the present day it is not actually destroyed, it is at any rate so completely disabled that we can scarcely assign to it any degree of influence on the course of affairs.

The democratic principle, on the contrary, has gained so much strength by time, by events, and by legislation, as to have become not only predominant, but all-powerful. No family or corporate authority can be perceived; very often one cannot even discover in it any very lasting individual influence.

America, then, exhibits in her social state an extraordinary phenomenon. Men are there seen on a greater equality in point of fortune and intellect, or, in other words, more equal in their strength, than in any other country of the world, or in any age of which history has preserved the remembrance.

### Political Consequences of the Social Condition of the Anglo-Americans

The political consequences of such a social condition as this are easily deducible.

It is impossible to believe that equality will not eventually find its way into the political world, as it does everywhere else. To conceive of men remaining forever unequal upon a single point, yet equal on all others, is impossible; they must come in the end to be equal upon all.

Now, I know of only two methods of establishing equality in the political world; rights must be given to every citizen, or none at all to anyone. For nations which are arrived at the same stage of social existence as the Anglo-Americans, it is, therefore, very difficult to discover a medium between the sovereignty of all and the absolute power of one man: and it would be vain to deny that the social condition which I have been describing is just as liable to one of these consequences as to the other.

There is, in fact, a manly and lawful passion for equality that incites men to wish all to be powerful and honored. This passion tends to elevate the humble to the rank of the great; but there exists also in the human heart a depraved taste for equality, which impels the weak to attempt to lower the powerful to their own level and reduces men to prefer equality in slavery to inequality with freedom. Not that those nations whose social condition is democratic naturally despise liberty; on the contrary, they have an instinctive love of it. But liberty is not the chief and constant object of their desires; equality is their idol: they make rapid and sudden efforts to obtain liberty and, if they miss their aim, resign themselves to their disappointment; but nothing can satisfy them without equality, and they would rather perish than lose it.

On the other hand, in a state where the citizens are all practically equal, it becomes difficult for them to preserve their independence against the aggressions of power. No one among them being strong enough to engage in the struggle alone with advantage, nothing but a general combination can protect their liberty. Now, such a union is not always possible.

From the same social position, then, nations may derive one or the other of two great political results; these results are extremely different from each other, but they both proceed from the same cause.

The Anglo-Americans are the first nation who, having been exposed to this formidable alternative, have been happy enough to escape the dominion of absolute power. They have been allowed by their circumstances, their origin, their intelligence, and especially by their morals to establish and maintain the sovereignty of the people.

## THE PRINCIPLE OF THE SOVEREIGNTY OF THE PEOPLE OF AMERICA

Whenever the political laws of the United States are to be discussed, it is with the doctrine of the sovereignty of the people that we must begin.

The principle of the sovereignty of the people, which is always to be found, more or less, at the bottom of almost all human institutions, generally remains there concealed from view. It is obeyed without being recognized, or if for a moment it is brought to light, it is hastily cast back into the gloom of the sanctuary.

"The will of the nation" is one of those phrases that have been most largely abused by the wily and the despotic of every age. Some have seen the expression of it in the purchased suffrages of a few of the satellites of power; others, in the votes of a timid or an interested minority; and some have even discovered it in the silence of a people, on the supposition that the fact of submission established the right to command.

In America the principle of the sovereignty of the people is neither barren nor concealed, as it is with some other nations; it is recognized by the customs and proclaimed by the laws; it spreads freely, and arrives without impediment at its most remote consequences. If there is a country in the world where the doctrine of the sovereignty of the people can be fairly appreciated, where it can be studied in its application to the affairs of society, and where its dangers and its advantages may be judged, that country is assuredly America.

I have already observed that, from their origin, the sovereignty of the people was the fundamental principle of most of the British colonies in America. It was far, however, from then exercising as much influence on the government of society as it now does. Two obstacles, the one external, the other internal, checked its invasive progress.

It could not ostensibly disclose itself in the laws of colonies which were still forced to obey the mother country; it was therefore obliged to rule secretly in the provincial assemblies, and especially in the townships.

American society at that time was not yet prepared to adopt it with all its consequences. Intelligence in New England and wealth in the country to the south of the Hudson... long exercised a sort of aristocratic influence, which tended to keep the exercise of social power in the hands of a few. Not all the public functionaries were chosen by popular vote, nor were all the citizens voters. The electoral franchise was everywhere somewhat restricted and made dependent on a certain qualification, which was very low in the North and more considerable in the South.

The American Revolution broke out, and the doctrine of the sovereignty of the people came out of the townships and took possession of the state. Every class was enlisted in its cause; battles were fought and victories obtained for it; it became the law of laws.

A change almost as rapid was effected in the interior of society, where the law of inheritance completed the abolition of local influences.

As soon as this effect of the laws and of the Revolution became apparent to every eye, victory was irrevocably pronounced in favor of the democratic cause. All power was, in fact, in its hands, and resistance was no longer possible. The higher orders submitted without a murmur and without a struggle to an evil that was thenceforth inevitable. The ordinary fate of falling powers awaited them: each of their members followed his own interest; and as it was impossible to wring the power from the hands of a people whom they did not detest sufficiently to brave, their only aim was to secure its goodwill at any price. The most democratic laws were consequently voted by the very men whose interests they impaired: and thus, although the higher classes did not excite the passions of the people against their order, they themselves accelerated the triumph of the new state of things; so that, by a singular change, the democratic impulse was found to be most irresistible in the very states where the aristocracy had the firmest hold. The state of Maryland, which had been founded by men of rank, was the first to proclaim universal suffrage and to introduce the most democratic forms into the whole of its government.

When a nation begins to modify the elective qualification, it may easily be foreseen that, sooner or later, that qualification will be entirely abolished. There is no more invariable rule in the history of society: the further electoral rights are extended, the greater is the need of extending them; for after each concession the strength of the democracy increases, and its demands increase with its strength. The ambition of those who are below the appointed rate is irritated in exact proportion to the great number of those who are above it. The exception at last becomes the rule, concession follows concession, and no stop can be made short of universal suffrage.

At the present day the principle of the sovereignty of the people has acquired in the United States all the practical development that the imagination can conceive. It is unencumbered by those fictions that are thrown over it in other countries, and it appears in every possible form, according to the exigency of the occasion. Sometimes the laws are made by the people in a body, as at Athens; and sometimes its representatives, chosen by universal suffrage, transact business in its name and under its immediate supervision.

In some countries a power exists which, though it is in a degree foreign to the social body, directs it, and forces it to pursue a certain track. In others the ruling force is divided, being partly within and partly without the ranks of the people. But nothing of the kind is to be seen in the United States; there society governs itself for itself. All power centers in its bosom, and scarcely an individual is to be met with who would venture to conceive or, still less, to express the idea of seeking it elsewhere. The nation participates in the making of its laws by the choice of its legislators, and in the execution of them by the choice of the agents of the executive government; it may almost be said to govern itself, so feeble and so restricted is the share left to the administration, so little do the authorities forget their popular origin and the power from which they emanate. The people reign in the American political world as the Deity does in the universe. They are the cause and the aim of all things; everything comes from them, and everything is absorbed in them.

*Alexis de Tocqueville*

## 1.3  ROBERT N. BELLAH ET AL.

# *Individualism*

*Habits of the Heart: Individualism and Commitment in American Life* (University of California Press, 1985), from which the following selection has been taken, established authors Robert N. Bellah (b. 1927), Richard Madsen (b. 1941), William M. Sullivan (b. 1945), Ann Swidler (b. 1944), and Steven M. Tipton as scholars of the communitarian school of American political thought. This school of thought links political theory to practical proposals for social and political reform of the American political system. In order to reestablish the connection between rights and duties, it emphasizes civic responsibilities and obligations, social commitments in the private and public sector, and the concept of a shared community or public interest. The communitarian philosophy insists that as social beings, citizens fulfill their lives by engaging in meaningful group activities and relations in their respective communities (e.g., religious, recreational, family, educational, and cultural activities).

*Habits of the Heart* was written in the context of the Ronald Reagan administration during a period of extreme individualism, egoism, and rejection of the welfare state. The book has been considered an influential analysis and critique of contemporary American political ideology. In the following selection, the authors contend that the forces of personal material gratification and self-fulfillment operating in contemporary American political culture result in shallow social relations, unfulfilled lives, and alienation. The prescribed remedy to a false conception of individualism is linked to a comprehensive strengthening of communal social bonds and associations.

Bellah is the Ford Professor of Sociology and Comparative Studies at the University of California, Berkeley, and a scholar of religious studies. Madsen is a professor of sociology and chairman of the Chinese studies program at the University of California, San Diego. Sullivan is a professor of philosophy at La Salle College in Philadelphia, Pennsylvania. Swidler is an associate professor of sociology at the University of California, Berkeley. Tipton is an associate professor of theology at Emory University in Atlanta, Georgia.

**Key Concept:** individualism as the core of American political culture

Individualism lies at the very core of American culture. Every one of the four traditions we have singled out is in a profound sense individualistic. There is a biblical individualism and a civic individualism as well as a utilitarian and an expressive individualism. Whatever the differences among the traditions and the consequent differences in their understandings of individualism, there are some things they all share, things that are basic to American identity. We believe in the dignity, indeed the sacredness, of the individual. Anything that would violate our right to think for ourselves, judge for ourselves, make our own decisions, live our lives as we see fit, is not only morally wrong, it is sacrilegious. Our highest and noblest aspirations, not only for ourselves, but for those we care about, for our society and for the world, are closely linked to our individualism. Yet, . . . some of our deepest problems both as individuals and as a society are also closely linked to our individualism. We do not argue that Americans should abandon individualism—that would mean for us to abandon our deepest identity. But individualism has come to mean so many things and to contain such contradictions and paradoxes that even to defend it requires that we analyze it critically, that we consider especially those tendencies that would destroy it from within.

Modern individualism emerged out of the struggle against monarchical and aristocratic authority that seemed arbitrary and oppressive to citizens prepared to assert the right to govern themselves. In that struggle, classical political philosophy and biblical religion were important cultural resources. Classical republicanism evoked an image of the active citizen contributing to the public good and Reformation Christianity, in both Puritan and sectarian forms, inspired a notion of government based on the voluntary participation of individuals. Yet both these traditions placed individual autonomy in a context of moral and religious obligation that in some contexts justified obedience as well as freedom.

In seventeenth-century England, a radical philosophical defense of individual rights emerged that owed little to either classical or biblical sources. Rather, it consciously started with the biological individual in a "state of nature" and derived a social order from the actions of such individuals, first in relation to nature and then in relation to one another. John Locke is the key figure and one enormously influential in America. The essence of the Lockean position is an almost ontological individualism. The individual is prior to society, which comes into existence only through the voluntary contract of individuals trying to maximize their own self-interest. It is from this position that we have derived the tradition of utilitarian individualism. But because one can only know what is useful to one by consulting one's desires and sentiments, this is also ultimately the source of the expressive individualist tradition as well.

Modern individualism has long coexisted with classical republicanism and biblical religion. The conflict in their basic assumptions was initially muted because they all, in the forms commonest in America, stressed the dignity and autonomy of the individual. But as modern individualism became more dominant in the United States and classical republicanism and biblical religion less effective, some of the difficulties in modern individualism began to become apparent. The therapeutic ethos to which we have devoted so much attention is suggestive of these because it is the way in which contemporary Americans live out the tenets of modern individualism. For psychology, as Robert Coles has written, the self is "the only or main form of reality."

The question is whether an individualism in which the self has become the main form of reality can really be sustained. What is at issue is not simply whether self-contained individuals might withdraw from the public sphere to pursue purely private ends, but whether such individuals are capable of sustaining either a public *or* a private life. If this is the danger, perhaps only the civic and biblical forms of individualism—forms that see the individual in relation to a larger whole, a community and a tradition—are capable of sustaining genuine individuality and nurturing both public and private life.

There are both ideological and sociological reasons for the growing strength of modern individualism at the expense of the civic and biblical traditions. Modern individualism has pursued individual rights and individual autonomy in ever new realms. In so doing, it has come into confrontation with those aspects of biblical and republican thought that accepted, even enshrined, unequal rights and obligations—between husbands and wives, masters and servants, leaders and followers, rich and poor. As the absolute commitment to individual dignity has condemned those inequalities, it has also seemed to invalidate the biblical and republican traditions. And in undermining these traditions, as Tocqueville warned, individualism also weakens the very meanings that give content and substance to the ideal of individual dignity.

We thus face a profound impasse. Modern individualism seems to be producing a way of life that is neither individually nor socially viable, yet a return to traditional forms would be to return to intolerable discrimination and oppression. The question, then, is whether the older civic and biblical traditions have the capacity to reformulate themselves while simultaneously remaining faithful to their own deepest insights.

Many Americans would prefer not to see the impasse as starkly as we have put it. Philosophical defenders of modern individualism have frequently presumed a social and cultural context for the individual that their theories cannot justify, or they have added ad hoc arguments that mitigate the harshness of their theoretical model.... Parents advocate "values" for their children even when they do not know what those "values" are. What this suggests is that there is a profound ambivalence about individualism in America among its most articulate defenders. This ambivalence shows up particularly clearly at the level of myth in our literature and our popular culture. There we find the fear that society may overwhelm the individual and destroy any chance of autonomy unless he stands against it, but also recognition that it is only in relation to society that the individual can fulfill himself and that if the break with society is too radical, life has no meaning at all.

A deep and continuing theme in American literature is the hero who must leave society, alone or with one or a few others, in order to realize the moral good in the wilderness, at sea, or on the margins of settled society. Sometimes the withdrawal involves a contribution to society, as in James Fenimore Cooper's *The Deerslayer.* Sometimes the new marginal community realizes ethical ends impossible in the larger society, as in the interracial harmony between Huckleberry Finn and Jim. Sometimes the flight from society is simply mad and ends in general disaster, as in *Moby Dick.* When it is not in and through society but in flight from it that the good is to be realized, as in the case of Melville's Ahab, the line between ethical heroism and madness vanishes, and the destructive potentiality of a completely asocial individualism is revealed.

America is also the inventor of that most mythic individual hero, the cowboy, who again and again saves a society he can never completely fit into. The cowboy has a special talent—he can shoot straighter and faster than other men —and a special sense of justice. But these characteristics make him so unique that he can never fully belong to society. His destiny is to defend society without ever really joining it. He rides off alone into the sunset like Shane, or like the Lone Ranger moves on accompanied only by his Indian companion. But the cowboy's importance is not that he is isolated or antisocial. Rather, his significance lies in his unique, individual virtue and special skill and it is because of those qualities that society needs and welcomes him. Shane, after all, starts as a real outsider, but ends up with the gratitude of the community and the love of a woman and a boy. And while the Lone Ranger never settles down and marries the local schoolteacher, he always leaves with the affection and gratitude of the people he has helped. It is as if the myth says you can be a truly good person, worthy of admiration and love, only if you resist fully joining the group. But sometimes the tension leads to an irreparable break. Will Kane, the hero of *High Noon,* abandoned by the cowardly townspeople, saves them from an unrestrained killer, but then throws his sheriff's badge in the dust and goes off into the desert with his bride. One is left wondering where they will go, for there is no longer any link with any town.

The connection of moral courage and lonely individualism is even tighter for that other, more modern American hero, the hard-boiled detective. From Sam Spade to Serpico, the detective is a loner. He is often unsuccessful in conventional terms, working out of a shabby office where the phone never rings. Wily, tough, smart, he is nonetheless unappreciated. But his marginality is also his strength. When a bit of business finally comes their way, Philip Marlowe, Lew Archer, and Travis McGee are tenacious. They pursue justice and help the unprotected even when it threatens to unravel the fabric of society itself....

Both the cowboy and the hard-boiled detective tell us something important about American individualism. The cowboy, like the detective, can be valuable to society only because he is a completely autonomous individual who stands outside it. To serve society, one must be able to stand alone, not needing others, not depending on their judgment, and not submitting to their wishes. Yet this individualism is not selfishness. Indeed, it is a kind of heroic selflessness. One accepts the necessity of remaining alone in order to serve the values of the group. And this obligation to aloneness is an important key to the American moral imagination. Yet it is part of the profound ambiguity of the mythology of American individualism that its moral heroism is always just a step away from despair. For an Ahab, and occasionally for a cowboy or a detective, there is no return to society, no moral redemption. The hero's lonely quest for moral excellence ends in absolute nihilism.

If we may turn from the mythical heroes of fiction to a mythic, but historically real, hero, Abraham Lincoln, we may begin to see what is necessary if the nihilistic alternative is to be avoided. In many respects, Lincoln conforms perfectly to the archetype of the lonely, individualistic hero. He was a self-made man, never comfortable with the eastern upper classes. His dual moral commitment to the preservation of the Union and the belief that "all men are created equal" roused the hostility of abolitionists and Southern sympathizers alike. In the war years, he was more and more isolated, misunderstood by Congress and cabinet, and unhappy at home. In the face of almost universal mistrust, he nonetheless completed his self-appointed task of bringing the nation through its most devastating war, preaching reconciliation as he did so, only to be brought down by an assassin's bullet. What saved Lincoln from nihilism was the larger whole for which he felt it was important to live and worthwhile to die. No one understood better the meaning of the Republic and of the freedom and equality that it only very imperfectly embodies. But it was not only civic republicanism that gave his life value. Reinhold Niebuhr has said that Lincoln's biblical understanding of the Civil War was deeper than that of any contemporary theologian. The great symbols of death and rebirth that Lincoln invoked to give meaning to the sacrifice of those who died at Gettysburg, in a war he knew to be senseless and evil, came to redeem his own senseless death at the hand of an assassin. It is through his identification with a community and a tradition that Lincoln became the deeply and typically American individual that he was.

## THE SOCIAL SOURCES OF AMBIVALENCE

... [I]ndividualism is deeply rooted in America's social history. Here the bond-servant became free, the tenant became a small landowner, and what Benjamin Franklin called the self-respecting "middling" condition of men became the norm. Yet the incipient "independent citizen" of colonial times found himself in a cohesive community, the "peaceable kingdoms" that were colonial towns, where ties to family and church and respect for the "natural leaders" of the community were still strong. Individualism was so embedded in the civic and religious structures of colonial life that it had not yet found a name, even though John Locke's ideas about individual autonomy were well known. It took the geographical and economic expansion of the new nation, especially in the years after 1800, to produce the restless quest for material betterment that led Tocqueville to use the word "individualism" to describe what he saw. The new social and economic conditions did not create the ideology of modern individualism, most of whose elements are considerably older than the nineteenth century, but those conditions did make it possible for what we have called utilitarian and, later, expressive individualism to develop their own inherent tendencies in relative independence from civic and religious forms of life, important though those still were.

Tocqueville was quick to point out one of the central ambiguities in the new individualism—that it was strangely compatible with conformism. He described the American insistence that one always rely on one's own judgment, rather than on received authority, in forming one's opinions and that one stand by one's own opinions. We have already heard many examples of this attitude ... in the assertion, for example, that compromise with others is desirable, but not if you sacrifice your own "values." But, as Tocqueville observed, when one can no longer rely on tradition or authority, one inevitably looks to others for confirmation of one's judgments. Refusal to accept established opinion and anxious conformity to the opinions of one's peers turn out to be two sides of the same coin. . . .

The ambiguity and ambivalence of American individualism derive from both cultural and social contradictions. We insist, perhaps more than ever before, on finding our true selves independent of any cultural or social influence, being responsible to that self alone, and making its fulfillment the very meaning of our lives. Yet we spend much of our time navigating through immense bureaucratic structures—multiversities, corporations, government agencies—manipulating and being manipulated by others. In describing this situation, Alasdair MacIntyre has spoken of "bureaucratic individualism," the form of life exemplified by the manager and the therapist. In bureaucratic individualism, the ambiguities and contradictions of individualism are frighteningly revealed, as freedom to make private decisions is bought at the cost of turning over most public decisions to bureaucratic managers and experts. A bureaucratic individualism in which the consent of the governed, the first demand of modern enlightened individualism, has been abandoned in all but form, illustrates the tendency of individualism to destroy its own conditions.

But in our interviews, though we saw tendencies toward bureaucratic individualism, we cannot say that it has yet become dominant. Rather we found all the classic polarities of American individualism still operating: the deep desire for autonomy and self-reliance combined with an equally deep conviction that life has no meaning unless shared with others in the context of community; a commitment to the equal right to dignity of every individual combined with an effort to justify inequality of reward, which, when extreme, may deprive people of dignity; an insistence that life requires practical effectiveness and "realism" combined with the feeling that compromise is ethically fatal. The inner tensions of American individualism add up to a classic case of ambivalence. We strongly assert the value of our self-reliance and autonomy. We deeply feel the emptiness of a life without sustaining social commitments. Yet we are hesitant to articulate our sense that we need one another as much as we need to stand alone, for fear that if we did we would lose our independence altogether. The tensions of our lives would be even greater if we did not, in fact, engage in practices that constantly limit the effects of an isolating individualism, even though we cannot articulate those practices nearly as well as we can the quest for autonomy.

# THE LIMITS OF INDIVIDUALISM

We have pointed out the peculiar resonance between middle-class life and individualism in America. We have also stressed the special nature of the middle class, the fact that it is not simply a "layer" in a "system of stratification" but rather a group that seeks to embody in its own continuous progress and advancement the very meaning of the American project. To a large extent, it has succeeded in this aspiration. It so dominates our culture that, as Schneider and Smith put it, "middle-class values can be said to encompass both lower- and upper-class values." This is true for the lower class in that not only are middle-class values understood and respected but "lower-class people explain their inferior position in terms of circumstances that have prevented them from behaving in a middle-class fashion." The upper class sometimes takes comfort in its special sense of family and tradition, but it does not try to substitute its values for the dominant ones. On the contrary, its members praise middle-class rationality and achievement as the values on which our society is based, even when they do not choose to follow them.

The nature of middle-class individualism becomes even clearer when we contrast it to lower-class and upper-class culture. Schneider and Smith describe the contrast very suggestively when they say that the middle class sees "individual and social behavior as predominantly determined by the application of technical rules to any situation that arises," whereas the lower class (and, interestingly enough, the upper class) have a more "dramaturgical view of social action." By "dramaturgical" they mean action that takes on meaning because of a particular history of relationships. Abstract rules are less important than the examples set by individuals. Schneider and Smith argue, for example, that it is in the lower class that ethnicity, as a specific pattern of cultural life, survives in America, and that as individuals enter the middle class, ethnicity loses distinctive social content even when it is symbolically emphasized. The point is not that lower- and upper-class Americans are not individualistic, but rather that their individualism is embedded in specific patterns of relationship and solidarity that mitigate the tendency toward an empty self and empty relationships in middle-class life. The contrast is expressed by middle-class Americans themselves when they entertain envious fantasies about more "meaningful community" among lower-class racial and ethnic groups or among (usually European) aristocracies.

Important though the distinctions we have been drawing are, we should not overemphasize the degree to which rationality and technical rules govern middle-class life. Children do not grow up through abstract injunctions. They identify with their parents, they learn through role modeling, and they are influenced by the historic specificity of their family, church, and local community. It is the middle-class orientation toward technical education, bureaucratic occupational hierarchies, and the market economy that encourages the greater emphasis on universal rules and technical rationality. The upper and lower classes can maintain greater cultural specificity (though in the United States that specificity is only relative) because they are less oriented to these rationalizing institutions.

Since middle-class people, too, are embedded in families, churches, and local communities, they also experience conflict between the more rational and the more dramaturgic spheres of life. The tensions that divide middle-class Americans from other Americans also exist within the middle class itself. Much is said about the cultural diversity and pluralism of American life. But perhaps what divides us most is not that diversity, but the conflict between the monoculture of technical and bureaucratic rationality and the specificity of our concrete commitments.

*Robert N.*
*Bellah et al.*

# Rights and the Common Good: The Communitarian Perspective

Amitai Etzioni (b. 1929) is University Professor at George Washington University and the founding editor of the communitarian journal *The Responsive Community*. He is also a former senior White House adviser to President Jimmy Carter. Etzioni has authored numerous articles and books on public policy, sociology, and philosophy. In 1967 he received the William Mosher Award for the most distinguished article, published in *Public Administration Review*, and was awarded a Guggenheim Fellowship in 1968.

Etzioni is considered by many political scientists to be a founder and scholarly proponent of the American communitarian school of thought. American communitarian political theory refers to a prescribed agenda of political and social reform. In particular, it emphasizes civic obligations and duties, social responsibilities in the private and public sectors, a concept of a shared community or public interest, and reestablishing the connection between rights and responsibilities. The term *communitarian* was selected to focus on the moral principle that citizens should fulfill their duties to their communities. Etzioni recognizes and condemns the excessive egoism, radical individualism, and the rejection of public authority pervasive in contemporary America. In the following selection, which is taken from *Rights and the Common Good: The Communitarian Perspective* (St. Martin's Press, 1995), Etzioni focuses on the delicate balance between civic obligations and individual rights. Due to the contemporary context of moral relativism and individualism, Etzioni contends that Americans should strengthen their collective moral foundations and ethical commitments to various communal associations (e.g., family, schools, religious institutions, and social clubs).

The theoretical works of Etzioni have had a practical impact upon American politics and public policy in that they have encouraged many public policymakers and academics to become actively involved in a communitarian movement to reform the American political system.

**Key Concept:** balance between social responsibilities and individual rights

$S$ocieties, like bicycles, teeter and need continuously to be pulled back to the center lest they lean too far toward anarchy or tyranny. The current legal and moral commitment to guaranteeing individual rights grew out of a concern about protecting persons from government excesses. The current commitment to advancing social responsibilities, on the other hand, reflects a concern that social institutions be properly nourished rather than abandoned. Because no society is ever perfectly balanced, communitarians seek to discern the direction a society is leaning at any one point in history and to cast their weight on the other side. Thus, in Albania, China, or even the former Soviet Union, a communitarian would fight for expanding and enshrining individual rights. In the United States, at the onset of the 1990s, communitarians felt that social responsibilities particularly needed shoring up.[1] Note that we do not suggest that responsibilities should replace rights or vice versa. On the contrary, they require one another. Strong rights presume strong responsibilities.

A finding from a poll illustrates the issue. The poll, reported by Morris Janowitz, found that young Americans believed that they had a right to trial by jury but were rather reluctant to serve on one.[2] This position is, first of all, illogical. It ignores the fact that if one's peers will not serve there will be no jury of one's peers. On a deeper level, it fails to recognize that rights and responsibilities are corollaries, two sides of the same coin: one person's right is a claim on another's responsibility. Finally, it is a morally defective viewpoint: people are seeking to take and not to give. No society can survive if people only want rights and are unwilling to assume responsibilities.

Where is the point of balance, the elusive center? How do we decide that in a particular area an imbalance needs to be corrected? Following are four criteria that must be applied together in making such a decision.

# ESTABLISHING A CLEAR AND PRESENT DANGER

No adjustments should be implemented unless there is a clear and present danger—a real, readily verifiable, sizable social problem or need. Unfortunately, in a media-centered society, prophets of alarm rapidly gain wide audiences. There are frequent calls on policymakers and citizens alike to tighten their belts and modify their life-styles, as well as demands for laws and constitutional protection to combat some imagined or anticipated scourge. For example, in the mid-1970s Americans were told that they must be forced out of cars and into mass transit because the United States was running out of oil. More recently, they were told that America must introduce central planning in the workplace in order to compete with the Japanese. And so on.

If policymakers and citizens were to respond to every cry of "wolf," society would frequently be run through the ringer, shaken, and rearranged at great cost. Unfortunately, on most issues it is nearly impossible to discern well in advance which dangers are real and which are wildly exaggerated, if not outrightly false. Hence, we reluctantly conclude that it is best to try not to predict too far into the future. Instead, we should embrace the humbler posture of not acting (especially in a grand way that involves major economic and human costs and diminutions of liberties) until a clear and present danger exists. Because the evidence that they endanger large numbers of lives, if not the very fabric of society is incontestable, we believe that nuclear weapons, handguns, AIDS, and drugs are clear and present dangers. Killer bees, on the other hand, are not clear and present dangers, and global warming may not justify the kind of draconian measures that have been advocated recently.

Clear and present danger can also be determined when there is a direct link between a cause and an effect. If a man points a machine gun at another person's head, for example, we have the right to take away the man's property —that is, the gun—and to wrestle him to the ground. The danger is clear and present. At the same time we would not condone, indeed we would penalize, the same conduct if we only suspected that the gun owner might so use his weapon.

An actual case illustrates the issue at hand. After several train wrecks involving engineers impaired by drugs and alcohol, the U.S. Department of Transportation maintained that random testing of train engineers for drugs and alcohol was warranted. Radical individualists opposed the policy for the usual reasons: only individualized case-by-case evidence of "probable cause" was proper ground, they said. They also claimed that it would even be improper to test an engineer stumbling away after a wreck unless there was evidence that he or she was drinking or was taking drugs. In February 1988, a federal appeals court in California agreed with these individualists, ruling that it was unconstitutional to administer drug tests to those who drive trains.

However, the following evidence suggests that there may be a direct link between the drug and alcohol abuse of train engineers and train wrecks. A 1979 study found that 23 percent of railroad operating employees were "problem drinkers," many of whom had gotten drunk on the job. Of all the train accidents between 1975 and 1984, drugs or alcohol were "directly effecting" causes in 48 of them, accounting for 37 fatalities and 80 injuries. Since then, the danger seems only to have become worse. Out of 179 railroad accidents in 1987, the engineers in 39 of the cases tested positive for drugs, 34 percent more than in 1986. In a January 1987 crash, 16 people died and 174 were injured when an Amtrak train was struck by a Conrail train. Both the engineer and brakeman on the train were under the influence of marijuana.

When 23 percent of railway employees—that is, nearly one out of four— is affected by this problem, and when railway employees directly deal with life and death, we would hold that *not* testing train engineers and other high-risk groups, such as airline pilots, for drugs and alcohol presents a clear and present danger to society.

# EXAMINING OPTIONS TO CONSTITUTIONAL REINTERPRETATIONS

Each year over 300,000 people in the United States die from smoking. Assume we agree as a community that because the human toll is so great, we should discourage smoking, especially among the young (over 87 percent of present-day smokers began before they were 21). Moreover, assume we agree that the link between smoking and ill health is sufficiently strong for smoking to be considered a direct cause, thereby justifying a publicly initiated effort to change behavior. Even if we accept the radical individualist notion that people ought to be free to choose their own purchases, even if self-injurious, we can argue that smoking harms others. Passive smoking accounts for approximately 2,400 cases of lung cancer per year, and in 1986 approximately 1,600 people died as a result of fires caused by smoking. And finally, people overwhelmingly show that their real preference is to stop; that 90 percent of smokers have tried to quit is a signal that they want help.

Now assume further that these findings, if they hold under continued scrutiny, indicate a clear and present danger; it does not yet follow that we need to reinterpret the Constitution. First, we ought to look for ways that do not require any tampering with the Constitution. Armed with this criterion, we might conclude that raising taxes on cigarettes is more justifiable than prohibiting cigarette ads. First, the result is more efficient; a 10 percent increase in price is reported to correlate with a 12 percent decrease in demand. Other studies corroborate this correlation by demonstrating that young people's taste for cigarettes is highly controlled by price. On the other hand, although advertising may persuade some young people to pick up the smoking habit, it is widely agreed that is main effect is to shift smokers from one brand to another.

Second, and more to our point, we should note that curbing ads raises constitutional issues of freedom of speech, whereas raising taxes does not. Hence, even if prohibiting ads proved to be more efficient, raising taxes would still be preferable as long as we could show that cigarette ads were not significantly more influential than prices.

# LIMITING ADJUSTMENTS AS MUCH AS POSSIBLE

If there is no effective alternative to adjusting the constitutional balance between individual rights and social responsibilities, we must look for options that will make the most minimal intrusion possible, rather than proceeding with a policy sledgehammer.

The debate over *Miranda* rights provides a good example of how we might find ways to trim rather than pound. In recent years, *Miranda* has been criticized for excessively favoring criminals. The extent to which the ruling actually hobbles the police and prosecutors is a much debated, much scrutinized topic. Whether recent court rulings have sharply or only moderately affected the reach of *Miranda* it is difficult to tell. However, over the last ten years, the balance has tilted somewhat away from rights for criminals and toward greater public safety. Our concern here is to illustrate what a reasonable intermediary position on *Miranda* would be rather than to examine the intricacies of these issues.

At one extreme of this discussion is the radical individualist position that no changes to *Miranda* should be made whatsoever, as if this rather recent legal tradition, one that did not go into effect until 1966, had the standing of the Bill of Rights and the sanction of the Founding Fathers. At the other extreme, authoritarians argue that many *Miranda* rights accord criminals more constitutional protection that is afforded their victims. Former Attorney General Edwin Meese wanted to do away with *Miranda* altogether because, he said, "it provides incentives for criminals not to talk" and "only helps guilty defendants." The Office of Legal Policy of the U.S. Attorney General under the Reagan administration even issued a position paper that called for a wholesale overturning of *Miranda*.

A reasonable intermediary position seems to be to let evidence stand, even if a technical error was made in its collection, as long as (1) there is no indication of bad faith and (2) the error is recorded in the relevant personnel file at the appropriate law enforcement agency to avoid any repetition of such error. This position was found acceptable in a 1985 Supreme Court case when a suspect had confessed to a crime before he was read his Miranda rights, was later informed of his rights, and then confessed again. The Court unanimously agreed that the first confession could not be used as evidence even if given voluntarily and without coercion, but it ruled 6 to 3 that the unsolicited admission of guilt did not taint the second confession. In a similar decision in 1987, the Supreme Court ruled that the police are not required to tell a suspect about each crime for which he or she may be questioned.

Another example of a carefully honed adjustment is the introduction of some restrictions on the inadmissibility of evidence uncovered by the police during a discovery procedure that was technically flawed. In *United States v. Leon*, the police believed they had a search warrant for a house in which they had gathered incriminating evidence. Later, they discovered that the clerk had written the address incorrectly on the warrant. In 1984 the Supreme Court ruled that the evidence gathered should not be excluded on the basis of the technical mistake. . . .

Although it is convenient to distinguish between legal and practical considerations of an adjustment, it should be noted that they are intertwined. To wit, burdens imposed by the government on a practice could rise to a point where they would become a form of undue government harassment—one of the main abuses against which the Bill of Rights is meant to protect us.

In short, far from yielding to demands that the authorities gun down any private airplane or speedboat that approaches a U.S. border unidentified, break down the doors of people's homes at midnight, quarantine all HIV-positive persons, and so on, to combat drugs and AIDS, we see justifications for introducing many measures that are minimally intrusive, in either legal or practical terms. Thus, sobriety checkpoints; searches of cars on public roads; roadblocks on roads leading to open-air drug markets; testing of train engineers, pilots, air traffic controllers, and other individuals whose jobs entail high risk to others;

and a requirement that people with AIDS disclose the identity of their sexual partners, if the precautions indicated are taken, are both overdue and legitimate.

*Amitai Etzioni*

## MAKING SPECIAL EFFORTS TO MINIMIZE OR AVOID SIDE EFFECTS

We should also take pains to reduce the deleterious impacts of a given policy. For example, if confidentiality is not maintained, AIDS testing and contact-tracing can lead to a person losing his or her job and health insurance. Hence, such a program should be accompanied by a thorough review of the controls limiting access to lists of the names of those tested; professional education programs on the need for confidentiality; and penalties for unauthorized disclosure of HIV status and for discrimination against people with AIDS or HIV carriers. These measures may seem cumbersome, but are clearly appropriate in view of the great danger AIDS poses for individuals and the high cost to society.

A good example of a limited crime-prevention program that has kept negative side effects to a minimum, and as a result has enhanced its own acceptability, are airport X rays and metal detectors. These devices allow for the confiscation of weapons that could otherwise be brought on board, and thus help prevent hijacking. The searches are deliberately not used to stop drug trafficking and other crimes.

Taken together, these criteria may guide policymakers, legislatures, judges, and fellow citizens as they ask which new social responsibilities they should add, which old ones they should honor, which individual rights are fundamental, and which ones must be trimmed to make room for new mores and policies, all in the name of enabling society—in which all rights ultimately are anchored—to be sustained. . . .

## THE ROLE OF VIRTUE

Another way to approach the same subject is to realize the deeper context of the issue before us. At stake is the question "What constitutes the good society, the virtuous society?" Not everybody agrees that this question should be asked, let alone answered. Radical individualists argue that once a certain conduct is defined as virtuous, then an essential foundation of our society is undermined. They fear that those members of society who fail to display the characteristics considered virtuous will be treated as inferior, if they are not discriminated against outright.

Communitarians argue that a society without some shared virtues cannot exist. A society cannot tolerate a condition in which all behavior is considered of equal merit. We must condemn not merely murder, rape, robbery, and other behaviors we call crimes (that is, counter to virtue), but also the destruction of the environment, discrimination against others, and many behaviors that endanger the sustainability of our communities and the values we hold dear. Moreover, the ultimate defense against intolerance is not to regard all behavior as equally meritorious but to consider mutual respect a key societal strength. It is within a healthy social context that social responsibilities and individual rights find their ultimate home. Struggling to ensure that both are well attended to goes a long way to make a society virtuous.[3]

## NOTES

1. See Amitai Etzioni, "What Fascists?" *The Responsive Community* (Winter 1990–1991), 1 (1), pp. 12–13 and the Communitarian Platform.

2. Morris Janowitz, *The Reconstruction of Patriotism: Education for Civic Consciousness* (Chicago: University of Chicago Press, 1983), p. 8.

3. For additional discussion, see Amitai Etzioni, *The Spirit of Community* (New York: Crown Publishers, 1993); Robert Bellah et al., *The Good Society* (New York: Alfred A. Knopf, 1991); and William Galston, *Liberal Purposes* (New York: Cambridge University Press, 1991).

# PART TWO

# *The Constitutional Framework and the Federalist System*

# On the Internet . . .

## Sites appropriate to Part Two

Through this Emory University site you can view scanned originals of the Declaration of Independence, the Constitution, and the Bill of Rights. The transcribed texts are also available, as are the *Federalist* papers.

>     http://www.law.emory.edu/FEDERAL/

This site of the Nonbeliever Antidiscrimination Project provides a frequently updated list of links to sites related to federalism.

>     http://www.infidels.org/~nap/
>        index.federalism.html

This page of links to U.S. federal government sites, provided by RAMS-FIE, includes multiple-agency sites, single-agency sites, and consortium sites.

>     http://www.fie.com/www/us_gov.htm

The mission of the National Archives and Records Administration is to ensure ready access to essential evidence that documents the rights of American citizens, the actions of federal officials, and the national experience. This site offers an online exhibit hall, historical records of government agencies, research tools, and much more.

>     http://www.nara.gov

CHAPTER **2** The
# Constitutional
# Foundation of
# American Government

## 2.1 JAMES MADISON

# Federalist, *Nos. 47, 48, and 51*

The framers of the U.S. Constitution, James Madison (1751–1836), Alexander Hamilton (1757–1804), and John Jay (1745–1829), wrote the *Federalist Papers* (1788) under the pseudonym "Publius" (identifying with Publius Valerius, a Roman emperor and defender of the Republic). This collection of 85 persuasive, political, theoretical articles and letters was published in New York City newspapers from October 1787 to March 1788 during New York's debates on the ratification of the U.S. Constitution. Although a pseudonym was used to conceal the identity of the authors during the publication of the essays, subsequent scholarly research has confirmed that Hamilton wrote 51 of them, Madison 26, Jay 5, and Hamilton and Madison collaborated on 3. The authors thought that it was necessary to publish the articles in this context due to New York's strong Anti-Federalist resistance to the ratification of

**34**

*Chapter 2*
*The*
*Constitutional*
*Foundation of*
*American*
*Government*

the U.S. Constitution. The papers had a powerful impact upon the ratification debates in New York and were immediately reprinted in several other critical states. The objective of this collection of essays was to critique the many significant defects of the Articles of Confederation and to forcefully argue for the proposed federal legal framework.

In the following selection from the *Federalist Papers* (1788), Madison dispassionately defends the U.S. Constitution. In *Federalist,* Nos. 47 and 48, Madison prescribes a national government with a configuration of three distinct, independent, and equal branches of public authority. He refers to the historical cases of state governments and the British Constitution to document the problems and limitations of the principle of separation of powers. These papers defend those constitutional principles that promote a strong unified national government and protect against the potential of any one branch usurping the powers and functions of the others, in addition to avoiding excessive consolidation or concentration of power in any one particular branch of the national government. In *Federalist,* No. 51, Madison focuses on the problems of the principle of separation of powers and the objective of avoiding governmental tyranny.

The *Federalist Papers* have had an enduring impact as the most comprehensive and substantive interpretation of the U.S. Constitution. They are considered by many scholars to be the most significant and creative work in American political philosophy.

**Key Concept:** proposed constitutional principles to avoid governmental tyranny

# NO. 47

Having reviewed the general form of the proposed government and the general mass of power allotted to it, I proceed to examine the particular structure of this government, and the distribution of this mass of power among its constituent parts.

One of the principal objections inculcated by the more respectable adversaries to the Constitution is its supposed violation of the political maxim that the legislative, executive, and judiciary departments ought to be separate and distinct. In the structure of the federal government no regard, it is said, seems to have been paid to this essential precaution in favor of liberty. The several departments of power are distributed and blended in such a manner as at once to destroy all symmetry and beauty of form, and to expose some of the essential parts of the edifice to the danger of being crushed by the disproportionate weight of other parts.

No political truth is certainly of greater intrinsic value, or is stamped with the authority of more enlightened patrons of liberty than that on which the objection is founded. The accumulation of all powers, legislative, executive, and judiciary, in the same hands, whether or one, a few, or many, and whether hereditary, self-appointed, or elective, may justly be pronounced the very definition of tyranny. Were the federal Constitution, therefore, really chargeable with this accumulation of power, or with a mixture of powers, having a dangerous tendency to such an accumulation, no further arguments would be necessary to inspire a universal reprobation of the system. I persuade myself, however, that it will be made apparent to everyone that the charge cannot be supported, and that the maxim on which it relies has been totally misconceived and misapplied. In order to form correct ideas on this important subject it will be proper to investigate the sense in which the preservation of liberty requires that the three great departments of power should be separate and distinct.

The oracle who is always consulted and cited on this subject is the celebrated Montesquieu. If he be not the author of this invaluable precept in the science of politics, he has the merit at least of displaying and recommending it most effectually to the attention of mankind....

From... facts, by which Montesquieu was guided, it may clearly be inferred that in saying "There can be no liberty where the legislative and executive powers are united in the same person, or body of magistrates," or, "if the power of judging be not separated from the legislative and executive powers," he did not mean that these departments ought to have no *partial agency* in, or no *control* over, the acts of each other. His meaning, as his own words import, and still more conclusively as illustrated by the example in his eye, can amount to no more than this, that where the *whole* power of one department is exercised by the same hands which possess the *whole* power of another department, the fundamental principles of a free constitution are subverted....

If we look into the constitutions of the several States we find that, notwithstanding the emphatical and, in some instances, the unqualified terms in which this axiom has been laid down, there is not a single instance in which the several departments of power have been kept absolutely separate and distinct....

The constitution of Massachusetts has observed a sufficient though less pointed caution in expressing this fundamental article of liberty. It declares "that the legislative department shall never exercise the executive and judicial powers, or either of them; the executive shall never exercise the legislative and judicial powers, or either of them; the judicial shall never exercise the legislative and executive powers, or either of them." This declaration corresponds precisely with the doctrine of Montesquieu... and is not in a single point violated by the plan of the convention. It goes no farther than to prohibit any one of the entire departments from exercising the powers of another department. In the very Constitution to which it is prefixed, a partial mixture of powers has been admitted. The executive magistrate has a qualified negative on the legislative body, and the Senate, which is a part of the legislature, is a court of impeachment for members both of the executive and judiciary departments. The members of the judiciary department, again, are appointable by the executive department, and removable by the same authority on the address of the two legislative branches....

# NO. 48

It was shown in the last paper that the political apothegm there examined does not require that the legislative, executive, and judiciary departments should be wholly unconnected with each other. I shall undertake, in the next place, to show that unless these departments be so far connected and blended as to give to each a constitutional control over the others, the degree of separation which the maxim requires, as essential to a free government, can never in practice be duly maintained.

It is agreed on all sides that the powers properly belonging to one of the departments ought not to be directly and completely administered by either of the other departments. It is equally evident that none of them ought to possess, directly or indirectly, an overruling influence over the others in the administration of their respective powers. It will not be denied that power is of an encroaching nature and that it ought to be effectually restrained from passing the limits assigned to it. After discriminating, therefore, in theory, the several classes of power, as they may in their nature be legislative, executive, or judiciary, the next and most difficult task is to provide some practical security for each, against the invasion of the others. What this security ought to be is the great problem to be solved.

Will it be sufficient to mark, with precision, the boundaries of these departments in the constitution of the government, and to trust to these parchment barriers against the encroaching spirit of power? This is the security which appears to have been principally relied on by the compliers of most of the American constitutions. But experience assures us that the efficacy of the provision has been greatly overrated; and that some more adequate defense is indispensably necessary for the more feeble against the more powerful members of the government. The legislative department is everywhere extending the sphere of its activity and drawing all power into its impetuous vortex. . . .

In a government where numerous and extensive prerogatives are placed in the hands of an hereditary monarch, the executive department is very justly regarded as the source of danger, and watched with all the jealousy which a zeal for liberty ought to inspire. In a democracy, where a multitude of people exercise in person the legislative functions and are continually exposed, by their incapacity for regular deliberation and concerted measures, to the ambitious intrigues of their executive magistrates, tyranny may well be apprehended, on some favorable emergency, to start up in the same quarter. But in a representative republic where the executive magistracy is carefully limited, both in the extent and the duration of its power; and where the legislative power is exercised by an assembly, which is inspired by a supposed influence over the people with an intrepid confidence in its own strength; which is sufficiently numerous to feel all the passions which actuate a multitude, yet not so numerous as to be incapable of pursuing the objects of its passions by means which reason prescribes; it is against the enterprising ambition of this department that the people ought to indulge all their jealousy and exhaust all their precautions.

The legislative department derives a superiority in our governments from other circumstances. Its constitutional powers being at once more extensive, and less susceptible of precise limits, it can, with the greater facility, mask, under complicated and indirect measures, the encroachments which it makes on the co-ordinate departments. It is not unfrequently a question of real nicety in legislative bodies whether the operation of a particular measure will, or will not, extend beyond the legislative sphere. On the other side, the executive power being restrained within a narrower compass and being more simple in its nature, and the judiciary being described by landmarks still less uncertain, projects of usurpation by either of these departments would immediately betray and defeat themselves. Nor is this all: as the legislative department alone has access to the pockets of the people, and has in some constitutions full discretion, and in all a prevailing influence, over the pecuniary rewards of those who fill the other departments, a dependence is thus created in the latter, which gives still greater facility to encroachments of the former....

# NO. 51

To what expedient, then, shall we finally resort, for maintaining in practice the necessary partition of power among the several departments as laid down in the Constitution? The only answer that can be given is that as all these exterior provisions are found to be inadequate the defect must be supplied, by so contriving the interior structure of the government as that its several constituent parts may, by their mutual relations, be the means of keeping each other in their proper places....

In order to lay a due foundation for that separate and distinct exercise of the different powers of government, which to a certain extent is admitted on all hands to be essential to the preservation of liberty, it is evident that each department should have a will of its own; and consequently should be so constituted that the members of each should have as little agency as possible in the appointment of the members of the others....

It is equally evident that the members of each department should be as little dependent as possible on those of the others for the emoluments annexed to their offices. Were the executive magistrate, or the judges, not independent of the legislature in this particular, their independence in every other would be merely nominal.

But the great security against a gradual concentration of the several powers in the same department consists in giving to those who administer each department the necessary constitutional means and personal motives to resist encroachments of the others. The provision for defense must in this, as in all other cases, be made commensurate to the danger of attack. Ambition must be made to counteract ambition. The interest of the man must be connected with the constitutional rights of the place. It may be a reflection on human nature that such devices should be necessary to control the abuses of government. But what is government itself but the greatest of all reflections on human nature? If men were angels, no government would be necessary. If angels were to govern men, neither external nor internal controls on government would be necessary. In framing a government which is to be administered by men over men, the

**38**

*Chapter 2*
*The*
*Constitutional*
*Foundation of*
*American*
*Government*

great difficulty lies in this: you must first enable the government to control the governed; and in the next place oblige it to control itself. A dependence on the people is, no doubt, the primary control on the government; but experience has taught mankind the necessity of auxiliary precautions.

This policy of supplying, by opposite and rival interests, the defect of better motives, might be traced through the whole system of human affairs, private as well as public. We see it particularly displayed in all the subordinate distributions of power, where the constant aim is to divide and arrange the several offices in such a manner as that each may be a check on the other—that the private interest of every individual may be a sentinel over the public rights. These inventions of prudence cannot be less requisite in the distribution of the supreme powers of the State.

But it is not possible to give to each department an equal power of self-defense. In republican government, the legislative authority necessarily predominates. The remedy for this inconveniency is to divide the legislature into different branches; and to render them, by different modes of election and different principles of action, as little connected with each other as the nature of their common functions and their common dependence on the society will admit. It may even be necessary to guard against dangerous encroachments by still further precautions. As the weight of the legislative authority requires that it should be thus divided, the weakness of the executive may require, on the other hand, that it should be fortified. An absolute negative on the legislature appears, at first view, to be the natural defense with which the executive magistrate should be armed. But perhaps it would be neither altogether safe nor alone sufficient. On ordinary occasions it might not be exerted with the requisite firmness, and on extraordinary occasions it might be perfidiously abused. May not this defect of an absolute negative be supplied by some qualified connection between this weaker department and the weaker branch of the stronger department, by which the latter may be led to support the constitutional rights of the former, without being too much detached from the rights of its own department?

## 2.2 CHARLES A. BEARD

# An Economic Interpretation of the Constitution of the United States

Charles A. Beard's *An Economic Interpretation of the Constitution of the United States* (Macmillan, 1935), from which the following selection is excerpted, offers a historical revisionist interpretation of the U.S. Constitution. This political study was controversial because it strongly rejected the conventional democratic interpretation of the nature of the Constitution and the public-spirited, virtuous motivation of the framers of the U.S. Constitution. In sharp contrast to alternative studies that focus on the pragmatic character of the framers and on the Constitution as a flexible and stable blueprint based upon negotiated compromises, Beard contended that the document is a reflection exclusively of the private economic self-interests of an elite, or minority, of the American population. Beard claimed that the delegate membership of the Constitutional Convention consisted in a social economic elite of wealthy and powerful individuals.

In the following selection, Beard contends that the fundamental objective of the framers was to consolidate and expand their property holdings. The delegates strongly desired to limit the power of the masses, or majority rule, and consequently to protect their private property from potential tyranny of the majority and mob rule. The Constitution was designed with provisions consisting of specific political procedures and governmental institutions with the purposes of limiting majority rule, reducing popular accessibility and influence on public policy, and preserving elite dominance.

Various political scientists and historians have offered a rebuttal to Beard's thesis due to theoretical and historical deficiencies of evidence. However, several contemporary political theorists have adopted Beard's thesis and antidemocratic interpretation of the political ideas of the framers.

**40**

*Chapter 2*
*The*
*Constitutional*
*Foundation of*
*American*
*Government*

Beard (1874–1948) was the author of numerous books on American political history, and his scholarly reputation was recognized by both political scientists and historians. He was elected president of the American Political Science Association in 1926 and president of the American Historical Association in 1933. He was also awarded the prestigious Gold Medal for distinguished achievement by the National Institute of Arts and Letters in 1948.

**Key Concept:** the economic intention of the framers of the U.S. Constitution

# A SURVEY OF ECONOMIC INTERESTS IN 1787

The whole theory of the economic interpretation of history rests upon the concept that social progress in general is the result of contending interests in society —some favorable, others opposed, to change. On this hypothesis, we are required to discover at the very outset of the present study what classes and social groups existed in the United States just previous to the adoption of the Constitution and which of them, from the nature of their property, might have expected to benefit immediately and definitely by the overthrow of the old system and the establishment of the new. On the other hand, it must be discovered which of them might have expected more beneficial immediate results, on the whole, from the maintenance of the existing legal arrangements.

The importance of a survey of the distribution of property in 1787 for economic as well as political history is so evident that it is strange that no attempt has been made to undertake it on a large scale. Not even a beginning has been made. It is, therefore, necessary for us to rely for the present upon the general statements of historians who have written more or less at length about the period under consideration; but in the meanwhile it can do no harm to suggest, by way of a preface, the outlines of such a survey and some of the chief sources of information....

A survey of the economic interests of the members of the Convention presents certain conclusions:

A majority of the members were lawyers by profession.

Most of the members came from towns, on or near the coast, that is, from the regions in which personalty was largely concentrated.

Not one member represented in his immediate personal economic interests the small farming or mechanic classes.

The overwhelming majority of members, at least five-sixths, were immediately, directly, and personally interested in the outcome of their labors at Philadelphia, and were to a greater or less extent economic beneficiaries from the adoption of the Constitution....

It cannot be said... that the members of the Convention were "disinterested." On the contrary, we are forced to accept the profoundly significant conclusion that they knew through their personal experiences in economic affairs the precise results which the new government that they were setting up was designed to attain. As a group of doctrinaires, like the Frankfort assembly of 1848, they would have failed miserably; but as practical men they were able to build the new government upon the only foundations which could be stable: fundamental economic interests.[1]

# THE CONSTITUTION AS AN ECONOMIC DOCUMENT

It is difficult for the superficial student of the Constitution, who has read only the commentaries of the legists, to conceive of that instrument as an economic document. It places no property qualifications on voters or officers; it gives no outward recognition of any economic groups in society; it mentions no special privileges to be conferred upon any class. It betrays no feeling, such as vibrates through the French constitution of 1791; its language is cold, formal, and severe.

The true inwardness of the Constitution is not revealed by an examination of its provisions as simple propositions of law; but by a long and careful study of the voluminous correspondence of the period, contemporary newspapers and pamphlets, the records of the debates in the Convention at Philadelphia and in the several state conventions, and particularly, *The Federalist*, which was widely circulated during the struggle over ratification. The correspondence shows the exact character of the evils which the Constitution was intended to remedy; the records of the proceedings in the Philadelphia Convention reveal the successive steps in the building of the framework of the government under the pressure of economic interests; the pamphlets and newspapers disclose the ideas of the contestants over the ratification; and *The Federalist* presents the political science of the new system as conceived by three of the profoundest thinkers of the period, Hamilton, Madison, and Jay.

Doubtless, the most illuminating of these sources on the economic character of the Constitution are the records of the debates in the Convention, which have come down to us in fragmentary form; and a thorough treatment of material forces reflected in the several clauses of the instrument of government created by the grave assembly at Philadelphia would require a rewriting of the history of the proceedings in the light of the great interests represented there. But an entire volume would scarcely suffice to present the results of such a survey, and an undertaking of this character is accordingly impossible here.

*The Federalist*, on the other hand, presents in a relatively brief and systematic form an economic interpretation of the Constitution by the men best fitted, through an intimate knowledge of the ideals of the framers, to expound the political science of the new government. This wonderful piece of argumentation by Hamilton, Madison, and Jay is in fact the finest study in the economic interpretation of politics which exists in any language; and whoever would understand the Constitution as an economic document need hardly go beyond it. It is true that the tone of the writers is somewhat modified on account of the fact that they are appealing to the voters to ratify the Constitution, but at the same time they are, by the force of circumstances, compelled to convince large economic groups that safety and strength lie in the adoption of the new system.

**42**

*Chapter 2
The
Constitutional
Foundation of
American
Government*

Indeed, every fundamental appeal in it is to some material and substantial interest. Sometimes it is to the people at large in the name of protection against invading armies and European coalitions. Sometimes it is to the commercial classes whose business is represented as prostrate before the follies of the Confederation. Now it is to creditors seeking relief against paper money and the assaults of the agrarians in general; now it is to the holders of federal securities which are depreciating toward the vanishing point. But above all, it is to the owners of personalty anxious to find a foil against the attacks of levelling democracy, that the authors of *The Federalist* address their most cogent arguments in favor of ratification. It is true there is much discussion of the details of the new frame-work of government, to which even some friends of reform took exceptions; but Madison and Hamilton both knew that these were incidental matters when compared with the sound basis upon which the superstructure rested.

In reading the pages of this remarkable work as a study in political economy, it is important to bear in mind that the system, which the authors are describing, consisted of two fundamental parts—one positive, the other negative:

I. A government endowed to certain positive powers, but so constructed as to break the force of majority rule and prevent invasions of the property rights of minorities.

II. Restrictions on the state legislatures which had been so vigorous in their attacks on capital. . . .

### The Powers Conferred Upon the Federal Government

1. The powers for positive action conferred upon the new government were few, but they were adequate to the purposes of the framers. They included, first, the power to lay and collect taxes; but here the rural interests were conciliated by the provision that direct taxes must be apportioned among the states according to population, counting three-fifths of the slaves. This, in the opinion of contemporaries eminently qualified to speak, was designed to prevent the populations of the manufacturing states from shifting the burdens of taxation to the sparsely settled agricultural regions. . . .

The taxing power was the basis of all other positive powers, and it afforded the revenues that were to discharge the public debt in full. Provision was made for this discharge in Article VI to the effect that "All debts contracted and engagements entered into before the adoption of this Constitution shall be valid against the United States under this Constitution as under the Confederation."

But the cautious student of public economy, remembering the difficulties which Congress encountered under the Articles of Confederation in its attempts to raise the money to meet the interest on the debt, may ask how the framers of the Constitution could expect to overcome the hostile economic forces which had hitherto blocked the payment of the requisitions. The answer is short. Under the Articles, Congress had no power to lay and collect taxes immediately; it could only make requisitions on the state legislatures. Inasmuch as most of the states relied largely on direct taxes for their revenues, the demands of Congress were keenly felt and stoutly resisted. Under the new system, however, Congress is authorized to lay taxes on its own account, but it is evident that the framers contemplated placing practically all of the national burden on the consumer. The provision requiring the apportionment of direct taxes on a basis of population obviously implied that such taxes were to be viewed as a last resort when indirect taxes failed to provide the required revenue.

With his usual acumen, Hamilton conciliates the freeholders and property owners in general by pointing out that they will not be called upon to support the national government by payments proportioned to their wealth.[2] Experience has demonstrated that it is impracticable to raise any considerable sums by direct taxation. Even where the government is strong, as in Great Britain, resort must be had chiefly to indirect taxation. The pockets of the farmers "will reluctantly yield but scanty supplies, in the unwelcome shape of impositions on their houses and lands; and personal property is too precarious and invisible a fund to be laid hold of in any other way than by the imperceptible agency of taxes on consumption." Real and personal property are thus assured a generous immunity from such burdens as Congress had attempted to impose under the Articles; taxes under the new system will, therefore, be less troublesome than under the old.

2. Congress was given, in the second place, plenary power to raise and support military and naval forces, for the defence of the country against foreign and domestic foes. These forces were to be at the disposal of the President in the execution of national laws; and to guard the states against renewed attempts of "desperate debtors" like Shays, the United States guaranteed to every commonwealth a republican form of government and promised to aid in quelling internal disorder on call of the proper authorities.

The army and navy are considered by the authors of *The Federalist* as genuine economic instrumentalities. As will be pointed out below, they regarded trade and commerce as the fundamental cause of wars between nations; and the source of domestic insurrection they traced to class conflicts within society. "Nations in general," says Jay, "will make war whenever they have a prospect of getting anything by it";[3] and it is obvious that the United States dissevered and discordant will be the easy prey to the commercial ambitions of their neighbors and rivals.

The material gains to be made by other nations at the expense of the United States are so apparent that the former cannot restrain themselves from aggression. France and Great Britain feel the pressure of our rivalry in the fisheries; they and other European nations are our competitors in navigation and the carrying trade; our independent voyages to China interfere with the monopolies enjoyed by other countries there; Spain would like to shut the Mississippi against us on one side and Great Britain fain would close the St. Lawrence on the other. The cheapness and excellence of our productions will excite their jealousy, and the enterprise and address of our merchants will not be consistent with the wishes or policy of the sovereigns of Europe. But, adds the commentator, by way of clinching the argument, "if they see that our national government is efficient and well administered, our trade prudently regulated, our militia properly organized and disciplined, our resources and finances discreetly managed, our credit re-established, our people free, contented, and

**44**

*Chapter 2
The
Constitutional
Foundation of
American
Government*

united, they will be much more disposed to cultivate our friendship than provoke our resentment."[4]

All the powers of Europe could not prevail against us. "Under a vigorous national government the natural strength and resources of the country, directed to a common interest, would baffle all the combinations of European jealousy to restrain our growth.... An active commerce, an extensive navigation, and a flourishing marine would then be the offspring of moral and physical necessity. We might defy the little arts of the little politicians to control or vary the irresistible and unchangeable course of nature."[5] In the present state of disunion the profits of trade are snatched from us; our commerce languishes; and poverty threatens to overspread a country which might outrival the world in riches.

The army and navy are to be not only instruments of defence in protecting the United States against the commercial and territorial ambitions of other countries; but they may be used also in forcing open foreign markets. What discriminatory tariffs and navigation laws may not accomplish the sword may achieve. The authors of *The Federalist* do not contemplate that policy of mild and innocuous isolation which was later made famous by Washington's farewell address. On the contrary—they do not expect the United States to change human nature and make our commercial classes less ambitious than those of other countries to extend their spheres of trade. A strong navy will command the respect of European states....

3. In addition to the power to lay and collect taxes and raise and maintain armed forces on land and sea, the Constitution vests in Congress plenary control over foreign and interstate commerce, and thus authorizes it to institute protective and discriminatory laws in favor of American interests, and to create a wide sweep for free trade throughout the whole American empire. A single clause thus reflects the strong impulse of economic forces in the towns and young manufacturing centres. In a few simple words the mercantile and manufacturing interests wrote their *Zweck im Recht;* and they paid for their victory by large concessions to the slave-owning planters of the south.

While dealing with commerce in *The Federalist*[6] Hamilton does not neglect the subject of interstate traffic and intercourse. He shows how free trade over a wide range will be to reciprocal advantage, will give great diversity to commercial enterprise, and will render stagnation less liable by offering more distant markets when local demands fall off. "The speculative trader," he concludes, "will at once perceive the force of these observations and will acknowledge that the aggregate balance of the commerce of the United States would bid fair to be much more favorable than that of the thirteen states without union or with partial unions." ...

These are the great powers conferred on the new government: taxation, war, commercial control, and disposition of western lands. Through them public creditors may be paid in full, domestic peace maintained, advantages obtained in dealing with foreign nations, manufactures protected, and the development of the territories go forward with full swing. The remaining powers are minor and need not be examined here. What implied powers lay in the minds of the framers likewise need not be inquired into; they have long been the subject of juridical speculation.

None of the powers conferred by the Constitution on Congress permits a direct attack on property. The federal government is given no general authority to define property. It may tax, but indirect taxes must be uniform, and these are to fall upon consumers. Direct taxes may be laid, but resort to this form of taxation is rendered practically impossible, save on extraordinary occasions, by the provision that they must be apportioned according to population—so that numbers cannot transfer the burden to accumulated wealth. The slave trade may be destroyed, it is true, after the lapse of a few years; but slavery as a domestic institution is better safeguarded than before.

# NOTES

1. The fact that a few members of the Convention, who had considerable economic interests at stake, refused to support the Constitution does not invalidate the general conclusions here presented.
2. *The Federalist*, Number 12.
3. *The Federalist*, No. 4.
4. *Ibid.*
5. *The Federalist*, No. 11.
6. No. 11.

# The Intellectual Origins of the American Constitution

Gordon S. Wood (b. 1933) has taught with great distinction as a professor of history at numerous institutions, including the College of William and Mary, Harvard University, and the University of Michigan, and he was the Pitt Professor at Cambridge University in 1982–1983. From 1969 to the present he has taught at Brown University, where he is currently University Professor and a professor of history. He has received several awards and honors, including the John H. Dunning Prize from the American Historical Association and the Bancroft Award in 1970 for his book *The Creation of the American Republic, 1776–1787* (University of North Carolina Press, 1969). His book *The Radicalism of the American Revolution* (Random House, 1991) won a Pulitzer Prize. Wood has also published many scholarly articles in various American historical journals.

In the following selection from "The Intellectual Origins of the American Constitution," *National Forum: The Phi Kappa Phi Journal* (Fall 1984), Wood emphasizes the central ideological and intellectual role and dominant historical significance of classical republican political thought during the American Revolution and the designing of the Constitution. Classical republicanism refers to a political theory or ideology that is articulated through such values as civic virtue, governmental accountability, civic education, citizen obligations, and the public good as the ultimate criterion evaluating the worth of public policy. Wood develops the claim that the republican value of civic virtue performed a central role in the political culture of the American Revolution and in the period of the drafting of the U.S. Constitution. However, Wood also identifies other intellectual sources that influenced the Founders, such as a political theory of balanced or mixed government, a political theory of separation of powers, and a commitment to a particular interpretation of liberty.

**Key Concept:** the political culture of the U.S. Constitution

*T*he Constitution was created at a stroke in the summer of 1787, but its intellectual origins and sources, like those of all great events, reached back deep into the past. The Constitution has been described as the climax of the Enlightenment—that great eighteenth-century attempt to apply the results of Western science and learning to human affairs. As the product of Western "enlightened" thinking, the Constitution could scarcely have sprung simply from a summer's meeting. Its sources have often seemed to be the whole of previous history. No thinker, no idea, has been too remote, too obscure, to have been involved somehow in the making of the Constitution. Thus historians and political theorists have rummaged through the past looking for the particular philosopher or book that might have especially influenced the Framers of the Constitution. Some have seized on the Englishman John Locke; others, the Frenchman Montesquieu; still others, the Scot David Hume or the Swiss Burlamaqui; and some have even made a case for the ancient Greek Polybius....

Although isolating the influence of any one thinker on the Founding Fathers may be impossible, describing the currents of the political culture in which they were immersed in 1787 is not. The Founders were experienced, pragmatic political leaders, but they were not such practical, down-to-earth men that they could not be bothered by questions of political philosophy and theory. On the contrary, they were men intensely interested in ideas and especially concerned with making theoretical sense of what they were doing. They were participants in a rich, dynamic political culture that helped determine the nature of the Constitution they created. Understanding the Constitution requires an understanding of that political culture.

# REPUBLICANISM

The most pervasive characteristic of that political culture was republicanism, a body of ideas and values so deeply rooted that it formed the presuppositions of American thinking. This body of thought not only determined the elective political system the Founders believed in; it also determined their moral and social goals. To become republican was what the American Revolution had been about.

... Republicanism was the ideology of the democratic revolutions of the late eighteenth century; it was the ideology of the people against monarchs and hereditary aristocracies. Even the English who held on to their king and their House of Lords through the upheavals of this period nevertheless felt compelled to claim that, because of the power of the House of Commons, their constitution was already greatly republicanized. By the last quarter of the eighteenth century, being enlightened in the Western world, it seemed, was nearly equivalent to believing in republican values.

The deepest origins of these civic and moral values went all the way back to ancient Rome and the great era of the Roman Republic....

This great body of classical literature was revived and updated by the Renaissance, especially in the writings of the Italian philosopher Machiavelli. All was blended into a tradition of what has been called "civic humanism."...

**48**

*Chapter 2*
*The*
*Constitutional*
*Foundation of*
*American*
*Government*

What precisely did this body of ideas mean? It meant most obviously the elimination of a king and the institution of an electoral system of government. But these were just incidental means to a larger end. Republicanism really meant creating a political system concerned with the *res publica*, public things, the welfare of the people. Liberal critics of eighteenth-century monarchism believed that kings had become too wrapped up in their own selfish dynastic purposes and were ignoring the good of their people. By eliminating hereditary kings and instituting governments in which the people themselves would elect their political leaders, liberal reformers hoped that governments at last would promote only the public's welfare.

This civic culture, however, had more than political significance; it had social and moral significance as well. Republics required a particular sort of egalitarian and virtuous people: independent, property-holding citizens without artificial hereditary distinctions who were willing to sacrifice many of their private, selfish interests for the good of the whole community. This dependence on a relatively equal and virtuous populace was what made republics such fragile and often short-lived polities. Monarchies were long-lasting; they could maintain order from the top down over large, diverse, and stratified populations through their use of hereditary privilege, executive power, standing armies, and religious establishments. But republics had to be held together from below, from the consent and sacrifice of the people themselves; and therefore, as Montesquieu and other theorists had warned, republics necessarily had to be small in territory and homogeneous and moral in character....

Americans of 1787 were not the republican enthusiasts they had been in 1776. In a decade's time many of them had had their earlier dreams and illusions about republicanism considerably dampened. Experience with popular government, especially in the state legislatures, had cast doubt on the American people's capacity for virtue and disinterestedness. By 1787 many leaders, therefore, were ready for what James Madison called a "systematic change" of government, a change that resulted in the creation of the federal Constitution. But dissatisfied as many American leaders were with the Confederation and with the state legislatures, none of them—not even Alexander Hamilton who was the most monarchically minded among them—was prepared to give up on republican government. They knew, as Madison said, that "no other form would be reconcileable with the genius of the people of America; with the fundamental principles of the revolution; or with that honorable determination, which animates every votary of freedom, to rest all our political experiments on the capacity of mankind for self-government." Hence in the new Constitution, the Framers provided for periodically elected officers of the executive and legislative branches, and they made the federal government guarantee a republican form of government for each state (Article IV, Section 4), and forbade the United States from granting any titles of nobility (Article I, Section 9).

Still, the new federal government was sufficiently different from the Confederation and the governments of the states to arouse fears among many people that it was not "strictly republican." Did it not have a strong king-like executive and a powerful Senate with an aristocratic bearing? Unlike the Confederation, did it not operate directly on diverse peoples over half a continent despite the warnings of theorists and experience that such a large republic could not last? Fears and questions like these are what led Hamilton, Madison, and John Jay to spend so much time in *The Federalist* trying to prove that the Constitution was really "conformable to the true principles of republican government." In the process they helped to develop and shape further American ideas of republicanism.

# BALANCED GOVERNMENT

In 1787, classical republicanism was the basic premise of American thinking—the central presupposition behind all other ideas. However, it alone was not responsible for the peculiar structure of the revolutionary governments, including that of the federal government created by the Constitution. There was another set of ideas encapsulated in the theory of balanced or mixed government. It came likewise out of antiquity and was closely if not inextricably entwined with the tradition of classical republicanism. The classical theory of balanced government provided much more than the foundational ideas for the structures of the several state governments. The classical theory also included the notion of an independent president, the aristocratic Senate, and the popular House of Representatives.

Since at least the time of Aristotle, theorists had categorized forms of government into three ideal types—monarchy, aristocracy, and democracy. These types were derived from the number of rulers in each: for monarchy, one person; for aristocracy, a few nobles; for democracy, all the people. Aristotle and others believed that each of these rulers when alone entrusted with political power tended to run amok and to become perverted. By itself monarchy became tyranny; aristocracy became oligarchy; and democracy became anarchy. Only by mixing each of these types together in the same constitution, only by balancing the tendencies of each of them, could order be maintained and the perfections of each type of simple government be achieved. The result would be a governmental system in equilibrium—the very kind of static model that the eighteenth-century Enlightenment admired.

For most enlightened thinkers of the eighteenth century, including those of the American colonies, there already existed at least in theory such a perfectly balanced government—the English constitution....

When Americans in 1776 revolted from this perfect English constitution, most of them had no intention of repudiating the classical ideal behind it. Nor did they believe that this ideal of balanced government was incompatible with republicanism.... They and other English critics, speaking out of the civic humanist tradition of republicanism, thought that in the course of the eighteenth century the ideal English constitution had degenerated and become corrupted. The king was using his power to appoint men to crown offices in order to bribe and influence members of the House of Lords and House of Commons....

Most of America's revolutionary state governments created in 1776–77 were meant to be miniature republican copies of the ideal English constitution. Although elected, the governors, senates, and houses of representatives of the several states were intended to resemble the king, House of Lords, and House

**50**

*Chapter 2
The
Constitutional
Foundation of
American
Government*

of Commons of the English constitution; indeed, they still do. But in order to prevent their balanced governments from degenerating in the way the English constitution had, most of the states in 1776 severely limited the appointing powers of the governors or chief executives; and, more important for American constitutional development, all of them forbade members of both houses of the legislature and the judiciary from simultaneously holding office in the executive branch. In justifying this prohibition, some of the states in 1776 invoked a doctrine made famous by Montesquieu of separating the executive, legislative, and judicial powers from each other. This triad of functioning powers was really not the same as the classical triad of ruling elements—governors, senates, and houses of representatives—but the goal of the two triads—the prevention of corruption—was the same.

There is no exaggerating the importance of this American exclusion of the legislators from simultaneous executive or ministerial office. This fundamentally divided America's constitutional tradition from that of the former mother country. By this prohibition alone, Americans prevented the development of an English or European-style parliamentary cabinet form of government. Members of America's executive branch, unlike those of most of the democracies in the world, cannot at the same time hold seats in the legislatures. The separation of the legislature from what was thought to be the perverse, corrupting influence of the executive was written into the revolutionary state constitutions of 1776–77. This division was instituted for the sake of maintaining the independence of the ruling parts and the balance that an ideal government ought to have. Since separation of powers was often used to justify the maintenance of this independence and balance, there was the likelihood that separating powers and balancing parts of the government would blend in people's minds.

## Separation of Powers

By the time Americans came to form the federal Constitution in 1787–88, the two sets of ideas had become thoroughly confused. Undoubtedly most of the Framers at Philadelphia thought they were creating a balanced government much in the form of the several state governments—only with a stronger chief executive and Senate than in most of the states. Although the ultimate source of this structure was the ideal English constitution, by 1787 few American political leaders felt comfortable any longer saying so in public. (John Adams was a conspicuous exception.) Referring to the chief executive as the monarchical element and the Senate as the aristocracy in a balanced government was politically impossible in the popular atmosphere of the 1780s. Thus the Framers had to find justifications for their two-house legislature and their strong, independent president in some place other than the English constitution and the classical ideal of mixed government.

What they did was blend the notion of separating the functional powers of government—executive, legislative, and judicial—with the older theory of balanced government; and they used both indiscriminately to describe the now incredibly fragmented and countervailing character of America's political system. "The constant aim," wrote Madison in *The Federalist* No. 51, which summed up the Founders' thinking on their parcelling of power, "is to divide and arrange the several offices in such a manner as that each may be a check on the other." Bicameralism, the presidential veto power, the independent judiciary, even federalism itself—the apportioning of authority between the national and state governments—all became various means of dividing, checking, and balancing a mistrusted political power.

# LIBERTY

... Although the classical traditions of republicanism and mixed government formed the presuppositions of American thinking, they were presuppositions shared by the whole Western world. Other nations, such as eighteenth-century France, were influenced by republicanism; indeed, most countries in the world now have republican governments. Other states also have attempted balanced governments, two-house legislatures, independent executives, and separated powers. But few of them have our particular concern for personal and political liberty: for the rule of law, for private personal and property rights, for constitutional and judicial limitations on the use of governmental power. If the origins of these concerns are to be found in sources other than America's own experience, then they must be found neither in the ideas of classical antiquity nor in those of Renaissance civic humanism but in the peculiarities of the English legal tradition.

Nothing was more important for the development of American constitutionalism in 1787 and in the years following than the fact that most of the Founders had been reared as Englishmen and had thus shared in the English preoccupation with liberty and in the unique protections of the English common law. England was, as Montesquieu said in 1731, "the freest country that exists in the world," and eighteenth-century Englishmen on both sides of the Atlantic prided themselves on that reputation. The colonists began the Revolution in defense of their English liberties. Liberty was an English obsession before it was an American one.

... Whatever Americans did to extend liberty and protect individual rights from the encroachments of governmental power, the English had done it first: trial by jury, writs of *habeas corpus*, concern for property rights, fear of standing armies, bills of rights—all were English before they were American. Without the influence of the English constitutional and legal tradition, it is inconceivable that Americans in 1787 or later would have believed and acted as they did.

Yet ultimately, of course, the American political and legal system is not the English system, and this difference should make us aware that looking for intellectual origins and tracing intellectual influences are only part of the explanation of how we have come to be what we are. More important perhaps is what Americans have done with these inherited ideas, how they have used, expanded, and reshaped their intellectual legacies to fit the dynamics of their changing experience.

# CHAPTER 3 The Evolution of American Federalism

## 3.1 JOHN MARSHALL

# McCulloch v. Maryland

The 1819 landmark decision *McCulloch v. Maryland* (4 Wheaton 316), from which the following selection is taken, had major constitutional and political consequences, including the dramatic growth of the federal government. The opinion of the U.S. Supreme Court reflected a fundamental attempt to identify the legitimate relationship between the federal and state governments. In 1791, after an intense national partisan debate, Congress chartered the First National Bank of the United States. As a leader of the Federalist political party and a strong advocate for the construction of the bank, Alexander Hamilton defended the bank, interpreting its legitimate existence to be based upon an implied power. As a leader of the Anti-Federalist political party and a strong opponent of the bank, Thomas Jefferson contended that any congressional power must be explicitly expressed. However, the First National Bank's constitutionality was not challenged in the courts, and its charter expired in 1811. In 1816 Congress created the Second National Bank of the United States, and it met immediate intense political opposition by various state legislatures. In 1818 the state of Maryland passed legislation designed to tax a branch of the National Bank in Baltimore. The cashier of the bank, James McCulloch, refused to pay the tax, so Maryland sued. A Maryland state court upheld the tax legislation; McCulloch subsequently appealed the decision to the U.S. Supreme Court.

Chief Justice John Marshall articulated that in addition to the expressed or enumerated powers listed in the Constitution, the federal government, and Congress in particular, have implied powers due to the "elastic" or "necessary and proper clause" of the Constitution. Thus, Marshall established the constitutionality of Congress's establishment of the bank and the illegitimacy of Maryland's legislation to tax the bank. The Court's decision had a highly significant impact upon the general expansion of the federal government's power. In particular, *McCulloch v. Maryland* established a legal foundation and a precedent for the expanded commercial powers of the national government.

**Key Concept:** implied powers of the national government under the "necessary and proper clause"

*M*r. Chief Justice Marshall delivered the opinion of the Court, saying in part:

In the case now to be determined, the defendant, a sovereign State, denies the obligation of a law enacted by the legislature of the Union; and the plaintiff, on his part, contests the validity of an Act which has been passed by the legislature of that State. The Constitution of our country, in its most interesting and vital parts, is to be considered; the conflicting powers of the government of the Union and of its members, as marked in that Constitution, are to be discussed; and an opinion given, which may essentially influence the great operations of the government. . . .

The first question made in the cause is, has Congress power to incorporate a bank? . . .

In discussing this question, the counsel for the State of Maryland have deemed it of some importance, in the construction of the Constitution, to consider that instrument not as emanating from the people, but as the act of sovereign and independent states. The powers of the general government, it has been said, are delegated by the states, who alone are truly sovereign; and must be exercised in subordination to the states, who alone possess supreme dominion. . . .

If any one proposition could command the universal assent of mankind, we might expect it would be this: that the government of the Union, though limited in its powers, is supreme within its sphere of action. This would seem to result necessarily from its nature. It is the government of all; its powers are delegated by all; it represents all, and acts for all. Though any one State may be willing to control its operations, no State is willing to allow others to control. them. The nation, on those subjects on which it can act, must necessarily bind its component parts. But this question is not left to mere reason: the people have, in express terms, decided it, by saying, "this Constitution, and the laws of the United States, which shall be made in pursuance thereof," "shall be the supreme law of the land," and by requiring that the members of the State legislatures, and the officers of the executive and judicial departments of the States, shall take the oath of fidelity to it.

The government of the United States, then, though limited in its powers, is supreme; and its laws, when made in pursuance of the Constitution, form the supreme law of the land, "anything in the Constitution or laws of any State to the contrary notwithstanding."

Among the enumerated powers, we do not find that of establishing a bank or creating a corporation. But there is no phrase in the instrument which, like the Articles of Confederation, excludes incidental or implied powers; and which requires that everything granted shall be expressly and minutely described. Even the Tenth Amendment, which was framed for the purpose of quieting the excessive jealousies which had been excited, omits the word "expressly," and declares only that the powers "not delegated to the United States, nor prohibited to the States, are reserved to the States or to the people"; thus leaving the question, whether the particular power which may become the subject of contest, has been delegated to the one government, or prohibited to the other, to depend on a fair construction of the whole instrument. The men who drew and adopted this amendment, had experienced the embarrassments resulting from the insertion of this word in the Articles of Confederation, and probably omitted it to avoid those embarrassments. A constitution, to contain an accurate detail of all the subdivisions of which its great powers will admit, and of all the means by which they may be carried into execution, would partake of the prolixity of a legal code, and could scarcely be embraced by the human mind. It would probably never be understood by the public. Its nature, therefore, requires, that only its great outlines should be marked, its important objects designated, and the minor ingredients which compose those objects be deduced from the nature of the objects themselves. That this idea was entertained by the framers of the American Constitution, is not only to be inferred from the nature of the instrument, but from the language. . . .

Although, among the enumerated powers of government, we do not find the word "bank," or "incorporation," we find the great powers to lay and collect taxes; to borrow money; to regulate commerce; to declare and conduct a war; and to raise and support armies and navies. The sword and the purse, all the external relations, and no inconsiderable portion of the industry of the nation, are entrusted to its government. It can never be pretended that these vast powers draw after them others of inferior importance, merely because they are inferior. Such an idea can never be advanced. But it may, with great reason, be contended, that a government, entrusted with such ample powers, on the due execution of which the happiness and prosperity of the nation so vitally depends, must also be entrusted with ample means for their execution. The power being given, it is the interest of the nation to facilitate its execution. It can never be their interest, and cannot be presumed to have been their intention, to clog and embarrass its execution by withholding the most appropriate means. Throughout this vast republic, from the St. Croix to the Gulf of Mexico, from the Atlantic to the Pacific, revenue is to be collected and expended, armies are to be marched and supported. The exigencies of the nation may require, that the treasure raised in the North should be transported to the South, that raised in the East conveyed to the West, or that this order should be reversed. Is that construction of the Constitution to be preferred which would render these operations difficult, hazardous, and expensive? Can we adopt that construction (unless the words imperiously require it) which would impute to the framers of that instrument, when granting these powers for the public good, the intention of impeding their exercise by withholding a choice of means? If, indeed, such be the mandate of the Constitution, we have only to obey; but that instrument does not profess to enumerate the means by which the powers it confers may be executed; nor does it prohibit the creation of a corporation, if the existence of such a being be essential to the beneficial exercise of those powers. It is, then, the subject of fair inquiry, how far such means may be employed. . . .

But the Constitution of the United States has not left the right of Congress to employ the necessary means, for the execution of the powers conferred on the government, to general reasoning. To its enumeration of powers is added that of making "all laws which shall be necessary and proper, for carrying into execution the foregoing powers, and all other powers vested by this Constitution, in the government of the United States, or in any department thereof." . . .

But the argument on which most reliance is placed, is drawn from the peculiar language of this clause. Congress is not empowered by it to make all laws, which may have relation to the powers conferred on the government, but such only as may be "necessary and proper" for carrying them into execution. The word "necessary" is considered as controlling the whole sentence, and as limiting the right to pass laws for the execution of the granted powers, to such as are indispensable, and without which the power would be nugatory. That it excludes the choice of means, and leaves to Congress, in each case, that only which is most direct and simple.

Is it true, that this is the sense in which the word "necessary" is always used? Does it always import an absolute physical necessity, so strong, that one thing, to which another may be termed necessary, cannot exist without that other? We think it does not. If reference be had to its use, in the common affairs of the world, or in approved authors, we find that it frequently imports no more than that one thing is convenient, or useful, or essential to another. To employ the means necessary to an end, is generally understood as employing any means calculated to produce the end, and not as being confined to those single means, without which the end would be entirely unattainable. . . .

This provision is made in a constitution intended to endure for ages to come, and, consequently, to be adapted to the various crises of human affairs. To have prescribed the means by which government should, in all future time, execute its powers, would have been to change, entirely, the character of the instrument, and give it the properties of a legal code. It would have been an unwise attempt to provide, by immutable rules, for exigencies which, if foreseen at all, must have been seen dimly, and which can be best provided for as they occur. To have declared that the best means shall not be used, but those alone without which the power given would be nugatory, would have been to deprive the legislature of the capacity to avail itself of experience, to exercise its reason, and to accommodate its legislation to circumstances. . . .

But the argument which most conclusively demonstrates the error of the construction contended for by the counsel for the State of Maryland, is founded on the intention of the convention, as manifested in the whole clause. To waste time and argument in proving that, without it, Congress might carry its powers into execution, would be not much less idle than to hold a lighted taper to the sun. As little can it be required to prove, that in the absence of this clause, Congress would have some choice of means. That it might employ those which, in its judgment, would most advantageously effect the object to be accomplished. That any means adapted to the end, any means which tended directly to the execution of the constitutional powers of the government, were in themselves constitutional. This clause, as construed by the State of Maryland, would abridge and almost annihilate this useful and necessary right of the legislature to select its means. That this could not be intended, is, we should think, had it not been already controverted, too apparent for controversy. We think so for the following reasons:

1st. The clause is placed among the powers of Congress, not among the limitations on those powers.

2d. Its terms purport to enlarge, not to diminish the powers vested in the government. It purports to be an additional power, not a restriction on those already granted. No reason has been or can be assigned, for thus concealing an intention to narrow the discretion of the national legislature, under words which purport to enlarge it. The framers of the Constitution wished its adoption, and well knew that it would be endangered by its strength, not by its weakness. Had they been capable of using language which would convey to the eye one idea, and after deep reflection, impress on the mind another, they would rather have disguised the grant of power, than its limitation. If then, their intention had been, by this clause, to restrain the free use of means which might otherwise have been implied, that intention would have been inserted in another place, and would have been expressed in terms resembling these: "In carrying into execution the foregoing powers, and all others," etc., "no laws shall be passed but such as are necessary and proper." Had the intention been to make this clause restrictive, it would unquestionably have been so in form as well as in effect.

The result of the most careful and attentive consideration bestowed upon this clause is, that if it does not enlarge, it cannot be construed to restrain the powers of Congress, or to impair the right of the legislature to exercise its best judgment in the selection of measures, to carry into execution the constitutional powers of the government. If no other motive for its insertion can be suggested, a sufficient one is found in the desire to remove all doubts respecting the right to legislate on that vast mass of incidental powers which must be involved in the Constitution, if that instrument be not a splendid bauble.

We admit, as all must admit, that the powers of the government are limited, and that its limits are not to be transcended. But we think the sound construction of the Constitution must allow to the national legislature that discretion, with respect to the means by which the powers it confers are to be carried into execution, which will enable that body to perform the high duties assigned to it, in the manner most beneficial to the people. Let the end be legitimate, let it be within the scope of the Constitution, and all means which are appropriate, which are plainly adapted to that end, which are not prohibited, but consist with the letter and spirit of the Constitution, are constitutional....

It being the opinion of the court that the act incorporating the bank is constitutional; and that the power of establishing a branch in the State of Maryland might be properly exercised by the bank itself, we proceed to inquire:

2. Whether the State of Maryland may, without violating the Constitution, tax that branch?

That the power of taxation is one of vital importance; that it is retained by the States; that it is not abridged by the grant of a similar power to the government of the Union; that it is to be concurrently exercised by the two governments: are truths which have never been denied. But, such is the paramount character of the Constitution, that its capacity to withdraw any subject from the action of even this power, is admitted. The States are expressly forbidden to lay any duties on imports or exports, except what may be absolutely necessary for executing their inspection laws. If the obligation of this prohibition must be conceded—if it may restrain a State from the exercise of its taxing power on imports and exports; the same paramount character would seem to restrain, as it certainly may restrain, a State from such other exercise of this power, as is in its nature incompatible with, and repugnant to, the constitutional laws of the Union. A law, absolutely repugnant to another, as entirely repeals that other as if express terms of repeal were used.

On this ground the counsel for the bank place its claim to be exempted from the power of a State to tax its operations. There is no express provision for the case, but the claim has been sustained on a principle which so entirely pervades the Constitution, is so intermixed with the materials which compose it, so interwoven with its web, so blended with its texture, as to be incapable of being separated from it, without rending it into shreds.

This great principle is, that the Constitution and the laws made in pursuance thereof are supreme; that they control the Constitution and laws of the respective States, and cannot be controlled by them. From this, which may be almost termed an axiom, other propositions are deduced as corollaries, on the truth or error of which, and on their application to this case, the cause has been supposed to depend. These are, 1st. That a power to create implies a power to preserve. 2d. That a power to destroy, if wielded by a different hand, is hostile to, and incompatible with, these powers to create and preserve. 3d. That where this repugnancy exists, that authority which is supreme must control, not yield to that over which it is supreme. . . .

If we apply the principle for which the State of Maryland contends, to the Constitution generally, we shall find it capable of changing totally the character of that instrument. We shall find it capable of arresting all the measures of the government and of prostrating it at the foot of the States. The American people have declared their Constitution, and the laws made in pursuance thereof, to be supreme; but this principle would transfer the supremacy, in fact, to the States. . . .

The court has bestowed on this subject its most deliberate consideration. The result is a conviction that the States have no power, by taxation or otherwise, to retard, impede, burden or in any manner control, the operations of the constitutional laws enacted by Congress to carry into execution the powers vested in the general government. This is, we think, the unavoidable consequence of that supremacy which the Constitution has declared.

We are unanimously of opinion, that the law passed by the legislature of Maryland, imposing a tax on the Bank of the United States, is unconstitutional and void.

# Federalism, Nationalism, and Democracy in America

Samuel H. Beer (b. 1911) received his Ph.D. from Harvard University, where he has served as professor of government since 1938 and where he is presently the Eaton Professor of Science of Government. He has received several awards and honors, including a Rhodes Scholarship from 1932 to 1935, Fulbright and Guggenheim Fellowships from 1953 to 1954, and a Woodrow Wilson Foundation Award in 1966 for his work *British Politics in the Collectivist Age* (Alfred A. Knopf, 1965). Beer is a prolific author who has published numerous books on American government, comparative politics, and British politics, such as *The City of Reason* (Harvard University Press, 1968) and *Treasury Control: The Coordination of Financial and Economic Policy in Great Britain* (Clarendon Press, 1956). He has published numerous scholarly articles in various political science and public policy journals. Beer has also served as associate editor of the journal *American Political Science Review*.

In the following selection, which is excerpted from "Federalism, Nationalism, and Democracy in America," *American Political Science Review* (March 1978), Beer analyzes the apparently contradictory developments of centralization and decentralization, which have occurred simultaneously with the dramatic expansion of American governmental institutions in recent decades. He argues that the most dramatic development of American federalism has been the emergence of multiple contexts of cooperative interaction and interdependence among distinct layers of government. This, he feels, represents the most significant transformation of American federalism, more so than any of particular transference of public authority or governmental roles and responsibilities among levels of government. The recently accelerated blurring of distinction between national and state powers and functions is referred to as *cooperative federalism*. Beer contends that these new developments closely conform to the framers' original model of representational federalism. The original design of representation was based upon a theory of territorial diffusion of powers as a preventative measure against a highly centralized tyrannical government and as a means to promote expanded political representation.

Beer's analysis, a critical addition and necessary contribution to the literature on federalism, helped shift the focus of debate and analysis on this topic.

**Key Concept:** the impact of intergovernmental relations upon representation

$D$uring the 1960s in the United States, as in most advanced countries, there was a large and sudden surge upward in the growth of the public sector, largely under the impetus of the central government. Supporters of this new phase of centralization sometimes see it as one more, and perhaps the final, stage in the transformation of the American polity into virtually a unitary system. Critics, on the other hand, seek to revive federalism, frequently proposing a reallocation of functions between levels of government. Some find evidence of such a revival in the decentralization accomplished by recent less restrictive schemes of federal aid.

I should like to present a third position. My thesis is that more important than any shifts of power or function between levels of government has been the emergence of new arenas of mutual influence among levels of government. Within the field of intergovernmental relations a new and powerful system of representation has arisen, as the federal government has made a vast new use of state and local governments and these governments in turn have asserted a new direct influence on the federal government. What is interesting about American federalism today is not its particular allocation of functions or powers between levels of government, but rather what it is adding to our national system of representation.

Moreover, I should say that these developments, while new, are in harmony with the original design of the federal system. Federalism as the mutually exclusive allocation of powers between the general and the state governments —dual federalism it may be called—belongs to the past. Dual federalism was indeed a feature of the original design and, broadly speaking, characterized our system of multilevel government until the New Deal. Federalism in this sense does not apply, and given the realities of our times, could not be made to apply, to that system today.

But dual federalism was only one and a secondary feature of the original design. The theory governing that design made its territorial allocation of powers an instrument of a far more important purpose. That purpose was so to divide and organize power as to avert the evils and realize the benefits of free government. Within this general scheme, the federal division of powers served a representative function by creating a structure of mutual balance and influence between the two main levels of government. In this manner, dual federalism was a means to representational federalism.

In the first part of this article I shall, therefore, be talking about the original federal design, in order, in the second part, to direct attention to the way that representational federalism has been reconstituted by recent developments in intergovernmental relations. Since these developments have parallels in other countries, I shall conclude with a few questions for comparative study suggested by American experience.

# THE ORIGINAL FEDERAL DESIGN

THE DEMOCRATIC PURPOSE.   To see the original federal design as the solution to a problem of representation links it directly and intimately to the great cause that led to the American Revolution. That cause was liberty. To the colonial dissidents liberty meant certain personal rights, such as freedom of conscience, but above all political liberty, the right to government by "the consent of the governed." And by "consent" they meant not some presumed agreement to a form of government delivered by social contract in the distant past, but rather a consent that closely and actively joined voter and representative. Ambiguities in this idea permitted various degrees of control by voters over representatives, ranging from strict delegation to a fiduciary relationship subject to frequent accountability. Sometimes the two tendencies were mixed, as when the town meeting of Boston in May 1764 at the height of the Stamp Act crisis delegated to their representatives in the provincial assembly "the power of acting in their public concerns in general as your own prudence shall direct you, always reserving to themselves the constitutional right of expressing their mind and giving you such instruction upon particular matters as they at any time shall judge proper." One part of the charge leads toward legislative discretion, the other toward popular sovereignty. Either makes government crucially dependent on the will of the voters....

THE NATIONAL QUESTION.   When this failure had led to independence, the national question came suddenly and urgently to the fore. What was the source of the authority of the new government? Obviously, the consent of the people—that and nothing more. But was this consent given by one people or by several peoples, by the nation or by the states? The Declaration of Independence described itself in Jefferson's words as the act of "one people" and eleven years later the Constitution similarly declared that it was ordained and established by "We, the people." According to Abraham Lincoln, the unity of the nation asserted in these documents dated back to the time of the Continental Congress when the colonists chose to form the Union, which is, in his words, "older than any of the States, and, in fact... created the States" and "produced their independence and liberty."

This version of events provides the historical basis for the national theory of American federalism. According to that theory, a single sovereign power, the people of the United States, created both the federal and state governments, delegating to each a certain limited authority. In this theory of the juridical basis of the American polity popular sovereignty appears as a single national will acting as the constituent power. The compact theory, on the other hand, takes a different view of the same events and arrives at a different view of the Constitution and of federalism. According to this view, the colonies became separate, independent polities when they cast loose from Britain and only thereafter entered into an agreement to have a general government for certain limited purposes. From this theory justifications have been deduced for secession, interposition, or at least extensive "states' rights."

The national theory, I should say, is a superior interpretation of what actually happened, an interpretation incidentally which has been given further powerful support by recent historical research. The important thing, however, for the present inquiry into the original design of American federalism, is that the men who conceived and elaborated that design worked from the premises of the national theory. Their federalism presupposes their nationalism. In their view the constituent power was on people, the nation. What they sought to produce in the constitution of the new polity was a scheme by which that nation would act not only as the constituent power, but also as the continuous controlling and directing influence in the political life of the new polity. In seeking to give such effect to this idea of national democracy, they were consistently carrying out the belief in government by consent that had rationalized and impelled the resistance to Great Britain in prerevolutionary days. The problem of representation which had preoccupied the energies of that long struggle continued to be central to the shaping of the federal structure.

THE FRAMERS' THEORY.    Theory had powerfully directed their labors of resistance and theory powerfully directed their labors of construction. In the later as in the earlier phase, the orienting ideology consisted of those same liberal democratic ideas that had come down from the seventeenth century. In their work of construction, however, the Americans also made wide use of "the new science of politics" which had blossomed in the early eighteenth century. This new study was by no means conceived as value-free, but was dominated by the new hope of the time, free government. Its main concern was how to protect liberty by dividing and balancing power within a polity. The premise of this concern and of its consequent technique was a certain distrust of human nature. Although many of these authors, as in the case of the Americans, had had a Protestant upbringing, I would not say that this distrust was Calvinist—it did not approach that black despair—nor even that it was distinctively Christian or biblical. It was more modern, more secular, a workable pessimism which saw a love of power in all men and feared any monopoly of the instruments of power, but which held that if control over these instruments were properly divided and balanced, power could be made to check power so that it would be used only for the common good. One technique was a separation of powers according to the "natural" functions of government or according to the ranks and orders of society. Another consisted in a division of powers between a general government and a number of provincial governments. It was, of course, this latter sort of balancing that the framers sought to achieve in their federal design.

That design was unique. At Philadelphia in 1787, it is generally recognized, the Americans invented federalism as it has come to be understood since that time. The scheme had no precedent. Its authors were not, as some have claimed, attempting to restore an allocation of powers between central and provincial governments like that the colonists had experienced in the days of "benign and salutary neglect" under the old empire before the Sugar Act. They were surely not trying to imitate the Dutch, Swiss or German regimes, a type of polity which they regarded as "the cause of incurable disorder and imbecility." Their new creation was theory-based. Yet even in drawing generously on the political science of their time, they did not follow their authorities slavishly. Indeed, their inventivenesss consisted precisely in combining elements taken from two incompatible constructions of, respectively, Montesquieu and Hume.

Montesquieu's contribution came principally from his famous discussion of the confederate republic in Books VIII and IX of *The Spirit of the Laws*. There he was trying to reconcile the conflicting conditions conducive respectively to liberty and to security. In conformity with the conventional view, he held that "republican government" could flourish only in a small state where "the public good" is "more obvious, better understood, and more within the reach of every citizen." In an extensive republic, on the other hand, although its defensive posture would be stronger, the public good would be "sacrificed to a thousand private views" and encroachments on liberty would be able to grow without arousing general resistance. Distance, size or—more properly—scale would present the man of ambition with his opportunity and his temptation. Montesquieu proposed to realize the respective advantages of smallness and largeness of scale without introducing their disadvantages by means of a confederate republic. Formed by "a convention" among a number of small republics, such a polity could amass defensive power without making itself vulnerable to the internal corruption of despotism, because the member states would retain the independent force to prevent the abuse of power by the general government. The territorial pluralism of these continuing small governments would counteract tendencies toward corruption in the wider polity.

Montesquieu's confederate republic alone was clearly not the model for the constitution makers at Philadelphia. It was rather the sort of regime which in their eyes had proved to be both inefficient and dangerous to liberty under the Articles of Confederation. Their radical transformation was to impose on it certain features of a unitary regime. For the sake of "stability and energy" they gave the general government a new instrument of power by enabling it to act directly on individuals. But their main concern was to add a further protection of "republican liberty" by providing for the representation of individuals in the federal legislature.

The significance of this new scheme of representation was given its classical exposition in Madison's Tenth Federalist. His idea is an adaptation of a proposal put forward by Hume in his essay on the "Idea of a Perfect Commonwealth." In that essay, first published in 1752, Hume sketched an elaborate system of representative government and against this background attacked the "common opinion" that republican government is more likely to survive in a small than a large polity. On the contrary, he argued, the "near habitation" of the citizens of a small polity will make even their division into small parties vulnerable to "the force of popular tides and currents." In the large representative republic, however, not only will the "higher magistrates" "refine" the opinions of the voters, but also the various parts will be less likely to unite against "the public interest." Madison improves on this model by stressing the diversity of social and economic interests that will be embraced in the more extensive republic. Thanks to the greater differentiation that goes with larger scale, the social pluralism of the general government will counteract tendencies toward a factional abuse of power in the subordinate governments.

The invention at Philadelphia transformed Montesquieu's model by integrating with it this Humean construction. The new unitary features meant that now the social pluralism of the nation as a whole would be represented in the general government, which, within limits, would be able to avert the dangers of faction within the states, while the continued existence of the states meant that, as in Montesquieu's model, territorial pluralism would constitute a safeguard against encroachments by the general government. It was a unified, internally coherent and highly original model of a new kind of government. This invention resulted from compromise, to be sure—not the compromise of stalemate, however, but of social learning.

FEDERALISM AS REPRESENTATIONAL.    In the *Federalist* papers and the ratification debates, the new model was set forth and defended. It had a military version in which the possession of instruments of coercive force by each level held the balance for free government. "Power being almost always the rival of power," wrote Hamilton, "the general government will at all times stand ready to check the usurpations of the state governments, and these will have the same disposition towards the general government." His next sentence revealed the motor in the mechanism: "The people, by throwing themselves into either scale, will infallibly make it preponderate. If their rights are invaded by either, they can make use of the other as the instrument of redress." In short, the same force which, according to the national theory, had brought the Constitution into existence and formed its juridical foundation, the sovereign people, would continue to guarantee its free operation.

This military version of how the federal design would operate is hardly more than an historical curiosity today. But its authors were, of course, also thinking in larger terms and of a more political application. They expected the social pluralism of the general government to operate not only in emergencies, but also in day-to-day decision making. Nor did they see this function as merely negative—to prevent narrow and oppressive majorities from forming or acting. Their political science taught them that "the larger the society . . . the more duly capable it will be of self-government." They therefore expected that the majority coalitions which did form within the general government not only would respect "the rights of every class of citizens," but also would positively express "principles . . . of justice and the general good." The framers were not some sort of early-day laissez-fairists. Indeed, Turgot gave them a famous scolding for their interventionism. They lived in an age of state-building and mercantilism and fully recognized the need for active government in their developing economy. They saw no need, however, to trade off liberty for development and, although by no means utopians, they had high hopes for their political engineering, believing that its processes of mutual balance and influence would not only break the violence of faction, but also produce decisions worthy of general assent.

In the *Federalist* papers and the ratification debates, discussion of the military aspects of the federal balance shade off into a more political version, which tells us a good deal about how the American system has actually worked and which is still vividly relevant to its operation today. "Notwithstanding the different modes in which [the federal and state governments] are appointed," Madison wrote in the 46th *Federalist*, "we must consider both of them as substantially dependent on the great body of the citizens of the United States.... The federal and the State governments are in fact but different agents and trustees of the people, constituted with different powers, and designed for different purposes." "The people" is "the ultimate authority," the "common superior" of both. Nor does he mean this only in the sense of juridical foundation or military balance. He is also concerned to show how the people, acting as the common electorate of all levels of government, bring state perspectives to bear on federal decisions and federal perspectives to bear on state decisions. The three main propositions in his analysis are that these perspectives will not merely reflect the immediate wishes of the voters, but will be shaped by the processes of self-government in which the voters take part; that the influence between levels will pass from state to general government, but also from general government to state government; and finally that the medium through which this influence will be transmitted will be the common electorate of the two sets of governments.

The essence of the invention of 1787 was the use of the same electorate to choose two sets of governments, each with constitutional protection. As in the military version of the new federal system, where the people were to maintain the balance for free government by casting their weight in one or the other scale, in this political version the medium of interaction was the common electorate. Governing himself through two different governments, the voter views the political world from two perspectives, one shaped by the social pluralism of the general government, the other shaped by the territorial pluralism of state government. In his political life, as a member of one nation, he does not separate from one another the two perspectives and the interests each elicits in him. His state perspective affects his choices and decisions in federal politics as his federal perspective affects his choices and decisions in state politics. One may call this process "representational federalism" because it gives representation in the general government to the territorial pluralism of the states and representation in the state governments to the social pluralism of the general government.

In framing and debating the new federal structure, Americans of the time were concerned with the same central problem that had stirred them to criticism, resistance and rebellion a generation before: the problem of representation. Now as then their interest in the allocation of specific powers between levels of government was secondary to this overriding concern. They did believe that certain government functions were more effectively exercised at one rather than the other level. Defense, for instance, was more properly a function of the general government. Yet, guided by their primary concern for liberty, they did not hesitate to divide authority over this function, giving important military powers to the states.

Federalism has often been advocated primarily as a means of accommodating levels of government to territorial diversity. The compact theory would lead one to expect this to be the major subject of debate during the framing and ratification of the Constitution. Supporters as well as critics did recognize that the "sentiments, habits, and customs" of the states were diverse and that, therefore, "a government which might be very suitable for one might not be agreeable to the other." Yet the great mass of utterance at Philadelphia and the ratifying conventions displays remarkably little concern with this fact. Even the most ardent champions of greater powers for the states gave little or no weight to the argument from territorial diversity. Luther Martin, for instance, did not ground his advocacy of state power in his identification with Maryland as a distinctive community or in its need for authority commensurate with its special values or way of life. When he attacked the new powers of the federal government, he, as much as Madison or Hamilton, saw liberty as his goal and the new science of politics as the means for reaching that goal. He differed from them only in clinging to the conventional wisdom of the time as put forward in an unalloyed version of Montesquieu's theory of the confederate republic. It is consistent with this ground of the differences among Americans of that day over the Constitution that a bill of rights, which protected the liberties most valued by their common ideology and which was, as John Hancock said, "in no wise local, but calculated to give security and ease alike to all the states," served to win over critics and produce the quick subsidence of opposition that followed ratification.

## NEW STRUCTURES OF REPRESENTATIONAL FEDERALISM

In summary, my historical thesis is: that in making a democratic revolution, the American rebels created a nation and invented representational federalism as a means of governing their new national democracy.

A RATIONALE FOR THE STATES.   The reason for looking at this history and especially at its theoretical component is that they tell us something important about how the American polity has actually worked and continues to work. This perspective, in the first place, throws light on what we can and cannot expect of the states today. Any modern polity will have one or more levels of government. The smaller governments may be designed simply as administrative districts under the central authority. They may be set up for an economic purpose, and, accordingly, endowed with powers and boundaries suited to a distinctive complex of agricultural, commercial or industrial activity. They may be so laid out as to match patterns of cultural differentiation, as in the case of linguistic boundaries or other indicators of diversity in community values.

None of these rationales, administrative, economic or cultural, makes sense of the American states, except occasionally and accidentally. Look at the map. It must make you wonder whether there could have been a United States, if the rectangle had not been invented. Typically, those boundaries were not laid out to fit some pre-existing community of value or complex of interests, nor has it been possible to adapt them to territorial diversities as these have emerged. Most of the boundaries were dictated by Act of Congress, usually when the area was sparsely populated and had only the status of a territory. If the purpose of the states had been to provide a level of self-government functional to territorial diversity, then it would have been imperative, in this rapidly growing and developing society, that their boundaries be changed from time to time. On the contrary, however, our national policy toward federalism has been to freeze the boundaries of the states into a virtually unchangeable form by giving them constitutional protection.

Michael Reagan observes that the constitutional meaning of federalism still has importance in only one respect: the guarantee of the independent existence of the states. This may be so, but it does not mean that federalism is dead. Such a guarantee, to be sure, is dysfunctional to an administrative, economic or cultural role for the states. It is, however, highly functional and, I should say, indispensable to their political role in representational federalism. Even if state and federal power were completely overlapping, even if our society were perfectly homogeneous, it would still be necessary, in the light of the original design, that state government have its constitutionally protected existence. The rigidities of our federal system may often frustrate the purposes of public administration, economic efficiency and community living, but they make political sense as the foundation of a major and distinctive element of our representative system.

THE DUAL ROLE OF PARTY.   Over the course of time, both state and general governments have performed in various ways the roles assigned them in this system by representational federalism. When one asks what specific forms these processes have taken, the answer, until very recently, I suggest, would be found mainly in the mode of operation of the major political parties. The original federal design endowed the voter with two basic roles, a federal role and a state role. Typically, any major American party has reflected this dualism. The territorial pluralism of the federal structure has had such great and obvious effect as to lead us often to speak of the parties as coalitions of state and local organizations. At the same time, we recognize that their participation in the politics of the general government draws them into a competition which addresses problems and appeals to group interests transcending state and local boundaries. In spite of the resulting territorial and social pluralism, each party is also national, as a body of voters possessing at all levels of government common symbols which focus sentiments of party identification and ideas of party principle. This affectual and cognitive identification is a bond of cohesion that helps make each party a forum within which federal and state perspectives mutually influence one another, instead of merely finding expression in separate spheres.

The politics of civil rights during the past generation provides striking illustration of how the Madisonian mechanism may work through the medium of party. I will merely suggest the outlines of this very complicated process. After World War II, the movement of southern blacks to Northern cities admitted them for the first time to effective political participation in the social pluralism of the more extensive republic. The competition of Republicans and Democrats for this vote led to intervention by the federal government to remedy the denial by state governments of rights generally enjoyed by American citizens. At the same time, within the Democratic party an interaction between federal and state levels was producing political changes tending toward the same result. Action by the national party organs supported and stimulated within some southern state parties the rise of loyalist groups favorable to civil rights. These groups fought the old leadership, won power in state parties and influence on state government and so were able in some degree to ease the acceptance of federal initiatives. Thanks to the party system the pluralism of the more extensive republic helped bring about a universalistic result....

## COMPARATIVE PERSPECTIVES

In spite of overpowering forces making for centralization, the modern state seems to be unable to do without territorial subunits. Nor are these mere branch offices of administration, but rather governmental units with a political capacity. Much has been said, but little done in any country about decentralizing power to them or enlarging their autonomy. They have been widely used, however, as vehicles for carrying out the programs of central governments and, at the same time, have taken an increasingly active role as agents of representation before, and indeed, within those central governments. In other countries, both unitary and federal, the equivalent of the American intergovernmental lobby has appeared and flourishes. These varieties of topocratic representation are many and complex and light up major contrasts among the different versions of the modern state.

As we will want to look into the relation of technocratic representation to older processes of pressure group politics and functional representation, we shall also ask what are the conflicts and connections between topocratic representation and the older structures of territorial representation. In the U.S., for instance, the political relations of mayors and members of Congress are one of the great unexplored mysteries.

Moreover, whom does the topocrat represent when he formulates the presumed needs of his government before central authorities? He will commonly speak on behalf of groups among his constituents. He may know and be responsive to them. He might even have been chosen by them in part because he was expected to be a good lobbyist in the national capital. Yet he is subject not only to their wishes, but also to an array of influences proceeding from his position as the agent of a bureaucratic and political body. This governmental position will affect and may dominate his representative role.

I can communicate my unease at these technocratic and topocratic dilutions of the popular will by saying that the new structures have a strong connotation of corporate rather than personal representation. They do add real strengths to the modern state. But this may be at some cost to free government.

# Opening the Third Century of American Federalism: Issues and Prospects

Daniel J. Elazar (b. 1934) received his M.A. and his Ph.D. from the University of Chicago. He has been a professor of political science at numerous prestigious universities, including the University of Illinois and the University of Minnesota, and he was a Fulbright senior lecturer and visiting professor of political science and American studies at the Hebrew University of Jerusalem. He is currently teaching at Temple University, where he has served as director of the Center for the Study of Federalism since 1967. A member of the U.S. Advisory Commission on Intergovernmental Relations, Elazar has received numerous awards and honors, including a Guggenheim Fellowship, a Fulbright Fellowship, and the Leonard D. White Award from the American Political Science Association in 1960.

Elazar's scholarly writings have focused on American federalism, federal-state relations, and comparative studies of federalism. His works include *The American Partnership: Intergovernmental Cooperation in the Nineteenth-Century United States* (University of Chicago Press, 1962) and *Federalism and Political Integration* (Turtledove Publishing, 1979). Elazar is also the editor of *Publius, The Journal of Federalism,* a unique scholarly journal with an interdisciplinary research focus on federalism.

In the following selection, which is taken from "Opening the Third Century of American Federalism: Issues and Prospects," *The Annals of the American Academy of Political and Social Science* (May 1990), Elazar analyzes the most significant recent changes concerning American federalism, in particular the contradictory forces of centralization and decentralization operative in the contemporary American federal system. Elazar's evidence confirming the relentless forces behind an evolving centralization consists of recent U.S. Supreme Court decisions authorizing Congress as the final decision maker over federal-state relations concerning issues of commerce. Elazar also cites congressional mandates sanctioned by the U.S. Supreme Court as another strong force behind the recent trend toward centralization. In sharp contrast, Elazar cites President Ronald Reagan's dual-federalism, or his plan for highly decentralized and diffused public authority in conjunction with a states' rights ideology, as a major factor behind the contemporary movement toward decentralization.

*Daniel J. Elazar*

The following selection contributed to the literature on intergovernmental relations as it opened up a dialogue on the ambiguities and complexities of contemporary American federalism.

**Key Concept:** the contradictory forces of centralization and decentralization in contemporary American federalism

*A*t the beginning of its third century, the condition of American federalism is best characterized as ambiguous but promising. This, in itself, represents a great advance for noncentralized government over the situation that prevailed between 1965 and 1980, during which the trend was rather unambiguously centralizing.

In an earlier *Annals* article, I set out the shifting patterns of American intergovernmental relations in the twentieth century.[1] ... In the intervening 25 years, federal intervention into state and local affairs reached its apogee and then began to collapse of its own weight, assisted by the electoral triumph of Ronald Reagan and his dual-federalism, states' rights ideology. At the most, the various New Federalisms that preceded the Reagan administration sought to replace noncentralization—the constitutional diffusion of power among federal, state, and local centers that makes the relationships between those centers ones of true partnership—with decentralization—namely, a federal center deciding what the states and localities should or should not do.[2]

The most striking aspect of American federalism in the 1980s was the existence of very strong contradictory trends within the federal system. On one hand, in its *Garcia* and *South Carolina* decisions, the U.S. Supreme Court compounded all of its previous errors with regard to the proper constitutional relationship between the federal government and the states.[3] The Court stood the Constitution on its head so as to give the Congress of the United States the last word in determining the federal-state relationship in matters deemed to be within the purview of the federal government under the commerce clause of the federal Constitution. In doing so, the Court threw over 200 years of constitutional understanding and nearly that many years of precedent. The Court did exactly what the Constitution pledged not to do, that is to say, make one of the parties to any intergovernmental controversy the arbiter of the results.

If the states and localities, through their political influence in Congress, have been able to hold the line on a number of the issues directly confronted in U.S. Supreme Court decisions, they have lost the battle with regard to congressional mandates, whereby the Congress, in Court-justified actions, orders the states to do this and that without any pretense of winning them over through federal aid or making those orders contingent upon accepting federal grants. This is prefectorial federalism. A decade ago, prefectorial federalism seemed to be emanating from the executive branch of the federal government.[4] In the intervening years, the executive branch, headed by President Reagan, turned out to be generally a friend of federalism while Congress, increasingly detached as it is from state and local ties, turned out to be unfriendly, in a manner that once seemed characteristic only of the U.S. Supreme Court.

The transformation of American politics from a state and local party-based system to a free-for-all among individuals supported by various national economic, cultural, social, and political interests through political action committees has meant that fewer members of Congress have had direct experience in state and local government. Increasingly, candidates for Congress are new to the political arena and depend on projecting their personalities by raising enough funds from political action committees and individuals to meet today's outrageous campaign costs. Hence they come to Washington without state and local political roots. They settle their families within the Beltway year round, and, although they continue to work their districts, they do so as visitors more than as residents. Thus they have no strong personal commitments to state and local government interests, much less to the constitutional rights of the states.

## THE STATES REASSERT THEMSELVES AS POLITIES

Nevertheless, within this deteriorating constitutional and political framework, the states have become stronger and more vigorous than ever. They have reasserted themselves as polities and have become the principal source of governmental innovation in the United States as well as the principal custodians of most domestic programs. In this extraordinary turnaround, they have been helped by the catastrophes that have befallen previous presidents and by the positive efforts of the Reagan administration to have the federal government turn over certain functions to the states, free certain revenue sources to accompany them, and reduce federal regulatory interventions in state affairs and the processes of state governance.

[In the early 1970s], the crisis of the Nixon administration—Watergate, the Arab oil embargo, the national truckers' strike, and the collapse of South Vietnam—paralyzed the federal government. The states, particularly the governors, acted to fill the vacuum in the true spirit of federalism, and in a manner that demonstrated the virtues of federalism as providing useful redundancy and fail-safe mechanisms, so that when one part of the political system cannot function, other parts can take over. The states organized the distribution of limited oil and gas resources, governors settled the truckers' strike, and state and local agencies came to the fore in resettling Southeast Asian refugees. State officials discovered that they had powers of their own derived from the very existence of their states as states and did not need to wait for federal initiatives or permission, in other words, that the states are indeed polities. Moreover, they enjoyed exercising those powers and did so well.

By 1975, as the United States was about to enter a new political generation, the states were off and running. The states' innovative role continued to expand through the late 1970s, in part because of the relative paralysis of the Carter administration, which was sympathetic to fostering a greater state role in the federal system and whose relations with the states were generally good and constructive.

*Daniel J. Elazar*

At the same time, in the years following the Warren Court, the formerly unambiguously activist U.S. Supreme Court entered a period of rather diffuse retrenchment. Many state supreme courts began to pick up the slack through the development of a new, vibrant state constitutional law, building state constitutional foundations for public policy in everything from individual rights to relations between religion, state, and society, and to fairer distributions of public services. The constitutional legitimacy of these grounds was increasingly recognized by liberals and conservatives alike on the U.S. Supreme Court, each for his own reasons. State constitutional law became a field of academic and legal interest beyond the courts, a sure sign of its new importance....

## THE REAGAN BALANCE SHEET

President Reagan, from the moment of his election, began to reshape American attitudes toward the federal government and the states in particular. The president enunciated a traditional dual federalist view of the American system, but by enunciating it forcefully, he compelled even committed centralists to respond in federalist terms and to justify their extraordinary reliance on federal intervention in those terms. With his flare for communication, Reagan brought federalism into the headlines in a way unexcelled by any president in this century.

By its decisive actions in so many fields, the Reagan administration demonstrated that it was still possible to take hold of the reins of government and begin to reverse seemingly irreversible trends, including the at least seventy-year-long thrust toward greater government permeation of society. Yet fulfilling Reagan's promise to strengthen the states within that system, and thereby strengthen the system as a whole, has not been easy. There are several reasons why this is so.

First, even when there was general agreement in principle, there was great disagreement around the country and even in the administration as to what should be turned over to the states. The Reagan administration was no more immune to this problem than was any other. Indeed, its people suggested new federal interventions almost as frequently as they suggested federal withdrawals. Second, the states were not necessarily willing to accept added responsibilities as solely theirs if the costs—fiscal or political—were high. Third, there was a tendency in the administration to rely on simple notions of separating federal and state functions as a basis for making policy rather than on gaining an understanding of the possibilities of strengthening the states by restoring classic patterns of intergovernmental cooperation. Much of the problem relates to a misunderstanding of the principles of federalism and how they informed the American political system in better days.

The Reagan administration failed to secure the adoption of the most visible portions of its New Federalism program, but by shifting federal government priorities, reorganizing existing grant programs, and reducing federal domestic expenditures as a proportion of the total federal budget, it did succeed in introducing new attitudes among state and local officials and their constituents. The latter learned that it was no longer possible to turn to Washington for solutions to most of their problems and that, therefore, it was necessary to rely on their own efforts. All this was accompanied by a shift in the orientation of the federal departments and regulatory agencies in favor of loosening or reducing federal regulation of state and local activities and oversight of intergovernmental programs.

On the other hand, the Reagan administration did not succeed in restoring anything approximating dual federalism, even in the limited areas in which it made proposals. Quite to the contrary, the general sense that cooperative federalism was the only kind of federalism possible was much strengthened from both directions, that is to say, among those who would have hoped for more federal activity and those who hoped for less.

Moreover, whenever an issue came forward in which an increased federal role was perceived by the administration to be beneficial to its interests, it acted in what has by now become the usual way of opting for the expansion of federal powers. Three examples of this will suffice: the federal act allowing tandem trailer-trucks on most federally aided highways, thereby preempting state standards; the enactment of a requirement that states raise the minimum drinking age to 21 or lose a percentage of their federal highway funds; and further federal preemption of state banking laws, thereby initiating a process of nationalization of the banking system. Still, all told, the Reagan administration pointed the United States in a new direction. In doing so, it galvanized and focused the shift that had begun to be evident even earlier.

## A NEW DIRECTION

The twentieth century has been a time in which objective conditions have fostered centralization. Whether the states and localities acted responsibly or not in meeting the century's challenges, they found the federal government stepping in. Especially during the first postwar generation (1946–76), there was an environmental basis for centralization. The nation's economic system became increasingly centralized as locally owned firms were purchased by national—and multinational—corporations. The civil rights revolution led to substantial federal intervention in the legal and educational systems. Even organized religion underwent centralization as the various denominations developed strong national offices with extensive bureaucracies. The country's mass communications system, which so influences the public, led the pack toward an almost exclusive focus on Washington as the single center of political power.[5]

There are many signs that objective conditions in the twenty-first century will require different responses. Conditions of size and scale will reduce the utility of the federal government as a problem solver and increase that of the states. The idea that new models of intergovernmental, interorganizational, and public-private activity are needed has attracted increasing attention across the entire political spectrum, from Robert Reich's *Next American Frontier* to John Naisbit's *Megatrends*[6] and from conservative advocates of old-fashioned states' rights to environmentalists interested in the greening of America. Even ten years ago, similar ideas, whatever their intellectual value, ran against the realities of American civil society....

What is characteristic of this new noncentralization is that it does not represent a retreat from nationalization to an older style of territorial democracy but a movement to a new stage that combines territorially based and nonterritorially based actors in a multidimensional matrix. Technological change has made much of the old centralization obsolete, or is rapidly doing so, but the new technology is certainly not restoring the simpler territorial democracy of a more rural age. American civil society is becoming more multidimensional than ever, having to accommodate great diversity in an urbanized environment, people with different life-styles rubbing shoulders with one another as well as different stages of economic growth, educational aspiration, religious commitment, and social group expression.

If the system has become too complex simply to turn things back to the states, it has also become too complex simply to rely upon the federal government. There are too many forces in a country of 250 million people spread over 3.5 million square miles. States, localities, and sections offer points of identification and expression that have vitality in their own right and offer real opportunities to deal with the challenges of a multidimensional society.

Changes in the patterns of urban settlement will continue to reinforce that trend. At the beginning of the century, urbanization had encouraged centralization; at mid-century, metropolitanization helped to shift government in the direction of decentralization. Now the spread of low-density urban settlement in the countryside is restoring the impulse for noncentralization. Finally, the closer integration of an international community whose members will increasingly rely on federal principles in their own organization will increase the international role of the states, including a closer relationship with their counterparts in other federal systems. Today over 70 percent of the world's population lives under federal arrangements of one kind or another, from the United States of America to the European Community. The 160-plus politically sovereign states are interacting with the 300-plus federal states in ways that are diminishing the differences between them....

## REFOCUSING ON THE STATES

There was a time when the American public—reformers and conservatives, interested parties of all kinds—looked to their states as the arenas in which to fight great battles and do great things. Indeed, that was the case even though American society was in many respects a national society from the first and certainly became more intertwined nationwide in the wake of the Industrial Revolution. Now that is happening again. The New Deal quite properly represented a recognition that the states could not go it alone, at least not after the U.S. Supreme Court had so limited their powers that reform was stymied unless Congress acted. But—to carry the principles of the New Deal to absurd extremes—to assume that, because the states cannot go it alone in some things, they cannot go it alone in any or that they cannot lead in those things that are done cooperatively is simply to misread American reality and American aspirations.

On the other hand, because powers really are diffused throughout the matrix, usually in a rather untidy way, it is very difficult to decide to transfer power from Washington. In the past, presidents who tried to do so discovered that in order to decentralize, they first had to centralize. Today, in an age of hierarchy assumers, a president can be a successful centralizer to a great degree, but there is no guarantee that an administration strong enough to overcome the noncentralization inherent in the system will so willingly part with hard-won powers. For those who believe in the utility and virtues of federalism, the substitution of decentralization for noncentralization is not an advance. The Reagan administration grasped the idea apparently lost in the previous generation that while, under normal circumstances, the elements in the matrix do work together to develop common policies and programs, the secret of a successful federal system lies precisely in the right of the elements not to act under certain conditions.

## FEDERALISM AND THE CURSES OF BIGNESS

Through bitter experience, it has been discovered that, in very large bureaucracies, coordination is well-nigh impossible at the top because the people on the top can barely control and are frequently at the mercy of their own organizations. Moreover, in a system of interlocking arenas—which is what exists in the United States despite all the talk about levels—there is no real top to do the coordinating. Similarly, students of public administration have begun to note the failure of managerial techniques widely touted as means to come to grips with contemporary problems. Certainly, the idea that such techniques would automatically result in efficiency and economy has long since gone by the boards. We now know how bureaucracies create their own inefficiencies and diseconomies. Beyond that, there has been a discovery that the new management techniques—the planning-programming-budgeting system and zero-based budgeting are prime examples—often are inappropriate to the political arena with its lack of precise, agreed-upon goals and its basic purposes of conciliating the irreconcilable and managing conflict.

On a different but closely related plane, Americans are beginning to sense the failure of consumerism, namely, the redefinition of people primarily as consumers and their institutions primarily as vehicles for the satisfaction of consumer wants. At the very least, the redefinition of government as a service-delivery mechanism and citizens as consumers leads to an unmanageable acceleration of public demands. It also leads to the evaluation of all institutions by a set of standards that, being human institutions, they are bound not to meet. Not the least of the problems of the consumer model is the abandonment of the principle that people have responsibilities as well as rights, and that they have obligations to each other, if not to the polity in the abstract, which, when neglected, imperil democracy by undermining its very foundations.

Simultaneously, the actions of the U.S. Supreme Court and, to some extent, the Congress offer vigorous testimony to the danger faced by the states and the federal system, demonstrating once again the need for strong constitutional protections for federalism even where there is the best will in the world on the part of those actively engaged in the political arena to be good federalists. The founding fathers understood this need, which is why they wrote such protections into the Constitution.

The possibilities of an increased role for the states are better for yet another reason. Until the mid-1970s, states' rights were inevitably associated with arguments on behalf of slavery, racial segregation, and discrimination against nonwhites. However erroneous such arguments may have been in principle, in practice states' rights were used effectively as a shield for racism and discrimination. That problem has been overcome as a constitutional issue. It is clear that the federal Constitution and, for that matter, the vast majority of state constitutions are color-blind. This is the constitutionally correct position in a civil society dedicated to the proposition that "all men are created equal and endowed by their Creator with certain inalienable rights." For the first time in American history, believers in federalism can argue that protecting the rights of the states is important for the sake of liberty and is not entangled with racism and discrimination. Hence, as the United States moves into the third century of American federalism, within the limits of a reality that will never conform as closely to our models as we would like and that might not pass certain aesthetic tests, there is a serious opportunity to strengthen the basic noncentralization of the American system in new ways.

## NOTES

1. Daniel J. Elazar, "The Shaping of Intergovernmental Relations in the Twentieth Century," *The Annals* of the American Academy of Political and Social Science, 359:10–22 (May 1965).

2. Cf. Jeffrey L. Mayer, ed., *Dialogues on Decentralization,* vol. 6, *Publius: The Journal of Federalism* (Fall 1976); Robert B. Hawkins, Jr., and George Packard, eds., *Government Reorganization and the Federal System,* vol. 8, *Publius: The Journal of Federalism* (Spring 1978).

3. *Garcia v. San Antonio Metropolitan Transit Authority,* 469 U.S. 528 (1985); *South Carolina v. Baker,* 56 U.S.L.W. 4311 (1988).

4. Daniel J. Elazar, "Is Federalism Compatible with Prefectorial Administration?" *Publius: The Journal of Federalism,* 11:3–22 (Spring 1981).

5. Daniel J. Elazar, "Cursed by Bigness or Toward a Post-Technocratic Federalism," *Publius: The Journal of Federalism,* 3:239 (Fall 1973).

6. Robert Reich, *The Next American Frontier* (New York: Penguin, 1983); John Naisbit, *Megatrends: Ten New Directions Transforming Our Lives,* 6th ed. (New York: Warner, 1983).

# The Dream, the Reality, and Some Solutions

Alice M. Rivlin (b. 1931) has earned the reputation of integrating her sophisticated scholarly expertise and insights on economics and public policy with her extensive experiences in public service. Her book *Reviving the American Dream: The Economy, the States and the Federal Government* (Brookings Institution, 1992), from which the following selection is excerpted, has solidified this reputation. Rivlin received her M.A. and her Ph.D. from Radcliffe College. In her distinguished career, Rivlin has held numerous positions with the Brookings Institution in Washington, D.C., including research fellow, staff member of the Economics Studies Division, and senior staff economist. She is currently a senior fellow in the Economics Studies Program at the Brookings Institution. She was also the first director of the Congressional Budget Office as well as president of the American Economic Association. She served as deputy assistant secretary for program coordination, assistant secretary for planning and evaluation for the U.S. Department of Health, Education, and Welfare, and consultant to the U.S. House Committee on Education and Labor and to the U.S. Secretary of the Treasury.

Rivlin's scholarly writings have focused on American federalism and budgetary, fiscal, and taxation policies. Some of her other published works include *The Role of the Federal Government in Financing Higher Education* (Brookings Institution, 1961), *Systematic Thinking for Social Action* (Brookings Institution, 1971), *Economics Choices 1984* (Brookings Institution, 1984) and, coauthored with Joshua M. Wiener, *Caring for the Disabled Elderly: Who Will Pay?* (Brookings Institution, 1988). She has also been a frequent contributor to *The Progressive, New York Times Sunday Magazine,* and numerous political science and economics journals.

In *Reviving the American Dream,* Rivlin raises challenging questions about economic public policy and serious national economic problems, and she prescribes a reconfiguration of the responsibilities, roles, and relationships between the federal and state governments. She contends that the flexible and evolutionary nature of American federalism enables the political system to adapt to changing critical political and social needs. This book is considered a classic analysis of the American political economy, federalism, and public policy. It had a profound impact on contemporary scholarly thought and on the Clinton administration's vision of federalism, revision of major public programs (such as welfare reform), and the abolition of the federal budget deficit.

The basic objectives of Rivlin's prescribed fundamental revision of American federalism include the revitalization of the economy, an increase in governmental efficiency, and a restoration of Americans' trust in government. According to Rivlin, this reform proposal requires a devolution of public authority from the federal government to the state governments. This striking recommendation would dramatically reduce the federal government's direct involvement in major public programs and social services —including education, housing, highways, employment training, and economic development—and shift these responsibilities and initiatives to the state and local governments. Such a shift in responsibilities would enable the federal government to focus on critical national issues, such as the need to develop a comprehensive health insurance program, which would also limit escalating health costs. In addition, according to Rivlin's analysis, the complexity of contemporary global interdependence requires attention by the federal government.

**Key Concept:** a prescribed redesign of American federalism

# THE CASE FOR RETHINKING FEDERALISM

The argument about which functions should be exercised by the federal government and which by the states has been going on for more than two hundred years. There are no "right" answers. The prevailing view shifts with changing perceptions of the needs of the country and the relative competence and responsiveness of the states and the federal government.

Until the 1930s, the federal government had limited powers and spent relatively little money except in time of war. Government services were not as extensive as they are now, and most were performed by states and their localities. In this period of "dual federalism," the powers of the federal government and the states were viewed as separate and distinct, not overlapping. Then, over the half century between 1930 and 1980, Americans laid increasing responsibilities on the central government. All levels of government grew, but the power, functions, and budget of the federal government grew most rapidly.

Americans turned to Washington for two distinct sets of reasons. First, the collapse of the economy in the Great Depression convinced many people of the need for national institutions to strengthen the economy and deal with problems that states could not be expected to handle on their own. The federal government created social security, set up the unemployment insurance system, developed river basins to control flooding and produce power, supported agricultural prices, strengthened banking and credit systems, and began regulating many economic activities.

Second, activists and reformers turned to Washington, especially in the 1960s, out of frustration with the way states and localities were performing their traditional functions. Compared with the federal government, states had limited capacities and resources. Their staffs were unsophisticated and unprofessional. Their legislatures, dominated by rural members, were unresponsive to city dwellers and minorities. Many state governments were overtly racist. Hence the federal government enacted a range of programs designed to influence the level and nature of state spending in areas that had traditionally been states' responsibilities, such as education, job training, health services, waste treatment, and housing. Many federal grants bypassed states entirely and went directly to local governments, especially big cities.

The surge of federal activities had many positive results, but it also diffused accountability and directed the energies of reformers toward Washington. Citizens concerned about improving state and local services began joining national organizations to lobby for federal money, rather than working at the state or local level. States and localities, even universities, established Washington offices, hired consultants, and acquired expertise in federal grantsmanship.

The proliferation of federal programs, projects, offices, and agencies in so many parts of the country made the federal government increasingly unmanageable. It resembled a giant conglomerate that has acquired too many different kinds of businesses and cannot coordinate its own activities or manage them all effectively from central headquarters.

Then the reaction set in. The flood of federal funds for state and local government crested in the late 1970s and ebbed in the 1980s. Tax cuts and defense spending increases created a huge federal budget deficit that precluded new federal domestic activities. States and cities had to rely more on their own resources. Moreover, the perception of superior federal competence, which had propelled Washington into many traditionally state areas, faded. Reforms gave states stronger governors, more representative legislatures, and more professional and sophisticated civil servants. Meanwhile, the federal government lost some of its former luster. The savings and loan debacle and scandals in defense procurement and housing programs undermined the presumption that the federal government managed more effectively than the states. The intertwining of state and local responsibilities and the diffusion of accountability remained, however.

In the 1990s the United States faces an urgent need to revitalize its economy and to get its political system off dead center and functioning responsively again. There are at least four reasons to think that reraising the fundamental questions of federalism—which level of government should do what and where the revenues should come from—would help in meeting these challenges.


### The Impact of Global Interdependence


The first reason is that dramatic changes in the world are radically altering the tasks facing national governments. Rapid advances in the technology of transportation, communications, and weaponry have shrunk distances and intertwined the United States with the rest of the world, intimately and irreversibly. Goods, services, money, and people are flowing easily across oceans and borders. So are economic, political, and environmental problems.

Global interdependence requires international cooperation to solve common problems and some delegation of sovereignty to supranational authorities. The Gulf war and growing nuclear capacity in developing nations leave no doubt that stronger international controls are needed on sophisticated weapons. The rapidly thinning ozone layer dramatizes the stake that all nations have in controlling harmful atmospheric emissions.

Despite its political appeal, isolationism is no longer a viable option. If the United States is to protect its own citizens and help shape a more habitable world, it must take an active part in international partnerships focused on everything from chemical weapons to acid rain to narcotics traffic. These partnerships are already demanding increasing attention from both the executive and legislative branches of the federal government.

Global interdependence creates a paradox for the U.S. government. On the one hand, since both the president and Congress will be spending greater time and energy on international affairs, domestic policy will get less attention in Washington. At the same time, global interdependence makes domestic policy more important than ever. The United States needs rising productivity, a skilled labor force, and modern physical capital, both public and private, if it is to generate the improved standard of living necessary not only to foster domestic well-being, but also to play an effective role in international partnerships. The added complexity of Washington's international role strengthens the case for sorting out domestic responsibilities more clearly. Washington cannot do everything and should not try. The states should take responsibility for a larger and more clearly defined segment of the domestic agenda.

## Top-Down and Bottom-Up Reform

A second and more important reason for rethinking the division of responsibilities is that some of the policies needed to revitalize the American economy require bottom-up community effort that cannot be imposed from the top down. They require experimentation and adaptation to local and regional conditions, and that can come only from the state and local level, not from Washington.

Improving education will take bottom-up reform. Presidential speeches and photo opportunities, national testing and assessment, federally funded experimental schools, even new grants spent in accordance with federal guidelines, can make only marginal contributions to fixing the schools. Education in America will not improve significantly until states and communities decide they want better schools. Making education more effective will take parents who care, committed teachers, community support, and accountable school officials. An "education president" can help focus media attention on schooling, but he risks diluting state and local responsibility by implying that Washington can actually produce change.

The popular federal Head Start program demonstrates that preschool education helps children from poor families cope better in school. The negative legacy of Head Start, however, is that states and communities have come to believe that the responsibility for preschool education lies with Washington, not with them. Change would come more rapidly if concerned citizens, parents, and educators worked to improve their own preschools instead of lobbying Washington to allocate more funds for Head Start.

Street crime, drug use, and teenage pregnancy are all examples of problems that the federal government can deplore but cannot fix. A resurgence of community concern and effort is needed. Social services, housing, community development, and most infrastructure also must be carefully adapted to the needs of particular places. Federal grants can help defray the costs, but at the price of confusing the issue of who is responsible and who needs to take action.

On the other hand, there are important public functions that Washington performs well and state and local governments cannot address effectively. First, there are inherently central responsibilities, like national defense and foreign affairs, for which the federal government must represent and defend the interests of the country as a whole. Second, there are activities whose benefits clearly spill over state lines—such as air traffic control, basic scientific research, and prevention of river pollution or acid rain. Individual states have little incentive to undertake these programs because so much of the benefit would go to people in other states. Third, there are programs whose workability depends on having a uniform national system, such as social security.

Social security is perhaps the federal government's greatest domestic success. It is well administered and immensely popular. People are less resentful of social security taxes than other taxes, because they know what the money goes for and they expect benefits themselves. Because it involves tracking people over a lifetime, social security could not easily be handled by the states; too many people would move in and out of state systems and end up with conflicting and overlapping coverage.

The federal government is also best adapted to solving the double problem of controlling rapidly rising health costs and providing health insurance to the whole population. The U.S. health care system is the most expensive in the world, now consuming more than one-eighth of everything the nation produces, but it does not provide commensurate benefits. Millions of people are left out or inadequately insured. State-by-state efforts to expand insurance coverage and control medical costs are not likely to be successful. Sentiment is growing for some kind of national health insurance system that would provide universal coverage for basic health services and would control costs by setting reimbursement rates for doctors, hospitals, and other medical providers.

Another important role that the federal government is uniquely positioned to play at the moment is increasing national saving. Americans are saving by contributing to social security. The social security system is currently running significant annual surpluses because taxes collected exceed benefits paid out. These reserves will be needed to pay benefits to the large baby boom generation when its members retire. They ought to be used to help finance the productive investment needed to generate higher incomes in the future. At present, however, the social security surpluses are simply being lent to the rest of the government to offset part of the huge federal budget deficit. . . .

The third reason for focusing on the assignment of tasks to federal and state governments is that all levels of government are in serious financial difficulties. Even if some services are cut back and others are run more efficiently, more revenues are needed to eliminate deficits at the federal, state, and local levels, to accomplish the productivity agenda, and to reform health care financing. If taxes must go up, it is important to consider which level of government will make best use of the revenues....

*Alice M. Rivlin*

*The state fiscal crisis.*    Increasing the responsibilities of state and local governments is a dubious proposition because they too are in fiscal trouble. At first glance, their fiscal distress seems more temporary than that of the federal government. State and local governments generally suffer serious fiscal stress in recessions. Their revenues fall off as sales, income, and property values stop growing or decline while claims on their services continue to increase. Because, unlike the federal government, states and localities cannot normally borrow to cover operating expenses, they are forced to raise taxes and cut services as soon as their reserves are exhausted.

Even after the economy returns to moderate growth, however, there are reasons for pessimism about the prospects for state and local finance in the 1990s. The fiscal health of state and local governments declined in the second half of the 1980s. Pressures for spending outran revenues. The fiscal stress, especially in cities, reflected the growth in crime, drug addiction, AIDS, homelessness, and poverty, all of which continued to increase through the long recovery from the recession of the early 1980s. Moreover, a major villain of the federal budget drama appears again at the state and local level. Rising medical care costs, especially for medicaid, have put enormous pressure on state and local budgets that seems unlikely to abate.

Thus all levels of government will probably face continuing fiscal stress in the 1990s. Policies to revitalize the economy—increased public investment, a federal surplus, health financing reform—cannot be undertaken without more revenue at some level of government. The public seems angry and dissatisfied with government, however, and unwilling either to increase its support or to accept a lower level of services.

### Dissatisfaction With Government

The fourth reason for questioning the jobs assigned to various levels of government in the 1990s is the American public's dissatisfaction with politics and politicians. Many Americans have "tuned out" political debate and stopped participating in elections. Polls reveal declining confidence in political leaders, rising skepticism that public officials care about the views of ordinary people, disgust at political campaigns, and cynicism about the democratic process.

There are many possible reasons for the disparagement of government: the need to blame someone for the stresses of a faltering economy, the influence of big money on political campaigns, the negativism of political advertising, and the insensitivity of politicians to the damage done to their collective image by even minor peccadillos such as getting parking tickets fixed. Some blame the ideological polarization of the major parties—the capture of the Republicans by ultraconservatives and the Democrats by extreme liberals—for leaving the pragmatic, middle-of-the-road majority without leadership.[1] Others point to the widening gulf between elites, who see public policy as a matter of technical control, and a general public that correctly perceives the elites' contempt for citizens' opinions.[2]

The blurring of state and federal roles contributes to cynicism about politics. For example, much of the rhetoric in the 1988 presidential campaign concerned issues over which presidents have little control—crime, drugs, education, child care, and industrial development. Voters care about these issues, but they also know that Washington is too remote from them to make a difference. Candidates for federal office undermine their credibility by implying these problems have national solutions and by refusing to address serious federal issues, such as the budget deficit.

Voters also appear more willing to pay taxes if they know that revenues will be used for identifiable services important to them. Polls show voters opposed to paying more taxes for undisclosed purposes but willing to pay for improved schools or increased environmental protection. In recent years the federal government's general revenues (other than social security and medicare payroll taxes) have declined as a percentage of GNP, while state and local revenues have increased substantially. Perhaps taxpayers are clearer about their need for state and local services and are more willing to pay for them than for the more remote services of the federal government. Despite substantial increases in payroll taxes for social security and medicare in recent decades, polls show these taxes are less unpopular than the federal income tax, presumably because taxpayers know what the payroll taxes buy and value the benefits. Hence the most feasible way to increase revenue may be to earmark new taxes for a particular federal benefit such as health insurance or for improved services at the state and local level.

## PROPOSALS FOR THE FUTURE

This focus on federalism suggests several quite drastic proposals aimed at reenergizing the American economy and restoring confidence in the political system. Their basic theme is that the federal and state governments should divide the jobs to be done and get moving.

- *The productivity agenda.* The states should take charge of the primary public investment needed to increase productivity and raise incomes, especially to improve education and skill training and modernize infrastructure.

- *Devolution.* The federal government should eliminate most of its programs in education, housing, highways, social services, economic development, and job training.

- *Common shared taxes.* With federal blessing, or even the assistance of the federal government, states should strengthen their revenue systems by cooperating in collecting common taxes to be shared among them on a formula basis.

- *Health care financing.* The federal government should adopt a plan that will ensure basic health insurance coverage for everyone and control the increase in health costs.

- *Federal budget surplus.* The federal government should run a surplus in its whole budget (counting social security), thus reducing federal debt service costs and adding to the pool of saving available to finance private investment.

These proposals fit together. State responsibility for the productivity agenda would sharpen the distinction between federal and state tasks, making it easier for citizens to understand what each level of government does and to blame the right set of officials for poor performance. Devolution would take whole areas of public spending out of the federal budget, making it easier to move that budget toward surplus. More important, making clear that the devolved functions belong to the states, not the federal government, would transfer pressure for increased spending in these areas from Washington to state capitals and help keep federal deficits from recurring.

The resulting fiscal pressure on states and localities would be alleviated in two ways. First, federal responsibility for health care financing, coupled with strong cost controls, would relieve states and localities of the escalating burden of medicaid and reduce the cost of other public medical care. Second, the adoption of one or more common shared taxes would improve the states' collective revenue-raising capacity.

One example of a common shared tax would be a uniform state sales tax (or value-added tax) collected at the same rate on the same items and shared on the basis of population. A uniform corporation income tax, collected along with the federal income tax and shared on a formula basis, would make tax compliance simpler for multistate corporations. A common state energy tax could reduce pollution and promote conservation as well as raising revenue.

The idea of states sharing common taxes is a radical departure from the American tradition that each state must go it alone it levying taxes. In other federal systems, tax sharing is more usual. In Germany, for example, the central government collects most of the taxes and shares the proceeds with the *Länder* (states). German taxpayers, individual and corporate, fill out only one income tax return, for both federal and state taxes. German firms pay a value-added tax whose proceeds are shared between the federal government and the states, with disproportionate shares going to the least affluent states to help equalize services.

As the American economy becomes more national and international, the case for more coordination of state taxation increases. People, companies, sales, and services move with greater ease across borders. One consequence is that states and localities have to worry about keeping their tax rates from getting out of line with those of other jurisdictions. Another is that more and more companies, and even individuals, owe taxes in multiple jurisdictions. The resulting complexity is costly for both taxpayers and tax collectors.

Like federal grants, common shared taxes could be designed to improve the relative position of the least affluent states. Unlike federal grants, however, they would not cause confusion about which level of government has responsibility for particular programs or impose federal rules and guidelines on state and local authorities.

To revive the American dream, citizens must find new energy and commitment to revitalize the myriad institutions that influence American life—families, businesses, schools, unions, churches, clubs, and government at all levels. They must be willing to experiment, restructure, and try new approaches to old and new problems. In the words of David Osborne and Ted Gaebler, they must even "reinvent government" by breaking out of old hierarchical patterns and empowering those closest to the problems to participate in finding solutions.[3]

A first step is to reexamine that peculiarly American institution, federalism. The current confusion of responsibilities between federal and state government is undermining confidence in government and impeding the implementation of policies needed to restore a healthy economy. Sorting out the roles more clearly could break the logjam, help both levels function more effectively, and improve both domestic and foreign policy.

## NOTES

1. E. J. Dionne, Jr., *Why Americans Hate Politics* (Simon and Schuster, 1991).
2. Daniel Yankelovich, *Coming to Public Judgment: Making Democracy Work in a Complex World* (Syracuse University Press, 1991).
3. David Osborne and Ted Gaebler, *Reinventing Government: How the Entrepreneurial Spirit Is Transforming the Public Sector* (Addison-Wesley, 1992).

# PART THREE

# *Civil Liberties and Civil Rights*

# On the Internet . . .

## Sites appropriate to Part Three

The American Civil Liberties Union (ACLU) is America's foremost advocate of individual rights—litigating, legislating, and educating the public on a broad array of issues affecting individual freedom in the United States. This site offers information on civil rights issues in the courts and in Congress; current news and events; specific ACLU issues, such as "cyber liberties," the death penalty, and racial equality; and the ACLU itself.

```
http://www.aclu.org/textpg.html
```

Click on "Civil Rights" in the topic list to see a list of key civil rights Supreme Court cases, from *Scott v. Sandford* (1856) to *Martin v. Wilks* (1989), the text and opinions of which are provided.

```
http://supct.law.cornell.edu/supct/cases/
   topic.htm
```

Maintained by the National Women's History Project, this site provides a history of the civil rights movement, from the first women's rights convention in 1848 to the complex rights issues that women face today.

```
http://www.legacy98.org/move-hist.html
```

# CHAPTER 4 Civil Liberties

## 4.1 JOHN STUART MILL

# *Of the Liberty of Thought and Discussion*

John Stuart Mill (1806–1873) was a classical liberal British political philosopher, logician, political economist, and social and political reformer. Classical liberalism refers to a political theory or ideology based upon a commitment to such fundamental normative principles or values as limited government, constitutionalism or rule of law, toleration, individualism, individual rights and freedoms, privacy, and voluntarism. Mill's philosophical work *On Liberty* (New American Library, 1968), from which the following selection is excerpted, had a profound impact upon the development of modern liberal democratic political thought in the United States.

Utilitarianism refers to an ethical or political theory that identifies an action or public policy as right or wrong, good or bad, just or unjust, based upon the consequences of such acts or policies, particularly in proportion to the degree of human happiness or societal benefit promoted. The greatest good for the greatest number is often cited as an ultimate or fundamental utilitarian moral principle. In *On Liberty* (1859), Mill's central argument and justification of liberty of thought and discussion is primarily utilitarian, in reflection of the desirable social consequences resulting from a policy of freedom of expression and the exposure of truth.

In the following selection, Mill defends freedom of thought and expression. He theorizes that the repression of any opinion or thought is bad policy, independent of the truth of such opinions or thoughts. Mill claims that the suppression of a true opinion deprives humanity from learning the truth.

In addition to the fundamental significance of freedom of thought and expression for a free democratic society, the American political system also has been influenced by Mill's defense of the self-development of the individual. Mill contends that an individual's acts should only be limited by the state or society if such acts are determined to cause injury to others.

**Key Concept:** freedom of thought and expression

*T*he time, it is to be hoped, is gone by, when any defence would be necessary of the "liberty of the press" as one of the securities against corrupt or tyrannical government. No argument, we may suppose, can now be needed, against permitting a legislature or an executive, not identified in interest with the people, to prescribe opinions to them, and determine what doctrines or what arguments they shall be allowed to hear. This aspect of the question, besides, has been so often and so triumphantly enforced by preceding writers, that it needs not be specially insisted on in this place. Though the law of England, on the subject of the press, is as servile to this day as it was in the time of the Tudors, there is little danger of its being actually put in force against political discussion, except during some temporary panic, when fear of insurrection drives ministers and judges from their propriety, and, speaking generally, it is not, in constitutional countries, to be apprehended, that the government, whether completely responsible to the people or not, will often attempt to control the expression of opinion, except when in doing so it makes itself the organ of the general intolerance of the public. Let us suppose, therefore, that the government is entirely at one with the people, and never thinks of exerting any power of coercion unless in agreement with what it conceives to be their voice. But I deny the right of the people to exercise such coercion, either by themselves or by their government. The power itself is illegitimate. The best government has no more title to it than the worst. It is as noxious, or more noxious, when exerted in accordance with public opinion, than when in opposition to it. If all mankind minus one were of one opinion, and only one person were of the contrary opinion, mankind would be no more justified in silencing that one person, than he, if he had the power, would be justified in silencing mankind. Were an opinion a personal possession of no value except to the owner; if to be obstructed in the enjoyment of it were simply a private injury, it would make some difference whether the injury was inflicted only on a few persons or on many. But the peculiar evil of silencing the expression of an opinion is, that it is robbing the human race; posterity as well as the existing generation; those who dissent from the opinion, still more than those who hold it. If the opinion is right, they are deprived of the opportunity of exchanging error for truth: if wrong, they lose, what is almost as great a benefit, the clearer perception and livelier impression of truth, produced by its collision with error.

It is necessary to consider separately these two hypotheses, each of which has a distinct branch of the argument corresponding to it. We can never be sure that the opinion we are endeavouring to stifle is a false opinion; and if we were sure, stifling it would be an evil still.

First: the opinion which it is attempted to suppress by authority may possibly be true. Those who desire to suppress it, of course deny its truth; but they are not infallible. They have no authority to decide the question for all mankind, and exclude every other person from the means of judging. To refuse a hearing to an opinion, because they are sure that it is false, is to assume that *their* certainty is the same thing as *absolute* certainty. All silencing of discussion is an assumption of infallibility. Its condemnation may be allowed to rest on this common argument, not the worse for being common.

Unfortunately for the good sense of mankind, the fact of their fallibility is far from carrying the weight in their practical judgment which is always allowed to it in theory; for while every one well knows himself to be fallible, few think it necessary to take any precautions against their own fallibility, or admit the supposition that any opinion, of which they feel very certain, may be one of the examples of the error to which they acknowledge themselves to be liable. Absolute princes, or others who are accustomed to unlimited deference, usually feel this complete confidence in their own opinions on nearly all subjects. People more happily situated, who sometimes hear their opinions disputed, and are not wholly unused to be set right when they are wrong, place the same unbounded reliance only on such of their opinions as are shared by all who surround them, or to whom they habitually defer; for in proportion to a man's want of confidence in his own solitary judgment, does he usually repose, with implicit trust, on the infallibility of "the world" in general. And the world, to each individual, means the part of it with which he comes in contact; his party, his sect, his church, his class of society; the man may be called, by comparison, almost liberal and large-minded to whom it means anything so comprehensive as his own country or his own age. Nor is his faith in this collective authority at all shaken by his being aware that other ages, countries, sects, churches, classes, and parties have thought, and even now think, the exact reverse. He devolves upon his own world the responsibility of being in the right against the dissentient worlds of other people; and it never troubles him that mere accident has decided which of these numerous worlds is the object of his reliance, and that the same causes which make him a Churchman in London, would have made him a Buddhist or a Confucian in Peking. Yet it is as evident in itself, as any amount of argument can make it, that ages are no more infallible than individuals; every age having held many opinions which subsequent ages have deemed not only false but absurd; and it is as certain that many opinions now general will be rejected by future ages, as it is that many, once general, are rejected by the present.

The objection likely to be made to this argument would probably take some such form as the following. There is no greater assumption of infallibility in forbidding the propagation of error, than in any other thing which is done by public authority on its own judgment and responsibility. Judgment is given to men that they may use it. Because it may be used erroneously, are men to be told that they ought not to use it at all? To prohibit what they think pernicious, is not claiming exemption from error, but fulfilling the duty incumbent on them, although fallible, of acting on their conscientious conviction. If we were never to act on our opinions, because those opinions may be wrong, we should leave all our interests uncared for, and all our duties unperformed. An objection which applies to all conduct can be no valid objection to any conduct in particular. It is the duty of governments, and of individuals, to form the truest opinions they can; to form carefully, and never impose them upon others unless they are quite sure of being right. But when they are sure (such reasoners may say), it is not conscientiousness but cowardice to shrink from acting on their opinions, and allow doctrines which they honestly think dangerous to the welfare of mankind, either in this life or in another, to be scattered abroad without restraint, because other people, in less enlightened times, have persecuted opinions now believed to be true. Let us take care, it may be said, not to make the same mistake: but governments and nations have made mistakes in other things, which are not denied to be fit subjects for the exercise of authority: they have laid on bad taxes, made unjust wars. Ought we therefore to lay on no taxes, and, under whatever provocation, make no wars? Men and governments, must act to the best of their ability. There is no such thing as absolute certainty, but there is assurance sufficient for the purposes of human life. We may, and must, assume our opinion to be true for the guidance of our own conduct: and it is assuming no more when we forbid bad men to pervert society by the propagation of opinions which we regard as false and pernicious.

I answer, that it is assuming very much more. There is the greatest difference between presuming an opinion to be true, because, with every opportunity for contesting it, it has not been refuted, and assuming its truth for the purpose of not permitting its refutation. Complete liberty of contradicting and disproving our opinion is the very condition which justifies us in assuming its truth for purposes of action; and on no other terms can a being with human faculties have any rational assurance of being right.

When we consider either the history of opinion, or the ordinary conduct of human life, to what is it to be ascribed that the one and the other are no worse than they are? Not certainly to the inherent force of the human understanding; for, on any matter not self-evident, there are ninety-nine persons totally incapable of judging of it for one who is capable; and the capacity of the hundredth person is only comparative; for the majority of the eminent men of every past generation held many opinions now known to be erroneous, and did or approved numerous things which no one will now justify. Why is it, then, that there is on the whole a preponderance among mankind of rational opinions and rational conduct? If there really is this preponderance—which there must be unless human affairs are, and have always been, in an almost desperate state—it is owing to a quality of the human mind, the source of everything respectable in man either as an intellectual or as a moral being, namely, that his errors are corrigible. He is capable of rectifying his mistakes, by discussion and experience. Not by experience alone. There must be discussion, to show how experience is to be interpreted. Wrong opinions and practices gradually yield to fact and argument; but facts and arguments, to produce any effect on the mind, must be brought before it. Very few facts are able to tell their own story, without comments to bring out their meaning. The whole strength and value, then, of human judgment, depending on the one property, that it can be set right when it is wrong, reliance can be placed on it only when the means of setting it right are kept constantly at hand. In the case of any person whose judgment is really deserving of confidence, how has it become so? Because he has kept his mind open to criticism on his opinions and conduct. Because it has been his practice to listen to all that could be said against him; to profit by as much of it as was just, and expound to himself, and upon occasion to others, the fallacy of what was fallacious. Because he has felt, that the only way in which a human being can make some approach to knowing the whole of a subject, is by hearing what can be said about it by persons of every variety of opinion, and studying all modes in which it can be looked at by every character of mind. No wise man ever acquired his wisdom in any mode but this; nor is it in the nature of human intellect to become wise in any other manner. The steady habit of correcting and completing his own opinion by collating it with those of others, so far from causing doubt and hesitation in carrying it into practice, is the only stable foundation for a just reliance on it: for, being cognisant of all that can, at least obviously, be said against him, and having taken up his position against all gainsayers—knowing that he has sought for objections and difficulties, instead of avoiding them, and has shut out no light which can be thrown upon the subject from any quarter—he has a right to think his judgment better than that of any person, or any multitude, who have not gone through a similar process.

It is not too much to require that what the wisest of mankind, those who are best entitled to trust their own judgment, find necessary to warrant their relying on it, should be submitted to by that miscellaneous collection of a few wise and many foolish individuals, called the public. The most intolerant of churches, the Roman Catholic Church, even at the canonisation of a saint, admits, and listens patiently to, a "devil's advocate." The holiest of men, it appears, cannot be admitted to posthumous honours, until all that the devil could say against him is known and weighed. If even the Newtonian philosophy were not permitted to be questioned, mankind could not feel as complete assurance of its truth as they now do. The beliefs which we have most warrant for have no safeguard to rest on, but a standing invitation to the whole world to prove them unfounded. If the challenge is not accepted, or is accepted and the attempt fails, we are far enough from certainty still; but we have done the best that the existing state of human reason admits of; we have neglected nothing that could give the truth a chance of reaching us: if the lists are kept open, we may hope that if there be a better truth, it will be found when the human mind is capable of receiving it; and in the meantime we may rely on having attained such approach to truth as is possible in our own day. This is the amount of certainty attainable by a fallible being, and this the sole way of attaining it....

We have now recognised the necessity to the mental well-being of mankind (on which all their other well-being depends) of freedom of opinion, and freedom of the expression of opinion, on four distinct grounds; which we will now briefly recapitulate.

First, if any opinion is compelled to silence, that opinion may, for aught we can certainly know, be true. To deny this is to assume our own infallibility.

Secondly, though the silenced opinion be an error, it may, and very commonly does, contain a portion of truth; and since the general or prevailing opinion on any subject is rarely or never the whole truth, it is only by the collision of adverse opinions that the remainder of the truth has any chance of being supplied.

Thirdly, even if the received opinion be not only true, but the whole truth; unless it is suffered to be, and actually is, vigorously and earnestly contested, it will, by most of those who receive it, be held in the manner of a prejudice, with little comprehension or feeling of its rational grounds. And not only this, but, fourthly, the meaning of the doctrine itself will be in danger of being lost, or enfeebled, and deprived of its vital effect on the character and conduct; the dogma becoming a mere formal profession, inefficacious for good, but cumbering the ground, and preventing the growth of any real and heartfelt conviction, from reason or personal experience.

Before quitting the subject of freedom of opinion, it is fit to take some notice of those who say that the free expression of all opinions should be permitted, on condition that the manner be temperate, and do not pass the bounds of fair discussion. Much might be said on the impossibility of fixing where these supposed bounds are to be placed; for if the test be offence to those whose opinions are attacked, I think experience testifies that this offence is given whenever the attack is telling and powerful, and that every opponent who pushes them hard, and whom they find it difficult to answer, appears to them, if he shows any strong feeling on the subject, an intemperate opponent. But this, though an important consideration in a practical point of view, merges in a more fundamental objection. Undoubtedly the manner of asserting an opinion, even though it be a true one, may be very objectionable, and may justly incur severe censure. But the principal offences of the kind are such as it is mostly impossible, unless by accidental self-betrayal, to bring home to conviction. The gravest of them is, to argue sophistically, to suppress facts or arguments, to misstate the elements of the case, or misrepresent the opposite opinion. But all this, even to the most aggravated degree, is so continually done in perfect good faith, by persons who are not considered, and in many other respects may not deserve to be considered, ignorant or incompetent, that it is rarely possible, on adequate grounds, conscientiously to stamp the misrepresentation as morally culpable; and still less could law presume to interfere with this kind of controversial misconduct. With regard to what is commonly meant by intemperate discussion, namely invective, sarcasm, personality and the like, the denunciation of these weapons would deserve more sympathy if it were ever proposed to interdict them equally to both sides; but it is only desired to restrain the employment of them against the prevailing opinion: against the unprevailing they may not only be used without general disapproval, but will be likely to obtain for him who uses them the praise of honest zeal and righteous indignation. Yet whatever mischief arises from their use is greatest when they are employed against the comparatively defenceless; and whatever unfair advantage can be derived by any opinion from this mode of asserting it, accrues almost exclusively to received opinions. The worst offence of this kind which can be committed by a polemic is to stigmatise those who hold the contrary opinion as bad and immoral men. To calumny of this sort, those who hold any unpopular opinion are peculiarly exposed, because they are in general few and uninfluential, and nobody but themselves feels much interested in seeing justice done them; but this weapon is, from the nature of the case, denied to those who attack a prevailing opinion: they can neither use it with safety to themselves, nor, if they could, would it do anything but recoil on their own cause. In general, opinions contrary to those commonly received can only obtain a hearing by studied moderation of language, and the most cautious avoidance of unnecessary offence, from which they hardly ever deviate even in a slight degree without losing ground: while unmeasured vituperation employed on the side of the prevailing opinion really does deter people from professing contrary opinions, and from listening to those who profess them. For the interest, therefore, of truth and justice, it is far more important to restrain this employment of vituperative language than the other; and, for example, if it were necessary to choose, there would be much more need to discourage offensive attacks on infidelity than on religion. It is, however, obvious that law and authority have no business with restraining either, while opinion ought, in every instance, to determine its verdict by the circumstances of the individual case; condemning every one, on whichever side of the argument he places himself, in whose mode of advocacy either want of candour, or malignity, bigotry, or intolerance of feeling manifest themselves; but not inferring these vices from the side which a person takes, though it be the contrary side of the question to our own; and giving merited honour to every one, whatever opinion he may hold, who has calmness to see and honesty to state what his opponents and their opinions really are, exaggerating nothing to their discredit, keeping nothing back which tells, or can be supposed to tell, in their favour. This is the real morality of public discussion: and if often violated, I am happy to think that there are many controversialists who to a great extent observe it, and a still greater number who conscientiously strive towards it.

# Gideon v. Wainwright

In the 1963 landmark decision *Gideon v. Wainwright* (372 U.S. 335), from which the following selection is taken, the U.S. Supreme Court expressed an opinion that had major constitutional and political consequences upon the interpretation of civil liberties and the application of the Bill of Rights to the state governments. Clarence Earl Gideon, a 51-year-old drifter with an extensive criminal record, was convicted of breaking into the Bay Harbor Poolroom in Panama City, Florida, with the intent of committing a misdemeanor, considered a felony under Florida law. Gideon appeared in court for his trial without an attorney and without the means to afford one, and he requested the trial court to appoint an attorney for him. The trial court judge rejected Gideon's request for legal counsel, referring to a Florida law that authorized the appointment of lawyers exclusively in capital cases (offenses punishable by death). Gideon served as his own defense counselor, and he was promptly found guilty by the jury and sentenced to five years in the Florida State Prison for petty larceny.

While in prison, Gideon became a "jail-house lawyer" and filed numerous unsuccessful lower-court actions disputing the constitutionality of his imprisonment and directed against Wainwright, the state director of corrections. Gideon's petition to the Florida Supreme Court was denied relief without opinion, but his poorly handwritten petition and case were accepted by the U.S. Supreme Court for review. Gideon argued that the trial judge's refusal to appoint legal counsel for him was a denial of rights guaranteed by the Sixth and Fourteenth Amendments.

Justice Hugo L. Black delivered the opinion of the Court. The opinion had a fundamental and profound impact upon state criminal cases by requiring state courts to appoint attorneys for all individuals accused of felony charges if they cannot afford counsel. Black argued that the Sixth Amendment right to counsel should be incorporated among the fundamental rights protected under the Fourteenth Amendment. Following the decision of this case, the Supreme Court expanded the rights of the accused, even requiring lawyers to be provided for individuals charged with offenses less severe than felonies in order to promote fair trials.

**Key Concept:** the right to counsel

$M$r. Justice Black delivered the opinion of the Court, saying in part:

Petitioner was charged in a Florida state court with having broken and entered a poolroom with intent to commit a misdemeanor. This offense is a felony under Florida law. Appearing in court without funds and without a lawyer, petitioner asked the court to appoint counsel for him, whereupon the following colloquy took place:

"The Court: Mr. Gideon, I am sorry, but I cannot appoint Counsel to represent you in this case. Under the laws of the State of Florida, the only time the Court can appoint Counsel to represent a Defendant is when that person is charged with a capital offense. I am sorry, but I will have to deny your request to appoint Counsel to defend you in this case."

"The Defendant: The United States Supreme Court says I am entitled to be represented by Counsel."

Put to trial before a jury, Gideon conducted his defense about as well as could be expected from a layman. He made an opening statement to the jury, cross-examined the State's witnesses, presented witnesses in his own defense, declined to testify himself, and made a short argument "emphasizing his innocence to the charge contained in the Information filed in this case." The jury returned a verdict of guilty, and petitioner was sentenced to serve five years in the state prison.... Since 1942, when Betts v. Brady was decided by divided Court, the problem of a defendant's federal constitutional right to counsel in a state court has been a continuing source of controversy and litigation in both state and federal courts....

The facts upon which Betts claimed that he had been unconstitutionally denied the right to have counsel appointed to assist him are strikingly like the facts upon which Gideon here bases his federal constitutional claim. Betts was indicted for robbery in a Maryland state court. On arraignment, he told the trial judge of his lack of funds to hire a lawyer and asked the court to appoint one for him. Betts was advised that it was not the practice in that county to appoint counsel for indigent defendants except in murder and rape cases. He then pleaded not guilty, had witnesses summoned, cross-examined the State's witnesses, examined his own, and chose not to testify himself. He was found guilty by the judge, sitting without a jury, and sentenced to eight years in prison. Like Gideon, Betts sought release by habeas corpus, alleging that he had been denied the right to assistance of counsel in violation of the Fourteenth Amendment. Betts was denied any relief, and on review this Court affirmed. It was held that a refusal to appoint counsel for an indigent defendant charged with a felony did not necessarily violate the Due Process Clause of the Fourteenth Amendment, which for reasons given the Court deemed to be the only applicable federal constitutional provision. The Court said:

"Asserted denial [of due process] is to be tested by an appraisal of the totality of facts in a given case. That which may, in one setting, constitute a denial of fundamental fairness, shocking to the universal sense of justice, may, in other circumstances, and in the light of other considerations, fall short of such denial."

Treating due process as "a concept less rigid and more fluid than those envisaged in other specific and particular provisions of the Bill of Rights," the Court held that refusal to appoint counsel under the particular facts and circumstances in the Betts Case was not so "offensive to the common and fundamental ideas of fairness" as to amount to a denial of due process. Since the facts and circumstances of the two cases are so nearly indistinguishable, we think the Betts v. Brady holding if left standing would require us to reject Gideon's claim that the Constitution guarantees him the assistance of counsel. Upon full reconsideration we conclude that Betts v. Brady should be overruled.

The Sixth Amendment provides, "In all criminal prosecutions, the accused shall enjoy the right... to have the Assistance of Counsel for his defence." We have construed this to mean that in federal courts counsel must be provided for defendants unable to employ counsel unless the right is competently and intelligently waived. Betts argued that this right is extended to indigent defendants in state courts by the Fourteenth Amendment. In response the Court stated that, while the Sixth Amendment laid down "no rule for the conduct of the States, the question recurs whether the constraint laid by the Amendment upon the national courts expresses a rule so fundamental and essential to a fair trial, and so, to due process of law, that it is made obligatory upon the States by the Fourteenth Amendment." In order to decide whether the Sixth Amendment's guarantee of counsel is of this fundamental nature, the Court in Betts set out and considered "[r]elevant data on the subject... afforded by constitutional and statutory provisions subsisting in the colonies and the States prior to the inclusion of the Bill of Rights in the national Constitution, and in the constitutional, legislative, and judicial history of the States to the present date." On the basis of this historical data the Court concluded that "appointment of counsel is not a fundamental right, essential to a fair trial." It was for this reason the Betts Court refused to accept the contention that the Sixth Amendment's guarantee of counsel for indigent federal defendants was extended to or, in the words of that Court, "made obligatory upon the States by the Fourteenth Amendment." Plainly, had the Court concluded that appointment of counsel for indigent criminal defendant was "a fundamental right, essential to a fair trial," it would have held that the Fourteenth Amendment requires appointment of counsel in a state court, just as the Sixth Amendment requires in a federal court.

We think the Court in Betts had ample precedent for acknowledging that those guarantees of the Bill of Rights which are fundamental safeguards of liberty immune from federal abridgment are equally protected against state invasion by the Due Process Clause of the Fourteenth Amendment. This same principle was recognized, explained and applied in Powell v. Alabama (1932), a case upholding the right of counsel, where the Court held that despite sweeping language to the contrary in Hurtado v. California (1884), the Fourteenth Amendment "embraced" those "fundamental principles of liberty and justice which lie at the base of all our civil and political institutions," even though they had been "specifically dealt with in another part of the federal Constitution." In many cases other than Powell and Betts, this Court has looked to the fundamental nature of original Bill of Rights guarantees to decide whether the

Fourteenth Amendment makes them obligatory on the States. Explicitly recognized to be of this "fundamental nature" and therefore made immune from state invasion by the Fourteenth, or some part of it, are the First Amendment's freedoms of speech, press, religion, assembly, association, and petition for redress of grievances. For the same reason, though not always in precisely the same terminology, the Court has made obligatory on the States the Fifth Amendment's command that private property shall not be taken for public use without just compensation, the Fourth Amendment's prohibition of unreasonable searches and seizures, and the Eighth's ban on cruel and unusual punishment. On the other hand, this Court in Palko v. Connecticut (1937), refused to hold that the Fourteenth Amendment made the double jeopardy provision of the Fifth Amendment obligatory on the States. In so refusing, however, the Court, speaking through Mr. Justice Cardozo, was careful to emphasize that "immunities that are valid as against the federal government by force of the specific pledges of particular amendments have been found to be implicit in the concept of ordered liberty, and thus, through the Fourteenth Amendment, become valid as against the states" and that guarantees "in their origin... effective against the federal government alone" had by prior cases "been taken over from the earlier articles of the federal bill of rights and brought within the Fourteenth Amendment by a process of absorption."

We accept Betts v. Brady's assumption, based as it was on our prior cases, that a provision of the Bill of Rights which is "fundamental and essential to a fair trial" is made obligatory upon the States by the Fourteenth Amendment. We think the Court in Betts was wrong, however, in concluding that the Sixth Amendment's guarantee of counsel is not one of these fundamental rights. Ten years before Betts v. Brady, this Court, after full consideration of all the historical data examined in Betts, had unequivocally declared that "the right to the aid of counsel is of this fundamental character." ... While the Court at the close of its Powell opinion did by its language, as this Court frequently does, limit its holding to the particular facts and circumstances of that case, its conclusions about the fundamental nature of the right to counsel are unmistakable. Several years later, in 1936, the Court reemphasized what it had said about the fundamental nature of the right to counsel in this language:

"We concluded that certain fundamental rights, safeguarded by the first eight amendments against federal action, were also safeguarded against state action by the due process of law clause of the Fourteenth Amendment, and among them the fundamental right of the accused to the aid of counsel in a criminal prosecution." Grosjean v. American Press Co. (1936).

And again in 1938 this Court said:

"[The assistance of counsel] is one of the safeguards of the Sixth Amendment deemed necessary to insure fundamental human rights of life and liberty.... The Sixth Amendment stands as a constant admonition that if the constitutional safeguards it provides be lost, justice will not 'still be done,'" Johnson v. Zerbst (1938)....

In light of these many other prior decisions of this Court, it is not surprising that the Betts Court, when faced with the contention that "one charged with crime, who is unable to obtain counsel, must be furnished counsel by the State," conceded that "[e]xpressions in the opinions of this court lend color to the argument...." The fact is that in deciding as it did—that "appointment of counsel is not a fundamental right, essential to a fair trial"—the Court in Betts v. Brady made an abrupt break with its own well-considered precedents. In returning to these old precedents, sounder we believe than the new, we but restore constitutional principles established to achieve a fair system of justice. Not only these precedents but also reason and reflection require us to recognize that in our adversary system of criminal justice, any person haled into court, who is too poor to hire a lawyer, cannot be assured a fair trial unless counsel is provided for him. This seems to us to be an obvious truth. Governments, both state and federal, quite properly spend vast sums of money to establish machinery to try defendants accused of crime. Lawyers to prosecute are everywhere deemed essential to protect the public's interest in an orderly society. Similarly, there are few defendants charged with crime, few indeed, who fail to hire the best lawyers they can get to prepare and present their defenses. That government hires lawyers to prosecute and defendants who have the money hire lawyers to defend are the strongest indications of the widespread belief that lawyers in criminal courts are necessities, not luxuries. The right of one charged with crime to counsel may not be deemed fundamental and essential for fair trials in some countries, but it is in ours. From the very beginning, our state and national constitutions and laws have laid great emphasis on procedural and substantive safeguards designed to assure fair trials before impartial tribunals in which every defendant stands equal before the law. This noble ideal cannot be realized if the poor man charged with crime has to face his accusers without a lawyer to assist him. A defendant's need for a lawyer is nowhere better stated than in the moving words of Mr. Justice Sutherland in Powell v. Alabama:

"The right to be heard would be, in many cases, of little avail if it did not comprehend the right to be heard by counsel. Even the intelligent and educated layman has small and sometimes no skill in the science of law. If charged with crime, he is incapable, generally, of determining for himself whether the indictment is good or bad. He is unfamiliar with the rules of evidence. Left without the aid of counsel he may be put on trial without a proper charge, and convicted upon incompetent evidence, or evidence irrelevant to the issue or otherwise inadmissable. He lacks both the skill and knowledge adequately to prepare his defense, even though he have a perfect one. He requires the guiding hand of counsel at every step in the proceedings against him. Without it, though he be not guilty, he faces the danger of conviction because he does not know how to establish his innocence."

The Court in Betts v. Brady departed from the sound wisdom upon which the Court's holding in Powell v. Alabama rested. Florida, supported by two other States, has asked that Betts v. Brady be left intact. Twenty-two States, as friends of the Court, argue that Betts was "an anachronism when handed down" and that it should now be overruled. We agree.

The judgment is reversed and the cause is remanded to the Supreme Court of Florida for further action not inconsistent with this opinion.

Reversed.

Mr. Justice Douglas, while joining the opinion of the Court, wrote a separate opinion, saying in part:

My Brother Harlan is of the view that a guarantee of the Bill of Rights that is made applicable to the States by reason of the Fourteenth Amendment is a lesser version of that same guarantee as applied to the Federal Government. Mr. Justice Jackson shared the view. But that view has not prevailed and rights protected against state invasion by the Due Process Clause of the Fourteenth Amendment are not watered-down versions of what the Bill of Rights guarantees.

Mr. Justice Clark, concurring in the result, wrote a separate opinion.

*Hugo L. Black*

## 4.3  ANTHONY M. KENNEDY ET AL.

# Lee v. Weisman

In the 1992 decision of *Lee v. Weisman* (112 S. Ct. 2649), from which the following selection is taken, the U.S. Supreme Court articulated an opinion that had fundamental constitutional and political ramifications upon the interpretation of civil liberties and the establishment of religion by government. The judgment of the Court was a landmark decision because of its interpretation of the establishment clause of the First Amendment of the Constitution; specifically, the Court found unconstitutional and banned the delivery of religious invocations and benediction prayers at public school graduation ceremonies.

The First Amendment consists of two statements regarding religion, the establishment clause and the free exercise clause. The establishment clause prohibits Congress from imposing religion upon citizens through legislation and from drafting legislation denying religious freedom. The free exercise clause prohibits states from passing legislation denying the free exercise of religious beliefs since the First Amendment has been applied to the state governments through the due process clause of the Fourteenth Amendment. A strict separation of church and state is derived from the establishment clause, which has required the creation of a secular state.

On behalf of his daughter Deborah, Daniel Weisman sued school board officials in the public middle and high schools of Providence, Rhode Island, for authorizing clergy-led benediction prayers and invocations at school graduation ceremonies. The federal district and appellate courts ruled that religious prayers and the citing of God during public school graduation ceremonies were in violation of the establishment clause. The school board appealed the decision to the U.S. Supreme Court. Justice Anthony M. Kennedy delivered the opinion of the Court, affirming the rulings of the lower courts. The following selection includes two concurring opinions and a dissenting opinion, indicating that there was substantial disagreement in this case. The Supreme Court remains deeply divided in articulating precise and explicit guidelines defining church-state relations, and it continues to struggle in its opinions to lower or raise the wall between church and state.

**Key Concept:** the establishment clause of the First Amendment

*J*ustice KENNEDY delivers the opinion of the Court.

This case does not require us to revisit the difficult questions dividing us in recent cases, questions of the definition and full scope of the principles governing the extent of permitted accommodation by the State for the religious beliefs and practices of many of its citizens. See *Allegheny County v. Greater Pittsburgh ACLU,* 492 U.S. 573 (1989); *Wallace v. Jaffree,* 472 U.S. 38 (1985); *Lynch v. Donnelly,* 465 U.S. 668 (1984). For without reference to those principles in other contexts, the controlling precedents as they relate to prayer and religious exercise in primary and secondary public schools compel the holding here that the policy of the city of Providence is an unconstitutional one. We can decide the case without reconsidering the general constitutional framework by which public schools' efforts to accommodate religion are measured. Thus we do not accept the invitation of petitioners and amicus the United States to reconsider our decision in *Lemon v. Kurtzman,* [403 U.S. 602 (1971)]. The government involvement with religious activity in this case is pervasive, to the point of creating a state-sponsored and state-directed religious exercise in a public school. Conducting this formal religious observance conflicts with settled rules pertaining to prayer exercises for students, and that suffices to determine the question before us.

The principle that government may accommodate the free exercise of religion does not supersede the fundamental limitations imposed by the Establishment Clause. It is beyond dispute that, at a minimum, the Constitution guarantees that government may not coerce anyone to support or participate in religion or its exercise, or otherwise act in a way which establishes a [state] religion or religious faith, or tends to do so. *Lynch.* The State's involvement in the school prayers challenged today violates these central principles....

We need not look beyond the circumstances of this case to see the phenomenon at work. The undeniable fact is that the school district's supervision and control of a high school graduation ceremony places public pressure, as well as peer pressure, on attending students to stand as a group or, at least, maintain respectful silence during the Invocation and Benediction. This pressure, though subtle and indirect, can be as real as any overt compulsion. Of course, in our culture standing or remaining silent can signify adherence to a view or simple respect for the views of others. And no doubt some persons who have no desire to join a prayer have little objection to standing as a sign of respect for those who do. But for the dissenter of high school age, who has a reasonable perception that she is being forced by the State to pray in a manner her conscience will not allow, the injury is no less real. There can be no doubt that for many, if not most, of the students at the graduation, the act of standing or remaining silent was an expression of participation in the Rabbi's prayer. That was the very point of the religious exercise. It is of little comfort to a dissenter, then, to be told that for her the act of standing or remaining in silence signifies mere respect, rather than participation. What matters is that, given our social conventions, a reasonable dissenter in this milieu could believe that the group exercise signified her own participation or approval of it....

The injury caused by the government's action, and the reason why Daniel and Deborah Weisman object to it, is that the State, in a school setting, in effect required participation in a religious exercise. It is, we concede, a brief exercise during which the individual can concentrate on joining its message, meditate on her own religion, or let her mind wander. But the embarrassment and the intrusion of the religious exercise cannot be refuted by arguing that these prayers, and similar ones to be said in the future, are of a de minimis character. To do so would be an affront to the Rabbi who offered them and to all those for whom the prayers were an essential and profound recognition of divine authority. And for the same reason, we think that the intrusion is greater than the two minutes or so of time consumed for prayers like these....

Inherent differences between the public school system and a session of a State Legislature distinguish this case from *Marsh v. Chambers*, 463 U.S. 783 (1983). The considerations we have raised in objection to the invocation and benediction are in many respects similar to the arguments we considered in *Marsh*. But there are also obvious differences. The atmosphere at the opening of a session of a state legislature where adults are free to enter and leave with little comment and for any number of reasons cannot compare with the constraining potential of the one school event most important for the student to attend. The influence and force of a formal exercise in a school graduation are far greater than the prayer exercise we condoned in *Marsh*. The *Marsh* majority in fact gave specific recognition to this distinction and placed particular reliance on it in upholding the prayers at issue there. Today's case is different. At a high school graduation, teachers and principals must and do retain a high degree of control over the precise contents of the program, the speeches, the timing, the movements, the dress, and the decorum of the students. In this atmosphere the state-imposed character of an invocation and benediction by clergy selected by the school combine to make the prayer a state-sanctioned religious exercise in which the student was left with no alternative but to submit....

For the reasons we have stated, the judgment of the Court of Appeals is Affirmed.

Justice BLACKMUN, with whom Justice STEVENS and Justice O'CONNOR join, concurring.

The Court holds that the graduation prayer is unconstitutional because the State "in effect required participation in a religious exercise." Although our precedents make clear that proof of government coercion is not necessary to prove an Establishment Clause violation, it is sufficient. Government pressure to participate in a religious activity is an obvious indication that the government is endorsing or promoting religion.

But it is not enough that the government restrain from compelling religious practices: it must not engage in them either. The Court repeatedly has recognized that a violation of the Establishment Clause is not predicated on coercion. The Establishment Clause proscribes public schools from "conveying or attempting to convey a message that religion or a particular religious belief is favored or preferred," *County of Allegheny v. ACLU* (1989), even if the schools do not actually "impose pressure upon a student to participate in a religious activity." *Westside Community Bd. of Ed. v. Mergens*, 496 U.S. 226 (1990) (KENNEDY, J., concurring).

There is no doubt that attempts to aid religion through government coercion jeopardize freedom of conscience....

Our decisions have gone beyond prohibiting coercion, however, because the Court has recognized that "the fullest possible scope of religious liberty," *Schempp,* entails more than freedom from coercion. The Establishment Clause protects religious liberty on a grand scale; it is a social compact that guarantees for generations a democracy and a strong religious community—both essential to safeguarding religious liberty....

Justice SOUTER, with whom Justice STEVENS and Justice O'CONNOR join, concurring.

That government must remain neutral in matters of religion does not foreclose it from ever taking religion into account. The State may "accommodate" the free exercise of religion by relieving people from generally applicable rules that interfere with their religious callings. See, e.g., *Corporation of Presiding Bishop of Church of Jesus Christ of Latter-Day Saints v. Amos,* 483 U.S. 327 (1987); see also *Sherbert v. Verner,* 374 U.S. 398 (1963). Contrary to the views of some, such accommodation does not necessarily signify an official endorsement of religious observance over disbelief....

Whatever else may define the scope of accommodation permissible under the Establishment Clause, one requirement is clear: accommodation must lift a discernible burden on the free exercise of religion. Concern for the position of religious individuals in the modern regulatory state cannot justify official solicitude for a religious practice unburdened by general rules; such gratuitous largesse would effectively favor religion over disbelief. By these lights one easily sees that, in sponsoring the graduation prayers at issue here, the State has crossed the line from permissible accommodation to unconstitutional establishment.

Justice SCALIA, with whom the CHIEF JUSTICE, Justice WHITE, and Justice THOMAS join, dissenting.

From our Nation's origin, prayer has been a prominent part of governmental ceremonies and proclamations. The Declaration of Independence, the document marking our birth as a separate people, "appealed to the Supreme Judge of the world for the rectitude of our intentions" and avowed "a firm reliance on the protection of divine Providence." In his first inaugural address, after swearing his oath of office on a Bible, George Washington deliberately made a prayer a part of his first official act as President.... Such supplications have been a characteristic feature of inaugural addresses ever since....

[A] tradition of Thanksgiving Proclamations—with their religious theme of prayerful gratitude to God—has been adhered to by almost every President....

The Court presumably would separate graduation invocations and benedictions from other instances of public "preservation and transmission of religious beliefs" on the ground that they involve "psychological coercion." I find it a sufficient embarrassment that our Establishment Clause jurisprudence regarding holiday displays, has come to "require scrutiny more commonly associated with interior decorators than with the judiciary." *American Jewish Congress v. Chicago, 827* F. 2d 120 (Easterbrook,J., dissenting). But interior decorating is a rock-hard science compared to psychology practiced by amateurs. A few citations of "research in psychology" that have no particular bearing upon the precise issue here, cannot disguise the fact that the Court has gone beyond the realm where judges know what they are doing. The Court's argument that state officials have "coerced" students to take part in the invocation and benediction at graduation ceremonies is, not to put too fine a point on it, incoherent.

The Court identifies two "dominant facts" that it says dictate its ruling that invocations and benedictions at public-school graduation ceremonies violate the Establishment Clause. Neither of them is in any relevant sense true.

The Court declares that students' "attendance and participation in the [invocation and benediction] are in a fair and real sense obligatory." But what exactly is this "fair and real sense"? According to the Court, students at graduation who want "to avoid the fact or appearance of participation," in the invocation and benediction are psychologically obligated by "public pressure, as well as peer pressure, ... to stand as a group or, at least, maintain respectful silence" during those prayers. This assertion—the very linchpin of the Court's opinion— is almost as intriguing for what it does not say as for what it says. It does not say, for example, that students are psychologically coerced to bow their heads, place their hands in a Drer-like prayer position, pay attention to the prayers, utter "Amen," or in fact pray. (Perhaps further intensive psychological research remains to be done on these matters.) It claims only that students are psychologically coerced "to stand ... or, at least, maintain respectful silence." Both halves of this disjunctive (both of which must amount to the fact or appearance of participation in prayer if the Court's analysis is to survive on its own terms) merit particular attention.

To begin with the latter: The Court's notion that a student who simply sits in "respectful silence" during the invocation and benediction (when all others are standing) has somehow joined—or would somehow be perceived as having joined—in the prayers is nothing short of ludicrous. We indeed live in a vulgar age. But surely "our social conventions" have not coarsened to the point that anyone who does not stand on his chair and shout obscenities can reasonably be deemed to have assented to everything said in his presence. Since the Court does not dispute that students exposed to prayer at graduation ceremonies retain (despite "subtle coercive pressures") the free will to sit, there is absolutely no basis for the Court's decision. It is fanciful enough to say that "a reasonable dissenter," standing head erect in a class of bowed heads, "could believe that the group exercise signified her own participation or approval of it." It is beyond the absurd to say that she could entertain such a belief while pointedly declining to rise.

But let us assume the very worst, that the nonparticipating graduate is "subtly coerced" ... to stand! Even that half of the disjunctive does not remotely establish a "participation" (or an "appearance of participation") in a religious exercise. The Court acknowledges that "in our culture standing ... can signify adherence to a view or simple respect for the views of others." (Much more often the latter than the former, I think, except perhaps in the proverbial town meeting, where one votes by standing.) But if it is a permissible inference that one who is standing is doing so simply out of respect for the prayers of others that are in progress, then how can it possibly be said that a "reasonable dissenter... could believe that the group exercise signified her own participation or approval"? Quite obviously, it cannot. I may add, moreover, that maintaining respect for the religious observances of others is a fundamental civic virtue that government (including the public schools) can and should cultivate—so that even if it were the case that the displaying of such respect might be mistaken for taking part in the prayer, I would deny that the dissenter's interest in avoiding even the false appearance of participation constitutionally trumps the government's interest in fostering respect for religion generally.

The opinion manifests that the Court itself has not given careful consideration to its test of psychological coercion. For if it had, how could it observe, with no hint of concern or disapproval, that students stood for the Pledge of Allegiance, which immediately preceded Rabbi Gutterman's invocation? The government can, of course, no more coerce political orthodoxy than religious orthodoxy. *West Virginia Board of Education v. Barnette*, 319 U.S. 624 (1943). Moreover, since the Pledge of Allegiance has been revised since *Barnette* to include the phrase "under God," recital of the Pledge would appear to raise the same Establishment Clause issue as the invocation and benediction. If students were psychologically coerced to remain standing during the invocation, they must also have been psychologically coerced, moments before, to stand for (and thereby, in the Court's view, take part in or appear to take part in) the Pledge. Must the Pledge therefore be barred from the public schools (both from graduation ceremonies and from the classroom)? In *Barnette* we held that a public-school student could not be compelled to recite the Pledge; we did not even hint that she could not be compelled to observe respectful silence—indeed, even to stand in respectful silence—when those who wished to recite it did so. Logically, that ought to be the next project for the Court's bulldozer....

The deeper flaw in the Court's opinion does not lie in its wrong answer to the question whether there was state-induced "peer-pressure" coercion; it lies, rather, in the Court's making violation of the Establishment Clause hinge on such a precious question. The coercion that was a hallmark of historical establishments of religion was coercion of religious orthodoxy and of financial support by force of law and threat of penalty. Typically, attendance at the state church was required; only clergy of the official church could lawfully perform sacraments; and dissenters, if tolerated, faced an array of civil disabilities....

Our religion-clause jurisprudence has become bedeviled (so to speak) by reliance on formulaic abstractions that are not derived from, but positively conflict with, our long-accepted constitutional traditions. Foremost among these has been the so-called *Lemon* test, see *Lemon v. Kurtzman*, 403 U.S. 602 (1971), which has received well-earned criticism from many members of this Court. The Court today demonstrates the irrelevance of *Lemon* by essentially ignoring it, and the interment of that case may be the one happy byproduct of the Court's otherwise lamentable decision. Unfortunately, however, the Court has replaced *Lemon* with its psycho-coercion test, which suffers the double disability of having no roots whatever in our people's historic practice, and being as infinitely expandable as the reasons for psychotherapy itself....

The reader has been told much in this case about the personal interest of Mr. Weisman and his daughter, and very little about the personal interests on the other side. They are not inconsequential....

The narrow context of the present case involves a community's celebration of one of the milestones in its young citizens' lives, and it is a bold step for this Court to seek to banish from that occasion, and from thousands of similar celebrations throughout this land, the expression of gratitude to God that a majority of the community wishes to make. The issue before us today is not the abstract philosophical question whether the alternative of frustrating this desire of a religious majority is to be preferred over the alternative of imposing "psychological coercion," or a feeling of exclusion, upon nonbelievers. Rather, the question is whether a mandatory choice in favor of the former has been imposed by the United States Constitution. As the age-old practices of our people show, the answer to that question is not at all in doubt.... For the foregoing reasons, I dissent.

# *Roe v. Wade*

In the 1973 landmark decision *Roe v. Wade* (410 U.S. 113), from which the following selection is taken, the U.S. Supreme Court expressed an opinion on probably the most controversial issue in American politics of the twentieth century. The Court's decision in this case had enormous constitutional and political implications for the interpretation of civil liberties. The reasoning of the U.S. Supreme Court reflected the classic decision that a woman's right to obtain an abortion is protected by the U.S. Constitution—specifically, that a linkage exists between the right to terminate a pregnancy and the constitutional right to privacy. Although the Constitution does not explicitly articulate a concept of privacy or its potential substantive range, Americans share a deep ideological commitment to such a right and assume its existence.

The Supreme Court's most comprehensive expression of the right to privacy was formulated in 1965 in a case filed by Planned Parenthood, *Griswold v. Connecticut* (381 U.S. 479). In this case, the Court found unconstitutional a Connecticut law banning the use of birth control methods. The *Griswold* decision provided a conceptual framework and an immediate Court precedent for *Roe v. Wade*.

Norma McCorvey was a poor, 21-year-old, pregnant carnival employee and the mother of one child. Since she was unable to obtain a legal abortion due to Texas's very strict law, McCorvey gave up her child for adoption. Under the pseudonym Jane Roe, McCorvey permitted Texas attorney Sarah Weddington to challenge the Texas statute before the U.S. Supreme Court in her behalf. Justice Harry A. Blackmun delivered the opinion of the Court, ruling that the Texas law violated a woman's constitutionally protected right to privacy, specifically, the right to terminate a pregnancy. The Court argued that the Fourteenth Amendment's guarantee of life, liberty, and property does not apply to an unborn fetus.

Pro-life organizations have vigorously fought to overturn *Roe v. Wade* and have lobbied state legislatures to impose stricter regulations on abortions. Although the Court has generally upheld *Roe v. Wade* and a woman's constitutional right to secure an abortion, recent decisions have greatly limited the scope of *Roe v. Wade* by permitting states to impose some restrictions.

**Key Concept:** privacy as a constitutional right

$M$r. Justice Blackmun delivered the opinion of the Court, saying in part:

The principal thrust of appellant's attack on the Texas statutes is that they improperly invade a right, said to be possessed by the pregnant woman, to choose to terminate her pregnancy. Appellant would discover this right in the concept of personal "liberty" embodied in the Fourteenth Amendment's Due Process Clause; or in personal, marital, familial, and sexual privacy said to be protected by the Bill of Rights or its penumbras, see Griswold v. Connecticut (1965); Eisenstadt v. Baird (1972); (White, J., concurring); or among those rights reserved to the people by the Ninth Amendment, Griswold v. Connecticut (Goldberg, J., concurring). Before addressing this claim, we feel it desirable briefly to survey, in several aspects, the history of abortion, for such insight as that history may afford us, and then to examine the state purposes and interests behind the criminal abortion laws.

It perhaps is not generally appreciated that the restrictive criminal abortion laws in effect in a majority of States today are of relatively recent vintage. Those laws, generally proscribing abortion or its attempt at any time during pregnancy except when necessary to preserve the pregnant woman's life, are not of ancient or even of common law origin. Instead, they derive from statutory changes effected, for the most part, in the latter half of the 19th century....

Three reasons have been advanced to explain historically the enactment of criminal abortion laws in the 19th century and to justify their continued existence.

It has been argued occasionally that these laws were the product of a Victorian social concern to discourage illicit sexual conduct. Texas, however, does not advance this justification in the present case, and it appears that no court or commentator has taken the argument seriously. The appellants and amici contend, moreover, that this is not a proper state purpose at all and suggest that, if it were, the Texas statutes are overbroad in protecting it since the law fails to distinguish between married and unwed mothers.

A second reason is concerned with abortion as a medical procedure. When most criminal abortion laws were first enacted, the procedure was a hazardous one for the woman. This was particularly true prior to the development of antisepsis. Antiseptic techniques, of course, were based on discoveries by Lister, Pasteur, and others first announced in 1867, but were not generally accepted and employed until about the turn of the century. Abortion mortality was high. Even after 1900, and perhaps until as late as the development of antibiotics in the 1940's, standard modern techniques such as dilation and curettage were not nearly so safe as they are today. Thus it has been argued that a State's real concern in enacting a criminal abortion law was to protect the pregnant woman, that is, to restrain her from submitting to a procedure that placed her life in serious jeopardy.

Modern medical techniques have altered this situation. Appellants and various amici refer to medical data indicating that abortion in early pregnancy, that is, prior to the end of first trimester, although not without its risk, is now relatively safe. Mortality rates for women undergoing early abortions, where the procedure is legal, appear to be as low as or lower than the rates for normal childbirth. Consequently, any interest of the State in protecting the woman from an inherently hazardous procedure, except when it would be equally dangerous for her to forego it, has largely disappeared. Of course, important state interests in the area of health and medical standards do remain. The State has a legitimate interest in seeing to it that abortion, like any other medical procedure, is performed under circumstances that insure maximum safety for the patient. This interest obviously extends at least to the performing physician and his staff, to the facilities involved, to the availability of after-care, and to adequate provision for any complication or emergency that might arise. The prevalence of high mortality rates at illegal "abortion mills" strengthens, rather than weakens, the State's interest in regulating the conditions under which abortions are performed. Moreover, the risk to the woman increases as her pregnancy continues. Thus the State retains a definite interest in protecting the woman's own health and safety when an abortion is proposed at a late stage of pregnancy.

The third reason is the State's interest—some phrase it in terms of duty—in protecting prenatal life. Some of the argument for this justification rests on the theory that a new human life is present from the moment of conception. The State's interest and general obligation to protect life then extends, it is argued, to prenatal life. Only when the life of the pregnant mother herself is at stake, balanced against the life she carries within her, should the interest of the embryo or fetus not prevail. Logically, of course, a legitimate State interest in this area need not stand or fall on acceptance of the belief that life begins at conception or at some other point prior to live birth. In assessing the State's interest, recognition may be given to the less rigid claim that as long as at least *potential* life is involved, the State may assert interests beyond the protection of the pregnant woman alone.

Parties challenging state abortion laws have sharply disputed in some courts the contention that a purpose of these laws, when enacted, was to protect prenatal life. . . .

It is with these interests, and the weight to be attached to them, that this case is concerned.

The Constitution does not explicitly mention any right of privacy. In a line of decisions, however, going back perhaps as far as Union Pacific R. Co. v. Botsford (1891), the Court has recognized that a right of personal privacy, or a guarantee of certain areas or zones of privacy, does exist under the Constitution. In varying contexts the Court or individual Justices have indeed found at least the roots of that right in the First Amendment, Stanley v. Georgia (1969); in the Fourth and Fifth Amendments, Terry v. Ohio (1968), Katz v. United States (1967) . . . ; in the penumbras of the Bill of Rights, Griswold v. Connecticut (1965); in the Ninth Amendment; or in the concept of liberty guaranteed by the first section of the Fourteenth Amendment, see Meyer v. Nebraska (1923). These decisions make it clear that only personal rights that can be deemed "fundamental" or "implicit in the concept of ordered liberty," Palko v. Connecticut (1937), are included in this guarantee of personal privacy. They also make it clear that the right has some extension to activities relating to marriage, Loving v. Virginia (1967), procreation, Skinner v. Oklahoma (1942), contraception, Eisenstadt v. Baird (1972)....

This right of privacy, whether it be founded in the Fourteenth Amendment's concept of personal liberty and restrictions upon state action, as we feel it is, or, as the District Court determined, in the Ninth Amendment's reservation of rights to the people, is broad enough to encompass a woman's decision whether or not to terminate her pregnancy. The detriment that the State would impose upon the pregnant woman by denying this choice altogether is apparent. Specific and direct harm medically diagnosable even in early pregnancy may be involved. Maternity, or additional offspring, may force upon the woman a distressful life and future. Psychological harm may be imminent. Mental and physical health may be taxed by child care. There is also the distress, for all concerned, associated with the unwanted child, and there is the problem of bringing a child into a family already unable, psychologically and otherwise, to care for it. In other cases, as in this one, the additional difficulties and continuing stigma of unwed motherhood may be involved. All these are factors the woman and her responsible physician necessarily will consider in consultation....

We therefore conclude that the right of personal privacy includes the abortion decision, but that this right is not unqualified and must be considered against state interests in regulation.

Where certain "fundamental rights" are involved, the Court has held that regulation limiting these rights may be justified only by a "compelling state interest," Kramer v. Union Free School District (1969), Shapiro v. Thompson (1969), ... and that legislative enactments must be narrowly drawn to express only the legitimate state interests at stake. Griswold v. Connecticut (1965)....

The District Court held that the appellee failed to meet his burden of demonstrating that the Texas statute's infringement upon Roe's rights was necessary to support a compelling state interest.... Appellee argues that the State's determination to recognize and protect prenatal life from and after conception constitutes a compelling state interest. As noted above, we do not agree fully with either formulation.

A. The appellee and certain amici argue that the fetus is a "person" within the language and meaning of the Fourteenth Amendment. In support of this they outline at length and in detail the well-known facts of fetal development. If this suggestion of personhood is established, the appellant's case, of course, collapses, for the fetus' right to life is then guaranteed specifically by the Amendment. The appellant conceded as much on reargument. On the other hand, the appellee conceded on reargument that no case could be cited that holds that a fetus is a person within the meaning of the Fourteenth Amendment.

The Constitution does not define "person" in so many words. Section 1 of the Fourteenth Amendment contains three references to "person." The first, in defining "citizens," speaks of "persons born or naturalized in the United States." The word also appears both in the Due Process Clause and in the Equal Protection Clause. "Person" is used in other places in the Constitution.... But in nearly all these instances, the use of the word is such that it has application only postnatally. None indicates, with any assurance, that it has any possible prenatal application. All this, together with our observation, that throughout the major portion of the 19th century prevailing legal abortion practices were far freer than they are today, persuades us that the word "person," as used in the Fourteenth Amendment, does not include the unborn....

B. The pregnant woman cannot be isolated in her privacy. She carries an embryo and, later, a fetus, if one accepts the medical definitions of the developing young in the human uterus.... The situation therefore is inherently different from marital intimacy, or bedroom possession of obscene material, or marriage, or procreation, or education, with which Eisenstadt, Griswold, Stanley, Loving, Skinner, Pierce, and Meyer were respectively concerned. As we have intimated above, it is reasonable and appropriate for a State to decide that at some point in time another interest, that of health of the mother or that of potential human life, becomes significantly involved. The woman's privacy is no longer sole and any right of privacy she possesses must be measured accordingly.

Texas urges that, apart from the Fourteenth Amendment, life begins at conception and is present throughout pregnancy, and that, therefore, the State has a compelling interest in protecting that life from and after conception. We need not resolve the difficult question of when life begins. When those trained in the respective disciplines of medicine, philosophy, and theology are unable to arrive at any consensus, the judiciary, at this point in the development of man's knowledge, is not in a position to speculate as to the answer.

It should be sufficient to note briefly the wide divergence of thinking on this most sensitive and difficult question....

In view of all this, we do not agree that, by adopting one theory of life, Texas may override the rights of the pregnant woman that are at stake. We repeat, however, that the State does have an important and legitimate interest in preserving and protecting the health of the pregnant woman, whether she be a resident of the State or a nonresident who seeks medical consultation and treatment there, and that it has still *another* important and legitimate interest in protecting the potentiality of human life. These interests are separate and distinct. Each grows in substantiality as the woman approaches term and, at a point during pregnancy, each becomes "compelling."...

To summarize and to repeat:

1. A state criminal abortion statute of the current Texas type, that excepts from criminality only a *life saving* procedure on behalf of the mother, without regard to pregnancy stage and without recognition of the other interests involved, is violative of the Due Process Clause of the Fourteenth Amendment.

(a) For the stage prior to approximately the end of the first trimester, the abortion decision and its effectuation must be left to the medical judgment of the pregnant woman's attending physician.

(b) For the stage subsequent to approximately the end of the first trimester, the State, in promoting its interest in the health of the mother, may, if it chooses, regulate the abortion procedure in ways that are reasonably related to maternal health.

(c) For the stage subsequent to viability the State, in promoting its interest in the potentiality of human life, may, if it chooses, regulate, and even proscribe, abortion except where it is necessary, in appropriate medical judgment, for the preservation of the life or health of the mother.

2. The State may define the term "physician," as it has been employed in the preceding numbered paragraphs of this Part XI of this opinion, to mean only a physician currently licensed by the State, and may proscribe any abortion by a person who is not a physician as so defined.

In Doe v. Bolton procedural requirements contained in one of the modern abortion statutes are considered. That opinion and this one, of course, are to be read together. . . .

Mr. Chief Justice Burger concurred.

Mr. Justice Douglas concurred. . . .

Mr. Justice Rehnquist, dissenting, said in part:

. . . I have difficulty in concluding, as the Court does, that the right of "privacy" is involved in this case. Texas by the statute here challenged bars the performance of a medical abortion by a licensed physician on a plaintiff such as Roe. A transaction resulting in an operation such as this is not "private" in the ordinary usage of that word. . . .

If the Court means by the term "privacy" no more than that the claim of a person to be free from unwanted state regulation of consensual transactions may be a form of "liberty" protected by the Fourteenth Amendment, there is no doubt that similar claims have been upheld in our earlier decisions on the basis of that liberty. I agree with the statement of Mr. Justice Stewart in his concurring opinion that the "liberty," against deprivation of which without due process the Fourteenth Amendment protects, embraces more than the rights found in the Bill of Rights. But that liberty is not guaranteed absolutely against deprivation, but only against deprivation without due process of law. The test traditionally applied in the area of social and economic legislation is whether or not a law such as that challenged has a rational relation to a valid state objective. . . . But the Court's sweeping invalidation of any restrictions on abortion during the first trimester is impossible to justify under that standard, and the conscious weighing of competing factors which the Court's opinion apparently substitutes for the established test is far more appropriate to a legislative judgment than to a judicial one.

The Court eschews the history of the Fourteenth Amendment in its reliance on the "compelling state interest" test. . . . But the Court adds a new wrinkle to this test by transposing it from the legal considerations associated with the Equal Protection Clause of the Fourteenth Amendment to this case arising under the Due Process Clause of the Fourteenth Amendment. Unless I misapprehend the consequences of this transplanting of the "compelling state interest test," the Court's opinion will accomplish the seemingly impossible feat of leaving this area of the law more confused than it found it.

While the Court's opinion quotes from the dissent of Mr. Justice Holmes in Lochner v. New York (1905), the result it reaches is more closely attuned to the majority opinion of Mr. Justice Peckham in that case. As in Lochner and similar cases applying substantive due process standards to economic and social welfare legislation, the adoption of the compelling state interest standard will inevitably require this Court to examine the legislative policies and pass on the wisdom of these policies in the very process of deciding whether a particular state interest put forward may or may not be "compelling." . . .

The fact that a majority of the States, reflecting after all the majority sentiment in those States, have had restrictions on abortions for at least a century is a strong indication, it seems to me, that the asserted right to an abortion is not "so rooted in the traditions and conscience of our people as to be ranked as fundamental," Snyder v. Massachusetts (1934). . . .

Mr. Justice White, with whom Mr. Justice Rehnquist joins, dissented.

*Harry A. Blackmun*

# CHAPTER 5 Civil Rights

## 5.1 RICHARD KLUGER

# *Simple Justice*

Richard Kluger (b. 1934) is an American author, editor, and social critic who has focused much of his writing on problematic issues pertaining to social justice and inequality in America. Kluger has served on the editorial staff of several New York papers and magazines, including the *Wall Street Journal, County Citizen,* and *Forbes.* In addition, Kluger established Charterhouse Books, where he served as president and publisher from 1972 to 1973. Kluger has received numerous awards and honors, including the 1976 Sidney Hillman Prize for his book *Simple Justice: The History of* Brown v. Board of Education *and Black America's Struggle for Equality* (Alfred A. Knopf, 1987) and the 1987 George Polk Prize for *The Paper: The Life and Death of the New York Herald Tribune* (Alfred A. Knopf, 1986).

Kluger has selected the problems of social justice and inequality in the United States as the central themes in his social commentary. His book *Simple Justice* has been regarded by American government scholars as one of the most insightful, meticulously researched accounts of one of the most divisive issues in American political history. Kluger's scholarly analysis focused on the 1954 landmark U.S. Supreme Court decision *Brown v. Board of Education of Topeka, Kansas* (347 U.S. 483).

Linda Brown was a seven-year-old African American whose father attempted to enroll her in a segregated white public school in Topeka, Kansas. Brown's request was rejected because of the public school racial segregation policy. Linda Brown was required to attend the African American school, since a federal district court decided that the African American school was relatively equal to the white school. Brown's appeal to the U.S. Supreme Court was supported by NAACP attorneys headed by Thurgood Marshall. Marshall argued before the Court that severe psychological, intellectual, and economic harm impacted upon African Americans due to the policy of segregation and that any claim of equality between the races is invalid.

Marshall also challenged the separate-but-equal doctrine as unconstitutional according to the equal protection clause of the Fourteenth Amendment.

*Richard Kluger*

Chief Justice Earl Warren spoke for a unanimous Court when he delivered the opinion in *Brown*. The Court's ruling focused on social science evidence linking racial segregation to a psychological feeling of inferiority that is irreversible. The Court ruled that separate-but-equal in education violates the equal protection clause of the Fourteenth Amendment.

Kluger's unique analysis of *Brown* focuses on multiple complex dimensions of the case, including the legal and cultural context of the case, as well as the human drama behind it. In particular, Kluger examines Warren's skills of negotiation and diplomacy, which dramatically prompted a unanimous decision. The following selection from *Simple Justice* analyzes the delivery of Warren's opinion itself. Kluger's work has had a profound impact upon the development of contemporary scholarly social commentary and political journalism in the United States.

**Key Concept:** *Brown v. Board of Education of Topeka, Kansas*

*I* have for announcement," said Earl Warren, "the judgment and opinion of the Court in No. 1—*Oliver Brown et al. v. Board of Education of Topeka.*" It was 12:52 p.m. In the press room, the Associated Press wire carried the first word to the country: "Chief Justice Warren today began reading the Supreme Court's decision in the public school segregation cases. The court's ruling could not be determined immediately." The bells went off in every news room in America. The nation was listening.

It was Warren's first major opinion as Chief Justice. He read it, by all accounts, in a firm, clear, unemotional voice. If he had delivered no other opinion but this one, he would have won his place in American history.

Considering its magnitude, it was a short opinion. During its first part, no one hearing it could tell where it would come out.

These four state cases had reached the Court by different routes, the opinion began, but had been consolidated because each dealt with "minors of the Negro race" who sought admission to public schools closed to them under "the so-called 'separate but equal' doctrine announced by this Court in *Plessy v. Ferguson,* 163 U.S. 537." The Justices had heard reargument that "exhaustively" considered the circumstances surrounding the adoption of the Fourteenth Amendment, the reach and intention of which were at the core of the segregation dispute. "This discussion and our own investigation convince us," announced Warren, "that although these sources cast some light, it is not enough to resolve the problem with which we are faced. At best, they are inconclusive." Thurgood Marshall had won his "nothin'-to-nothin'" standoff on the historical question.

Another reason why the amendment's history did not much help the Court resolve the issue was the primitive nature of public education at the time of its adoption, the Chief Justice said. In the South, where the movement to free common schools supported by general taxation had not yet taken hold, the education of white children was largely in the hands of private groups, while education of Negroes was almost non-existent, "and practically all of the race were illiterate. In fact, any education of Negroes was forbidden by law.... Today, in contrast, many Negroes have achieved outstanding success in the arts and sciences as well as in the business and professional world." It was not surprising, then, that "there should be so little in the history of the Fourteenth Amendment relating to its intended effect on public education."

Warren then turned to the Court's understanding of the amendment. In the first cases coming to it soon after the adoption of the amendment, "the Court interpreted it as proscribing all state-imposed discriminations against the Negro race," the Chief Justice said, citing in a footnote the *Slaughterhouse Cases* and *Strauder v. West Virginia* decisions and quoting from the latter the well-known passage that "the law in the States shall be the same for the black as for the white...." That was the way the Court had originally construed the reach of the amendment; "separate but equal" did not surface as a doctrine of the Court until two decades later, and when it did, it involved not education but transportation. "American courts have since labored with the doctrine for over half a century."

Having established that *Plessy* was a relative johnny-come-lately, Warren sounded as if he were about to direct criticism at it for its departure from the Court's earlier view of the amendment as prohibiting all racial discriminations under law. But he did not do that. Indeed, he seemed to take pains to establish the longevity of the separate-but-equal doctrine, which he said in a footnote had apparently had its genesis in *Roberts v. City of Boston* in 1849. He did not choose to note that the Massachusetts case had antedated the Fourteenth Amendment by nineteen years, though he did indicate that the state legislature had ended school segregation six years after the decision. With scrupulous fairness, though, the note added: "But elsewhere in the North segregation in public education has persisted until recent years. It is apparent that such segregation has long been a nationwide problem, not merely one of sectional concern." The Court was clearly taking pains not to level a finger at the South.

Six times after *Plessy*, the Court had dealt with cases involving the separate-but-equal doctrine in the field of education, the opinion continued. In two of the cases, *Cumming* and *Gong Lum*, "the validity of the doctrine itself was not challenged," the Chief Justice noted. He cited *Berea College v. Kentucky* in a footnote without comment, though he might have remarked that in that case, too, the doctrine itself was involved only tangentially. In the more recent cases—*Gaines, Sipuel, Sweatt,* and *McLaurin*—it had not proven necessary to re-examine "the doctrine to grant relief to the Negro plaintiff." In fact, the Court in *Sweatt* had "expressly reserved decision on the question of whether *Plessy v. Ferguson* should be held inapplicable to public education." But that question was now presented directly to the Court in the instant cases, where the courts below had found that the Negro and white schools had been—or were being—equalized in terms of the school buildings, curricula, qualifications and salaries of the teachers, and other "tangible" factors. To settle the question of *Plessy's* applicability, said Warren, the Court could therefore not compare merely the tangible factors: "We must look instead to the effect of segregation itself on public education."

Without in any way becoming technical and rhetorical, Warren then proceeded to demonstrate the dynamic nature and adaptive genius of American constitutional law:

> In approaching this problem, we cannot turn the clock back to 1868 when the Amendment was adopted, or even to 1896 when *Plessy v. Ferguson* was written. We must consider public education in the light of its full development and its present place in American life throughout the Nation....
>
> Today, education is perhaps the most important function of state and local governments. Compulsory school attendance laws and the great expenditures for education both demonstrate our recognition of the importance of education to our democratic society. It is required in the performance of our most basic public responsibilities, even service in the armed forces. It is the very foundation of good citizenship....

Having declared its essential value to the nation's civic health and vitality, he then argued for the central importance of education in the private life and aspirations of every individual:

> ...Today it is a principal instrument in awakening the child to cultural values, in preparing him for later professional training, and in helping him to adjust normally to his environment. In these days, it is doubtful that any child may reasonably be expected to succeed in life if he is denied the opportunity of an education. Such an opportunity, where the state has undertaken to provide it, is a right which must be made available to all on equal terms.

That led finally to the critical question: "Does segregation of children in public schools solely on the basis of race ... deprive the children of the minority group of equal educational opportunities?"

To this point, nearly two-thirds through the opinion, Warren had not tipped his hand. Now, in the next sentence, he showed it by answering that critical question: "We believe that it does." ...

Earl Warren read on.

In *Sweatt v. Painter*, the Chief Justice declared, the Court had relied on "those qualities which are incapable of objective measurement" in holding that the all-black law school did not provide the plaintiff with an educational opportunity equal to that offered white students at the University of Texas. In *McLaurin v. Oklahoma State Regents*, similarly, the treatment given to the plaintiff caused him to suffer by affecting him in such intangible areas as " ... his ability to study, to engage in discussions and exchange views with other students, and, in general, to learn his profession." Now Warren swept aside the argument by the South that unsegregated higher education, involving mature young people, was quite a different story from compulsory schooling in the more formative years. Extending the *Sweatt-McLaurin* line of logic, he asserted: "Such considerations apply with added force to children in grade and high schools." In the only soaring passage in the opinion, he went on:

> To separate them from others of similar age and qualifications solely because of their race generates a feeling of inferiority as to their status in the community that may affect their hearts and minds in a way unlikely ever to be undone.

To brace this compassionate declaration, he invoked the finding of the Kansas court, which in turn had been based largely on the testimony of the witness Louisa Holt: Segregation, with its detrimental effect on colored children, had a still more severe impact "when it has the sanction of the law; for the policy of separating the races is usually interpreted as denoting the inferiority of the Negro group. A sense of inferiority affects the motivation of a child to learn. Segregation with the sanction of law, therefore, has a tendency to retard the educational and mental development of Negro children..."

This finding flew directly in the face of *Plessy*. And here, finally, Warren collided with the 1896 decision. But he did so in such an economical and uncontentious way that the basic dishonesty of *Plessy* was allowed to escape censure and seemed instead to be dismissed as simply no longer fashionable thinking. *Plessy* had said that "the underlying fallacy" of the Negro plaintiff's complaint was its "assumption that the enforced separation of the two races stamps the colored race with a badge of inferiority. If this be so, it is not by reason of anything found in the act, but solely because the colored race chooses to put that construction upon it." Warren, in response now to this piece of enshrined disingenuousness, said simply: "Whatever may have been the extent of psychological knowledge at the time of *Plessy v. Ferguson*, this finding [by the Kansas court in *Brown* that segregation denotes inferiority and diminishes learning motivation] is amply supported by modern authority. Any language in *Plessy v. Ferguson* contrary to this finding is rejected."

To buttress such a brisk dismissal of *Plessy's* essence, Warren added a footnote—the eleventh in the opinion and destined to become one of the most debated in the annals of the Court. Footnote #11 was merely a list of seven works by contemporary social scientists, all of which had been cited in the NAACP briefs during litigation of the school cases. First on the list, and the highest tribute to his contribution to the overall NAACP effort, was "K. B. Clark, *Effect of Prejudice and Discrimination on Personality Development* (Midcentury White House Conference on Children and Youth, 1950)." A bit farther down on the list was "Deutscher and Chein, *The Psychological Effects of Enforced Segregation: A Survey of Social Science Opinion*, 26 J. Psychol. 259 (1948)." It was Isidor Chein's reward for withstanding the personal and professional assault made on him on the witness stand in Richmond by Justin Moore in the name of the commonwealth of Virginia. The footnote wound up with two massive books: "[E. Franklin] Frazier, *The Negro in the United States* (1949).... And see generally Myrdal, *An American Dilemma*."

To Warren, it had seemed an innocuous enough item to insert in the opinion. "We included it because I thought the point it made was the antithesis of what was said in *Plessy*," he later commented. "They had said there that if there was any harm intended, it was solely in the mind of the Negro. I thought these things—these cited sources—were sufficient to note as being in contradistinction to that statement in *Plessy*." Then he added, by way of stressing that the sociology was merely supportive and not the substance of the holding, "It was only a note, after all." Warren's clerk Earl Pollock, one of those closest to the writing of the opinion, puts it more bluntly: "The only reason to have included footnote #11 was as a rebuttal to the cheap psychology of *Plessy* that said inferiority was only in the mind of the Negro. The Chief Justice was saying in effect that we know a lot more now about how human beings work than they did back then and can therefore cast doubt on that preposterous line of argument."

But the footnote apparently provoked at least mild concern among several members of the Court, especially the last part of the listed authorities. "I questioned the Chief's going with Myrdal in the opinion," recalls retired Justice Tom Clark. "I told him—and Hugo Black did, too—that it wouldn't go down well in the South. And he didn't need it." Myrdal's compendious assault on the brutalities of American racism had by then, a decade after its publication, become a dagger in the flesh of the white South; its author, moreover, was both foreign and leftward-tilting in his political orientation and therefore prone to ready vilification throughout the old Confederacy. That two of the three Southerners on the Court may have cautioned Warren[1] against the very mention of Myrdal's scholarly masterwork underscored both the wisdom and the necessity of the Chief Justice's insistence on making the opinion as bland and non-accusatory as possible. Any pointed language would almost surely have shattered the unanimity Warren had won. "You know," adds Justice Clark, "we don't have money at the Court for an army and we can't take ads in the newspapers, and we don't want to go out on a picket line in our robes. We have to convince the nation by the force of our opinions." ...

The balance of the Chief Justice's opinion consisted of just two paragraphs. The first began: "We conclude"—and here Warren departed from the printed text before him to insert the word "unanimously," which sent a sound of muffled astonishment eddying around the courtroom—"that in the field of public education the doctrine of 'separate but equal' has no place. Separate educational facilities are inherently unequal." The plaintiffs and others similarly situated—technically meaning Negro children within the segregated school districts under challenge—were therefore being deprived of the equal protection of the laws guaranteed by the Fourteenth Amendment.

The concluding paragraph of the opinion revealed Earl Warren's political adroitness both at compromise and at the ready use of the power of his office for ends he thought worthy. "Because these are class actions, because of the wide applicability of this decision, and because of the great variety of local conditions," he declared, "these cases present problems of considerable complexity.... In order that we may have the full assistance of the parties in formulating decrees," the Court was scheduling further argument for the term beginning the following fall. The attorneys general of the United States and all the states requiring or permitting segregation in public education were invited to participate. In a few strokes, Warren thus managed to (1) proclaim "the wide applicability" of the decision and make it plain that the Court had no intention of limiting its benefits to a handful of plaintiffs in a few outlying districts; (2) reassure the South that the Court understood the emotional wrench desegregation would cause and was therefore granting the region some time to get accustomed to the idea; and (3) invite the South to participate in the entombing of Jim Crow by joining the Court's efforts to fashion a temperate implementation decree—or to forfeit that chance by petulantly abstaining from the Court's further deliberations and thereby run the risk of having a harsh decree imposed upon it. It was such dexterous use of the power available to him and of the circumstances in which to exploit it that had established John Marshall as a judicial statesman and political tactician of the most formidable sort. The Court had not seen his like since. Earl Warren, in his first major opinion, moved now with that same sure purposefulness.

He turned next to the District of Columbia case, *Boiling v. Sharpe,* and disposed of it in similar fashion in six paragraphs.

"Classifications based solely upon race must be scrutinized with particular care, since they are contrary to our traditions and hence constitutionally suspect," the Chief Justice asserted, pursuing a line of argument that had been basic to the entire NAACP legal effort but that Warren had not bothered to introduce into the opinion on the state cases that he had just delivered. As source for his warning against racial classifications, he cited with unspoken irony the Court's decisions in *Korematsu v. United States* and *Hirabayashi v. United States,* upholding the mass wartime removal of Japanese-Americans from their West Coast homes—an act of dishonor that Earl Warren had promoted as vigorously as any other man in the nation. Now he declared that such a wholesale deprivation of due process of law was involved in the imposition of segregated education in the District of Columbia, where the protections of the Fourteenth Amendment did not extend.

It was 1:20 p.m. The wire services proclaimed the news to the nation. Within the hour, the Voice of America would begin beaming word to the world in thirty-four languages: In the United States, schoolchildren could no longer be segregated by race. The law of the land no longer recognized a separate equality. No Americans were more equal than any other Americans. Jim Crow was on the way to the burial ground.

## NOTES

1. Warren's clerk Earl Pollock believes that if any of the other Justices had objected strongly to the footnote—especially Hugo Black—it would most likely have been struck by the Chief Justice.

## REFERENCES

*Books:* Allport, *The Nature of Prejudice;* Ashmore, *The Negro and the Schools;* Berman. *It Is So Ordered;* Blaustein and Ferguson, *Desegregation and the Law;* Friedman and Israel, *The Justices of the Supreme Court* (see Norman Dorsen's sketch of John Marshall Harlan, 2803–2820); Greenberg, *Race Relations and American Law;* Hill and Greenberg, *Citizen's Guide to Desegregation;* Lewis, *Portrait of a Decade;* Peltason, *Fifty-eight Lonely Men;* and Smith, *They Closed Their Schools.*

*Interviews and Correspondence:* Almond, J. Lindsay; Bickel, Alexander M.; Clark, Kenneth B.; Clark, Tom C.; Elman, Philip; Fassett, John D.; Huston, Luther; McKay, Ellis H.; Mickum, George V., III; Pollock, Earl E.; Prettyman, E. Barrett, Jr.; Rogers, S. Emory; and Rubenstein, Ernest.

*Articles and Documents:* Clark, Kenneth B., "Desegregation: An Appraisal of the Evidence," *Journal of Social Issues,* IX, No. 4 (1953), entire issue; Clark's report on desegregation in Milford, Delaware, in September 1954 is in the LDF files. Justice Frankfurter's letter to Justice Reed, May 20, 1954, offering the writer's impression of the Court's disposition on *Brown* a year earlier, and his letter to Paul A. Freund, July 22, 1958, ruminating on Holmes's use of "all deliberate speed," are in the Library of Congress. The *New York Times's* massive coverage of the *Brown* decision in its May 18, 1954, issue shows why it is the leading newspaper in the United States.

*Quotations:* Chief Justice Warren's remarks on Footnote #11 were made to the author in an interview in his chambers. I made no tape of this or any other interview I had, but typed up my notes at the first possible moment.

# Why We Lost the ERA

Jane J. Mansbridge (b. 1939) received her Ph.D. from Harvard University in 1971. A professor of political science and sociology at Northwestern University, she has been recognized by her peers as a leading scholar and expert on feminist political theory and history, gender politics and social movements, and political psychology and socialization. Her teaching and research have also focused on political thought and philosophy, American government and politics, and political behavior, and she is the author of *Beyond Adversary Democracy* (Basic Books, 1980). Mansbridge has also published numerous scholarly articles in various political science journals.

In the following selection, which is excerpted from Mansbridge's classic case study of the defeated Equal Rights Amendment (ERA) entitled *Why We Lost the ERA* (University of Chicago Press, 1986), Mansbridge examines the causal linkage between political attitudes or public opinion and actual legislative voting behavior. In particular, Mansbridge provides detailed data to support her claim that although most Americans expressed support for the ERA in general, many of them articulated attitudes that reflected deep reservations about the amendment's potential consequences upon widely shared social norms (i.e., women's traditional roles). A decline in ERA support occurred to a great extent because of a highly successful backlash among conservative women's groups (e.g., Phyllis Schlafly's Eagle Forum) and fundamentalist religious associations committed to traditional female roles within the family. These groups persuaded the American public to fear substantive changes in women's roles and behavior that they claimed would occur upon the ratification of the ERA. Opponents of the ERA focused their efforts at the state level and convinced many state legislators that support of the amendment involved serious political risks.

The critical provision of the ERA amendment simply declared that "equality of rights under the law shall not be denied or abridged by the United States or by any State on account of sex." Although the ERA failed to gain ratification, it did have an immediate impact upon the awareness of American women concerning their social status and gender issues. The movement to ratify the ERA also encouraged a greater number of women to participate in politics, and it led to the passage of serious legislation affecting women.

**Key Concept:** the failure to ratify the ERA

1. Equality of rights under the law shall not be denied or abridged by the United States or by any State on account of sex.
2. The Congress shall have the power to enforce, by appropriate legislation, the provisions of this article.
3. This amendment shall take effect two years after the date of ratification.

—Complete text of the Equal Rights Amendment

In March 1972 the Equal Rights Amendment to the United States Constitution —the ERA—passed the Senate of the United States with a vote of 84 to 8, fifteen votes more than the two-thirds required for constitutional amendments. In the ensuing ten years—from 1972 to 1982—a majority of Americans consistently told interviewers that they favored this amendment to the Constitution. Yet on June 30, 1982, the deadline for ratifying the amendment passed with only thirty-five of the required thirty-eight states having ratified.

How did this happen? . . .

Contrary to widespread belief, public support for the ERA did not increase in the course of the ten-year struggle. In key wavering states where the ERA was most debated, public support actually declined. Much of the support for the Amendment was superficial, because it was based on a support for abstract rights, not for real changes. Many nominal supporters took strong antifeminist positions on other issues, and their support evaporated when the ERA became linked in their minds to feminist positions they rejected.

The irony in all this is that the ERA would have had much less substantive effect than either proponents or opponents claimed. Because the ERA applied only to the government and not to private businesses and corporations, it would have had no noticeable effect, at least in the short run, on the gap between men's and women's wages. Furthermore, during the 1970s, the Supreme Court began to use the Fourteenth Amendment to the Constitution to declare unconstitutional almost all the laws and practices that Congress had intended to make unconstitutional when it passed the ERA in 1972. The exceptions were laws and practices that most Americans approved. Thus, by the late 1970s it was hard to show that the ERA would have made any of the substantive changes that most Americans favored.

While the ERA would have had few immediate, tangible effects, I nonetheless believe that its defeat was a major setback for equality between men and women. Its direct effects would have been slight, but its indirect effects on both judges and legislators would probably have led in the long run to interpretations of existing laws and enactment of new laws that would have benefited women. The lack of immediate benefits did, however, deeply influence the course of the public debate. Because ERA activists had little of an immediate, practical nature to lose if the ERA was defeated, they had little reason to describe it in a way that would make it acceptable to middle-of-the-road legislators. As a consequence, the most influential leaders in the pro-ERA organizations and many of the activists in those organizations chose to interpret the ERA as delivering radical results....

The only possible way to have persuaded three more state legislatures to ratify the ERA would have been to insist—correctly—that it would do relatively little in the short run, and to insist equally strongly—and correctly—on the importance of placing the principle in the Constitution to guide the Supreme Court in its long-run evolution of constitutional law. In addition, the pro-ERA movement would have had to develop an ongoing, district-based political network capable of turning generalized public sympathy for reforms that benefit women into political pressure on specific legislators in the marginal unratified states. But even this strategy might not have worked. Comparatively few state legislators were open to persuasion on this issue, and the troops for district-based organizing were often hard to mobilize—or keep mobilized.

The movement away from principle and the increasing focus on substantive effects was probably an inevitable result of the ten-year struggle for the ERA. Inevitable or not, the shift did occur. In the near future, therefore, the only way to convince legislators that the ERA would not have undesirable substantive effects would be to add explicit amendments limiting its application to the military, abortion, and so on. No principled feminist, including myself, favors an ERA that includes such "crippling" amendments. In the present political climate, therefore, the future of the ERA looks even dimmer than its past.

The death of the ERA was, of course, also related to broader changes in American political attitudes. Two of these changes were especially relevant: growing legislative skepticism about the consequences of giving the U.S. Supreme Court authority to review legislation, and the growing organizational power of the new Right....

## A VERY BRIEF HISTORY

The major women's organizations were able to persuade two-thirds of the states to approve women's suffrage in 1920. In the same year these organizations began to discuss an Equal Rights Amendment. Alice Paul and her militant National Woman's Party had gained national notoriety by picketing the White House and staging hunger strikes for women's suffrage. Now the same group proposed a constitutional amendment, introduced in Congress in 1923, that read: "Men and women shall have equal rights throughout the United Stats and in every place subject to its jurisdiction. Congress shall have power to enforce this article by appropriate legislation."[1]

From the beginning, "equal rights" meant "ending special benefits." An ERA would have made unconstitutional the protective legislation that socialists and social reformers like Florence Kelley, frustrated by the lack of a strong working-class movement in America, had struggled to erect in order to protect at least women and children from the worst ravages of capitalism. Against Kelley and women like her, the National Woman's Party leaders, primarily professional and upper- or upper-middle-class women,[2] argued that "a maximum hour law or a minimum wage law which applied to women but not to men was bound to hurt women more than it could possibly help them." Kelley in turn dubbed the ERA "topsy-turvy feminism," and declared that "women cannot achieve true equality with men by securing identity of treatment under the law."[3]

After a 1921 meeting between Alice Paul, Florence Kelley, and others, the board of directors of the National Consumers' League voted to oppose the Equal Rights Amendment. The League, a powerful Progressive organization of which Kelley was general secretary, thereafter made opposition to the ERA a consistent plank in its program.[4] The strong opposition of Progressive and union feminists meant that when the Equal Rights Amendment was introduced in Congress in 1923 it was immediately opposed by a coalition of Progressive organizations and labor unions. And although the Amendment was introduced in every subsequent Congress for the next twenty years, opposition from this coalition and from most conservatives ensured its repeated defeat.

During the 1930s, the National Association of Women Lawyers and the National Federation of Business and Professional Women's Clubs (BPW) decided to sponsor the ERA, and in 1940 the Republican party revitalized the ERA by placing it in the party's platform. In 1944, despite strong opposition from labor, the Democratic party followed suit. Nonetheless, the ERA never came close to passing until 1950 and 1953, when the U.S. Senate passed it, but with the "Hayden rider," which provided that the Amendment "shall not be construed to impair any rights, benefits, or exemptions now or hereinafter conferred by law upon persons of the female sex."[5] In both years the House of Representatives recessed without a vote. Because the women's organizations supporting the ERA knew that special benefits were incompatible with equal rights, they had tried to block the amended ERA in the House and were relieved when their efforts succeeded.

Support widened during the 1950s—primarily among Republicans, although among the Democrats Eleanor Roosevelt and some other prominent women dropped their opposition to the ERA in order to support the United Nations charter, which affirmed the "equal rights of men and women." In 1953 President Dwight Eisenhower replaced the unionist head of the Federal Women's Bureau with a Republican businesswoman who, having sponsored Connecticut's equal pay law, moved the bureau from active opposition into a neutral position regarding the ERA. In later speeches Eisenhower also stressed the pro-ERA planks of both parties and stated his support for "equal rights" for women.[6] . . .

The crucial step in building progressive and liberal support for the ERA was the passage of Title VII of the Civil Rights Act of 1964, which prohibited job discrimination on the basis of sex. Title VII had originally been designed to prevent discrimination against blacks, but a group of southern congressmen added a ban on discrimination against women in a vain effort to make the bill unacceptable to northern conservatives. Initially, Title VII had no effect on "protective" legislation. Unions, accordingly, continued to oppose the ERA because they thought it would nullify such legislation. In 1967, when the newly formed National Organization for Women (NOW) gave the ERA first place on its Bill of Rights for Women, several union members immediately resigned. But by 1970 both the federal courts and the Equal Employment Opportunity Commission (EEOC) had interpreted Title VII as invalidating protective legislation, and had extended most traditional protections to men rather than removing them for women. With their long-standing concern now for the most part made moot, union opposition to the ERA began to wane.

In 1970, the Pittsburgh chapter of NOW took direct action. The group disrupted Senator Birch Bayh's hearings on the nineteen-year-old vote, getting Bayh to promise hearings on the ERA the following spring. This was the moment. Labor opposition was fading, and, because few radical claims had been made for the ERA, conservatives had little ammunition with which to oppose it. In April, the United Auto Workers' convention voted to endorse the ERA. In May, Bayh began Senate hearings on the ERA, and for the first time in its history the U.S. Department of Labor supported the ERA. In June, Representative Martha Griffiths succeeded in collecting enough signatures on a discharge petition to pry the ERA out of the House Judiciary Committee, where for many years the liberal chair of the committee, Emanuel Celler, had refused to schedule hearings because of the persistent opposition by labor movement traditionalists. After only an hour's debate, the House of Representatives passed the ERA by a vote of 350 to 15.

The next fall, the ERA came to the Senate, which, after several days of debate, added by a narrow majority a provision exempting women from the draft.[7] This provision eliminated the only consequence proponents claimed for the ERA that might not have received support from a majority of Americans. However, having consistently insisted on bearing the responsibilities of citizenship as well as the rights, the women's organizations promoting the ERA had decided that women must be drafted. Because an ERA amended to exempt women from the draft was not acceptable to any of the organizations promoting the ERA, Senator Bayh did not bring it to a vote. Instead, without consulting those organizations, he proposed a new wording for the ERA that mirrored the words of the Fourteenth Amendment: "Neither the United States nor any State shall, on account of sex, deny to any person within its jurisdiction the equal protection of the laws." Bayh described his new wording as "recognizing the need for a flexible standard" and "meeting the objections of [the ERA's] most articulate critics,"[8] and he said in a subsequent press interview that the new wording would permit excluding women from the draft.[9] Fearing, on the basis of these remarks, that Bayh would be too flexible in his interpretation of this new wording, the major women's organizations told him that this substitute was not acceptable to them.

In the spring of 1971, the House Judiciary Committee returned to the original 1970 wording of the ERA but adopted the "Wiggins amendment," which said that the ERA would "not impair the validity of any law of the United States which exempts a person from compulsory military service or any other law of the United States or any state which reasonably promotes the health and safety of the people."[10] The women's organizations supporting an ERA concluded, correctly, that the standard of "reasonably" promoting health and safety was no more stringent than the standard the Supreme Court was already using to judge constitutional many laws discriminating against women. Accordingly, they opposed the Wiggins amendment, and under their urging the House rejected it, voting 354 to 23 to adopt the original ERA.

Having passed the House, the ERA went to the Senate, where the Subcommittee on Constitutional Amendments, chaired by ERA opponent Senator Sam Ervin, adopted another substitute: "Neither the United States nor any State shall make any legal distinction between the rights and responsibilities of male and female persons unless such distinction is based on physiological or functional differences between them." A majority of the full Committee on the Judiciary, chaired by Senator Bayh, rejected this attempt, so similar to the previous two, and adopted the original wording of the ERA in its definitive March 1972 report.

In the immediately ensuing Senate debate, Senator Ervin introduced eight amendments to the ERA relating to draft and combat, marital and family support, privacy, protections and exemptions, and homosexuality. His goal was twofold. First, he hoped to tempt a majority in the Senate into adopting one or more of the amendments, which would have divided the ERA proponents and at the very least would have delayed the ERA's passage. Second, if the ERA did pass in the Senate, he hoped to focus the upcoming debates in the states on the potentially unpalatable substantive consequences of the ERA.... Bayh succeeded in persuading a majority to vote down all the Ervin amendments. On March 22, 1972, the ERA passed the Senate of the United States with a vote of 84 to 8.

As soon as the Senate voted, a secretary in the office of the senator from Hawaii contacted the Hawaii legislative reference bureau, and within twenty minutes the president of the Hawaii state senate presented a resolution to ratify. Five minutes later the resolution, unanimously passed, came before the Hawaii house, receiving equally quick and unanimous treatment. Thus on the very day that the U.S. Senate passed the ERA, Hawaii became the first state to ratify. Delaware, Nebraska, and New Hampshire ratified the next day, and on the third day Idaho and Iowa ratified. Twenty-four more states ratified in 1972 and early 1973. The very earliest states to ratify were all unanimous, and in the other early states the votes were rarely close. Moreover,

> rules were suspended in order to avoid referral to committee. Frequently no or only perfunctory hearings were held on the subject. Floor debate too was brief.... Even in those states where open hearings were held, it was not uncommon for only proponents of the amendment to appear as witnesses.[11]

By late 1973, however, the ERA's proponents had lost control of the ratification process. While the national offices of the various pro-ERA organizations could relatively easily coordinate their Washington activities to get the ERA through Congress, they were slow in organizing coalitions in the states. At the end of the 1973 state legislative sessions, only a few states even had active ERA coalitions.

Moreover, in 1973 the Supreme Court decided, in *Roe v. Wade,* that state laws forbidding abortion violated the "right to privacy" implicit in the Constitution. Although the ERA had no obvious direct bearing on whether "abortion is murder," the two issues nonetheless became politically linked. The *Roe* decision took power out of the hands of relatively parochial, conservative state legislators and put it in the hands of a relatively cosmopolitan, liberal U.S. Supreme Court. The ERA would have done the same thing. Furthermore, both were sponsored by what was at that time still called the "women's liberation" movement. Traditionalists saw the "women's libbers" both as rejecting the notion that motherhood was a truly important task and as endorsing sexual hedonism instead of moral restraint. The *Roe* decision seemed to constitute judicial endorsement for these values. Since NOW was not only the leading sponsor of the ERA but the leading defender of abortion on demand, conservative activists saw abortion and the ERA as two prongs of the "libbers'" general strategy for undermining traditional American values. Unable to overturn the *Roe* decision directly, many conservatives sought to turn the ERA into a referendum on that decision. To a significant degree, they succeeded. The opponents began to organize and convinced the first of several states to rescind ratification—a move that had no legal force but certainly made a political difference in unratified states.

Three more states ratified in 1974, one in 1975, and one—Indiana—in 1977, bringing the total to thirty-five of the required thirty-eight. No state ratified after 1977 despite the triumph of ERA proponents in 1978 in getting Congress to extend the original 1979 deadline until 1982.[12] In 1982 this extension ran out, and the Amendment died. Alabama, Arizona, Arkansas, Florida, Georgia, Illinois, Louisiana, Mississippi, Missouri, Nevada, North Carolina, Oklahoma, Utah, and Virginia had not ratified. All were Mormon or southern states, except Illinois, which required a three-fifths majority for ratifying constitutional amendments and which had a strongly southern culture in the third of the state surrounded by Missouri and Kentucky.[13]

# NOTES

1. *S.J. Res. 21* and *H.J. Res. 75*, 68th Cong., 1st sess.

2. Eleanor Flexner, *Centuries of Struggle: The Women's Rights Movement in the United States* (Cambridge, Mass.: Harvard University Press, 1959), p. 328.

3. Josephine Goldmark, *Impatient Crusader: Florence Kelley's Life Story* (Urbana: University of Illinois Press, 1953), pp. 182, 183. . . .

4. Clement E. Vose, *Constitutional Change: Amendment Politics and Supreme Court Litigation since 1900* (Lexington, Mass.: D. C. Heath, 1972), p. 254. . . .

5. Marguerite Rawalt, "The Equal Rights Amendment," in Tinker, ed., p. 53.

6. Rawalt, pp. 54–55. . . .

7. The vote on this provision, proposed by Senator Ervin, was 36–33. A 50–20 majority also added a school prayer amendment, presumably intended to kill the ERA. The Amendment's supporters did not fight the school prayer amendment because they "felt that with the passage of the Ervin amendment we'd had it" ("Snarl in Senate All But Kills Women's Rights Amendment," *Washington Post*, October 14, 1970, p. 1).

8. *Congressional Record,* (hereafter *Cong. Rec.*), October 14, 1970, p. 36863.

9. Senator Birch Bayh, press interview, "Men's Lib Pending," *Washington Daily News,* October 15, 1970, p. 25.

10. Janet K. Boles, *The Politics of the Equal Rights Amendment: Conflict and the Decision Process* (New York: Longman, 1979), p. 39.

11. Ibid., pp. 143–144.

12. I have taken this account largely from Boles, *Politics,* passim, and her table 1.1, pp. 2–3.

13. The states that refused to ratify were also relatively poor.

*Jane J.
Mansbridge*

# *Korematsu v. United States*

In the 1944 case *Korematsu v. United States* (323 U.S. 214), from which the following selection is taken, the U.S. Supreme Court articulated an opinion on a divisive racial issue in American domestic and defense policy during World War II. The Court's decision in this case had fundamental constitutional and political consequences upon the interpretation of civil rights. In particular, the judgment of the Court was a landmark decision in that it reinterpreted the equal protection clause of the Fourteenth Amendment and the government's authority to override conventional civil rights of American citizens. The equal protection clause forbids any state to deny equal protection of the laws to any individual within its jurisdiction. The Court, however, specifically found constitutional President Franklin Roosevelt's policy of compulsory mass evacuation and internment of 135,000 citizens of Japanese descent during World War II so as to promote American national defense and safety.

Roosevelt had issued an executive order authorizing the construction of military or defense areas from which particular American citizens could be excluded in order to avoid potential sabotage or espionage. (It is interesting to note that not one Japanese American citizen was ever found guilty of either of these crimes.) Toyosaburo Korematsu, an American citizen of Japanese descent, refused to leave his California home and was subsequently convicted in a federal district court for violating the exclusion order. After his conviction was upheld by a circuit court of appeals, Korematsu brought the case to the U.S. Supreme Court. The Court has consistently overturned laws that distinguish between citizens upon the criterion of race. However, the Court's ruling in *Korematsu v. United States* was a rare exception to this principle, as the Court deliberately sustained a government policy (i.e., evacuation and internment) that promoted discrimination upon the criterion of race and, in effect, denied the application of the equal protection clause of the Fourteenth Amendment to a particular minority group of American citizens. Justice Hugo L. Black delivered the opinion of the Court.

In 1988 Congress formally apologized to the survivors and passed legislation that provided $20,000 in compensation to all former camp inhabitants or their survivors.

**Key Concept:** the evacuation and internment of Japanese American citizens

$M$r. Justice Black delivered the opinion of the Court, saying in part:

The petitioner, an American citizen of Japanese descent, was convicted in a federal district court for remaining in San Leandro, California, a "Military Area," contrary to Civilian Exclusion Order No. 34 of the Commanding General of the Western Command, U. S. Army, which directed that after May 9, 1942, all persons of Japanese ancestry should be excluded from that area. No question was raised as to petitioner's loyalty to the United States. The Circuit Court of Appeals affirmed, and the importance of the constitutional question involved caused us to grant certiorari.

It should be noted, to begin with, that all legal restrictions which curtail the civil rights of a single racial group are immediately suspect. That is not to say that all such restrictions are unconstitutional. It is to say that courts must subject them to the most rigid scrutiny. Pressing public necessity may sometimes justify the existence of such restrictions; racial antagonism never can.

In the instant case prosecution of the petitioner was begun by information charging violation of an Act of Congress, of March 21, 1942, which provides that " . . . whoever shall enter, remain in, leave, or commit any act in any military area or military zone prescribed, under the authority of an Executive order of the President, by the Secretary of War, or by any military commander designated by the Secretary of War, contrary to the restrictions applicable to any such area or zone or contrary to the order of the Secretary of War or any such military commander, shall, if it appears that he knew or should have known of the existence and extent of the restrictions or order and that his act was in violation thereof, be guilty of a misdemeanor and upon conviction shall be liable to a fine of not to exceed $5,000 or to imprisonment for not more than one year, or both, for each offense."

Exclusion Order No. 34, which the petitioner knowingly and admittedly violated was one of a number of military orders and proclamations, all of which were substantially based upon Executive Order No. 9066. That order, issued after we were at war with Japan, declared that "the successful prosecution of the war requires every possible protection against espionage and against sabotage to national-defense material, national-defense premises, and national-defense utilities. . . ."

One of the series of orders and proclamations, a curfew order, which like the exclusion order here was promulgated pursuant to Executive Order 9066, subjected all persons of Japanese ancestry in prescribed West Coast military areas to remain in their residences from 8 p.m. to 6 a.m. As is the case with the exclusion order here, that prior curfew order was designed as a "protection against espionage and against sabotage." In Kiyoshi Hirabayashi v. United States [1943], we sustained a conviction obtained for violation of the curfew order. The Hirabayashi conviction and this one thus rest on the same 1942 Congressional Act and the same basic executive and military orders, all of which orders were aimed at the twin dangers of espionage and sabotage.

The 1942 Act was attacked in the Hirabayashi case as an unconstitutional delegation of power; it was contended that the curfew order and other orders on which it rested were beyond the war powers of the Congress, the military authorities and of the President, as Commander in Chief of the Army; and finally that to apply the order against none but citizens of Japanese ancestry amounted to a constitutionally prohibited discrimination solely on account of race. To these questions, we gave the serious consideration which their importance justified. We upheld the curfew order as an exercise of the power of the government to take steps necessary to prevent espionage and sabotage in an area threatened by Japanese attack.

In the light of the principles we announced in the Hirabayashi case, we are unable to conclude that it was beyond the war power of Congress and the Executive to exclude those of Japanese ancestry from the West Coast war area at the time they did. True, exclusion from the area in which one's home is located is a far greater deprivation than constant confinement to the home from 8 p.m. to 6 a.m. Nothing short of apprehension by the proper military authorities of the gravest imminent danger to the public safety can constitutionally justify either. But exclusion from a threatened area, no less than curfew, has a definite and close relationship to the prevention of espionage and sabotage. The military authorities, charged with the primary responsibility of defending our shores, concluded that curfew provided inadequate protection and ordered exclusion. They did so, as pointed out in our Hirabayashi opinion, in accordance with Congressional authority to the military to say who should, and who should not, remain in the threatened areas.

In this case the petitioner challenges the assumptions upon which we rested our conclusions in the Hirabayashi case. He also urges that by May 1942, when Order No. 34 was promulgated, all danger of Japanese invasion of the West Coast had disappeared. After careful consideration of these contentions we are compelled to reject them.

Here, as in the Hirabayashi case, "... we cannot reject as unfounded the judgment of the military authorities and of Congress that there were disloyal members of that population, whose number and strength could not be precisely and quickly ascertained. We cannot say that the war-making branches of the Government did not have ground for believing that in a critical hour such persons could not readily be isolated and separately dealt with, and constituted a menace to the national defense and safety, which demanded that prompt and adequate measures be taken to guard against it."

Like curfew, exclusion of those of Japanese origin was deemed necessary because of the presence of an unascertained number of disloyal members of the group, most of whom we have no doubt were loyal to this country. It was because we could not reject the finding of the military authorities that it was impossible to bring about an immediate segregation of the disloyal from the loyal that we sustained the validity of the curfew order as applying to the whole group. In the instant case, temporary exclusion of the entire group was rested by the military on the same ground. The judgment that exclusion of the whole group was for the same reason a military imperative answers the contention that the exclusion was in the nature of group punishment based on antagonism to those of Japanese origin. That there were members of the group who retained loyalties to Japan has been confirmed by investigations made subsequent to the exclusion. Approximately five thousand American citizens of Japanese ancestry refused to swear unqualified allegiance to the United States and to renounce allegiance to the Japanese Emperor, and several thousand evacuees requested repatriation to Japan.

We uphold the exclusion order as of the time it was made and when the petitioner violated it.... In doing so, we are not unmindful of the hardships imposed by it upon a large group of American citizens.... But hardships are part of war, and war is an aggregation of hardships. All citizens alike, both in and out of uniform, feel the impact of war in greater or lesser measure. Citizenship has its responsibilities as well as its privileges, and in time of war the burden is always heavier. Compulsory exclusion of large groups of citizens from their homes, except under circumstances of direst emergency and peril, is inconsistent with our basic governmental institution. But when under conditions of modern warfare our shores are threatened by hostile forces, the power to protect must be commensurate with the threatened danger....

It is said that we are dealing here with the case of imprisonment of a citizen in a concentration camp solely because of his ancestry, without evidence or inquiry concerning his loyalty and good disposition towards the United States. Our task would be simple, our duty clear, were this a case involving the imprisonment of a loyal citizen in a concentration camp because of racial prejudice. Regardless of the true nature of the assembly and relocation centers—and we deem it unjustifiable to call them concentration camps with all the ugly connotations that term implies—we are dealing specifically with nothing but an exclusion order. To cast this case into outlines of racial prejudice, without reference to the real military dangers which were presented, merely confuses the issue. Korematsu was not excluded from the Military Area because of hostility to him or his race. He was excluded because we are at war with the Japanese Empire, because the properly constituted military authorities feared an invasion of our West Coast and felt constrained to take proper security measures, because they decided that the military urgency of the situation demanded that all citizens of Japanese ancestry be segregated from the West Coast temporarily, and finally, because Congress, reposing its confidence in this time of war in our military leaders—as inevitably it must—determined that they should have the power to do just this. There was evidence of disloyalty on the part of some, the military authorities considered that the need for action was great, and time was short. We cannot—by availing ourselves of the calm perspective of hindsight—now say that at that time these actions were unjustified.

Affirmed.

# PART FOUR

# *Democratic Participatory Organizations*

# On the Internet . . .

## Sites appropriate to Part Four

This University of Houston Libraries site offers a valuable collection of links to campaign, conservative/liberal perspective, and political party sites. Included are Democratic party sites, Republican party sites, third-party sites, nonpartisan voter information, and much more.

```
http://info.lib.uh.edu/politics/
   markind.htm
```

The Political Communication Research Center is a virtual research center created by Dr. Kenneth L. Hacker, associate professor of communication studies at New Mexico State University. This center is designed to provide high-quality, valid, and reliable information regarding political communication in the United States.

```
http://web.nmsu.edu/~comstudy/
   polcomm.html
```

At this site, the Federal Election Commission (FEC) provides a history of campaign finance laws, explains how they work, and outlines the FEC's role.

```
http://www.fec.gov/pages/fecfeca.htm
```

## CHAPTER 6

Interest Groups

## 6.1 JAMES MADISON

# Federalist, *No. 10*

The *Federalist Papers* are a collection of 85 essays written by James Madison (1751–1836), Alexander Hamilton (1757–1804), and John Jay (1745–1829) under the pseudonym "Publius." American government scholars agree that these papers reveal in a systematic and comprehensive way the intentions of the framers of the U.S. Constitution as they designed a Federalist legal framework in conjunction with a representative, or popular, form of government. Since there existed a strong Anti-Federalist partisan sentiment in New York, the authors thought that a massive printing of these essays written in powerful political rhetoric would persuade many to vote for ratification of the Constitution. However, some scholars argue that the *Federalist Papers* had only a minor impact on the successful ratification of the Constitution. Their enduring value is in their comprehensive analysis of the configuration of the institutions and processes of the new government.

Madison's *Federalist,* No. 10 (1788) is the most frequently cited of all the *Federalist Papers.* It is recognized by political science scholars as America's unique contribution to political theory. In the following selection from *Federalist,* No. 10, Madison analyzes a prescribed set of solutions to the fundamental governmental problem of maintaining a delicate balance between the establishment of a representative government and popular majority rule, and the simultaneous fulfillment of individual and minority rights and freedoms.

The primary goal of *Federalist,* No. 10 is to demonstrate how a "well-constructed Union" can "break and control the violence of faction" or limit "the mischiefs of faction." Madison defines *factions* as competitive economic special interest groups that often conflict with the interests of other citizens or the public good of the entire community or nation. Factions naturally evolve in any society due to the unequal distribution of property and the natural inclination of individuals to join private voluntary associations due to self-interested human nature. Instead of abolishing factions, which would destroy individual liberty, Madison recommends regulating the excesses of factions through a Federalist division of public authority and a republican, or representative, form of government.

Madison correctly projected that the division of governmental powers among several branches; the levels of federal, state, and local governments; the numerous checks and balances in the Constitution; and the intense competition between the factions themselves would all assist to limit or work against the negative and dangerous effects of factions.

**Key Concept:** the regulation of factions

*A*mong the numerous advantages promised by a well-constructed Union, none deserves to be more accurately developed than its tendency to break and control the violence of faction. The friend of popular governments never finds himself so much alarmed for their character and fate as when he contemplates their propensity to this dangerous vice. He will not fail, therefore, to set a due value on any plan which, without violating the principles to which he is attached, provides a proper cure for it. The instability, injustice, and confusion introduced into the public councils have, in truth, been the mortal diseases under which popular governments have everywhere perished, as they continue to be the favorite and fruitful topics from which the adversaries to liberty derive their most specious declamations. The valuable improvements made by the American constitutions on the popular models, both ancient and modern, cannot certainly be too much admired; but it would be an unwarrantable partiality to contend that they have as effectually obviated the danger on this side, as was wished and expected. Complaints are everywhere heard from our most considerate and virtuous citizens, equally the friends of public and private faith and of public and personal liberty, that our governments are too unstable, that the public good is disregarded in the conflicts of rival parties, and that measures are too often decided, not according to the rules of justice and the rights of the minor party, but by the superior force of an interested and Overbearing majority. However anxiously we may wish that these complaints had no foundation, the evidence of known facts will not permit us to deny that they are in some degree true. It will be found, indeed, on a candid review of our situation, that some of the distresses under which we labor have been erroneously charged on the operation of our governments; but it will be found, at the same time, that other causes will not alone account for many of our heaviest misfortunes; and, particularly, for that prevailing and increasing distrust of public engagements and alarm for private rights which are echoed from one end of the continent to the other. These must be chiefly, if not wholly, effects of the unsteadiness and injustice with which a factious spirit has tainted our public administration.

By a faction I understand a number of citizens, whether amounting to a majority or minority of the whole, who are united and actuated by some common impulse of passion, or of interest, adverse to the rights of other citizens, or to the permanent and aggregate interests of the community.

There are two methods of curing the mischiefs of faction: the one, by removing its causes; the other, by controlling its effects.

*James Madison*

There are again two methods of removing the causes of faction: the one, by destroying the liberty which is essential to its existence; the other, by giving to every citizen the same opinions, the same passions, and the same interests.

It could never be more truly said than of the first remedy that it was worse than the disease. Liberty is to faction what air is to fire, an aliment without which it instantly expires. But it could not be a less folly to abolish liberty, which is essential to political life, because it nourishes faction than it would be to wish the annihilation of air, which is essential to animal life, because it imparts to fire its destructive agency.

The second expedient is as impracticable as the first would be unwise. As long as the reason of man continues fallible, and he is at liberty to exercise it, different opinions will be formed. As long as the connection subsists between his reason and his self-love, his Opinions and his passions will have a reciprocal influence on each other; and the former will be objects to which the latter will attach themselves. The diversity in the faculties of men, from which the rights of property originate, is not less an insuperable obstacle to a uniformity of interests. The protection of these faculties is the first object of government. From the protection of different and unequal faculties of acquiring property, the possession of different degrees and kinds of property immediately results; and from the influence of these on the sentiments and views of the respective proprietors ensues a division of the society into different interests and parties.

The latent causes of faction are thus sown in the nature of man; and we see them everywhere brought into different degrees of activity, according to the different circumstances of civil society. A zeal for different opinions concerning religion, concerning government, and many other points, as well of speculation as of practice; an attachment to different leaders ambitiously contending for pre-eminence and power; or to persons of other descriptions whose fortunes have been interesting to the human passions, have, in turn, divided mankind into parties, inflamed them with mutual animosity, and rendered them much more disposed to vex and oppress each other than to cooperate for their common good. So strong is this propensity of mankind to fall into mutual animosities that where no substantial occasion presents itself the most frivolous and fanciful distinctions have been sufficient to kindle their unfriendly passions and excite their most violent conflicts. But the most common and durable source of factions has been the various and unequal distribution of property. Those who hold and those who are without property have ever formed distinct interests in society. Those who are creditors, and those who are debtors, fall under a like discrimination. A landed interest, a manufacturing interest, a mercantile interest, a moneyed interest, with many lesser interests, grow up of necessity in civilized nations, and divide them into different classes, actuated by different sentiments and views. The regulation of these various and interfering interests forms the principal task of modern legislation and involves the spirit of party and faction in the necessary and ordinary operations of government.

No man is allowed to be a judge in his own cause, because his interest would certainly bias his judgment, and, not improbably, corrupt his integrity. With equal, nay with greater reason, a body of men are unfit to be both judges and parties at the same time; yet what are many of the' most important acts of legislation but so many judicial determinations, not indeed concerning the rights of single persons, but concerning the rights of large bodies of citizens? And what are the different classes of legislators but advocates and parties to the causes which they determine? Is a law proposed concerning private debts? It is a question to which the creditors are parties on one side and the debtors on the other. Justice ought to hold the balance between them. Yet the parties are, and must be, themselves the judges; and the most numerous party, or in other words, the most powerful faction must be expected to prevail. Shall domestic manufacturers be encouraged, and in what degree, by restrictions on foreign manufacturers? are questions which would be differently decided by the landed and the manufacturing classes, and probably by neither with a sole regard to justice and the public good. The apportionment of taxes, on the various descriptions of property is an act which seems to require the most exact impartiality; yet there is, perhaps, no legislative act in which greater opportunity and temptation are given to a predominant party to trample on the rules of justice. Every shilling with which they overburden the inferior number is a shilling saved to their own pockets.

It is in vain to say that enlightened statesmen will be able to adjust these clashing interests and render them all subservient to the public good. Enlightened statesmen will not always be at the helm. Nor, in many cases, can such an adjustment be made at all without taking into view indirect and remote considerations, which will rarely prevail, over the immediate interest which one party may find in disregarding the rights of another or the good of the whole.

The inference to which we are brought is that the *causes* of faction cannot be removed and that relief is only to be sought in the means of controlling its *effects*.

If a faction consists of less than a majority, relief is supplied by the republican principle, which enables the majority to defeat its sinister views by regular vote. It may clog the administration, it may convulse the society; but it will be unable to execute and mask its violence under the forms of the Constitution. When a majority is included in a faction, the form of popular government, on the other hand, enables it to sacrifice to its ruling passion or interest both the public good and the rights of other citizens. To secure the public good and private rights against the danger of such a faction, and at the same time to preserve the spirit and the form of popular government, is then the great object to which our inquiries are directed. Let me add that it is the great desideratum by which alone this form of government can be rescued from the opprobrium under which it has so long labored and be recommended to the esteem and adoption of mankind.

By what means is this object attainable? Evidently by one of two only. Either the existence of the same passion or interest in a majority at the same time must be prevented, or the majority, having such coexistent passion or interest, must be rendered, by their number and local situation, unable to concert and carry into effect schemes of oppression. If the impulse and the opportunity be suffered to coincide, we well know that neither moral nor religious motives can be relied on as an adequate control. They are not found to be such on the injustice and violence of individuals, and lose their efficacy in proportion to the number combined together, that is, in proportion as their efficacy becomes needful.

From this view of the subject it may be concluded that a pure democracy, by which I mean a society consisting of a small number of citizens, who assemble and administer the government in person, can admit of no cure for the mischiefs of faction. A common passion or interest will, in almost every case, be felt by a majority of the whole; a communication and concert results from the form of government itself; and there is nothing to check the inducements to sacrifice the weaker party or an obnoxious individual. Hence it is that such democracies have ever been spectacles of turbulence and contention; have ever been found incompatible with personal security or the rights of property; and have in general been as short in their lives as they have been violent in their deaths. Theoretic politicians, who have patronized this species of government, have erroneously supposed that by reducing mankind to a perfect equality in their political rights, they would at the same time be perfectly equalized and assimilated in their possessions, their opinions, and their passions.

A republic, by which I mean a government in which the scheme of representation takes place, opens a different prospect and promises the cure for which we are seeking. Let us examine the points in which it varies from pure democracy, and we shall comprehend both the nature of the cure and the efficacy which it must derive from the Union.

The two great points of difference between a democracy and a republic are: first, the delegation of the government, in the latter, to a small number of citizens elected by the rest; secondly, the greater number of citizens and greater sphere of country over which the latter may he extended.

The effect of the first difference is, on the one hand, to refine and enlarge the public views by passing them through the medium of a chosen body of citizens, whose wisdom may best discern the true interest of their country and whose patriotism and love of justice will be least likely to sacrifice it to temporary or partial considerations. Under such a regulation it may well happen that the public voice, pronounced by the representatives of the people, will be more consonant to the public good than if pronounced by the people themselves, convened for the purpose. On the other hand, the effect may be inverted. Men of factious tempers, of local prejudices, or of sinister designs, may, by intrigue, by corruption, or by other means, first obtain the suffrages, and then betray the interests of the people. The question resulting is, whether small or extensive republics are most favorable to the election of proper guardians of the public weal; and it is clearly decided in favor of the latter by two obvious considerations.

In the first place it is to be remarked that however small the republic may be the representatives must be raised to a certain number in order to guard against the cabals of a few; and that however large it may be they must be limited to a certain number in order to guard against the confusion of a multitude. Hence, the number of representatives in the two cases not being in proportion to that of the constituents, and being proportionally greatest in the small republic, it follows that if the proportion of fit characters be not less in the large than in the small republic, the former will present a greater option, and consequently a greater probability of a fit choice.

In the next place, as each representative will be chosen by a greater number of citizens in the large than in the small republic, it will be more difficult for unworthy candidates to practise with success the vicious arts by which elections are too often carried; and the suffrages of the people being more free, will be more likely to center on men who possess the most attractive merit and the most diffusive and established characters.

It must be confessed that in this, as in most other cases, there is a mean, on both sides of which inconveniencies will be found to lie. By enlarging too much the number of electors, you render the representative too little acquainted with all their local circumstances and lesser interests; as by reducing it too much, you render him unduly attached to these, and too little fit to comprehend and pursue great and national objects. The federal Constitution forms a happy combination in this respect; the great and aggregate interests being referred to the national, the local and particular to the State legislatures.

The other point of difference is the greater number of citizens and extent of territory which may be brought within the compass of republican than of democratic government; and it is this circumstance principally which renders factious combinations less to be dreaded in the former than in the latter. The smaller the society, the fewer probably will be the distinct parties and interests composing it; the fewer the distinct parties and interests, the more frequently will a majority be found of the same party; and the smaller the number of individuals composing a majority, and the smaller the compass within which they are placed, the more easily will they concert and execute their plans of oppression. Extend the sphere and you take in a greater variety of parties and interests; you make it less probable that a majority of the whole will have a common motive to invade the rights of other citizens; or if such a common motive exists, it will be more difficult for all who feel it to discover their own strength and to act in unison with each other. Besides other impediments, it may be remarked that, where there is a consciousness of unjust or dishonorable purposes, communication is always checked by distrust in proportion to the number whose concurrence is necessary.

Hence, it clearly appears that the same advantage which a republic has over a democracy in controlling the effects of faction is enjoyed by a large over a small republic—is enjoyed by the Union over the States composing it. Does this advantage consist in the substitution of representatives whose enlightened views and virtuous sentiments render them superior to local prejudices and to schemes of injustice? It will not be denied that the representation of the Union will be most likely to possess these requisite endowments. Does it consist in the greater security afforded by a greater variety of parties, against the event of any one party being able to outnumber and oppress the rest? In an equal degree does the increased variety of parties comprised within the Union increase this security. Does it, in fine, consist in the greater obstacles opposed to the concert and accomplishment of the secret wishes of an unjust and interested majority? Here again the extent of the Union gives it the most palpable advantage.

The influence of factious leaders may kindle a flame within their particular States but will be unable to spread a general conflagration through the other States. A religious sect may degenerate into a political faction in a part of the Confederacy; but the variety of sects dispersed over the entire face of it must secure the national councils against any danger from that source. A rage for paper money, for an abolition of debts, for an equal division of property, or for any other improper or wicked project, will be less apt to pervade the whole body of the Union than a particular member of it, in the same proportion as such a malady is more likely to taint a particular county or district than an entire State.

In the extent and proper structure of the Union, therefore, we behold a republican remedy for the diseases most incident to republican government. And according to the degree of pleasure and pride we feel in being republicans ought to be our zeal in cherishing the spirit and supporting the character of federalists.

# The Changing Nature of Interest Group Politics

The book *Interest Group Politics* established editors Burdett A. Loomis and Allan J. Cigler as leading scholars of American interest group politics and theory. By focusing on the behavior of political interest groups, interest group theory expresses a set of assumptions about the development and implementation of public policy. According to this perspective, adopted by Loomis and Cigler, intense competition among organized special interests results in some policy output. The authors also contend that interest groups that are successful in influencing governmental decisions tend to rely upon contemporary technological developments (e.g., cable television and computer-based operations).

Loomis (b. 1945) received his M.A. and Ph.D. from the University of Wisconsin. He has taught at Indiana University, Knox College, and the University of Kansas, where he served as chairman of the political science department from 1986 to 1989. His research has focused on legislative politics, political parties, and interest groups. His other published works include *Setting Course: A Congressional Management Guide* (American University, 1984) and *The New American Politician* (Basic Books, 1988).

Cigler (b. 1943) received his M.A. from the University of Maryland and his Ph.D. from Indiana University. A professor of political science at the University of Kansas, Cigler's research interests have included political behavior, political parties and interest groups, elections, and public opinion. He has written numerous scholarly articles for various political science journals, and he is the coeditor, with William P. Browne, of *U.S. Agricultural Groups: Institutional Profiles* (Greenwood Press, 1990).

In the following selection from the fifth edition of *Interest Group Politics* (CQ Press, 1998), Loomis and Cigler focus on fundamental developments that have occurred in interest group political behavior during the past few decades. In particular, they emphasize the most significant changes in the character, function, and impact of political interest groups. The authors discuss the development of special, or single-issue, interest groups (e.g., the National Rifle Association [NRA] and Mothers Against Drunk Driving [MADD]) as a highly significant trend. Loomis and Cigler also analyze the impact of federal election campaign finance reform legislation in the early 1970s upon the proliferation of political action committees (PACs).

*Burdett A. Loomis and Allan J. Cigler*

**Key Concept:** the contemporary nature and influence of political interest groups

*F*rom James Madison to Madison Avenue, political interests have played a central role in American politics. But this great continuity in our political experience has been matched by the ambivalence with which citizens, politicians, and scholars have approached interest groups. James Madison's warnings on the dangers of faction echo in the rhetoric of reformers ranging from Populists and Progressives near the turn of the century to the so-called public interest advocates of today.

If organized special interests are nothing new in American politics, can today's group politics nevertheless be seen as having undergone some fundamental changes? Acknowledging that many important, continuing trends do exist, we seek to place in perspective a broad series of changes in the nature of modern interest group politics. Among the most substantial of these developments are:

1. A great proliferation of interest groups since the early 1960s
2. A centralization of group headquarters in Washington, D.C., rather than in New York City or elsewhere
3. Major technological developments in information processing that promote more sophisticated, more timely, and more specialized communication strategies, such as grassroots lobbying
4. The rise of single-issue groups
5. Changes in campaign finance laws (1971, 1974) and the ensuing growth of political action committees (PACs), and more recently, the growth of independent campaign expenditures by some interests
6. The increased formal penetration of political and economic interests into the bureaucracy (advisory committees), the presidency (White House group representatives), and the Congress (caucuses of members)
7. The continuing decline of political parties' abilities to perform key electoral and policy-related activities
8. The increased number, activity, and visibility of public-interest groups, such as Common Cause and the Ralph Nader-inspired public interest research organizations
9. The growth of activity and impact by institutions, including corporations, universities, state and local governments, and foreign interests
10. A continuing rise in the amount and sophistication of group activity in state capitals, especially given the devolution of some federal programs and substantial increases in state budgets. . . .

# CONTEMPORARY INTEREST GROUP POLITICS

Several notable developments mark the modern age of interest group politics. Of primary importance is the large and growing number of active groups and other interests. The data here are sketchy, but one major study found that most current groups came into existence after World War II and that group formation has accelerated substantially since the early 1960s.[1] Also since the 1960s groups have increasingly directed their attention toward the center of power in Washington, D.C., as the scope of federal policy making has grown, and groups seeking influence have determined to "hunt where the ducks are." As a result, the 1960s and 1970s marked a veritable explosion in the number of groups lobbying in Washington.

A second key change is evident in the composition of the interest group universe. Beginning in the late 1950s political participation patterns underwent some significant transformations. Conventional activities such as voting declined, and political parties, the traditional aggregators and articulators of mass interests, became weaker. Yet at all levels of government, evidence of citizen involvement has been apparent, often in the form of new or revived groups. Particularly impressive has been the growth of citizens' groups—those organized around an idea or cause (at times a single issue) with no occupational basis for membership. Fully 30 percent of such groups have formed since 1975, and in 1980 they made up more than one-fifth of all groups represented in Washington.[2]

In fact, a participation revolution has occurred in the country as many citizens have become active in an ever-increasing number of protest groups, citizens' organizations, and special interest groups. These groups often comprise issue-oriented activists or individuals who seek collective material benefits. The free-rider problem has proven not to be an insurmountable barrier to group formation, and many new interest groups do not use selective material benefits to gain support. Still, since the late 1970s, the number of these groups has remained relatively stable, and they have become well-established in representing the positions of consumers, environmentalists, and other public interest organizations.[3]

Third, government itself has had a profound effect on the growth and activity of interest groups. Early in this century, workers found organizing difficult because business and industry used government-backed injunctions to prevent strikes. By the 1930s, however, with the prohibition of injunctions in private labor disputes and the rights of collective bargaining established, most governmental actions directly promoted the growth of labor unions. In recent years changes in the campaign finance laws have led to an explosion in the number of PACs, especially among business, industry, and issue-oriented groups. Laws facilitating group formation certainly have contributed to group proliferation, but government policy in a broader sense has been equally responsible.

Fourth, not only has the number of membership groups grown in recent decades, but a similar expansion has occurred in the political activity of many other interests such as individual corporations, universities, churches, governmental units, foundations, and think tanks.[4] Historically, most of these interests have been satisfied with representation by trade or professional associations. Since the mid-1960s, however, many have chosen to employ their own Washington representatives. Between 1961 and 1982, for example, the number of corporations with Washington offices increased tenfold.[5] The chief beneficiaries of this trend are Washington-based lawyers, lobbyists, and public relations firms. The number of attorneys in the nation's capital, taken as a rough indicator of lobbyist strength, tripled between 1973 and 1983, and the growth of public relations firms was dramatic. The lobbying community of the 1990s is large, increasingly diverse, and part of the expansion of policy domain participation, whether in agriculture, the environment, or industrial development. Overall, political scientist James Thurber has calculated that, as of the early 1990s, 91,000 lobbyists and people associated with lobbying were employed in the Washington, D.C., area.[6] As of 1993, the *Encyclopedia of Associations* listed approximately 23,000 organizations, up more than 50 percent since 1980 and almost 40 percent since 1955.[7] ...

# THE GROWTH OF INTEREST GROUPS

Although it may be premature to formulate a theory that accounts for spurts of growth,[8] we can identify several factors fundamental to group proliferation in contemporary politics. Rapid social and economic changes, powerful catalysts for group formation, have developed new interests (for example, the recreation industry) and redefined traditional ones (for example, higher education). The spread of affluence and education, coupled with advanced communication technologies, further contributes to the translation of interests into formal group organizations. Postindustrial changes have generated a large number of new interests, particularly among occupational and professional groups in the scientific and technological arenas. For instance, genetic engineering associations have sprung up in the wake of recent DNA discoveries, to say nothing of the growing clout and sophistication of the computer industry, from Microsoft's Bill Gates on down.

Perhaps more important, postindustrial changes have altered the pattern of conflict in society and created an intensely emotional setting in which groups rise or fall in status. Ascending groups, such as members of the new professional–managerial–technical elite, have both benefited from and supported government activism; they represent the new cultural liberalism, politically cosmopolitan and socially permissive. At the same time, rising expectations and feelings of entitlement have increased pressures on government by aspiring groups and the disadvantaged. The 1960s and early 1970s witnessed wave after wave of group mobilization based on causes ranging from civil rights to women's issues to the environment to consumer protection.

Abrupt changes and alterations in status, however, threaten many citizens. Middle America, perceiving itself as downwardly mobile, has grown alienated from the social, economic, and cultural dominance of the postindustrial elites, on one hand, and resentful toward government attempts to aid minorities and other aspiring groups, on the other. The conditions of a modern technologically based culture also are disturbing to more traditional elements in society. Industrialization and urbanization can uproot people, cutting them loose from familiar life patterns and values and depriving them of meaning-ful personal associations. Fundamentalist elements feel threatened by various technological advances (such as use of fetal tissue for medical research) as well as by the more general secular liberalism and moral permissiveness of contem-porary life. In the 1990s, the growth of the Christian Coalition, both nationally and locally, has profoundly affected both electoral and legislative politics by mobilizing citizens and activists. In addition, the growth of bureaucracy, in and out of government, antagonizes everyone at one time or another.

Postindustrial threats are felt by elites as well. The nuclear arms race and its potential for mass destruction fostered the revived peace movement of the 1980s and its goal of a freeze on nuclear weapons. In addition, the excesses and errors of technology, such as oil spills and toxic waste disposal, have led to group formation among some of the most advantaged and ascending elements of society.

Illustrating the possibilities is the growth since the mid-1980s of the an-imal rights movement. Although traditional animal protection organizations such as the Humane Society have existed for decades, the past fifteen years have "spawned a colorful menagerie of pro-animal offspring" such as People for Eth-ical Treatment of Animals (PETA), Progressive Animal Welfare Society (PAWS), Committee to Abolish Sport Hunting (CASH), and the Animal Rights Network (ARN). Reminiscent of the 1960s, there is even the Animal Liberation Front, an extremist group that engages in direct actions that sometimes include violence.[9] Membership in the organizations that make up the animal rights movement has increased rapidly; founded in 1980, PETA grew from 20,000 in 1984 to 250,000 in 1988 and 370,000 by 1994.[10] One estimate places the number of animal rights organizations at 400, representing approximately ten million members.[11]

One major goal of these groups is to stop, or greatly retard, scientific ex-perimentation on animals. Using a mix of protest, lobbying, and litigation, the movement has contributed to the closing of several animal labs, including the Defense Department's Wound Laboratory and a University of Pennsylvania facility involved in research on head injuries. In 1988 Trans-Species, a recent addition to the animal rights movement, forced the Cornell University Medi-cal College to give up a $600,000 grant, which left unfinished a fourteen-year research project in which cats were fed barbiturates.[12]

As the most visible of the animal rights groups, PETA embarked on an in-tensive campaign in the early 1990s to influence children's attitudes and values toward society's treatment of animals. Using a seven-foot mascot, Chris P. Car-rot, to spread its message, PETA organizers have sought to visit public schools throughout the Midwest. Although some of their message is noncontroversial (for example, children should eat their vegetables), they also argue aggressively against consuming meat. Chris P. Carrot thus carries a placard stating, "Eat your veggies, not your friends," More prosaically, PETA produces publications denouncing hunting, trapping, and other practices that abuse animals. . . .

It is not surprising that threats to those involved in activities that PETA protests have spawned countermobilizations, as, for instance, in the growth of an anti-animal rights movement. In the forefront of such actions are organizations that support hunting as a sport. They must contend with a public that has become increasingly hostile to hunting; a 1993 survey reported that 54 percent of Americans were opposed to hunting, with the youngest respondents (ages 18 to 29) expressing the most negative sentiments.[13] In addition, farm and medical groups have mobilized against the animal rights movements, and a number of new organizations have been formed. Such groups range from the incurably ill for Animal Research (iiFAR), representing those who hope for medical breakthroughs in biomedical research, to the Foundation for Animal Health, organized by the American Medical Association in hopes of diverting funds away from animal rights groups.

The most visible group in the animal rights countermobilization, Putting People First (PPF), claimed more than 35,000 members and one hundred local chapters within one year of its formation. As well as its individual members, PPF counted hunting clubs, trapping associations, rodeos, zoos, circuses, veterinary hospitals, kennels/stables, and carriage horse companies among its membership. Taking a page from animal rights' public relations activities, PPF has begun a Hunters for the Hungry campaign that has provided 160,000 pounds of venison to economically disadvantaged families in the South. To PPF, the animal rights movement has declared war on much of America and is "seeking to destroy a way of life—to tell us we can no longer believe in the Judeo-Christian principles this country was founded on. They insist every form of life is equal: humans and dogs and slugs and cockroaches." PPF leaders see the organization as speaking for "the average American who eats meat and drinks milk, benefits from medical research, wears leather, wool, and fur, hunts and fishes, and owns a pet and goes to the zoo."[14]

The intensity of conflict between the animal rights advocates and their opponents typifies the deep cultural divisions of the postindustrial era. Similar differences affect many other key issues, from gun control to education (school choice) to immigration policy. Moreover, many of these conflicts do not lend themselves to compromise, whether because of vast policy differences or group leaders' desire to keep "hot" issues alive as a way to increase membership.

Although postindustrial conflicts generate the issues for group development, the spread of affluence also systematically contributes to group formation and maintenance. In fact, affluence creates a large potential for "checkbook" membership. Issue-based groups have done especially well. Membership in such groups as PETA and Common Cause might once have been considered a luxury, but the growth in discretionary income has placed the cost of modest dues within the reach of most citizens. For a $15 to $25 membership fee, people can make an "expressive" statement without incurring other organizational obligations. Increasing education also has been a factor in that "organizations become more numerous as ideas become more important."[15]

Reform groups and citizens' groups depend heavily upon the educated, suburban–urban, white middle-class for their membership and financial base. A Common Cause poll, for example, found that members' mean family income was $17,000 above the national average and that 43 percent of members had an advanced degree.[16] Animal rights groups display a similar membership profile, although they are disproportionately composed of college-educated, urban, professional women.[17] Other expressive groups, including those on the political Right, have been aided as well by the increased wealth of constituents and the community activism that result from education and occupational advancement.

Groups can overcome the free-rider problem by finding a sponsor who will support the organization and reduce its reliance upon membership contributions. During the 1960s and 1970s private sources (often foundations) backed various groups. Jeffrey Berry's 1977 study of eighty-three public interest organizations found that at least one-third received more than half of their funds from private foundations, and one in ten received more than 90 percent of its operating expenses from such sources.[18] Jack Walker's 1981 study of Washington-based interest groups confirmed many of Berry's earlier findings, indicating that foundation support and individual grants provide 30 percent of all citizens' group funding.[19] Such patterns produce many staff organizations with no members, raising major questions about the representativeness of the new interest group universe. Finally, groups themselves can sponsor other groups. The National Council of Senior Citizens (NCSC), for example, was founded by the AFL-CIO, which helped recruit members from the ranks of organized labor and still pays part of NCSC's expenses.

Patrons often are more than just passive sponsors who respond to group requests for funds. In many instances, group mobilization comes from the top down, rather than the reverse. The patron—whether an individual such as General Motors' heir Stewart Mott or the peripatetic conservative Richard Mellon Scaife, an institution, another group, or government entity—may serve as the initiator of group development, to the point of seeking entrepreneurs and providing a forum for group pronouncements.

Postindustrial affluence and the spread of education also have contributed to group formation and maintenance through the development of a large pool of potential group organizers. This group tends to be young, well educated, and from the middle-class, caught up in a movement for change and inspired by ideas or doctrine. The 1960s was a period of opportunity for entrepreneurs, as college enrollments skyrocketed and powerful forces such as civil rights and the antiwar movement contributed to an idea orientation in both education and politics. Communications-based professions—from religion to law to university teaching—attracted social activists, many of whom became involved in the formation of groups....

Compounding the effects of the growing number of increasingly active groups are changes in what organizations can do, largely as a result of contemporary technology. On a grand scale, technological change produces new interests, such as cable television and the silicon chip industry, which organize to protect themselves as interests historically have done. Beyond this, communications breakthroughs make group politics much more visible than in the past. Civil rights activists in the South understood this, as did many protesters against the Vietnam War. Of equal importance, however, is the fact that much of what contemporary interest groups do derives directly from developments in information-related technology. Many group activities, whether fund-raising or grassroots lobbying or sampling members' opinions, rely heavily on computer-based operations that can target and send messages and process the responses.

Although satellite television links and survey research are important tools, the technology of direct mail has had by far the greatest impact on interest group politics. With a minimum initial investment and a reasonably good list of potential contributors, any individual can become a group entrepreneur. These activists literally create organizations, often based on emotion-laden appeals about specific issues, from Sarah Brady's Handgun Control to Randall Terry's Operation Rescue.[20] To the extent that an entrepreneur can attract members and continue to pay the costs of direct mail, he or she can claim—with substantial legitimacy—to articulate the organization's positions on the issues, positions probably defined initially by the entrepreneur.

*Burdett A. Loomis and Allan J. Cigler*

In addition to helping entrepreneurs develop organizations that require few (if any) active members, information technology also allows many organizations to exert considerable pressure on elected officials. The Washington-based interests increasingly are turning to grassroots techniques to influence legislators. Indeed, after the mid-1980s these tactics had become the norm in many lobbying efforts, to the point that they were sometimes discounted as routine and "manufactured" by groups and consultants.

Communications technology is widely available but expensive. In the health care debate, most mobilized opinion has come from the best-financed interests, such as insurance companies, the drug industry, and the medical profession. Money remains the mother's milk of politics. Indeed, one of the major impacts of technology may be to inflate the costs of political action, whether for candidates engaged in increasingly expensive election campaigns or in public lobbying efforts that employ specifically targeted advertisements and highly sophisticated grassroots efforts. . . .

## CONTEMPORARY PRACTICES

Modern lobbying emphasizes information, often on complex and difficult subjects. Determining actual influence is, as one lobbyist noted, "like finding a black cat in the coal bin at midnight,"[21] but we can make some assessments about the overall impact of group proliferation and increased activity.

First, more groups are engaged in more forms of lobbying than ever before —both classic forms, such as offering legislative testimony, and newer forms, such as mounting computer-based direct mail campaigns to stir up grassroots support.[22] As the number of new groups rises and existing groups become more active, the pressure on decision makers—especially legislators—mounts at a corresponding rate. Thus, a second general point can be made: Congressional reforms that opened up the legislative process during the 1970s have provided a much larger number of access points for today's lobbyists. Most committee (and subcommittee) sessions, including the mark-ups at which legislation is written, remain open to the public, as do many conference committee meetings. More roll-call votes are taken, and congressional floor action is televised. Thus, interests can monitor the performance of individual members of Congress as never before. This does nothing, however, to facilitate disinterested decision making or foster graceful compromises on most issues.

In fact, monitoring the legions of Washington policy actors has become the central activity of many groups. As Robert Salisbury recently observed, "Before [organized interests] can advocate a policy, they must determine what position they wish to embrace. Before they do this, they must find out not only what technical policy analysis can tell them but what relevant others, inside and outside the government, are thinking and planning."[23] Given the volume of policy making, just keeping up can represent a major undertaking.

The government itself has encouraged many interests to organize and articulate their demands. The rise of group activity thus leads us to another level of analysis: the impact of contemporary interest group politics on society. Harking back to Lowi's description of interest group liberalism, we see the eventual result to be an immobilized society, trapped by its willingness to allow interests to help fashion self-serving policies that embody no firm criteria of success or failure. For example, even in the midst of the savings and loan debacle, the government continued to offer guarantees to various sectors, based not on future promise but on past bargains and continuing pressures.

The notion advanced by Olson that some such group-related stagnation affects all stable democracies makes the prognosis all the more serious. In summary form, Olson argued that the longer societies are politically stable, the more interest groups they develop; the more interest groups they develop, the worse they work economically.[24] The United Automobile Workers' protectionist leanings, the American Medical Association's fight against intervention by the Federal Trade Commission into physicians' business affairs, and the insurance industry's successful prevention of FTC investigations all illustrate the possible linkage between self-centered group action and poor economic performance—that is, higher automobile prices, doctors' fees, and insurance premiums for no better product or service.[25]

In particular, the politics of Social Security demonstrate the difficulties posed by a highly mobilized, highly representative set of interests. Virtually everyone agrees that the Social Security system requires serious reform; at the same time, many groups of elderly citizens (with the AARP among the most moderate) have resisted changes that might reduce their benefits over time. In the end, the Social Security system will have to be restructured to maintain its viability, but particular interests pose serious obstacles to pursuing the more general welfare of society as a whole.

# CONCLUSION

The ultimate consequences of the growing number of groups, their expanding activities both in Washington and in state capitals, and the growth of citizens' groups remain unclear. From one perspective, such changes have made politics more representative than ever before. Although most occupation-based groups traditionally have been well organized in American politics, many other interests have not. Population groupings such as African Americans, Hispanics, and women have mobilized since the 1950s and 1960s; even animals and the un-born are well represented in the interest group arena, as is the broader "public interest," however defined.

Broadening the base of interest group participation may have truly opened up the political process, thus curbing the influence of special inter-ests. For example, agricultural policy making in the postwar era was almost exclusively the prerogative of a tight "iron triangle" composed of congressional committee and subcommittee members from farm states, government officials representing the agriculture bureaucracy, and major agriculture groups such as the American Farm Bureau. Activity in the 1970s by consumer and envi-ronmental interest groups changed agricultural politics, making it more visible and lengthening the agenda to consider such questions as how farm subsidies affect consumer purchasing power and how various fertilizers, herbicides, and pesticides affect public health.

From another perspective, more interest groups and more openness do not necessarily mean better policies or ones that genuinely represent the national interest. "Sunshine" and more participants may generate greater complexity and too many demands for decision makers to process effectively. Moreover, the content of demands may be ambiguous and priorities difficult to set.

Finally, elected leaders may find it practically impossible to build the kinds of political coalitions necessary to govern effectively, especially in an era of divided government.

This second perspective suggests that the American constitutional system is extraordinarily susceptible to the excesses of minority faction—in an ironic way a potential victim of the Madisonian solution of dealing with the tyranny of the majority. Decentralized government, especially one that wields consid-erable power, provides no adequate controls over the excessive demands of special interest politics. Decision makers feel obliged to respond to many of these demands, and "the cumulative effect of this pressure has been the relent-less and extraordinary rise of government spending and inflationary deficits, as well as the frustration of efforts to enact effective national policies on most major issues."[26]

In sum, the problem of contemporary interest group politics is one of rep-resentation. For particular interests, especially those that are well defined and adequately funded, the government is responsive to the issues of their greatest concern. But representation is not just a matter of responding to specific inter-ests or citizens; the government also must respond to the collective needs of a society, and here the success of individual interests reduces the possibility of overall responsiveness. The very vibrancy and success of contemporary groups contribute to a society that finds it increasingly difficult to formulate solutions to complex policy questions.

# NOTES

1. Jack L. Walker, "The Origins and Maintenance of Interest Groups in America," *Amer-ican Political Science Review* 77 (June 1983): 390–406; for a conservative critique of this

trend, see James T. Bennett and Thomas Di Lorenzo, *Destroying Democracy* (Washington, D.C.: Cato Institute, 1986). See also many of the articles in *The Politics of Interests*, ed. Mark P. Petracca (Boulder, Colo.:Westview, 1992).

2. Walker, "Origins and Maintenance of Interest Groups," 16.

3. Robert H. Salisbury, "Interest Representation and the Dominance of Institutions," *American Political Science Review* 78 (March 1984): 64–77.

4. See Jeffery Berry, "The Power of Citizen Groups," unpublished manuscript.

5. Gregory Colgate, ed., *National Trade and Professional Associations of the United States 1982* (Washington, D.C.: Columbia Books, 1984).

6. Cited in Kevin Phillips, *Arrogant Capital* (Boston: Back Bay/Little, Brown, 1995), 43.

7. Jonathan Rauch, *Democlerosis* (New York: Times Books, 1994), 39.

8. But see Virginia Gray and David Lowery, *The Population Ecology of Interest Representation* (Ann Arbor: University of Michigan Press, 1996).

9. Kevin Kasowski "Showdown on the Hunting Ground," *Outdoor America* 51 (Winter 1986): 9.

10. Sarah Lyall, "Scientist Gives Up Grant to Do Research on Cats," *New York Times*, November 21, 1988, A12.

11. Lauristan R. King and Kimberly Stephens, "Politics and the Animal Rights Movement" (Paper delivered at the annual meeting of the Southern Political Science Association, Tampa, Florida, 1991).

12. Lyall, "Scientist Gives Up Grant."

13. "Americans Divided on Animal Rights," *Los Angeles Times*, December 17, 1993. This national survey of 1,612 adults also found that 50 percent opposed the wearing of fur.

14. Phil McCombs, "Attack of the Omnivore," *Washington Post*, March 27, 1992, B1, B4.

15. James Q. Wilson, *Political Organizations* (New York: Basic Books, 1973), 201.

16. Andrew S. McFarland, *Common Cause* (Chatham, N.J.: Chatham House, 1984), 48–49.

17. King and Stephens, "Politics and the Animal Rights Movement," 15.

18. Jeffrey M. Berry, *Lobbying for the People* (Princeton, N.J.: Princeton University Press, 1977), 72.

19. Walker, "Origins and Maintenance of Interest Groups," 400.

20. Sarah Brady, wife of former White House press secretary James Brady, organized Handgun Control after her husband was wounded in John Hinckley's 1981 attack on Ronald Reagan. Randall Terry formed Operation Rescue, which seeks to shut down abortion clinics through direct action (for example, blocking entrances), after concluding that other prolife groups were not effective in halting abortions.

21. Quoted in "A New Era: Groups and the Grass Roots," by Burdett A. Loomis, in *Interest Group Politics* 2d ed., ed. Allan J. Cigler and Burdett A. Loomis (Washington, D.C.: CQ Press, 1983), 184.

22. Kay Lehman Schlozman and John T. Tierney, "More of the Same: Washington Pressure Group Activity in a Decade of Change," *Journal of Politics* 45 (May 1983): 18.

23. Robert H. Salisbury, "The Paradox of Interest Groups in Washington—More Groups and Less Clout," in *The New American Political System*, 2d ed., ed. Anthony King (Washington, D.C.: American Enterprise Institute, 1990), 225–226.

24. For an expansion of this argument, see Rausch, *Democlerosis*.

25. Robert J. Samuelson's description in *National Journal*, September 25, 1982, 1642.

26. Everett Carll Ladd, "How to Tame the Special Interest Groups," *Fortune*, (October 1980), 6.

# CHAPTER 7 Political Parties

## 7.1 LARRY SABATO

# *New Campaign Techniques and the American Party System*

Larry Sabato is a contemporary scholar of campaign politics, electoral behavior, and political interest group analysis. He has researched the roles of the mass media, political consultants, and political action committees (PACs) in modern political campaigns and elections. His extensive publications have also focused on the impact of campaign finance reform legislation on contemporary elections. Sabato's classic work *The Rise of Political Consultants: New Ways of Winning Elections* (Basic Books, 1981) was recognized as an innovative study of modern political campaigns and elections. The following selection is from Sabato's "New Campaign Techniques and the American Party System," in Vernon Bogdanor, ed., *Parties and Democracy in Britain and America* (Praeger, 1984).

Sabato (b. 1952) has taught at Oxford University, and he has been a professor of government and foreign affairs at the University of Virginia for most of his professional career. Sabato was a Rhodes Scholar and a Danforth Fellow, and he is the author of 12 books and monographs, most of which focus on political campaigns and elections, the impact of the media on elections, political interest groups, state government and politics, and Virginia politics and government.

In the following selection, Sabato offers a detailed historical review and analysis of the most significant developments that have occurred among political parties and in electoral behavior. He claims that the political power and influence of political parties and party leaders have greatly declined in recent decades. Independent professional political consultants have become competitors of party leaders and political party organizations. The critical electoral functions once performed efficiently by political parties are presently provided by political consultants. Political consultants are individuals that remain independent of formal party organizations but are employed by candidates because of their professional expertise on contemporary campaign strategies such as polling, media advertising, and computerized direct-mail requests for campaign contributions. PACs have also become rivals of political parties, as they often perform basic electoral functions such as recruiting political candidates, developing the candidates' political skills, designing campaign strategies, organizing campaign staffs, and soliciting campaign contributions.

**Key Concept:** political parties and contemporary campaign methods

*T*he political parties have been weakened by a multitude of circumstances, and in many respects the influence party leaders once wielded in election campaigns now is exercised by independent political consultants, just as the vital electoral roles once performed almost exclusively by parties are now available to anyone who masters the new campaign technologies such as polling, media advertising, and direct mail. The growth of political consultancy and the development of advanced campaign techniques were combined with the new election finance laws that hurt the parties, favored the prospering consultants, and encouraged the mushrooming of party-rivaling political action committees. . . .

## FROM PARTY POLS TO POLITICAL CONSULTANTS

. . . To understand the transformation of the parties within the American electoral system, it is important first to understand how the perception that the electorate has of them has changed over the years. Martin P. Wattenberg has recently argued[1] that American voters have *not* grown more alienated from the parties (contrary to journalistic myth). Rather, voters have become more neutral in their evaluations of the parties. Why has this happened? As Wattenberg explains it:

> The reason for party decline has not been that people no longer see any important differences between the parties. . . . Rather the problem which the parties must face is that they are considered less relevant in solving the most important domestic and foreign policy issues of the day. *In the voters' minds, the parties are losing their association with the candidates and the issues which the candidates claim to stand for.* [Emphasis added.]

That association between parties and candidates is weakening partly because the parties have ceased to be very important in the process of electing their candidates. Since candidates are not beholden to the party for their elections, they are not responsive to the party's needs or platform once in office.

As the parties have moved to the sidelines, independent political consultants have rushed forward to replace them.[2] Pollster Patrick Caddell clearly identified the alternate nonparty route that consultants have provided to willing politicians:

> Parties traditionally provided the avenue by which candidates reached voters. What we've done with media, what we've done with polling, and what we've done with direct organizational techniques is that we have provided candidates who have the resources (and that's the important thing, the resources), the ability to reach the voters and have a direct contact with the electorate without regard to party or party organization.[3]

The value of consultants to candidates is perhaps best described by the technologies at the consultants' command. The design and production of media advertising is among the essential skills that consultants offer political aspirants. It is difficult to find a contested race for major office in the United States today which does not feature television and radio commercials, and even campaigns for minor posts such as city councilor and state legislator often employ professional advertising. Quite simply, the paid media advertisements (together with the "free" media of press coverage) have replaced the political party as the middleman between candidate and voter. The candidate no longer depends so heavily on party workers to present his case to voters in his constituency; television can do it more directly and efficiently. The media consultant who can design effective and pleasing advertisements is thus worth his weight in gold to the modern candidate.

Equally prominent in modern campaigns is another kind of political consultant, the pollster. At every stage of the campaign the pollster, his survey data in hand and his role as *vox populi* [voice of the people] foremost in mind, aids the candidate and staff in crucial decisions—whether to run at all, how to run, what issues to emphasize and which ones to avoid, which aspects of his opponent's platform and personality are vulnerable, and so on. In doing so, the pollster substitutes for party leaders, since it was exactly this kind of advice that the party kingpins used to dispense and their candidates used to follow. Once again, the new technology replaces the political party as the middleman between candidate and voter. Office seekers formerly depended on party workers to convey to them grassroots sentiment and the opinions of average voters in the constituency. Now random-sample surveys can perform the same chore, but with relative certainty and with a wealth of semiprecise detail that party wheel-horses could only guess at. For example, it would be difficult even for a modern-day George Washington Plunkitt to know which television shows are watched by a population sub-group targeted by the campaign. Simple crosstabulations of standard survey questions used by the political pollsters reveal this, and more, today. While the process of polling has many weaknesses[4] and is rarely as error-free as the unwittingly arrogant disclaimer accompanying most surveys suggests—"this poll is accurate to within a margin of error of plus or minus 4 percent"—survey sampling is usually more accurate and normally more directly useful than the surmises of party leaders. Candidates know it, and that is why polling consultants like Jimmy Carter's Patrick Caddell and Ronald Reagan's Richard Wirthlin have had far more influence on the course of their client's campaigns than have party chiefs. It should be noted, too, that the pollster's dominance has recently been extended to governance as well as campaigning. Caddell, for instance, clearly had major influence on a number of President Carter's decisions (including his crucial 1979 Camp David domestic summit and subsequent "crisis of confidence" speech[5]). Wirthlin's frequent polling studies on a wide range of subjects are reportedly closely studied by President Reagan and his key aides; Wirthlin himself is a frequent White House visitor....

Even the political party's greatest remaining strength, its precinct organization and network of volunteers, is being duplicated by independent consultants.[6] Some consultants use a technique called "Instant Organization" (IO), which utilizes paid callers to ring up voters from centralized banks of telephones. Using various tested scripts, block captains are recruited and office volunteers solicited. Subsequent mail and telephone contracts, as well as get-togethers with the candidate and his surrogate, keep the "instant" volunteers motivated.

# THE RELATIONSHIP OF CONSULTANTS TO THE POLITICAL PARTIES

The consultants and their new campaign technologies have, then, increasingly been replacing the parties as the middlemen between candidate and voter. If the relationship between the consultants and the parties is a symbiotic or mutually reinforcing one, little harm—and potentially much good—is done. Unfortunately for the political parties, few consultants are vitally interested in the health of the party system. It is fair to describe most political consultants as businessmen, not party ideologues. There are exceptions, and a few are fierce partisans, having had their political baptism as party functionaries and occasionally having had years of direct party employment. One of these, Robert Odell, is inclined to take on just about any Republican in his direct-mail firm because, "Democrats do little or nothing that I respect and Republicans do nearly everything I respect." Striking a rare pose for a private consultant, Odell declares, "The most important goal for me is to make the Republican party effective." Matt Reese holds the Democratic party in similar esteem, observing only half in jest that he is "a partisan without apology. I don't even *like* Republicans, except for Abraham Lincoln." And few professionals have shown as long and abiding a concern for a political party as Stuart Spencer and his partner, Bill Roberts, who both began their political careers as volunteers for the Republican party in California. Their consulting shop actually developed around the GOP and was encouraged by the party. Spencer explained that he and Roberts "wanted to be an extension of the party, a management tool that the party could use," and they viewed each of their early consultant outings as "an opportunity for the Republican party."

The greatest number of consultants, though, are simply not committed in any real sense to a political party. Michael Kaye, for instance, proclaims himself to be an Independent and the parties to be "bull."

Yet, for all of the danger supposedly involved in crossing party lines, consultants seem to yield frequently to the temptation. Democrat Peter Hart conducted Republican U.S. Senate nominee John Heinz's surveys in Pennsylvania in 1976 (and claimed he was told he could not take polls for Jimmy Carter as a consequence). Media consultant David Garth has been "all over the lot," as one of his detractors termed his tendency to take moderate-to-liberal Democrats and Republicans indiscriminately, and it was a surprise to no one in the profession when GOP Congressman John Anderson tapped Garth to help with his 1980 Independent presidential bid. Another Democratic-leaning liberal firm, Craver, Matthews, Smith, and Company, took on Anderson's direct-mail program. The now-defunct firm of Baus and Ross in California secured the accounts of Richard Nixon, Barry Goldwater, and Edmund G. "Pat" Brown, Sr., within a few years of one another. The survey firm of D.M.I. not only worked for both Democrats and Republicans, it actually polled both sides of the same congressional election district in 1966. Vincent Breglio, the D.M.I. vice president, took one side, and President Richard Wirthlin took the other. They ran the research independent of one another and provided consulting services to each side without crossing communications. Apparently the candidates were rather trusting souls who reportedly agreed to this outrageous arrangement (although it was quite a useful one for the firm's "win ratio"). D.M.I. converted permanently to Republicanism in 1967 when Michigan Governor George Romney asked the firm to join his presidential effort on condition that it work only for the GOP. Convinced that the move was good for business, Wirthlin and Breglio made the switch over the objections of the Democratic members of the firm, who nevertheless stayed....

Even though virtually all consultants identify with one of the parties (primarily for business purposes, as Michael Kaye suggested), most of them are at least passively hostile to the parties, some of them openly contemptuous. At times consultants can sound like the evangelical populists they often portray their candidates to be, railing against the evils of boss rule. "Really the only major function of the political party structure these days is to nominate the candidates for president, and my personal feeling is that we'd all be better off if this responsibility also were placed in the hands of the people," consultant Joe Napolitan has written.[7] Media consultant Bob Goodman, in tones echoed time and again by his fellow independent professionals, lauds consultants for unshackling candidates, putting them beyond the reach of the petty party barons:

> We have enabled people to come into a party or call themselves independent Democrats or Republicans and run for office without having to pay the dues of being a party member in a feudal way. Meaning kiss the ass of certain people and maybe down the line they'll give you a shot at public office.

Parties are usually viewed as one more obstacle in the way of the client's election. "In most places the party operation does not do a great deal to help a candidate get elected the first time, and [it] is more of a hassle than it's worth," concludes GOP media consultant Douglas Bailey. Many party-consultant relationships are marked by sharp conflict, explained by Napolitan as the result of party workers' jealousy of consultants, who "have replaced organization regulars in making important campaign decisions" and who are possible usurpers of "what they [party workers] consider their rights to patronage."[8]

A natural consequence of the consultant's antagonism toward the party is his willingness to run his candidates apart from, or even against, their party label. It was difficult to know whether GOP nominee John Heinz was a Democrat or Republican in his 1976 Pennsylvania Senate race, since media consultant David Garth fashioned his advertising campaign around an antiparty theme: "If you think Pennsylvania needs an *Independent* senator, elect John Heinz." One of Garth's spots actually featured a glowing "endorsement" of Heinz's character by Jimmy Carter (delivered in March of 1975), to further confuse the voter. Scrambling labels may seem unfortunate to those concerned about the role of party in elections, but at least the party is not under direct attack, a common tactic in party primaries. Milton Shapp, for instance, won the Democratic nomination for the Pennsylvania governorship in 1966 in a major upset, thanks to Joe Napolitan's "Man Against the Machine" theme.[9] ...

# THE GROWTH OF POLITICAL ACTION COMMITTEES

Possibly the most far-reaching change wrought by FECA was in its legitimizing the use of corporate funds to establish and administer Political Action Committees (PACs). Labor unions already had that right, and the PAC had long been an essential political tool for organized labor. Now business and trade interests could benefit as well.

Once the floodgates were opened, the growth of corporate and trade PACs was nothing short of phenomenal.

Just between 1976 and 1978, the number of PACs rose from 1,242 to 1,938 and by 1982 PACs totaled 3,371. Their total spending increased from $30.1 million in 1976 to $127.7 million in 1980 and on to $190.4 million in 1982.[10] New business PACs comprised by far the largest share of the growth. In 1978, for instance, when all PACs accounted for $34.1 million of the $199 million in contributions received by congressional candidates, one researcher estimated that business and business-related groups outspent labor by better than two to one.[11] Between 1976 and 1978, corporate PAC gifts to candidates more than doubled, while labor's PAC donations showed only a 25% gain.[12] Business and trade PACs, which at first favored incumbents (and thus gave more to Democratic candidates), have gradually moved to the GOP's banner.

Of far greater concern to the political parties is another increasingly prominent form of political action committee: the ideological PAC. The National Committee for an Effective Congress (NCEC) on the left and the Committee for the Survival of a Free Congress (CSFC) on the right are typical examples. Both provide organizational assistance to ideologically compatible candidates, irrespective of party. The NCEC is much the elder of the two and was founded in 1948. It describes itself as a "bipartisan progressive" group dedicated to civil rights, civil liberties, and internationalism. Rather than giving money, the NCEC provides specific services, such as the hiring and paying of the campaign manager, polling, targeting, and organizing. In a normal election year the NCEC will assist in some way up to 60 House candidates and a dozen Senate contenders. Russell Hemenway, executive director of the NCEC, sees his organization as a substitute for the Democratic National Committee, which "provides almost no services to candidates," and for political consultants who "are looking for campaigns that can pay hefty bills."

Many of the same goals are shared by the CSFC, which has sought to imitate somewhat the NCEC and the AFL–CIO's Committee on Political Education (COPE). "I make no secret of the fact that I admire their [COPE's] operations and have to some extent modeled our committee on the labor groups" says CSFC director Paul Weyrich.[13] Founded in 1974 with financial support from Joseph Coors, the conservative Colorado brewer, the CSFC plays a central role in the so-called "New Right," along with Richard Viguerie's direct-mail outfit and other political committees, such as Sen. Jesse Helms' Congressional Club and the National Conservative PAC.[14] Like the NCEC, the CSFC helps candidates assemble a skilled campaign team, usually contributing about $500 a month to pay the salary of a field organizer. The CSFC acts almost like a political party, recruiting candidates, refining candidates' political abilities, performing electoral organizational chores, devising strategy, and constructing campaign staffs. An extensive five-day "candidate school" is held by the CSFC four to six times every two years, and it is attended by prospective congressional contenders and campaign managers from the conservative wings of both parties, who pay a registration fee of $500 per person. The schools enlist incumbent congressmen and consultants as instructors and are organized around problem-solving groups that enable the CSFC directors to evaluate each political candidate's performance. At the end of the course, a simulated election is held, which sometimes serves as an informal primary of sorts since more than one candidate from the same district attends. In 1978, three Republican House contenders from the same Wisconsin constituency attended the CSFC school, and the PAC decided that one of them, Toby Roth, was clearly superior (and the most conservative). After the school's adjournment, Roth received the group's blessing, and he went on to win his party's nomination and to defeat an incumbent Democratic congressman in November.

Ideological PACs are proliferating and strengthening. In 1981–82, the six largest conservative PACs raised a combined total of $29.4 million, up by 25% from the previous election cycle.[15] Liberal PACs did less well, raising about $9.4 million, but five of the six top groups were new-formed in reaction to the conservative PACs' 1980 election successes—and the comparable liberal total was a scant $400,000.[16]

In explaining the explosive growth of all forms of PACs, most (but not all) roads lead to FECA. The 1974 lifting of the ban on corporate funding of PACs was crucial, and the tighter public disclosure requirements, by revealing the previously obscured extent of each corporation's involvement in politics, have produced a "keep up with the Joneses" mentality among business and trade association circles. FECA's $1,000 limitation on individual contributions and its more permissive $5,000 PAC limit encourage candidates to rely on PACs as a more generous source of funds. Also having an effect on the extent and pace of PAC expansion is a growing group of political consultants, who specialize in assisting PAC formation and activity. The professionals are finding PAC consulting to be more stable, continuous, and profitable than candidate work, and almost all consultants have advised at least one or a few PACs from time to time.

Even though PACs are clearly party rivals, both parties seem to be resigned to the age of PACs. Like Willie Sutton who robbed banks "because that's where they keep the money," the parties have begun to direct their attentions to the overflowing PAC treasuries and have hired consultants to ensure that they get their fair share of PAC money. The GOP assists its candidates in soliciting PACs, helping its nominees to secure appointments with PAC officials and directing them toward committees that are likely to donate to them. Behind the facade of cooperation, however, lies the inescapable incompatibility and competitiveness between parties and PACs. Many political action committees are slowly but surely developing into rival institutions that raise money, develop memberships, recruit candidates, organize campaigns, and influence officeholders just as the parties do (or are supposed to do). PACs already outfinance the parties, partly because they drain away potential gifts to them, permitting supporters to tell the Democratic or Republican committee that they have already given at the office. PACs also outspend the parties by a large margin. While the two parties were contributing $21.9 million to their congressional nominees in 1982, for instance, PACs mustered $83.1 million in congressional contributions.

PACs are not organized along party lines and are never likely to be. In the words of one PAC official, "We believe you have to be pretty cold-blooded concerning your giving policy. You simply have to support candidates who support you... regardless of party or philosophy."[17] The ideological PACs, of course, make no pretense about their aims. Most of them view the parties with undisguised hostility, attacking them for a lack of ideological clarity and working to defeat the more moderate choices of party leaders in primaries. Paul Weyrich of CSFC proudly cites the case of Republican right-wing political novice Gordon Humphrey of New Hampshire, a former airline pilot who upset incumbent Democratic U.S. Senator Thomas McIntyre in 1978. The GOP senatorial campaign committee gave assistance to Humphrey's more moderate primary opponent, but CSFC helped to engineer a primary victory for him. Now, reports Weyrich, "Gordon is less than enthusiastic about the party," which suits CSFC just fine. It is easy to agree with Weyrich's observation that "both political parties would have an all-night celebration if we were to go out of business." The problem for the parties can be succinctly stated: Groups like CSFC are in no danger of going out of business. In fact, they are flourishing.

# NOTES

1. Martin P. Wattenberg, "The Decline of Political Partisanship in the United States: Negativity or Neutrality?" *American Political Science Review* 75 (1981): 941–50.

2. Much of the following discussion of consultants and their technologies is derived from Sabato, *The Rise of Political Consultants* (New York: Basic Books, 1981).

3. This quotation, and the others of political consultants that follow, are taken from the author's personal interviews conducted in 1979 and 1980.

4. Ibid., pp. 92–102.

5. Ibid., pp. 74–75.

6. Ibid., pp. 200–4.

7. Joseph Napolitan, *The Election Game and How to Win It* (New York: Doubleday, 1972), pp. 17–18.

8. Ibid.

9. See ibid., pp. 162–208. Shapp lost the general election that year but came back to win the statehouse in 1970.

10. See *National Journal,* February 27, 1982, p. 391, and *Congressional Quarterly Weekly,* April 10, 1982, pp. 814–23; 1982 figures are from FEC press release "1981–82 PAC Giving Up 51%, April 29, 1983.

11. See Edwin M. Epstein, "An Irony of Electoral Reform: The Business PAC Phenomenon," *Regulation* (May/June, 1979): 35–41. Also see FEC release of April 29, 1983 (ibid.).

12. Labor's figures do not, however, include separate spending for registration, get-out-the-vote, and other activities, which may amount to as much as $20 million in an election year.

13. See Paul M. Weyrich, "The New Right: PACs and Coalition Politics," in Michael J. Malbin (ed.), *Parties, Interest Groups, and Campaign Finance Laws* (Washington, D.C.: American Enterprise Institute, 1980), pp. 68–81.

14. *National Journal,* October 23, 1976, p. 1514, and January 5, 1980, p. 20. See also *Congressional Quarterly Weekly,* December 24, 1977, p. 2652.

15. See FEC release of April 29, 1983. See also *National Journal,* January 21, 1978, pp. 33–92, and March 20, 1982, pp. 500–1; *Congressional Quarterly Weekly,* February 27, 1982, p. 482, and March 6, 1982, pp 499–505. The latter article closely examines the Helms group, which in 1981 became the country's largest PAC.

16. Ibid.

17. As quoted in *Campaigning Reports,* vol. 1, no. 6 (August 9, 1979): 10.

# Strengthening the National Parties

In 1950 the American Political Science Association's Committee on Political Parties identified American political parties as weak, decentralized organizations without coherent sets of beliefs or principles and without strong party loyalty or consensus on fundamental positions or policies. The committee strongly recommended that the parties should be transformed into two highly-centralized, disciplined organizations. These organizations should then construct two national councils to generate and articulate each national party's policies and platforms and to serve as a means of transition toward a more responsible two-party system. The proposed council would also attempt to influence congressional and presidential politics by making recommendations on party candidates and by sharing in the policy-making power of both national institutions. A disciplined, responsible party system is a model of political parties that conforms to the theory of majoritarian democracy by compelling the party leadership in government to comply directly to majority public opinion. In a responsible party government, political parties articulate identifiable and coherent policies to the electorate, and the victorious party attempts to implement its agenda while in office. This type of party system also assumes that the electorate will vote for candidates because of party policies and will hold the governing party accountable for its decisions.

James L. Sundquist (b. 1915) is recognized as an outstanding scholar of political parties, electoral behavior, federalism, and intergovernmental relations. He received his M.S. from Syracuse University, and he is a senior fellow emeritus of the Brookings Institution. His publications include *The Decline and Resurgence of Congress* (Brookings Institution, 1981) and *Constitutional Reform and Effective Government* (Brookings Institution, 1986).

The following selection is an excerpt from Sundquist's "Strengthening the National Parties," in A. James Reichley, ed., *Elections American Style* (Brookings Institution, 1987). In it, Sundquist examines the inadequacies of contemporary American parties and gives his recommendations for strengthening the parties. He also analyzes the historical evolution of American political parties, and he contends that a responsible party system is unlikely in the American political system. The Madisonian model for organizing government became dominant in the American political system and was intentionally designed to impede the formation and power of factions or parties. In particular, the principle of separation of powers designed by the U.S. Constitution's framers and the creation of a bicameral Congress are perceived by Sundquist as fundamental barriers to the strengthening of political parties. Although Sundquist is skeptical of the development of a responsible party system, his reform proposals for increasing the discipline and power of parties have influenced many scholars.

**Key Concept:** the responsible party model

$P$olitical parties have always occupied an ambiguous position in American public life. They are profoundly mistrusted—yet accepted. Their constant maneuvering for petty advantage is reviled and ridiculed, but millions of people call themselves either Democrats or Republicans and cherish the ideals of their party with a religious fervor. Parties have been credited with such supreme achievements as saving the Union and rescuing the country from the Great Depression. But they have also been accused of placing partisan advantage ahead of the national good, of failing to conceive farsighted programs, of running away from problems and responsibilities, and sometimes of deep and pervasive corruption....

## THE MADISONIAN MODEL: A SYSTEM WITHOUT PARTIES

The Constitution that emerged from the Convention of 1787 made no place for parties. At that time, only the faint forerunners of modern political parties had appeared anywhere in the world. Factions had taken shape within legislative bodies in both the American states and in England, but they were not formally organized, and political organizations formed by citizens of the new states for purposes of particular elections were still local and rudimentary. Insofar as the Constitution's framers at Philadelphia referred to these groupings at all, they condemned them. They were usually termed factions or cabals rather than parties, and they were denounced as responsible for the "corruption" and "intrigue" of legislative bodies.

Accordingly, in designing the institutions of the new government, the men of 1787 deliberately sought to erect barriers against the development and influence of parties. Indeed, the basic tripartite structure of the government, as well as the division of the legislative branch into two houses, can be seen as having that essential purpose. The framers scattered power in order to forestall the evils of concentration in any individual or group, that is, in any one faction or party. They feared that a transient popular majority might be able to seize the House of Representatives and try to impose its will on the country, but they designed the Senate as a body of elder statesmen with long, overlapping terms who would rise above factionalism, and conceived the presidency, possessed of a veto in the legislative process, as the very embodiment of the nonpartisan ideal....

# THE RESPONSIBLE-PARTY MODEL

The opposing model for organizing a government recognizes not only the inevitability but the necessity of parties and assigns them the role that they everywhere seek and come naturally to assume. This is the model that has been adopted in various forms by most of the other advanced democracies of the world, and it is the one that inspires the recommendations of such contemporary American reformist groups as the CPR and the CCS.

In this model, political parties are formed because groups of people, each sharing a philosophy and a set of goals, desire governmental power in order to carry out their programs. In competition with one another, they present their programs to the people in an open and free election. The party or coalition that wins the support of a majority of the people gains control of the government and enacts its program. The minority party or parties form an opposition, with power to criticize, debate, and delay but not to block. After a few years the voters in another election render a verdict on the majority's stewardship. If they approve what has been done, they return the ruling party or coalition to office. If they disapprove, they turn the incumbents out and entrust power to an opposition party or combination of parties. At all times, one of the parties, or a combination, is responsible for the government, possesses authority commensurate with its responsibility (subject to check by the judiciary if it exceeds its constitutional powers), and is fully accountable for whatever the government (except for the judiciary) does. In the metaphors of political science textbook writers, the political party is the tie that binds, the glue that fastens, the bridge or the web that unites the disparate institutions that make up the government. Without parties, democracy on a national scale simply could not work. . . .

# THE OBSTACLES TO STRENGTHENING PARTIES

The fundamental barrier to strengthening political parties is the survival in popular culture of the Madisonian model. Rejected almost unanimously by the country's political elite for two centuries, the Madisonian ideal of a factionless government has never lost its hold on the public. Factionalism is derided, and wherever possible averted, in the multitude of private organizations with which individual citizens are familiar. Why then, they ask, must politicians divide into factions that spend their energies in recrimination and petty squabbling rather than getting together to do what is best for the country?

The machines that were the target of antiparty legislation nearly a century ago have by now virtually disappeared, and the strongest political organizations in the country are those held together not by public jobs and other forms of patronage but by ideology and philosophy. Yet the antiparty rhetoric of the Progressive era still rings loudly in political campaigns. Both Jimmy Carter and Ronald Reagan trumpeted their antiestablishment sentiments, and candidates at every level still find their road to victory by running against a party organization wherever one exists—the "man against the machine." So advocates of stronger parties must struggle against the widespread and often prevailing view that powerful party organizations are more a menace than a boon.

A second obstacle, related to the first, is the self-interest of individual politicians. A stronger party is by definition one with a stronger center, possessing some institutional means of fostering unity and cohesion. But... the individual politician who does not aspire to national leadership usually finds more to lose than to gain by strengthening the center. With a loose, decentralized structure the state or local leader can follow the national party and its leaders when their policies are popular at home or defy them when they are not. The self-interest of thousands of politicians is a centrifugal force within the party structure that is operative constantly; centripetal political forces develop now and then, but most of the time they are overbalanced.

## RECENT PROGRESS TOWARD STRONGER PARTIES

Yet advocates of stronger parties are the beneficiaries of one profound trend in American politics and one series of deliberate actions, and both of these give hope.

The promising trend is that the two major parties have both become, and are still becoming, more homogeneous ideologically. This trend is the simple consequence of the party realignment that began in the 1930s and has been working its way, gradually but inexorably, through the political system. Simply put, the minority wings, once strong enough to disrupt the internal unity of the two parties, have been dying out. The "four-party system" James MacGregor Burns condemned a generation ago for producing "the deadlock of democracy" is now much more nearly a genuine two-party system.[1]

First to fade were the progressive Republicans. The progressive wing of the GOP, which spanned the generations from Theodore Roosevelt through the La Follettes and George Norris to Nelson Rockefeller and George Romney, was powerful enough as recently as twenty years ago to contest seriously for the presidential nomination. But the progressive Republicans are now an ineffectual remnant. Their counterparts, the conservative Democrats, have been vanishing as well, although more slowly. Virtually confined to the South since the New Deal era, they have from the 1960s been gradually losing their base there to the burgeoning Republican party. As conservative Democrats have ended their careers one by one—usually through retirement rather than defeat—their successors have typically been either conservative Republicans or Democrats cut in the mold of their national party. Thus Republicans occupy the seats once held by such archconservative senators as Harry F. Byrd and A. Willis Robertson of Virginia and James O. Eastland of Mississippi, while new Democratic senators arriving from the South tend to be moderates, such as Terry Sanford of North Carolina and Bob Graham of Florida, or even bear the liberal label, like Wyche Fowler of Georgia. A corresponding transformation has taken place in both parties in the House.

The deliberate actions are those taken by congressional Democrats... to impose discipline on party dissenters. Any article on strengthening political parties written earlier than [the mid-1960s] would have opened and closed with a call for destruction of the seniority system in the Congress. That has now been accomplished on the Democratic side. As long as seniority was automatically honored, any Democrat, no matter how out of step with the majority of the party in Congress, could acquire all the plenary power of a committee chairmanship through mere longevity. Through that device some of the Senate and House committees most crucial to the enactment of the Democratic party's program were turned over to conservative Democrats who voted regularly with the Republicans against the majority of their own party. Sooner or later the situation was bound to prove intolerable. Finally the revolution occurred: liberals in the House forced through the party caucus a series of rules changes that not only scrapped seniority but reduced the arbitrary power of committee chairmen. The revolt was solidified in 1975 when the caucus deposed three chairmen. And it has continued to exercise disciplinary power. In 1987 the caucus voted to remove Les Aspin of Wisconsin from the chairmanship of the House Armed Services Committee, reversing itself only after Aspin humbly promised to accept its guidance on major questions of military policy. The caucus has also assumed, and exercised, the power to instruct the Democratic committee majorities to bring specific measures to the House floor.

With this power of discipline, the caucus has been revived as an instrument for building policy consensus. In their drive to assert control over party policy, the liberals won a demand for regular monthly party caucuses plus additional meetings on petition of fifty members—a dramatic departure from the once-every-two-years tradition that had prevailed for a quarter of a century. The caucus has proved to be an effective consensus-building mechanism, particularly in the long and acrimonious debate over the Vietnam War when the passion of the antiwar Democratic majority eventually persuaded some reluctant senior party figures to abandon their support. Since then it has expressed itself on a wide range of measures, including the issues of defense policy that led to Aspin's pledge of conformity. In early February 1987 the caucus denounced the Reagan administration's resumption of underground nuclear testing and urged the administration instead to begin negotiations with the Soviet Union for an agreement banning such tests.

Institutional change has occurred less formally in the clublike Senate, but the arbitrary power of Democratic committee chairmen has been effectively curtailed there as well. Within the committee structures in both houses, democratic norms now prevail.

Finally, the new Democratic party rule that guarantees seats in the quadrennial presidential nominating convention to 80 percent of the party's members of Congress may prove to be an important move in the direction of greater party cohesion. While most members will no doubt be guided by the sentiment of their states' voters as expressed in primaries and caucuses, and while they are unlikely to vote as a bloc in any case, their influence will be enhanced. In a close convention contest a determined network of House and Senate leaders could conceivably be decisive in selecting a nominee experienced in dealing with Congress, as opposed to an outsider like Jimmy Carter whose misfortunes in his relationships with the legislators and the rest of the party establishment spurred the rules revision.

So, whenever the next Democratic president is elected, advocates of responsible-party government may yet expect to see a close approximation to their model. Given reasonable luck in the presidential nominating lottery, today's more homogeneous Democratic party should be able to attain a degree of cohesion under presidential leadership that observers of the party system have not seen—except for the honeymoon years of Lyndon Johnson—in half a century.

Perhaps that cohesion will provide a satisfactory enough version of responsible-party government. But if additional measures to strengthen parties could be taken, the possibilities are worth considering. Any such measures, however, are sure to be difficult. If they were easy, they would already have been adopted, for those who lead the two national parties would assuredly prefer to lead stronger organizations.

## THE LIMITED OPPORTUNITIES FOR FURTHER ACTION

The first obvious possibility for further action is for the majorities in Congress to impose party discipline not merely to get measures out of committee but to get them passed. The means to that end is the binding caucus, which both houses last used with full effectiveness in the first Congress of the Wilson administration, in 1913–14. Through that device two-thirds of the Democratic caucus could bind the entire membership to vote with the majority. When the rule was invoked, however, the Democrats laid themselves open to attack by the Republican opposition and its supporters in the media and elsewhere, as well as by independents revolted by the spectacle of coercion. Rule by "King Caucus" developed into a major political issue. Chastened by the public reaction and by intraparty opposition as well, Senate Democrats abandoned the device after the Wilson era. The House party discarded it, too, after a brief revival in the early New Deal period. Any proposal for its reintroduction would undoubtedly arouse an even more adverse response in today's climate of political individualism, which makes the suggestion futile at the outset.

Another instrument employed by strong parties in other countries also appears beyond consideration in the United States. That is control by the national party, in one or another degree, over the selection of candidates for the national legislature. On reflection, it has to appear anomalous that anyone, no matter how ideologically opposed to the program and philosophy of the Democratic or Republican party, may run for Congress as the party's candidate, take his or her seat with the party upon election, and receive choice committee assignments as a matter of right from the party caucus. Yet neither party has ever developed mechanisms at any level for screening candidacies. Even to design such a mechanism would be difficult. Some have suggested that the copyright laws be made the vehicle, with only persons authorized by the national party allowed to use the party label. But the idea of national control of nominations has too antidemocratic a ring—smacking, like the binding caucus, of thought control—ever to acquire noticeable support. In emergencies, like the one that developed in Illinois in 1986 when two unacceptable candidates won Democratic nominations for state office, the party can devise extraordinary remedies, as the Democrats did in that case by organizing a temporary new party. Moreover, the principal reason for advocating control of candidacies disappeared on the Democratic side when the seniority system was scrapped, for while a dissenter can win committee assignments, he or she can now be denied on ideological grounds the power of a chairmanship. This, if the issue arises, would be the easier solution for the GOP as well.

In its 1950 report the American Political Science Association Committee on Political Parties proposed creation of a national council in each party to set party policy as a means for moving toward a more responsible two-party system. The council, to consist of about fifty members from both inside and outside government, would draft the preliminary party platform and, after its adoption by the convention, interpret it. The council would also make recommendations "in respect to congressional candidates," and perhaps presidential candidates as well. But any such proposal also founders on the rock of self-interest. Why would a president and leading legislators who had won governmental office through arduous election campaigns voluntarily share their policymaking power with outsiders and submit to their restraints? That was the experience when the Democratic National Committee, influenced by the APSA committee report, established its Democratic Advisory Council after the 1956 election. The party's congressional leaders simply declined to join. The council issued well-considered policy pronouncements, but it spoke for only a segment of the party and could not serve its purpose as an institution to unify the party.

There remains one other instrument of discipline: money. Dependent as legislators are on campaign contributions, the power to grant or deny financial assistance can in theory be a powerful disciplinary tool. The national Republican party in recent years has demonstrated the capacity to raise and distribute an enormous treasury. The Democrats' capability is by no means comparable, but it has been improving. Is money a potential means, then, for tightening party discipline within Congress to achieve responsible-party government?

In theory, yes. In practice, probably not to a significant degree. Because discretionary power over congressional campaign funds would be a powerful device to achieve central control, the resistance that arises against central control of any aspect of party organization would in this case be commensurately potent. But even if discretion were granted to the national party committees, their self-interest would steer them away from exercising it as an instrument of party discipline. The overriding objective of the national party in congressional campaigns is to win a majority of seats. To this end, the party's self-interest is to support any candidate with a chance of victory, and to support most generously the candidates in the closest races, where additional spending is most likely to pay off in victories. In the heat of a campaign the national party officials making money decisions do not ask about the voting regularity of a party's incumbents or extract voting promises from nonincumbents. They ask only about election prospects. They take polls and are guided by the numbers.

So it is that in these days of Republican opulence no complaints have been heard that the national party has been using its funds in a discriminatory fashion to penalize legislators who have deviated from the Reagan party line. After the 1986 election the party was proud to announce that it had "maxed out" on every candidate, that is, given the maximum amount permissible by law to its nominee in every race. No one was disciplined. Indeed, one true believer in party discipline, Patrick J. Buchanan, the White House director of communications, could complain after the election that President Reagan had been "travelling the nation as no other president before him, fighting to save the Senate for ... Republicans, throwing his arm around men—some of whom had cut-and-run on him in every major engagement he has fought since he came to the White House."[2]

In any case, cash contributions to congressional campaigns by national party committees are now so tightly limited by law that the potential for monetary discipline is not great. In House campaigns a party committee is treated as just another political action committee limited to contributing the same $5,000 a race (in Senate contests the ceiling is $17,500). Compared with what the array of PACs can put into closely contested races, these sums are a pittance, particularly in the case of the senior members of key committees who—if any member needed discipline—might need it the most. Any major influence by party committees has to be exerted indirectly, through advice given by party officials to friendly PACs, rather than directly through the party's own funds.

The limits on party contributions could, of course, be raised by new legislation, but the Democrats are hardly likely to use their Senate and House majorities to enhance the advantage that the richer Republican party would get from freer spending. And if a large share of congressional campaign funds were to come from the public treasury, that would not change matters either. In the bill introduced in January 1987 as S. 2 by Democratic Senators David L. Boren of Oklahoma and Robert C. Byrd of West Virginia, the majority leader, the public funds would be distributed among candidates by formula, with the party not even serving as a channel.

Money, then, is not likely to become the powerful centralizing force within the parties that at first sight might appear possible. The handling of money has yielded to, and been conformed to, the prevailing pattern of decentralization in the party structure. And it is likely to remain that way, no matter how the sums at the disposal of the parties might be increased. The members of Congress who would write any public financing law and who already have the decisive voice in determining the national parties' policies for distributing congressional campaign funds will see to that.

Deliberate attempts, then, to strengthen political parties run counter to deep-seated public attitudes, to the self-interest of the politicians who would have to initiate change, and to the structure of governmental and political institutions, including the electoral system. The feasible actions have already been taken—notably the crucial decisions in the 1970s to assert majority rule within the congressional parties. There is a solid basis for hope, however, in political trends beyond the influence of even the political elite itself—the continuing realignment of the party system that is producing the homogeneity on which party cohesion and strength at the governmental level must rest.

If, when one party again wins single-party control of the presidency and Congress, it succeeds in coping effectively with the problems of the country, the value of the responsible-party concept will have been demonstrated and the model will win a wider public acceptance. More people will then see the role of parties as those who believe in the responsible party model see it—as institutions crucially necessary to formulate governmental programs, to enact and execute those programs, and to account for them to the electorate afterward.

Only such a period of success can provide the necessary popular support for institutional changes that will further the same ends. In the meantime, such changes of any consequence will simply have to wait.

## NOTES

1. Burns, *The Deadlock of Democracy* (Prentice-Hall, 1963).
2. *Washington Post*, December 8, 1986.

# PART FIVE

# *Democratic Participatory Processes*

# On the Internet . . .

## Sites appropriate to Part Five

Voter Information Services (VIS) is a nonpartisan, nonprofit organization dedicated to voter education. Its primary focus is on publishing VIS ratings of the U.S. Congress and providing voting records of the U.S. Congress in electronic form. These records, as well as a link to other politically related sites, can be found on this page.

```
http://www.vis.org
```

Through a citizens' toolkit of free services, programs, and materials, Project Vote Smart—a national, nonpartisan, nonprofit effort—researches, tracks, and provides to the public independent factual information on over 13,000 candidates and elected officials. Voting records, campaign issue positions, performance evaluations by special interests, campaign contributions, backgrounds, previous experience, and contact information are available. The system allows citizens to monitor and supervise their elected representatives and to compare their campaign promises with their actual job performance once in office.

```
http://www.vote-smart.org
```

The Media and the Dialogue of Democracy focus of the Annenberg Public Policy Center of the University of Pennsylvania analyzes the amount and quality of information available to the electorate, examining how broader elements of the public may become engaged in political affairs.

```
http://www.asc.upenn.edu/appc/dd.htm
```

# CHAPTER 8 Electoral Politics

## 8.1 V. O. KEY, JR.

# *The Voice of the People: An Echo*

V. O. Key, Jr., is considered one of the most influential American political scientists of the twentieth century. He has demonstrated expertise in such diverse areas of study as public opinion and polling analysis, political parties and electoral behavior, state politics (particularly southern states), and interest group theory. Key's book *The Responsible Electorate: Rationality in Presidential Voting, 1936–1960* (Harvard University Press, 1966), from which the following selection is excerpted, is a study of the nature of the American electorate and party organizations. This work relies extensively upon public opinion or polling data and reflects Key's scientific detachment and scrupulous approach, which became a model of precise research emulated by many other contemporary political scientists.

In the following selection, Key analyzes the electorate's voting behavior across party lines and public policy preferences in presidential elections between 1936 and 1960. Key uses this data analysis and historical study of presidential elections to refute the common presumption that American voters are primarily influenced by subjective, nonrational factors (e.g., a candidate's personality). In sharp contrast to this assumption of electoral behavior, Key claims that the general electorate is much more responsible and rational in their voting behavior. He contends that the data he collected indicate that voters are generally consistent in their evaluation of the

performance of incumbent presidents based upon their successful implementation of policies. This linkage between the voters' policy preferences
and electoral decisions to support or reject incumbents is referred to by Key
as retrospective voting.

Key (1908–1963), who received his Ph.D. from the University of
Chicago, has taught at Johns Hopkins University; Yale University, where he
was the Alfred Cowles Professor of Government and served as chairman
of the Department of Political Science; and Harvard University, where he
was the Jonathan Trumbull Professor of American History and Government.
Key is the author of numerous publications, including *The Initiative and
the Referendum in California* (University of California Press, 1939) and
*Public Opinion and American Democracy* (Alfred A. Knopf, 1962). In 1949
he received the prestigious Woodrow Wilson Foundation Award from the
American Political Science Association for his book *Southern Politics* (Alfred
A. Knopf, 1949).

**Key Concept:** the rational voter

*I*n his reflective moments even the most experienced politician senses a
nagging curiosity about why people vote as they do. His power and his position depend upon the outcome of the mysterious rites we perform as opposing
candidates harangue the multitudes who finally march to the polls to prolong
the rule of their champion, to thrust him, ungratefully, back into the void of
private life, or to raise to eminence a new tribune of the people. What kinds of
appeals enable a candidate to win the favor of the great god, The People? What
circumstances move voters to shift their preferences in this direction or that?
What clever propaganda tactic or slogan led to this result? What mannerism of
oratory or style of rhetoric produced another outcome? What band of electors
rallied to this candidate to save the day for him? What policy of state attracted
the devotion of another bloc of voters? What action repelled a third sector of the
electorate?

The victorious candidate may claim with assurance that he has the answers to all such questions. He may regard his success as vindication of his
beliefs about why voters vote as they do. And he may regard the swing of
the vote to him as indubitably a response to the campaign positions he took,
as an indication of the acuteness of his intuitive estimates of the mood of the
people, and as a ringing manifestation of the esteem in which he is held by a
discriminating public. This narcissism assumes its most repulsive form among
election winners who have championed intolerance, who have stirred the passions and hatreds of people, or who have advocated causes known by decent
men to be outrageous or dangerous in their long-run consequences. No func-
tionary is more repugnant or more arrogant than the unjust man who asserts,
with a color of truth, that he speaks from a pedestal of popular approbation.

It thus can be a mischievous error to assume, because a candidate wins,
that a majority of the electorate shares his views on public questions, approves
his past actions, or has specific expectations about his future conduct. Nor does

victory establish that the candidate's campaign strategy, his image, his television style, or his fearless stand against cancer and polio turned the trick. The election returns establish only that the winner attracted a majority of the votes —assuming the existence of a modicum of rectitude in election administration. They tell us precious little about why the plurality was his.

For a glaringly obvious reason, electoral victory cannot be regarded as necessarily a popular ratification of a candidate's outlook. The voice of the people is but an echo. The output of an echo chamber bears an inevitable and invariable relation to the input. As candidates and parties clamor for attention and vie for popular support, the people's verdict can be no more than a selective reflection from among the alternatives and outlooks presented to them. Even the most discriminating popular judgment can reflect only ambiguity, uncertainty, or even foolishness if those are the qualities of the input into the echo chamber. A candidate may win despite his tactics and appeals rather than because of them. If the people can choose only from among rascals, they are certain to choose a rascal.

Scholars, though they have less at stake than do politicians, also have an abiding curiosity about why voters act as they do. In the past quarter of a century they have vastly enlarged their capacity to check the hunches born of their curiosities. The invention of the sample survey—the most widely known example of which is the Gallup poll—enabled them to make fairly trustworthy estimates of the characteristics and behaviors of large human populations. This method of mass observation revolutionized the study of politics—as well as the management of political campaigns. The new technique permitted large-scale tests to check the validity of old psychological and sociological theories of human behavior. These tests led to new hunches and new theories about voting behavior, which could, in turn, be checked and which thereby contributed to the extraordinary ferment in the social sciences during recent decades.

The studies of electoral behavior by survey methods cumulate into an imposing body of knowledge which conveys a vivid impression of the variety and subtlety of factors that enter into individual voting decisions. In their first stages in the 1930's the new electoral studies chiefly lent precision and verification to the working maxims of practicing politicians and to some of the crude theories of political speculators. Thus, sample surveys established that people did, indeed, appear to vote their pocketbooks. Yet the demonstration created its embarrassments because it also established that exceptions to the rule were numerous. Not all factory workers, for example, voted alike. How was the behavior of the deviants from "group interest" to be explained? Refinement after refinement of theory and analysis added complexity to the original simple explanation. By introducing a bit of psychological theory it could be demonstrated that factory workers with optimistic expectations tended less to be governed by pocketbook considerations than did those whose outlook was gloomy. When a little social psychology was stirred into the analysis, it could be established that identifications formed early in life, such as attachments to political parties, also reinforced or resisted the pull of the interest of the moment. A sociologist, bringing to play the conceptual tools of his trade, then could show that those factory workers who associate intimately with like-minded persons on the average vote with greater solidarity than do social isolates. Inquiries conducted with great ingenuity along many such lines have enormously broadened our knowledge of the factors associated with the responses of people to the stimuli presented to them by political campaigns.[1]

Yet, by and large, the picture of the voter that emerges from a combination of the folklore of practical politics and the findings of the new electoral studies is not a pretty one. It is not a portrait of citizens moving to considered decision as they play their solemn role of making and unmaking governments. The older tradition from practical politics may regard the voter as an erratic and irrational fellow susceptible to manipulation by skilled humbugs. One need not live through many campaigns to observe politicians, even successful politicians, who act as though they regarded the people as manageable fools. Nor does a heroic conception of the voter emerge from the new analyses of electoral behavior. They can be added up to a conception of voting not as a civic decision but as an almost purely deterministic act. Given knowledge of certain characteristics of a voter—his occupation, his residence, his religion, his national origin, and perhaps certain of his attitudes—one can predict with a high probability the direction of his vote. The actions of persons are made to appear to be only predictable and automatic responses to campaign stimuli.

Most findings of the analysts of voting never travel beyond the circle of the technicians; the popularizers, though, give wide currency to the most bizarre— and most dubious—theories of electoral behavior. Public-relations experts share in the process of dissemination as they sell their services to politicians (and succeed in establishing that politicians are sometimes as gullible as businessmen). Reporters pick up the latest psychological secret from campaign managers and spread it through a larger public. Thus, at one time a goodly proportion of the literate population must have placed some store in the theory that the electorate was a pushover for a candidate who projected an appropriate "father image." At another stage, the "sincere" candidate supposedly had an overwhelming advantage. And even so kindly a gentleman as General Eisenhower was said to have an especial attractiveness to those of authoritarian personality within the electorate.

Conceptions and theories of the way voters behave do not raise solely arcane problems to be disputed among the democratic and antidemocratic theorists or questions to be settled by the elegant techniques of the analysts of electoral behavior. Rather, they touch upon profound issues at the heart of the problem of the nature and work-ability of systems of popular government. Obviously the perceptions of the behavior of the electorate held by political leaders, agitators, and activists condition, if they do not fix, the types of appeals politicians employ as they seek popular support. These perceptions—or theories affect the nature of the input to the echo chamber, if we may revert to our earlier figure, and thereby control its output. They may govern, too, the kinds of actions that governments take as they look forward to the next election. If politicians perceive the electorate as responsive to father images, they will give it father images. If they see voters as most certainly responsive to nonsense, they will give them nonsense. If they see voters as susceptible to delusion, they will delude them. If they see an electorate receptive to the cold, hard realities, they will give it the cold, hard realities.

In short, theories of how voters behave acquire importance not because of their effects on voters, who may proceed blithely unaware of them. They gain significance because of their effects, both potentially and in reality, on candidates and other political leaders. If leaders believe the route to victory is by projection of images and cultivation of styles rather than by advocacy of policies to cope with the problems of the country, they will project images and cultivate styles to the neglect of the substance of politics. They will abdicate their prime function in a democratic system, which amounts, in essence, to the assumption of the risk of trying to persuade us to lift ourselves by our bootstraps.

Among the literary experts on politics there are those who contend that, because of the development of tricks for the manipulation of the masses, practices of political leadership in the management of voters have moved far toward the conversion of election campaigns into obscene parodies of the models set up by democratic idealists. They point to the good old days when politicians were deep thinkers, eloquent orators, and farsighted statesmen. Such estimates of the course of change in social institutions must be regarded with reserve. They may be only manifestations of the inverted optimism of aged and melancholy men who, estopped from hope for the future, see in the past a satisfaction of their yearning for greatness in our political life.

Whatever the trends may have been, the perceptions that leadership elements of democracies hold of the modes of response of the electorate must always be a matter of fundamental significance. Those perceptions determine the nature of the voice of the people, for they determine the character of the input into the echo chamber. While the output may be governed by the nature of the input, over the longer run the properties of the echo chamber may themselves be altered. Fed a steady diet of buncombe, the people may come to expect and to respond with highest predictability to buncombe. And those leaders most skilled in the propagation of buncombe may gain lasting advantage in the recurring struggles for popular favor.

The perverse and unorthodox argument of this little book is that voters are not fools. To be sure, many individual voters act in odd ways indeed; yet in the large the electorate behaves about as rationally and responsibly as we should expect, given the clarity of the alternatives presented to it and the character of the information available to it. In American presidential campaigns of recent decades the portrait of the American electorate that develops from the data is not one of an electorate strait-jacketed by social determinants or moved by subconscious urges triggered by devilishly skillful propagandists. It is rather one of an electorate moved by concern about central and relevant questions of public policy, of governmental performance, and of executive personality. Propositions so uncompromisingly stated inevitably represent overstatements. Yet to the extent that they can be shown to resemble the reality, they are propositions of basic importance for both the theory and the practice of democracy.

To check the validity of this broad interpretation of the behavior of voters, attention will center on the movements of voters across party lines as they reacted to the issues, events, and candidates of presidential campaigns between 1936 and 1960. Some Democratic voters of one election turned Republican at the next; others stood pat. Some Republicans of one presidential season voted Democratic four years later; others remained loyal Republicans. What motivated these shifts, sometimes large and sometimes small, in voter affection? How did the standpatters differ from the switchers? What led them to stand firmly by their party preference of four years earlier? Were these actions governed by images, moods, and other irrelevancies; or were they expressions of judgments about the sorts of questions that, hopefully, voters will weigh as they responsibly cast their ballots? On these matters evidence is available that is impressive in volume, if not always so complete or so precisely relevant as hindsight would wish. If one perseveres through the analysis of this extensive body of information, the proposition that the voter is not so irrational a fellow after all may become credible.

## NOTES

1. The principal books are: Paul F. Lazarsfeld, Bernard Berelson, and Hazel Gaudet, *The People's Choice* (New York: Duell, Sloan and Pearce, 1944); Angus Campbell, Gerald Gurin, and Warren E. Miller, *The Voter Decides* (Evanston, Ill.: Row, Peterson, 1954); Bernard R. Berelson, Paul F. Lazarsfeld, and William N. McPhee, *Voting* (Chicago: University of Chicago Press, 1954); Angus Campbell, Philip E. Converse, Warren E. Miller, and Donald E. Stokes, *The American Voter* (New York: Wiley, 1960). The periodical literature is almost limitless. The footnotes in Robert E. Lane's *Political Life* (Glencoe, Ill.: Free Press, 1959) constitute a handy guide to most of it.

## 8.2  WALTER DEAN BURNHAM

# Critical Elections and the Mainsprings of American Politics

Walter Dean Burnham's classic study *Critical Elections and the Mainsprings of American Politics* (W. W. Norton, 1970), from which the following selection is taken, is a political analysis and historical overview of American voting behavior.

Burnham (b. 1930) received his M.A. and Ph.D. from Harvard University. He has taught at Kenyon College, Haverford College, Washington University, and the Massachusetts Institute of Technology. He is currently a professor of government at the University of Texas at Austin. In addition to his fellowship at the Center for Advanced Study in the Behavioral Sciences, Burnham has received a Social Science Research Council Fellowship, a grant from the National Science Foundation, and a Guggenheim Fellowship. His expertise and research areas of specialization have included presidential politics, political parties, and electoral behavior. Burnham is coauthor and coeditor, with William N. Chambers, of *The American Party System* (Oxford University Press, 1967) and the author of *Presidential Ballots, 1836–1892* (Johns Hopkins University Press, 1955). He has also published numerous scholarly articles in professional journals of American government.

Burnham used quantitative techniques and presidential and congressional electoral voting data to confirm his cyclical theory of national elections. Using the categories of national election analysis first constructed by V. O. Key, Jr., and several other political scientists at the Survey Research Center at the University of Michigan, Burnham contends that national elections can be scientifically studied through an understanding of the political party identification of the electorate. These national elections conform to a pattern or sequence of recurring events.

A "maintaining election" is the most common type of election and one that preserves the previously established majority party identification of the electorate. It promotes stability and preserves the status quo as far as the existent party balance of power is concerned. In a "deviating election," the electorate's party identification remains stable, although the majority party loses the election. This type of election represents only a temporary shift in party power, and it occurs when a highly charismatic or popular presidential candidate of the minority party seeks office. The "realigning election," or "critical election," is very rare in American party history, as the electorate dramatically changes its party identification, and the majority party that loses in that election becomes the minority party. Burnham cites several classic examples of critical realignments that resulted in a shift of the party balance of power over a long period of time. Most of Burnham's analysis is focused on this type of election, which occurs because of some economic crisis and often results in a decline in voting participation.

**Key Concept:** "realigning elections"

# TOWARD A DEFINITION OF CRITICAL REALIGNMENT

For many decades it has been generally recognized that American electoral politics is not quite "all of a piece" despite its apparent diverse uniformity. Some elections have more important long—range consequences for the political system as a whole than others, and seem to "decide" substantive issues in a more clear-cut way. There has long been agreement among historians that the elections of those of 1800, 1828, 1860, 1896, and 1932, for example, were fundamental turning points in the course of American electoral politics.

Since the appearance in 1955 of V. O. Key's seminal article, "A Theory of Critical Elections," political scientists have moved to give this concept quantitative depth and meaning. In his article, Key isolated New England data in order to demonstrate the differential impact of a compressing sectionalism in the 1890's and of a class-ethnic polarity which emerged in the 1928–36 period.[1] ...

[T]he authors of *The American Voter* developed a typology of elections which included realigning elections—although, of course, on the basis of historical evidence rather than on grounds then observable in survey-research data.[2] Also writing in 1960, E. E. Schattschneider—employing little data but fertile insight—addressed our attention to the utility of viewing the structure of politics brought into being by realignments as systems of action: in the aftermath of realignment, not only voting behavior but institutional roles and policy outputs undergo substantial modifications.[3]

Work done by a number of scholars during the 1960's has fleshed out our empirical knowledge of some of the processes associated with critical realignment. For example, evidence has been brought forward that the adjustments of the 1890's were accompanied and followed by significant transformations in the rules of the game and in the behavioral properties of the American electorate. It has also been suggested that each era between realignments can be described as having its own "party system," even if the formal names of the major parties which form most of its organizational base happen to remain unchanged. A Schattschneiderian analysis has very recently been applied to California for the 1890–1910 period and found to work quite well.[4]

At the same time, there has been rather little effort directed to the task of exploring these phenomena in terms of their implications for effective analysis of American politics across time and space. While Key entitled his seminal article "A *Theory* of Critical Elections," and while both he and Schattschneider clearly regarded realignments of fundamental analytical importance, one is impressed with how little theorizing has been forthcoming in this area. One reason for this paucity may well be an annoying incompleteness in certain key ranges of data analysis; this often leaves us in controversy not only as to the, implications of the facts of change, but even as to the structure of those facts themselves.

It now seems time to attempt at least an interim assessment of the structure, function, and implications of critical realignments for the American political process. Such an effort is motivated in particular by the author's view that critical realignments are of fundamental importance not only to the system of political action called "the American political process" but also to the clarifications of some aspects of its operation. It seems particularly important in a period of obvious political upheaval not only to identify these phenomena and place them in time, but to integrate them into a larger (if still very modest) theory of movement in American politics.

Such a theory must inevitably emphasize the elements of stress and abrupt transformation in our political life at the expense of the consensual, gradualist perspectives which have until recently dominated the scholar's vision of American political processes and behavior. For the realignment phenomenon focuses our attention on "the dark side of the moon." It reminds us that politics as usual in the United States is not politics as always; that there are discrete types of voting behavior and quite different levels of voter response to political stimuli, depending on what those stimuli are and at what point in time they occur; and that American political institutions and leadership, once defined (or redefined) in a "normal phase" of our politics, seem to become part of the very conditions that threaten to overthrow them.

The work of survey research over the past generation has heavily confirmed what earlier students and practitioners of politics in the United States noted: once a stable pattern of voting behavior and of generalized leadership recruitment has been established, it tends to continue over time with only short-term deviations. As is well known, for example, party identification in the 1952–64 period showed only the most glacial movement, in sharp contrast to the actual partisan outcomes of elections....

It is enough to say for the present that any working definition of the concept "critical realignment" must, practically speaking, eliminate both deviating election situations—even landslides such as Theodore Roosevelt's in 1904 or Warren Harding's in 1920—and gradual secular realignments. It must also emphasize that while there are large historical, territorial, and stratification differences in the stability of "stable phases," they reveal comparatively far more of a component of political inertia at the mass base than do realigning eras.

In its "ideal-typical" form, the critical realignment differs from stable alignments eras, secular realignments, and deviating elections in the following basic ways.

1. The critical realignment is characteristically associated with short-lived but very intense disruptions of traditional patterns of voting behavior. Majority parties become minorities; politics which was once competitive becomes non-competitive or, alternatively, hitherto one-party areas now become arenas of intense partisan competition; and large blocks of the active electorate—minorities, to be sure, but perhaps involving as much as a fifth to a third of the voters—shift their partisan allegiance.

2. Critical elections are characterized by abnormally high intensity as well.

   *a.* This intensity typically spills over into the party nominating and platform-writing machinery during the upheaval and results in major shifts in convention behavior from the integrative "norm" as well as in transformations in the internal loci of power in the major party most heavily affected by the pressures of realignment. Ordinarily accepted "rules of the game" are flouted; the party's processes, instead of performing their usual integrative functions, themselves contribute to polarization.

   *b.* The rise in intensity is associated with a considerable increase in ideological polarizations, at first within one or more of the major parties and then between them. Issue distances between the parties are markedly increased, and elections tend to involve highly salient issue-clusters, often with strongly emotional and symbolic overtones, far more than is customary in American electoral politics. One curious property of established leadership as it drifts into the stress of realignment seems to be a tendency to become more rigid and dogmatic, which itself contributes greatly to the explosive "bursting stress" of realignment. Federalist leadership just before 1801 stands in marked contrast to the Jeffersonian afterward, for example. The same may be said (perhaps less certainly) of the inherited inner-circle political style of a John Quincy Adams as the antideferential democratic revolution got under way; of the inflexible leadership of a James Buchanan in 1857–61, which effectively foreclosed a middle-of-the-road northern Democratic alternative to the Republicans; of the rigid defense of the status quo waged by Grover Cleveland and Herbert Hoover in our two greatest depressions; and of Lyndon Johnson's unhappy second administration.

   *c.* The rise in intensity is also normally to be found in abnormally heavy voter participation for the time. This significant increase in political mobilization is not always or uniformly present, to be sure. It is particularly true of realigning cycles with a strong sectional thrust that the areas which are propelled most strongly to one party or the other tend to be those in which turnout does not increase much, or even declines. Similarly, while increases in participation during the 1928–36 period were very heavy in most of the country, they were slight or nonexistent in the South, because the restrictive structure of local politics which had been created at the turn of the century was not disturbed until long after World War II. Moreover, the net effect of the New Deal realignment was to make the South even more lopsidedly Democratic than it had been before. With such exceptions, however, there has still been a general tendency toward markedly increased participation during realigning eras.

3. Historically speaking, at least, national critical realignments have not occurred at random. Instead, there has been a remarkably uniform periodicity in their appearance. A variety of measures can be employed to examine this periodic phenomenon. Sudden shifts in the relationship between percentages

for a given political party in one election and the next can be easily detected through autocorrelation and may present strong evidence of realignment.[5] ...

4. It has been argued, with much truth, that American political parties are essentially constituent parties.[6] That is to say, the political-party subsystem is sited in a socioeconomic system of very great heterogeneity and diversity. For a variety of reasons this party system has tended to be preoccupied with performing the functions of integration and "automatic" aggregation of highly diverse and often antagonistic subgroupings in the population to the near exclusion of concern for development of "modern" mass organization in the European sense. It is neither structured nor widely perceived as a cohesive policy link between voters and officials. The conditions in which our political parties operate, and their normal operating styles and limitations, have produced not a little anguish among an older generation of political scientists who grew to professional maturity during the New Deal and who rightly saw the structure and functioning of our major political parties as a major obstacle to the realization of democratic accountability.[7] It has been well said that "electorally, American parties represent outcomes *in general;* parties seldom shape or represent outcomes *in particular.*"[8]

Critical realignments emerge directly from the dynamics of this constituent-function supremacy in American politics in ways and with implications which will be analyzed subsequently. Here we will only note that since they involve constitutional readjustments in the broadest sense of the term, they are intimately associated with and followed by transformations in large clusters of policy. This produces correspondingly profound alternations in policy and influences the grand institutional structures of American government. In other words, realignments are themselves constituent acts: they arise from emergent tensions in society which, not adequately controlled by the organization or outputs of party politics as usual, escalate to a flash point; they are issue-oriented phenomena, centrally associated with these tensions and more or less leading to resolution adjustments; they result in significant transformations in the general shape of policy; and they have relatively profound aftereffects on the roles played by institutional elites.[9] They are involved with redefinitions of the universe of voters, political parties, and the broad boundaries of the politically possible.

To recapitulate, then, eras of critical realignment are marked by short, sharp reorganizations of the mass coalitional bases of the major parties which occur at periodic intervals on the national level; are often preceded by major third-party revolts which reveal the incapacity of "politics as usual" to integrate, much less aggregate, emergent political demand; are closely associated with abnormal stress in the socioeconomic system; are marked by ideological polarizations and issue-distances between the major parties which are exceptionally large by normal standards; and have durable consequences as constituent acts which determine the outer boundaries of policy in general, though not necessarily of policies in detail. ...

# THE PERIODICITY OF AMERICAN CRITICAL REALIGNMENTS

The precise timing of the conditions which conduce to realignment is conditioned heavily by circumstance, of course: the intrusion of major crises in society and economy with which "politics as usual" in the United States cannot adequately cope, and the precise quality and bias of leadership decisions in a period of high political tension, cannot be predicted in specific time with any accuracy. Yet a broadly repetitive pattern of oscillation between the normal inertia of mass electoral politics and the ruptures of the normal which realignments bring about is clearly evident from the data. So evident is this pattern that one is led to suspect that the truly "normal" structure of American electoral politics at the mass base is precisely this dynamic, even dialectic polarization between long-term inertia and concentrated bursts of change in this open system of action. It may well be that American political institutions, including the major political parties, are so organized that they have a chronic, cumulative tendency toward underproduction of other than currently "normal" policy outputs. They may tend persistently to ignore, and hence not to aggregate, emergent political demand of a mass character until a boiling point of some kind is reached....

[C]ritical realignment emerges as decisively important in the study of the dynamics of American politics. It is as symptomatic of political nonevolution in this country as are the archaic and increasingly rudimentary structures of the political parties themselves. But even more importantly, critical realignment may well be defined as the chief tension-management device available to so peculiar a political system. Historically it has been the chief means through which an underdeveloped political system can be recurrently brought once again into some balanced relationship with the changing socioeconomic system, permitting a restabilization of our politics and a redefinition of the dominant Lockian political formula in terms which gain overwhelming support from the current generation. Granted the relative inability of our political institutions to make gradual adjustments along vectors of *emergent* political demand, critical realignments have been as inevitable as they have been necessary to the normal workings of American politics. Thus once again there is a paradox: the conditions which decree that coalitional negotiation, bargaining, and incremental, unplanned, and gradual policy change become the dominant characteristic of American politics in its normal state also decree that it give way to abrupt, disruptive change with considerable potential for violence. So central has this dialectic been to the workings of our "Tudor polity" across time that the disappearance of one of its key elements, the critical realignment, could only mean that the most fundamental turning point in the entire history of this political system has occurred.

Such a dynamically oriented frame of reference presupposes a holistic view of American politics which is radically different from that which until very recently has tended to dominate the professional literature. The models of American political life and political processes with which we are most familiar emphasize the well-known attributes of pluralist democracy. There are not stable policy majorities. Intense and focused minorities with well-defined interests exert influence on legislation and administrative rule making out of all proportion to their size. The process involves gradual, incremental change secured after bargaining has been completed among a wide array of interested groups who are prepared to accept the conditions of bargaining. It is true that such descriptions apply to a "politics as usual" which is an important fragment of political reality in the United States, but to describe this fragment as the whole of that reality is to assume an essentially ideological posture whose credibility can be maintained only by ignoring the complementary dynamics of American politics as a whole. The study of the electoral process and its relationship to the effectiveness of the system's integration of the demands made of it and to the political elites chosen through it provides an important key for a broader understanding.

The reality of this process taken as a whole seems quite different from the pluralist vision. It is one shot through with escalating tensions, periodic electoral upheavals, and repeated redefinitions of the rules and outcomes-in-general of the political game, as well as redefinitions—by no means always broadening ones—of those who are in fact permitted to play it. One very basic characteristic of American party politics which emerges from a contemplation of critical realignments is a profound incapacity of established political leadership to adapt itself sequentially—or even incrementally?—to emergent political demand generated by the losers in our stormy socioeconomic transformations. American political parties are not action instrumentalities of definable and broad social collectivities; as organizations they are, consequently, interested in control of offices but not of government in the broader sense of which we have been speaking. It follows from this that once successful routines are established or reestablished for winning office, there is no motivation among party leaders to disturb the routines of the game. These routines are disturbed not by adaptive change within the party-policy system, but by the application of overwhelming external force.

# NOTES

1. V. O. Key, Jr., "A Theory of Critical Elections," 17 *Journal of Politics*, pp. 3–18 (1955).

2. Angus Campbell *et al.*, *The American Voter* (New York: Wiley & Sons, 1960), pp. 531–38.

3. E. E. Schattschneider, *The Semisovereign People* (New York: Holt, Rinehart & Winston, 1960), especially pp. 78–96.

4. Michael Rogin, "California Populism and the 'System of 1896,'" 22 *Western Political Quarterly*, pp. 179–96 (1969).

5. Gerald Pomper, "Classification of Presidential Elections," 29 *Journal of Politics*, pp. 535–66 (1967); and Walter Dean Burnham, "American Voting Behavior and the 1964 Election," 12 *Midwest Journal of Political Science*, pp. 1–40 (1968).

6. Theodore J. Lowi, "Party, Policy, and Constitution" in William N. Chambers and Walter Dean Burnham (eds.), *The American Party Systems* (New York: Oxford University Press, 1967), pp. 238–76.

7. The *locus classicus* here is, of course, the report of the ASPA's Committee on Political Parties, *Toward a More Responsible Two-Party System* (1950).

8. Lowi, *op. cit.*, p. 263.

9. The most obviously plausible example of synchronization of institutional-role and policy-output change with critical realignment is the Supreme Court of the United States. The literature is voluminous if frequently inferential, and the subject merits a more explicit relational treatment that it has received. For an excellent account of elite attitudes under the pressure of the crisis of the 1890's and the enormous impetus this gave to judicial creativity in this period, see Arnold M. Paul, *Conservative Crisis and the Rule of Law* (Ithaca, N.Y.: Cornell University Press, 1960).

## 8.3 W. LANCE BENNETT

# The Postmodern Election

The book *The Governing Crisis: Media, Money, and Marketing in American Elections* (St. Martin's Press, 1992), from which the following selection is excerpted, has established W. Lance Bennett as a leading political science scholar. Bennett's systematic linkage of the roles of presidential campaign expenditures, marketing techniques, and the news media (particularly television) and their impact upon the quality of contemporary presidential campaigns and elections has greatly influenced the literature published by many scholars of electoral behavior.

Bennett received his Ph.D. from Yale University in 1974. He is presently a professor of political science at the University of Washington. His research areas of specialization and expertise have included the study of American governmental institutions and politics, electoral behavior and public opinion, political behavior, political psychology and socialization, and political communications and mass media politics. Bennett's other published works include *Public Opinion in American Politics* (Harcourt Brace Jovanovich, 1980) and *News: The Politics of Illusion* (Longman, 1986). He has also published numerous scholarly articles in such professional journals as the *Journal of Communication* and the *Quarterly Journal of Speech*.

In the following selection, Bennett interconnects the perspectives and methods of electoral analysis and voting behavior with communications and media studies. Bennett contends that in recent presidential elections, especially in 1988, there has been a dramatic decline in the electorate's serious interest and satisfaction in its electoral choices. The 1988 presidential campaing was a watershed election, or what Bennett refers to as the first "postmodern election," because the political dialogue of this election lacked any substantive discussion of policy priorities or potential governing agendas. Bennett identifies recent developments that have led to the growing importance of campaign funding, marketing techniques, and the news media in election campaigns. He links these significant campaign factors to the lack of any substantive exchange or communication in contemporary elections.

**Key Concept:** contemporary campaign rhetoric

# TOWARD AN EXPLANATION OF
# ELECTIONS WITHOUT CHOICES

Consider the possibility that tele-rhetoric is something known in academic circles as an epiphenomenon, or, in everyday parlance, as a symptom of something deeper. Television, after all, is a passive medium, having the capacity to show us everything from talking heads, the public affairs people, to Talking Heads, the rock band—everything from commentators trying to make sense of it all, to a rock concert video called "Stop Making Sense."

What this means for elections is that television could bring us an entirely different political reality. Debates could become true forensic exchanges. Conventions could be conferred special status rather than threatened with cancellation. Candidates could be grilled one at a time by journalists for extended periods under the television lights as they are in Sweden, for example.[1] Again as in Sweden and many other countries, networks could be required to provide free air time to candidates, and restrictions could be imposed on the length and format of political commercials (encouraged, of course, by appropriate legislation).

The list of "coulds" and "what ifs" is too long to continue. The point is that TV isn't an explanation; it is merely a medium. Who uses TV? Why do they use it? How do they employ its mediating potentialities? These are the underlying elements of an explanation of tele-rhetoric. As for television itself, it may be a worthy object of blame and a useful window on an important problem, but it is not a valid cause in an explanation. . . .

The decline of voter interest and satisfaction suggests that even the symbolic meanings of electoral choices have become undermined in recent elections, raising questions about this legitimation function of elections and the stability of public support for any elected governments put in office. The main reason for the loss of voter involvement and the declining legitimacy of elected government is an interesting one. Unlike audiences of other spectator media—even television—the political audience is a captive of a political system with no competition. . . .

In most other spectator arenas, decline of patronage and rise of antipathy would be more consequential. Whereas other cultural forums are responsive to the marketplace of popular taste, elections seem relatively immune from the most important market forces of consumer dissatisfaction and outright withdrawal from the marketplace. This curious feature of elections helps us recast traditional thinking about candidate–audience communication. The easy assumption is that the effectiveness of electoral rhetoric turns on some sort of meaningful, positive, responsive exchange between communicator and audience. Throwing out this assumption raises the question of what does shape the content of electoral language these days.

### Begin With Money . . .

Consider this possibility. Instead of competing with each other for audience approval, candidates increasingly compete for the support of a much more select and seldom recognized group: political campaign contributors. Presidential candidates spent more than $300 million in 1988. Although federal funding covers part of a candidate's immediate costs, campaigns must raise more than half these amounts from private backers. Competition for these staggering sums of money is stiff, and the nature of this offstage maneuvering does not reward those who expand the domain of issues and policy proposals. To simplify the point, a restricted range of political ideas makes backing a candidate a safer bet for big money interests. In fact, restricting the range of ideas enables backers to hedge their bets and support both candidates. This is, of course, a bad thing for the health of democracy but a very good thing for those who invest their money in elections....

### Next, Add Marketing...

This brings us to the second major constraint on campaign discourse: the wholesale use of marketing techniques and strategies to generate campaign content. Enter marketing experts into elections in a big way. Their task is to transform a product of diminished or dubious market value into one that wins the largest market share. The result is an emphasis on communication that short-circuits logic, reason, and linguistic richness in favor of image-making techniques. This means that candidates are not sold to a broad general public but to narrow slices or "market segments" of that public. These market segments need not understand the candidates; they need only vote for them. Thus, people are induced to vote for Candidate A over Candidate B much as soap buyers may favor Brand X over Brand Y without feeling they have established a meaningful relationship with their laundry detergent in the process. This further diminishes the importance of language, logic, and reason in the articulation of campaign issues.

Since at least 1980, the Democrats have encountered a difficult problem that once paralyzed the early Goldwater Republicans until the party solved it with the successful marketing of the "new" Richard Nixon and the even newer Ronald Reagan. The problem is simple: a narrow, unpalatable issue agenda that is hard to sell to the general public. The Republican secret was to turn the liability of voter avoidance into an asset by targeting key segments of the shrinking audience that continued to vote. Since votes aren't dollars, profitability isn't an issue. Only victory counts, no matter how many voters boycott the electoral process altogether.

In a classic commentary on the new political age, a Republican strategist ushered in the election of 1980 with these words: "I don't want everyone to vote. Our leverage in the election quite candidly goes up as the voting population goes down."[2] Borrowing this page from the Republican play book, the Democrats in the 1980s went after the narrow market segment of blue collar Republicans with a vengeance. Perhaps the most blatant example involved the Dukakis campaign's avoidance of anything resembling an overt appeal to Jesse Jackson's constituency. This market analysis, even though flawed, was followed to the end: the liberal Jackson wing of the party was not viewed as essential to victory, while the Reagan Democrats were. The constraints on campaign rhetoric and issue definition were equally clear: it was feared that anything said to liberal segments of the fragile voter market would send more conservative segments into the Republican camp. As it turned out, this feared pattern of conservative defection occurred anyway, owing in part to Dukakis' withering at the charge of being a "liberal" (the dreaded L-word), and in larger part to the inability of strategically hamstrung Democrats to compete rhetorically on remaining issues like prayer, patriotism, civil rights, and abortion. Such is political life without a credible rhetorical vision.

### Now, Try to Control the News Media...

In the three-factor model proposed here, the above two constraints necessarily engage a third limiting condition operating on electoral communication: the highly controlled use of the news media. The press, like the voters, generally regards issues and ideas as the most important grounds for electoral choice. Idea-less elections antagonize reporters searching for meaningful differences between the candidates to write home about. An aroused press can be expected to assume an adversarial role, leaping on inconsistencies, making much of candidate slips and blunders, seizing on anything inflammatory in the absence of much to say about policy positions. As a result, campaigns tend to isolate their candidates from the press corps, and stick to a tightly controlled and carefully scripted daily schedule. This means, in Roger Ailes' words,* that reporters are handed a lot of visuals and attacks, while mistakes (and ideas) are held to a minimum.

It is by now well accepted that good media strategy entails three requirements: keeping the candidate away from the press; feeding the press a simple, telegenic political line of the day; and making sure the daily news line echoes ("magnify" may be the better word) the images from campaign ads, thus blurring the distinction between commercials and "reality."[3] Candidates and their "handlers" vary in the ability to keep the press at bay, but when they succeed, reporters are left with little but an impoverished set of campaign slogans to report. As ABC reporter Sam Donaldson said on an election-week news analysis program in a tone that resembled that of the coroner disclosing an autopsy result: "When we cover the candidates, we cover their campaigns as they outline them."[4] Thus, a willing, if unhappy, press becomes a channel for much the same meaningless tele-rhetoric that emerges from the interplay of advertising strategy and the concessions made to campaign contributors.

In recent years the media have shown signs of becoming more critical of campaigns. Encouraged by a public that is angry at candidates and politicians, the news contains increased coverage of the celluloid world of marketed candidates and media manipulation. This increase in media coverage of media campaigns, however, has not brought candidates out of hiding or appreciably affected the way campaigns are run. The ironic result of media attempts to "deconstruct" candidate images and expose the techniques of news control

---

* [Roger Ailes was candidate George Bush's consultant during the 1988 presidential campaign.— Ed.]

may be to reinforce public cynicism about the whole process. Taking the public behind the political illusions has not succeeded in bringing the candidates out of hiding behind those illusions. The net result is still an election system dominated by mass-marketed, Madison Avenue messages that deliver quick emotional punches instead of lasting visions and governing ideas to voters. In other words, the way in which news organizations have exercised their critical skills may result less in changing the system than in reinforcing (albeit inadvertently) the public cynicism that helps keep it going.

One might think the press would do something bold to elevate election news content above the intellectual level of political commercials. For example, the various news organizations could separate themselves from the pack mentality and develop a thoughtful agenda of important issues (based, if need be, on opinion polls) and score the candidates on how well they address these issues. But that is not very likely. A news executive vetoed out of hand a very modest version of this suggestion. When asked why the media did not make more of George Bush's well-documented connections to the Iran–Contra arms scandal and the CIA hiring of Panamanian dictator Manuel Noriega, the producer of one of the three network evening newscasts explained simply, "We don't want to look like we're going after George Bush."[5]

Despite this reluctance to tackle candidates on the issues, it is apparently appropriate to go after them on grounds of health (Thomas Eagleton in 1972), character (Edmund Muskie, 1972), gaffes and malapropisms (Gerald Ford, 1976), family finances (Geraldine Ferraro, 1984), extramarital sex (Gary Hart, 1988), or hypocrisy and gall (Dan Quayle, 1988). However, the press draws the line when it comes to pursuing issues beyond where the candidates are willing to take them.

Never mind the resulting decline in the quality of campaign discourse and citizen interest in politics (not to mention public faith in the press), the media seem determined to steer a safe course of "objectivity." Elaborating the doctrine behind Sam Donaldson's earlier words, the ABC vice president in charge of campaign coverage in 1984 and 1988 said: "It's my job to take the news as they choose to give it to us and then, in the amount of time that's available, put it into the context of the day or that particular story.... The evening newscast is not supposed to be the watchdog on the Government."[6]

This self-styled impression of what the media are "supposed to be" has changed about 180 degrees from the hallowed role of the press defined by the likes of Peter Zenger and Thomas Jefferson. The new norm of press passivity enables increasingly profitable and decreasingly critical mass media to chase political candidates in dizzying circles like cats after their own tails. To wit, two-thirds of the coverage in 1988 was coverage of coverage: articles on the role of television, news about campaign strategy, and updates on voter fatigue in response to meaningless media fare. As the irrepressible French social critic Jacques Ellul said about the contemporary mass communications industry: "The media refer only to themselves."[7]

Each of these related constraints on political communication imposes a substantial limit on what candidates say to voters, creating, in turn, important limits on the quality of our most important democratic experience. Taken together, these limiting conditions go a long way toward explaining the alarming absence of meaningful choices and satisfied voters in recent elections. These restrictions on political speech also explain the mysterious elevation of tele-rhetoric to gospel standing in contemporary campaigns. With ideas safely out of the way and the press neutralized, television has little use other than as a medium for turning a seemingly endless election process into the world's longest running political commercial without programmatic interruption.

Other puzzles about the contemporary election scene also become less baffling. Take the rise of negative campaigning, for example. Because of the severe content restrictions imposed by the three limits outlined above, candidates suffer the marketing problem of appearing unattractive (i.e., negative). In this strange world, victory goes to the candidate who manages to appear the least unattractive or negative. The easiest strategy is to play up the opponent's negatives, in an effort to look less negative by comparison. (One can hardly hope to look positive in this context.) Hence, the obsession with the opponent's negatives, as emphasized in commercials and played up in news sound bites spoon–fed to the press.

All of the above—the rhetoric without vision, the telegenic sound bites, and commercialized advertising and news production—happen to play best (or, in keeping with the new spirit, less offensively) on television. In the words of a leading campaign consultant commenting on a race in California, "A political rally in California consists of three people around a television set."[8]

Considering the magnitude of these forces working against the traditional forms and contents of political communication, it is not surprising that candidates say so little these days. One marvels that they are able to say anything at all.

## ARE THE VOTERS BLAMELESS?

Where do citizens fit into this picture? On the one hand, the long list of public complaints makes it understandable why many have dropped out of the political process. Yet, without some sort of effective public input, little is likely to change. Even when signs of citizen life emerge, it is not always clear that people are tracking on the big picture. Led by Oklahoma, California, and Colorado, for example, a national stirring to limit the terms of state legislators has begun. In an action that raised constitutional questions, Colorado voters even approved limits on the length of time their national representatives can serve. There is little doubt that elected officials at all levels hear these signals from voters. The question is whether term limits will accomplish anything beyond signalling voter displeasure to lawmakers....

What are we to make of the whole collection of strange American voting habits, ranging from one of the lowest turnout rates among Western industrial democracies, to reelecting incumbents after blaming professional politicians as a group for the mess in Washington? Are these and other curious features of voter mentality signs of gross negligence and ignorance, or are they the results of people trying (unsuccessfully) to respond sensibly to a system that offers them few meaningful choices? This last question, it turns out, is one of the old-est and still unresolved debates about the American voter. There is evidence for both sides, suggesting that we are not dealing with an "either–or" type of choice, but a more complex relationship between individual voters and the political system in which they operate.

On the "voters are fools" side of the argument, there is considerable ev-idence that Americans possess little knowledge about the "who, what, when, where, and how" of government.[9] Moreover, voters do not tend to think in big-picture, ideological terms; instead they rely on party and group identifications, along with an occasional big issue to guide their choices.[10] Given this portrait of the voter, it is tempting to conclude that candidates have little incentive to ele-vate the level of national debate. Even if they did, there is little chance that such ignorant voters would approve of sophisticated political debates. Two leading students of American elections have described voters in the following terms:

> Most of them are not interested in most public issues most of the time. In a so-ciety like ours, it apparently is quite possible to live comfortably without being politically concerned. Political activity is costly and eats up time and energy at an astounding rate.... One must attend meetings, listen to or participate in discus-sions, write letters, attempt to persuade or be persuaded by others, and engage in other time-consuming labor. This means foregoing other activities, like devoting extra time to the job, playing with the children, and watching TV.[11]

"Wait a minute!" say proponents of the opposing "voters are *not* fools" school. If voters sometimes act like fools, it is because politicians treat them that way, offering few meaningful choices and seldom inviting the public inside the decision-making process. Supporting this claim is a long research tradition that attributes the failings inside voters' heads to the choices they are offered in the election taking place outside.[12] Viewed this way, voters make the best sense out of what little candidates may offer them. When few issues are solid enough to use for thinking about the future, voters look back and vote "retrospectively," based on their judgments about who did the best overall job in the past.[13] When there are no issues or ideas (whether forward- or backward-looking), voters tend to screen candidate personalities for information about leadership and emotional qualities.[14] When reliable information of any sort becomes scarce, voters continue to do the best they can, trying to decode political advertise-ments and well-staged public appearances for clues about what the candidates represent. All of this explains why many voters say they are increasingly un-happy with their choices these days, but remain willing and able to make them (and why other voters, finding nothing in the way of useful information, have simply given up).

Are voters a cause or a casualty in an electoral system that offers few meaningful choices? Probably both. The dual dangers of unsophisticated vot-ers and shallow candidates have been with us for some time. In recent years, the problem has been that these weaknesses in the electoral process have in-creasingly been moved to the center, institutionalized, if you will. As a result, candidates with ideas and voters who might want to think about them are less and less likely to find each other in the numbers required to create governing coalitions.

*Chapter 8*
*Electoral*
*Politics*

1. Erik Asard, "Election Campaigns in Sweden and the U.S.: Convergence or Divergence?," *American Studies in Scandinavia* 21, no. 2 (1989): 70–85.

2. Paul Weyrich quoted in Thomas Ferguson and Joel Rogers, "The Reagan Victory: Corporate Coalitions in the 1980 Campaign," in Ferguson and Rogers, eds., *The Hidden Election: Politics and Economics in the 1980 Presidential Campaign* (New York: Pantheon, 1981), p. 4.

3. See, for example, Mark Hertsgaard, *On Bended Knee: The Press and the Reagan Presidency* (New York: Farrar, Straus and Giroux, 1988).

4. "This Week with David Brinkley," ABC, November 6, 1988.

5. Unnamed source, cited in Mark Hertsgaard, "Electoral Journalism: Not Yellow, but Yellow-Bellied," *New York Times*, September 21, 1988, p. A15.

6. Ibid.

7. Jacques Ellul, "Preconceived Ideas about Mediated Information," in Everett M. Rogers and Francis Bolle, eds. *The Media Revolution in America and Western Europe* (Norwood, N. J.: Ablex Publishing Co., 1985), p. 107.

8. Robert Shrum, quoted in R. W. Apple, Jr. "Candidates Focus on Television Ads," *New York Times*, October 19, 1986, p. A16.

9. For a review of research on voter ignorance, see Eric R. A. N. Smith, *The Unchanging American Voter* (Berkeley: University of California Press, 1989), Ch. 4.

10. The classic work on this remains Angus Campbell, Philip E. Converse, Warren E. Miller, and Donald E. Stokes, *The American Voter* (New York: John Wiley, 1960). Smith's argument (ibid.) is that little has changed to warrant altering this portrait of our unsophisticated electorate.

11. Nelson W. Polsby and Aaron Wildavsky, *Presidential Elections*, 6th ed. (New York: Scribner's, 1984), pp. 5–6.

12. This tradition follows from the work of V. O. Key (with Milton C. Cummings), *The Responsible Electorate: Rationality in Presidential Voting 1936–1960* (New York: Vintage Books, 1966).

13. See Morris P. Fiorina, *Retrospective Voting in American National Elections* (New Haven, Conn.: Yale University Press, 1981).

14. See Benjamin Page, *Choices and Echoes in Presidential Elections* (Chicago: University of Chicago Press, 1978).

## CHAPTER 9

The Media and
Public Opinion

## 9.1 MICHAEL PARENTI

# *From Cronkite's Complaint to Orwell's Oversight*

Michael Parenti (b. 1933) has been a spokesperson for the American ideological left for the last 30 years. His book *Inventing Reality: The Politics of the Mass Media* (St. Martin's Press, 1986), from which the following selection is excerpted, is a study of the impact of mass media on public opinion in the American political context.

Parenti's work has been interpreted as a classic study of political elitism because Parenti emphasizes the conservative nature of the mass media in its uncritical support of established governmental and private powers and interests in American society. The political theory, or perspective, of political elitism is an interpretation of the division of power in the United States, which claims that a minority of the population representing the leadership of corporate, military, and governmental institutions makes the most significant policies for society. Parenti contends that in the American political system there is a concentration of power among an unelected elite who represent their own private interests and ignore the public interest.

In the following selection, Parenti argues that the contemporary mass media conform to the policy objectives of the dominant governmental and corporate leadership in the United States. In electoral campaigns, the media emphasizes trivial issues concerning candidates rather than issues of substantive significance for the electorate. As a consequence, according to

Parenti, the electorate remains passive, apathetic, and unlikely to mobilize around serious policy considerations. In addition, media political coverage focuses on the two major parties as the legitimate competitors in the electoral arena, while denying the significance of any substantive challenge of a minor or third party. Parenti concludes that the news media designs the political world for American citizens by controlling the public issue agenda.

Parenti received his M.A. from Brown University and his Ph.D. from Yale University. He has taught at numerous colleges and universities, including the State University of New York at Stony Brook and at Albany, Cornell University, and American University. He is the author of many innovative studies on American government, including *Democracy for the Few* (St. Martin's Press, 1974) and *Power and the Powerless* (St. Martin's Press, 1978). He has also been an active contributor of scholarly articles to various journals and periodicals, such as *Commonweal, The Progressive*, and *Society.*

**Key Concept:** the media's impact upon public discourse

# IMAGE POLITICS

The press sees the established governmental leadership as essential to the maintenance of social order; and it gives more credence to public officials, corporate representatives, church leaders and university officers that it does to protesters, taxpayers, consumers, workers, parishioners, and students.

The foremost leader in the United States is the president, "who is viewed as the ultimate protector of order."[1] A systematic examination of twenty-five years of presidential news in the *New York Times* and *Time* magazine, as well as ten years of CBS broadcasts, reveals a "consistent pattern of favorable coverage of the President," with sympathetic stories outnumbering critical ones by two to one.[2] More often than not, a president's viewpoint, especially if it has no liberal slant, is transmitted by the press with no opposing set of facts. Thus when President Reagan claimed credit for the 1982 extension of the Voting Rights Act and for appointing more minority members and females to administrative posts and waging a more vigorous enforcement of civil rights than previous administrations, the press faithfully reported his claims without pointing out that in fact he had threatened to veto the Voting Rights Act (and only signed it because it passed both houses by veto-proof majorities) and had actually cut back on minority and female appointments and on civil rights enforcement.[3] And in the 1984 campaign when President Reagan asserted he would "never" attack Social Security, most of the major media gave top play to his statement without noting that in previous years he had repeatedly attacked Social Security, equating it and other entitlement programs with welfare—which he hated....

By focusing on "human interest" trivia, on contest rather than content, the media make it difficult for the public to give intelligent expression to political life and to mobilize around the issues. Thus the media have—intentionally or not—a conservative effect on public discourse. Given short shrift are the concerns of millions of people regarding nuclear arms escalation, Pentagon spending, tax reform, war in Central America, unemployment, and poverty. The democratic input, the great public debate about the state of the Union and its national policies, the heightening of political consciousness and information levels—all the things democratic electoral campaigns are supposed to foster—are crowded off the stage by image politics.

Not only during election campaigns but just about on every other occasion the news media prefer surface to substance, emphasizing the eye-catching visuals, the attention-catching "special angle" report, and the reassuring and comforting stories, while slighting the deeper, more important but politically more troublesome and more controversial themes. There is so much concentration on surface events that we often have trouble grasping the content of things, so much focus on action and personality that we fail to see the purposive goal of the action. For instance, during 1981, President Reagan dismantled major portions of forty years of domestic social legislation, initiated enormous tax cuts for rich individuals and corporations, dramatically escalated an already huge military spending program, and launched a series of cold-war confrontations against the Soviet Union—all policies of great import. However, the theme that predominated in most of the stories about those crucial actions was whether Reagan was "winning" or "losing" in his contests with Congress, the bureaucracy, labor, and foreign governments. Thus momentous political issues were reduced to catchy but trivial questions about Reagan's political "score card," his efficacy as a leader, and his personal popularity.[4]

# MONOPOLY POLITICS

Such as it is, media electoral coverage is lavishly bestowed on the two major parties, while minor parties are totally ignored or allotted but a few minutes, if that, over the entire campaign. Thus the media help perpetuate the procapitalist, two-party monopoly.

In recent contests, presidential candidates of the Communist Party, the Citizens Party, the Socialist Workers Party, the Workers World Party, and others did all the things presidential candidates are supposed to do. They met thousands of voters on street corners, spoke on college campuses and at voter forums, issued position papers and press releases, traveled around the country, and probably spoke directly to more people than did the major candidates. But on election day, most voters had never heard of them. Deprived of mass media coverage, a third party cannot reach the voting masses. Most people remain unaware not only of its candidates but of its programs, issues, and critiques of status quo politics. . . .

Media exposure confers legitimacy on one's candidacy. By giving elaborate national coverage only to Republicans and Democrats, news organizations are letting us know that these are the only ones worth considering. Candidates who are not taken seriously by the media swiftly discover that they are not taken seriously by many voters. Even when they make face-to face contact with live audiences and with voters on street corners, they still lack legitimacy as candidates for national office, being more a curiosity than a serious choice. People may like what third-party candidates say, because often they are the only ones saying anything, but they usually won't vote for someone who doesn't have a chance. Since third-party candidates are not in the news, they are considered to be not really in the race; and since they are not in the race, this justifies treating them as if they are not news. . . .

## DO THE MEDIA MANAGE OUR MINDS?

Are the media independent of government influence? If not, what is the nature of that influence? Are the media dominated by particular class interests? If so, does this dominance carry over into news content? Does control of news content translate into propaganda? Does propaganda translate into indoctrination of the public mind? And does indoctrination translate into support for politics? These questions guide the present inquiry: let us run through them again, a little more slowly.

1. In the United States a free press is defined as one unhampered by repressive laws. As we shall find, government interference with the news is not the only or even the major problem. More often the danger is that the press goes along willingly with officialdom's view of things at home and abroad, frequently manifesting a disregard for accuracy equal to that of policymakers. To be sure, questions are sometimes raised and criticisms voiced, but most of these are confined to challenging the *efficacy* of a particular policy rather than its underlying interests especially if the interests are powerful ones.
2. The newspeople who participate in the many forums on freedom of the press usually concentrate on threats to the press from without, leaving untouched the question of coercion from within, specifically from media owners. Are the media free from censorial interference by their owners? Does ownership translate into actual control over information, or does responsibility for the news still rest in the hands of journalists and editors who are free to report what they want—limited only by professional canons of objectivity? As we shall see, the working press, including newspaper editors and television news producers and even the top media executives are beholden to media owners and corporate advertisers. More specifically, the owners exercise control through the power to hire and fire, to promote and demote anyone they want and by regularly intervening directly into the news production process with verbal and written directives.
3. But does control over media content and personnel translate into ruling class propaganda? Even if we allow that owners ultimately determine what is or is not publicized, can it be assumed that the end product serves their interests and gives only their viewpoint? I will argue that, except for momentary departures, a capitalist ideological perspective regarding events at home and abroad rather consistently predominates. The system of control works, although not with absolute perfection and

is not devoid of items that might at times be discomforting to the rich and powerful.

4. A final concern: Does ruling class propaganda translate into indoctrination of the public? It might be argued that even if the news is cast in a capitalist ideological mold, the public does not swallow it and has ways of withstanding the propaganda. The news may be manipulated by the press lords, but are we manipulated by the news? It is this last question I want to deal with here at some length. For if the press exercises only an inconsequential influence over the public, then we are dealing with a tempest in a teapot and are being unduly alarmist about "mind management."

Early studies of the media's impact on voting choices found that people seemed surprisingly immune from media manipulation. Campaign propaganda usually reinforced the public's preferences rather than altered them. People exposed themselves to media appeals in a selective way, giving more credence and attention to messages that bolstered their own views. Their opinions and information intake also were influenced by peers, social groups, and community, so the individual did not stand without a buffer against the impact of the media. The press, it was concluded, had only a "minimal effect."[5]

At first glance, these findings are reassuring: People seem fairly self-directed in their responses to the media and do not allow themselves to be mindlessly directed. Democracy is safe. But troublesome questions remain. If through "selective exposure" and "selective attention" we utilize the media mainly to reinforce our established predispositions, where do the predispositions themselves come from? We can point to various socializing agencies: family, school, peer groups, work place—and the media themselves. Certainly some of our internalized political predispositions come from the dominant political culture that the media have had a hand in shaping—and directly from earlier exposure to the media themselves.

Our ability to discriminate is limited in part by how we have been conditioned by previous media exposures. The selectivity we exercise is not an autonomous antidote to propaganda but may feed right into it, choosing one or another variation of the same establishment offering. Opinions that depart too far from the mainstream are likely to be rejected out of hand. In such situations, our "selectivity" is designed to *avoid* information and views that contradict the dominant propaganda, a propaganda we long ago implicitly embraced as representative of "the nature of things." Thus, an implanted set of conditioned responses are now mistakenly identified as our self-generated political perceptions, and the public's selective ingestion of the media's conventional fare is wrongly treated as evidence of the "minimal effect" of news organizations.

In addition, more recent empirical evidence suggest that, contrary to the earlier "minimal effects" theory, the news media are able to direct our attention to certain issues and shape our opinions about them. One study found that "participants exposed to a steady stream of news about defense or about pollution came to believe that defense or pollution were more consequential problems."[6] Other studies found that fluctuations in public concern for problems like civil rights, Vietnam, crime, and inflation over the last two decades reflected variations in the attention paid to them by the major media.[7]

Theorists who maintain that the media have only a minimal effect on campaigns ought to try convincing those political candidates who believe they survive and perish because of media exposure or the lack of it. And as we saw earlier, the inability to buy media time or attract press coverage consigns third-party candidates to the dim periphery of American politics. The power to ignore political viewpoints other than the standard two-party offerings is more than minimal, it is monumental. Media exposure frequently may be the single most crucial mobilizer of votes, even if certainly not the only one.

If much of our informational and opinion intake is filtered through our previously established mental predilections, these predilections are often not part of our conscious discernment but of our unexamined perceptual conditioning—which brings us back to an earlier point: *Rather than being rational guardians against propaganda, our predispositional sets, having been shaped by prolonged exposure to earlier outputs of that same propaganda, may be active accomplices....*

If the press cannot mold our every opinion, it can frame the perceptual reality around which our opinions take shape. Here may lie the most important effect of the news media: they set the issue agenda for the rest of us, choosing what to emphasize and what to ignore or suppress, in effect, organizing much of our political world for us. *The media may not always be able to tell us what to think, but they are strikingly successful in telling us what to think about.*[8]

Along with other social, cultural, and educational agencies, the media teach us tunnel vision, conditioning us to perceive the problems of society as isolated particulars, thereby stunting our critical vision. Larger causalities are reduced to immediately distinct events, while the linkages of wealth, power, and policy go unreported or are buried under a congestion of surface impressions and personalities. There is nothing too essential and revealing that cannot be ignored by the American press and nothing too trivial and superficial that cannot be accorded protracted play.

In sum, the media set the limits on public discourse and public understanding. They may not always mold opinion but they do not always have to. It is enough that they create opinion visibility, giving legitimacy to certain views and illegitimacy to others. The media do the same to substantive issues that they do to candidates, raising some from oblivion and conferring legitimacy upon them, while consigning others to limbo. This power to determine the issue agenda, the information flow, and the parameters of political debate so that it extends from ultra-right to no further than moderate center, is if not total, still totally awesome.

## NOTES

1. Herbert Gans, "The Message Behind the News," *Columbia Journalism Review,* January/February 1979, p. 45.
2. Michael Grossman and Martha Kumar, *Portraying the President* (Baltimore: Johns Hopkins University Press, 1981).

3. The above facts and figures are from James Nathan Miller, "Ronald Reagan and the Techniques of Deception," *Atlantic Monthly*, February 1984, pp. 62–68.

4. W. Lance Bennett, *News, The Politics of Illusion* (New York: Longman, 1983), pp. 9–10.

5. P. Lazarsfeld, B. Berelson, and H. Gaudet, *The People's Choice* (New York: Columbia University Press, 1948); C. I. Hovel et al., *Experiments on Mass Communication* (Princeton, N.J.: Princeton University Press, 1949).

6. S. Iyengar, M. Peters, and D. Kinder, "Experimental Demonstrations of the 'Not-So-Minimal' Consequences of Television News Programs," *American Political Science Review*, 76, December 1982, p. 852.

7. G. R. Funkhouser, "The Issues of the Sixties," *Public Opinion Quarterly*, 37, pp. 62–75; Michael MacKuen and Steven Coombs, *More than News* (Beverly Hills, Calif.: Sage Publications, 1981); also the essay by MacKuen therein.

8. The point was first made by B. Cohen, *The Press and Foreign Policy* (Princeton, N.J.: Princeton University Press, 1963), p. 16; a similar point is made in Maxwell Mc-Combs and Donald Shaw, *The Emergence of American Political Issues: the Agenda-Setting Function of the Press* (St. Paul, Minn.: West, 1977), p. 5.

## 9.2 KATHLEEN HALL JAMIESON AND KARLYN KOHRS CAMPBELL

# *News and Advertising in the Political Campaign*

In 1992 Kathleen Hall Jamieson and Karlyn Kohrs Campbell, two leading American experts on mass media, political communication, and political rhetoric, published *The Interplay of Influence: News, Advertising, Politics, and the Mass Media,* 3rd. ed. (Wadsworth, 1992). In the book, Jamieson and Campbell analyze the intricate interrelationships between presidential campaigns and elections, the media and political advertising, the media and the manipulation of news information, marketing techniques, recent media technological advances, and political journalism. Their analysis has been incorporated into the works of many other contemporary scholars of the mass media and public opinion.

Jamieson is a professor of communication and dean of the Annenberg School of Communication at the University of Pennsylvania. Her areas of research have included presidential and executive politics, electoral behavior and public opinion, and the mass media and political communication. Jamieson's scholarly publications include *Packaging the Presidency* (Oxford University Press, 1984), which received the 1985 Speech Communication Association Book Award; *Eloquence in an Electronic Age* (Oxford University Press, 1988), which received the 1989 Speech Communication Association Book Award; and *Dirty Politics: Deception, Distraction, and Democracy* (Oxford University Press, 1992).

Campbell (b. 1937) is a professor of speech communication at the University of Minnesota and a distinguished scholar in the field of rhetoric. She received the 1987 Charles M. Woolbert Award from the Speech Communication Association for scholarship of originality and influence. Campbell's scholarly works include *Critiques of Contemporary Rhetoric* (Wadsworth, 1972), *The Rhetorical Act* (Wadsworth, 1982), and *Man Cannot Speak for Her* (Praeger, 1989). Campbell has also published many articles on political rhetoric and the mass media in scholarly journals.

In the following selection from *The Interplay of Influence,* Jamieson and Campbell contend that many scholars often falsely distinguish between image and issues or character and positions as expressed through various messages conveyed by the mass media. They insist that such political communication factors are often closely intertwined in contemporary presidential election campaigns. The authors also emphasize the dramatic changes in the communication of political information because of television.

**Key Concept:** the impact of media on political information

THE CAMPAIGN    The media tend to see political campaigns as contests. The contest is described in battle metaphors, sports metaphors, or a combination of the two. If the electoral process is viewed as a game, it has contending sides, rules, and a goal.[1] Sports metaphors enable reporters to describe vividly the stages of the process (early primaries are the first innings or the first quarter), the intensity of the struggle (two outs in the ninth with the runner at bat, third down in the last quarter), the stakes (Super Bowl Sunday, the World Series), and the outcome (touchdown, home run).

Battle metaphors enable reporters to describe the staff and volunteers as troops, the primary as a battleground, the strategy as a process of mapping out options, and the outcome as analogous to such memorable names as Armageddon or Waterloo. Strategic options include a holding action, a retreat, a withdrawal, a first strike, or a pre-emptive strike. The outcome can be defeat, victory, or a rout. Candidates can declare a truce, sign an armistice, sign a peace treaty, declare war, or continue hostilities. Reporters can also dip into the biblical past to resurrect images of David and Goliath or, in the case of feuding among ideological kin, Cain and Abel. In 1988, for the first time in recent history, metaphors of the campaign as war occurred more often than sports metaphors.

THE CANDIDATES    In the linguistic world of the news media, there are front-runners, contenders, minor candidates, and also-rans. The criteria employed by reporters to determine to which category a candidate ought to be assigned vary from campaign to campaign. Before the Campaign Finance Law required that a candidate qualify in twenty states to receive matching funds, the presidential candidate with the most and the earliest "wins" was considered the front-runner. The new finance rules changed the criteria. To be a serious contender and not a minor candidate, a candidate has to qualify for matching funds.

Front-runners and contenders receive more news coverage than minor candidates and also-rans, and the type of coverage they receive differs. Also-rans are treated as human interest oddities. Their stands on issues are not probed; their chances of winning are not pondered. It is assumed they are going to lose.

Once classified a contender, a candidate is subject to comparison to past political figures. Is this candidate glamorous, dynamic, wealthy? Or cold, sneaky, untrustworthy? Like Roosevelt, Kennedy, Reagan, Nixon? Is this a common man like Truman? Or an innovator, a communicator, like FDR? Is this a bookish, intellectual candidate like Wilson or Stevenson? Democrats analogize Republicans to Hoover and Nixon; Republicans respond by tarring Democrats as Carteresque.

Candidates try to act so that journalists will associate their actions with those of admired historical figures such as Lincoln and FDR. They also identify with those people, places, and actions that the intended voters stereotype positively, and divorce themselves from those we negatively stereotype.

So, for example, in his successful 1990 campaign for the Democratic nomination for Cook County Board President, Richard Phelan sits at a *"Cheers"*-like bar, and tells how his parents "sacrificed" to enable him to study at Notre Dame. He worked at *"a one-lawyer firm,"* he says and *built it* into one of the largest in the Midwest. "The *boys in the backroom"* carp about his success, he notes, but adds that that is because he plans to work *for the taxpayers* and not *the professional politicians.*

When a candidate succeeds in sculpting an image consistent with a stereotype, it begins to play out in press coverage. For example, a report in the *Washington Post* described the 1990 Republican Texas gubernatorial nominee this way:

> Williams, a West Texas millionaire oilman, is the most colorful political character to appear on the Lone Star scene in years. He brags about his fistfights, loves to drink beer, rides horses in his TV commercials, designs his swimming pools in the shape of cowboy boots, paints all his possessions, including two airplanes, in the maroon and white colors of his beloved Texas A & M Aggies, says he wants to double the state's prison capacity and get more criminals "pounding rocks," and talks wistfully about Texas the way it was when his Daddy was around.[2]

But stereotypes can cut two ways. When Williams refused to debate Democratic nominee Ann Richards, she told the press, "You can't pretend to be John Wayne and run from a girl." [3]

## HOW HAS TELEVISION CHANGED POLITICS?

Television has changed politics by changing the way in which information is disseminated, by altering the way politics happens, and by changing our patterns of response to politics. By giving the electorate direct access to the candidates, television diminished the role of party in the selection of the major party nominees. By centering politics on the person of the candidate, television accelerated the electorate's focus on character rather than issues.

Television has altered the forms of political communication, as well. The messages on which most of us rely are briefer than they once were. The stump speech of $1\frac{1}{2}$ to 2 hours that characterized nineteenth-century political discourse has given way to the 30-second spot ad and the 10-second sound bite in broadcast news. Increasingly the audience for speeches is not that standing in front of the politician but the viewing audience that will hear and see a snippet of the speech on the news.

In these abbreviated forms, much of what constituted the traditional political discourse of earlier ages has been lost. In 15 or 30 seconds, a speaker cannot establish the historical context that shaped the issue in question, cannot detail the probable causes of the problem, cannot examine alternative proposals and argue that one is preferable to others. In snippets, politicians assert but do not argue.

Because television is an intimate medium, speaking through it required a changed political style that was more conversational, personal, and visual than that of old-style stump oratory. Reliance on television means that increasingly our political world contains memorable pictures rather than memorable words. And words increasingly have been spoken in places chosen to heighten their impact. "We have nothing to fear but fear itself" has given way to "Let them come to Berlin" and "Mr. Gorbachev, tear down this wall." Schools teach us to analyze words and print; in a world in which politics is increasingly visual, informed citizenship requires a new set of skills.

Recognizing the power of television's pictures, politicians craft televisual, staged events called pseudo-events designed to attract media coverage. Much of the political activity we see on television news has been crafted by politicians, their speechwriters, and their public relations advisers for televised consumption. Sound bites in news and answers to questions in debates increasingly sound like ads.

Political managers, termed "handlers" in 1988, spend large amounts of time ensuring that their clients appear in visually compelling settings so that the pictures seen in news will reinforce those seen in ads. In debates, candidates recall those staged pseudo-events.

By focusing on mainstream values, television mainstreams its viewers. Heavy viewers of television differ from light viewers in some politically relevant ways. The likelihood that a character in a prime-time program will be the victim of a crime is higher than it is in real life. Heavier viewers believe that they are more likely to be victims of crime than they actually are. Heavy viewers are also more conservative in their views about the socially appropriate response to crime. They are, for example, more likely than light viewers to favor heavy sentences and use of the death penalty. Heavy-viewing conservatives and heavy-viewing liberals are more likely to agree on how to respond to crime than are heavy- and light-viewing liberals.

But whereas heavy viewing makes liberals more conservative on crime, television's legitimation of government response to social problems draws conservatives closer to a more liberal view of the value of government solutions to social problems.

The quantity, quality, and audience for televised information about politics is changing. In the mid-1980s an increase in the quality of political programming on the Public Broadcasting Service and the rise of cable meant that the amount of substantive political information available on television increased. Until the mid-1980s those who sought extended political contact with candidates would have to give up their careers and become camp followers. Ads, news, and debates had all moved to highly abbreviated forms. By 1988, however, any citizen with a television set could tune to PBS and hear 10-minute excerpts from candidate stump speeches on the "MacNeil/Lehrer Newshour" and watch hour-long biographies on the two major party candidates by prize-winning author Garry Wills; those with cable could attend to the complete stump speeches of the major candidates on C-Span. In other words, in 1988, it was possible for an interested citizen to be more knowledgeable about the national race than in any time in the history of the United States.

The rise of cable meant that specialized audiences could now be addressed directly by candidates. What had been a broadcast medium, reaching a large undifferentiated mass audience, was increasingly becoming a narrowcast medium, reaching smaller, more homogenous audiences. What was once true only of radio and direct mail became true of television in the mid-1980s. Spanish-language cable reached Hispanics in large numbers; MTV reached young voters. Whereas broadcasting dictated that political messages speak to concerns that transcended our differences, the narrowcasting of cable meant that the special concerns of special segments of the audience could now be addressed.

But whereas the limited number of broadcast channels meant that reporters could easily eavesdrop on and critique candidate ads, the narrowcasting available on over 100 cable channels makes this increasingly difficult.

If the good news is that there is an unprecedented amount of televised political information available, the bad news is that the most educated electorate in human history is less disposed than ever to pay attention to it. The trend has been clear for quite a while. In 1964 viewers faced an evening of television that offered three choices. On one channel was that incarnation of high culture, the predecessor of "Dallas" and "Dynasty"—"Peyton Place." On the second channel was "Petticoat Junction." On the third was a paid political program featuring former President Dwight David Eisenhower discussing the future of the world with Republican party nominee Barry Goldwater. The next morning Goldwater's opponent, incumbent President Lyndon Johnson eagerly called reporters' attention to the fact that the audience had overwhelmingly chosen "Peyton Place" and "Petticoat Junction" over Goldwater.

In 1980, voters made an equally memorable choice. On CBS, Roger Mudd's documentary on Edward M. Kennedy. On the other channel *Jaws*. *Jaws* swallowed "Teddy." These examples are simply dramatic expressions of a statistical fact. Viewership for political substance is steadily declining and has been for well over a decade. More people watched the first Kennedy–Nixon debate of 1960 than watched the first Dukakis–Bush debate of 1988. In 1988, convention viewership was down as well. More people tuned in to the speeches of President Gerald Ford than to the speeches of President Jimmy Carter. The drop-off continued in the Reagan presidency. On most evenings, the "Mac-Neil/Lehrer Newshour" attracts such a small audience that a percent doesn't even appear in the ratings book.

Image versus issues; character versus positions. Scholars have wasted a lot of time trying to distinguish between messages that relate to candidate image and messages that relate to candidates' stands on issues. The problem, of course, is that almost every message says something that can be interpreted as an issue and tries to enhance the candidate's credibility, hence image. It is more useful to recognize that stands on issues produce an image and that such "image" questions as trustworthiness and competence often are issues.

A more useful distinction separates the character or natural temperamental dispositions and relevant biography of the candidate from the specific legislative action the candidate proposes. So a candidate might demonstrate her compassion, a facet of character, by indicating her strong support for Aid for Dependent Children, a policy position or stand on an issue. Since the early seventies, voters have been telling pollsters that the character of the candidates is more important to them than the candidates' policy positions or stands on issues.

## The Comparative Relevance of Character and Stands on Issues

In the 1960s and 1970s the electorate learned that judging a candidate on stands on issues was not a reliable predictor of his or her conduct in office. Some candidates acted against voter expectations: Lyndon Johnson, elected in 1964 as the peace candidate, escalated the war in Vietnam. Some presidents proved unable to meet their objectives. John Kennedy did not succeed in translating his campaign promises into law; only after his death did his successor secure passage of some of Kennedy's key initiatives. Jimmy Carter, elected to bring the budget into balance and lower inflation and unemployment, had not accomplished these goals by the end of his first term.

In this period, one campaign stood out for accurately forecasting a president's positions and accomplishments. Ronald Reagan campaigned promising a defense buildup and tax cuts and produced both.

Meanwhile, the character of a candidate seemed increasingly important in judging performance in office. Whether a person was truthful and trustworthy were focal concerns of those probing the failures of Johnson's handling of the Vietnam War and Nixon's handling of Watergate; whether a person was competent was central to those probing the failures of the presidencies of Ford and Carter; whether a person was candid about his health was of concern to those who learned of Kennedy's Addison's disease only after his death.

What can and does television tell us about issues and the character of presidential candidates?

DETERMINING WHICH ISSUES ARE THE LIKELY FOCUS OF A CAMPAIGN
In their own ads, in debates, and in news clips, candidates reveal their popular past positions and conceal their unpopular ones. At the same time, candidates reveal the unpopular past positions of their opponents. Public opinion polls and focus group tests (analysis of the response of small groups to various messages) help campaigns determine which issues will resonate with which voting group.

When an issue is controversial but, nonetheless, beneficial to one side or the other, that issue is more likely to be raised in the ads and news coverage of a Political Action Committee (PAC), not in the candidate's own messages.... [A] PAC is a group of like-minded citizens formed to advance a specific interest and unaffiliated with a party or candidate. A PAC contributes to candidacies and produces messages consistent with the self-interest of its members. Most major corporations have formed PACs as have a number of ideological groups.

When an issue hurts both candidates or both parties, as the savings and loan crisis did in 1988, it will be raised by neither side.

In general, at the presidential level the party affiliation of the contender has accurately predicted the likely positions on certain issues. Republicans will, for example, favor less government intervention and less taxation but will support greater defense spending than will Democrats.

In general, the issues on which news, advertising, and debates will focus are those advanced by major party nominees. Although in 1988 over 100 citizens filed the appropriate papers to be considered bona fide presidential contenders, public discussion focuses, with few exceptions, on the Democratic and Republican parties' nominees and on the issues they consider important.

Issues of general concern will receive treatment in the mass media; issues of less national concern or highly specialized issues will be treated in specialty publications and broadcasts. For example, those interested in a candidate's monetary philosophy are more likely to find such information on "Wall Street Week in Review" or in the *Wall Street Journal* than on the "NBC Nightly News" or in *USA Today*. Specific environmental policies are likely to be treated in magazines devoted to the subject.

Since television is a visual medium, the messages produced on it are more likely to speak to issues that lend themselves to visualization. This means that crime and environmental pollution are more likely to be the subject of political ads and of news coverage than is the national debt or international liquidity.

DETERMINING WHICH FACETS OF CHARACTER ARE THE LIKELY FOCUS IN A CAMPAIGN    The character defects of the most recent president are likely to shape the criteria by which the character of the candidates is judged. After Nixon's resignation, Carter won election campaigning as a candidate who would never lie and who would provide a government as good as its people.

Societal norms shape the criteria we set for candidate character. In the 50s and 60s, a divorced candidate was weakened by that fact. During their presidential runs, it was raised as an issue against Adlai Stevenson and Nelson Rockefeller. By the 1980s being divorced no longer carried a social stigma, and the country elected its first divorced president.

The press and public are in the process of determining which facets of character are relevant to governance. In the 1988 primaries we learned that having smoked marijuana in one's youth was not a disqualifier. In the Texas gubernatorial campaign of 1990, we learned that the press and public consider it inappropriate for a candidate for governor to have purchased the services of prostitutes in his youth.

Any form of hypocrisy any discrepancy between private behavior and public statement of politics, is likely to be scrutinized by the press. Pledging that they would find nothing, Gary Hart challenged the press to tail him. The press took him at his word and reported a weekend tryst with an aspiring actress that cost Hart his credibility as a presidential contender.

The resulting press scrutiny of itself is instructive. The reporting was justified on two grounds: Hart's hypocrisy and reporters' contentions that Hart's behavior showed a disposition toward risk-taking unacceptable in one who would head the country.

# NOTES

*Kathleen Hall Jamieson and Karlyn Kohrs Campbell*

1. For an excellent analysis of the function of metaphors in press coverage of the 1972 Democratic presidential campaign, see Jane Blankenship, "The Search for the 1972 Democratic Nomination: A Metaphoric Perspective," in *Rhetoric and Communication,* ed. Jane Blankenship and Hermann G. Stelzner (Urbana: University of Illinois Press, 1976), pp. 236–260.

2. David Maraniss, "In GOP Race, Money Takes Lead," *Washington Post,* 10 February 1990, p. A 7.

3. *Dallas Morning News,* 17 August 1990, p. 18 A.

# PART SIX

# Institutions of National Government

# On the Internet . . .

## Sites appropriate to Part Six

This page of the House of Representatives will lead you to information about current and past House members and agendas, the legislative process, and so on. You can learn about events on the House floor as they happen.

```
http://www.house.gov
```

This page of the U.S. Senate will lead you to information about current and past Senate members and agendas, legislative activities, committees, and so on.

```
http://www.senate.gov
```

Visit the White House page for direct access to information about commonly requested federal services, the White House Briefing Room, and the presidents and vice presidents. The Virtual Library allows you to search White House documents, listen to speeches, and view photos.

```
http://www.whitehouse.gov/WH/Welcome.html
```

Open this site of the Legal Information Institute (LII) for current and historical information about the Supreme Court. The LLI archive contains many opinions issued since May 1990 as well as a collection of nearly 600 of the most historical decisions of the Court.

```
http://supct.law.cornell.edu/supct/
   index.html
```

# CHAPTER 10 Congress

## 10.1 DAVID R. MAYHEW

# *The Electoral Incentive*

David R. Mayhew (b. 1937) has been recognized as an expert on Congress for the past three decades. His book *Congress: The Electoral Connection* (Yale University Press, 1974), from which the following selection has been excerpted, is considered a classic investigation of congressional motivation and behavior. The book has filled a gap in the contemporary literature on Congress and has shifted the theoretical focus of legislative research to emphasize the linkage between congressional elections and congressional public policy making.

In *Congress,* Mayhew argues that all members of Congress are primarily and continuously motivated and pressured by the impulse to be reelected, and they act accordingly. This is true regardless of whether they are representatives from safe congressional districts (i.e., lacking much party competition, rivalry, or turnover) or marginal congressional districts (i.e., marked by intensive party competition, rivalry, and turnover). Mayhew contends that the three basic types of political behavior that enable congresspersons to be successful include advertising, credit claiming, and position taking.

"Advertising" is expressed as any act, through any forum or medium and conveyed in messages with minimal substance, to publicize a candidate's positive image to the electorate. "Credit claiming" refers to a congressperson creating the perception among constituents of being personally responsible for providing desirable governmental programs or services or concrete benefits. Finally, "position taking" is a congressperson's public expression of a particular policy position or value judgment on policy priorities perceived to be of serious interest to one's constituents. This is concretely expressed in a congressperson's legislative voting record.

Mayhew received his Ph.D. from Harvard University. He is currently the Alfred Cowles Professor of Government at Yale University. His areas of expertise and research have included legislative politics, political parties, and interest groups. *Congress: The Electoral Connection* won *The Washington Monthly* Political Book Award in 1974. Mayhew is also the author of *Placing Parties in American Politics* (Princeton University Press, 1986) and *Divided We Govern* (Yale University Press, 1991).

**Key Concept:** congressional incumbent electoral strategies

$W$hether they are safe or marginal, cautious or audacious, congressmen must constantly engage in activities related to reelection. There will be differences in emphasis, but all members share the root need to do things—indeed, to do things day in and day out during their terms. The next step here is to present a typology, a short list of the *kinds* of activities congressmen find it electorally useful to engage in. The case will be that there are three basic kinds of activities....

One activity is *advertising,* defined here as any effort to disseminate one's name among constituents in such a fashion as to create a favorable image but in messages having little or no issue content. A successful congressman builds what amounts to a brand name, which may have a generalized electoral value for other politicians in the same family. The personal qualities to emphasize are experience, knowledge, responsiveness, concern, sincerity, independence, and the like. Just getting one's name across is difficult enough; only about half the electorate, if asked, can supply their House members' names. It helps a congressman to be known.... A vital advantage enjoyed by House incumbents is that they are much better known among voters than their November challengers. They are better known because they spend a great deal of time, energy, and money trying to make themselves better known. There are standard routines—frequent visits to the constituency, nonpolitical speeches to home audiences, the sending out of infant care booklets and letters of condolence and congratulation. Of 158 House members questioned in the mid-1960s, 121 said that they regularly sent newsletters to their constituents,[1] 48 wrote separate news or opinion columns for newspapers; 82 regularly reported to their constituencies by radio or television, 89 regularly sent out mail questionnaires.[2] ... [C]ongressional advertising is done largely at public expense. Use of the franking privilege has mushroomed in recent years; in early 1973 one estimate predicted that House and Senate members would send out about 476 million pieces of mail in the year 1974, at a public cost of $38.1 million—or about 900,000 pieces per member with a subsidy of $70,000 per member.[3] By far the heaviest mailroom traffic comes in Octobers of even-numbered years. There are some differences between House and Senate members in the ways they go about getting their names across. House members are free to blanket their constituencies with mailings for all boxholders; senators are not. But senators find it easier to appear on national television—for example, in short reaction statements on the nightly news shows. Advertising is a staple congressional activity, and there is no end to it. For each member there are always new voters to be apprised of his worthiness and old voters to be reminded of it.

A second activity may be called *credit claiming,* defined here as acting so as to generate a belief in a relevant political actor (or actors) that one is personally responsible for causing the government, or some unit thereof, to do something that the actor (or actors) considers desirable. The political logic of this, from the congressman's point of view, is that an actor who believes that a member can make pleasing things happen will no doubt wish to keep him in office so that he can make pleasing things happen in the future. The emphasis here is on individual accomplishment (rather than, say, party or governmental accomplishment) and on the congressman as doer (rather than as, say, expounder of constituency views). Credit claiming is highly important to congressmen, with the consequence that much congressional life is a relentless search for opportunities to engage in it.

Where can credit be found? If there were only one congressman rather than 535, the answer would in principle be simple enough. Credit (or blame) would attach in Downsian fashion to the doings of the government as a whole. But there are 535. Hence it becomes necessary for each congressman to try to peel off pieces of governmental accomplishment for which he can believably generate a sense of responsibility. For the average congressman the staple way of doing this is to traffic in what may be called "particularized benefits." Particularized governmental benefits, as the term will be used here, have two properties: (1) Each benefit is given out to a specific individual, group, or geographical constituency, the recipient unit being of a scale that allows a single congressman to be recognized (by relevant political actors and other congressmen) as the claimant for the benefit (other congressmen being perceived as indifferent or hostile). (2) Each benefit is given out in apparently ad hoc fashion (unlike, say, social security checks) with a congressman apparently having a hand in the allocation. A particularized benefit can normally be regarded as a member of a class. That is, a benefit given out to an individual, group, or constituency can normally be looked upon by congressmen as one of a class of similar benefits given out to sizable numbers of individuals, groups, or constituencies. Hence the impression can arise that a congressman is getting "his share" of whatever it is the government is offering....

In sheer volume the bulk of particularized benefits come under the heading of "casework"—the thousands of favors congressional offices perform for supplicants in ways that normally do not require legislative action. High school students ask for essay materials, soldiers for emergency leaves, pensioners for location of missing checks, local governments for grant information, and on and on. Each office has skilled professionals who can play the bureaucracy like an organ—pushing the right pedals to produce the desired effects.[4] But many benefits require new legislation, or at least they require important allocative decisions on matters covered by existent legislation. Here the congressman fills the traditional role of supplier of goods to the home district. It is a believable role; when a member claims credit for a benefit on the order of a dam, he may well receive it. Shiny construction projects seem especially useful. In the decades before 1934, tariff duties for local industries were a major commodity.[5] In recent years awards given under grant-in-aid programs have become more useful as they have become more numerous. Some quests for credit are ingenious; in 1971 the story broke that congressmen had been earmarking foreign aid money for specific projects in Israel in order to win favor with home constituents.[6] It should be said of constituency benefits that congressmen are quite capable of taking the initiative in drumming them up; that is, there can be no automatic assumption that a congressman's activity is the result of pressures brought to bear by organized interests. . . .

How much particularized benefits count for at the polls is extraordinarily difficult to say. But it would be hard to find a congressman who thinks he can afford to wait around until precise information is available. The lore is that they count—furthermore, given home expectations, that they must be supplied in regular quantities for a member to stay electorally even with the board. Awareness of favors may spread beyond their recipients, building for a member a general reputation as a good provider. "Rivers Delivers." "He Can Do More for Massachusetts." . . .

The third activity congressmen engage in may be called *position taking*, defined here as the public enunciation of a judgmental statement on anything likely to be of interest to political actors. The statement may take the form of a roll call vote. The most important classes of judgmental statements are those prescribing American governmental ends (a vote cast against the war; a statement that "the war should be ended immediately") or governmental means (a statement that "the way to end the war is to take it to the United Nations"). The judgments may be implicit rather than explicit, as in: "I will support the president on this matter." But judgments may range far beyond these classes to take in implicit or explicit statements on what almost anybody should do or how he should do it: "The great Polish scientist Copernicus has been unjustly neglected"; "The way for Israel to achieve peace is to give up the Sinai." The congressman as position taker is a speaker rather than a doer. The electoral requirement is not that he make pleasing things happen but that he make pleasing judgmental statements. The position itself is the political commodity. Especially on matters where governmental responsibility is widely diffused it is not surprising that political actors should fall back on positions as tests of incumbent virtue. For voters ignorant of congressional processes the recourse is an easy one. . . .

The ways in which positions can be registered are numerous and often imaginative. There are floor addresses ranging from weighty orations to mass-produced "nationality day statements." There are speeches before home groups, television appearances, letters, newsletters, press releases, ghostwritten books, *Playboy* articles, even interviews with political scientists. On occasion congressmen generate what amount to petitions; whether or not to sign the 1956 Southern Manifesto defying school desegregation rulings was an important decision for southern members. Outside the roll call process the congressman is usually able to tailor his positions to suit his audiences. A solid consensus in the constituency calls for ringing declarations; for years the late Senator James K. Vardaman (D., Miss.) campaigned on a proposal to repeal the Fifteenth Amendment. Division or uncertainty in the constituency calls for waffling; in the late 1960s a congressman had to be a poor politician indeed not to be able to come up with an inoffensive statement on Vietnam ("We must have peace with honor at the earliest possible moment consistent with the national interest"). On a controversial issue a Capitol Hill office normally prepares two form letters to send out to constituent letter writers—one for the pros and one (not directly contradictory) for the antis. . . .

Probably the best position-taking strategy for most congressmen at most times is to be conservative—to cling to their own positions of the past where possible and to reach for new ones with great caution where necessary. Yet in an earlier discussion of strategy the suggestion was made that it might be rational for members in electoral danger to resort to innovation. The form of innovation available is entrepreneurial position taking, its logic being that for a member facing defeat with his old array of positions it makes good sense to gamble on some new ones. It may be that congressional marginals fulfill an important function here as issue pioneers—experimenters who test out new issues and thereby show other politicians which ones are usable. An example of such a pioneer is Senator Warren Magnuson (D., Wash.), who responded to a surprisingly narrow victory in 1962 by reaching for a reputation in the area of consumer affairs.[7] Another example is Senator Ernest Hollings (D., S.C.), a servant of a shaky and racially heterogeneous southern constituency who launched "hunger" as an issue in 1969—at once pointing to a problem and giving it a useful nonracial definition. One of the most successful issue entrepreneurs of recent decades was the late Senator Joseph McCarthy (R., Wis.); it was all there—the close primary in 1946, the fear of defeat in 1952, the desperate casting about for an issue, the famous 1950 dinner at the Colony Restaurant where suggestions were tendered, the decision that "Communism" might just do the trick.[8]

The effect of position taking on electoral behavior is about as hard to measure as the effect of credit claiming. Once again there is a variance problem; congressmen do not differ very much among themselves in the methods they use or the skills they display in attuning themselves to their diverse constituencies. All of them, after all, are professional politicians. . . .

There can be no doubt that congressmen believe positions make a difference. An important consequence of this belief is their custom of watching each other's elections to try to figure out what positions are salable. Nothing is more important in Capitol Hill politics than the shared conviction that election returns have proven a point. Thus the 1950 returns were read not only as a rejection of health insurance but as a ratification of McCarthyism. When two North Carolina nonsigners of the 1956 Southern Manifesto immediately lost their primaries, the message was clear to southern members that there could be no straying from a hard line on the school desegregation issue. Any breath of life left in the cause of school bussing was squeezed out by House returns from the Detroit area in 1972. . . .

These, then, are the three kinds of electorally oriented activities congressmen engage in—advertising, credit claiming, and position taking.

# NOTES

1. These and the following figures on member activity are from Donald G. Tacheron and Morris K. Udall, *The Job of the Congressman* (Indianapolis: Bobbs-Merrill, 1966), pp. 281–288.

2. On questionnaires generally see Walter Wilcox, "The Congressional Poll—and Non-Poll," in Edward C. Dreyer and Walter A. Rosenbaum (eds.), *Political Opinion and Electoral Behavior* (Belmont, Calif.: Wadsworth, 1966), pp. 390–400.

3. Norman C. Miller, "Yes, You Are Getting More Politico Mail: And It Will Get Worse," *Wall Street Journal,* March 6, 1973, p. 1.

4. On casework generally see Kenneth G. Olson, "The Service Function of the United States Congress," pp. 337–74 in American Enterprise Institute, *Congress: The First Branch of Government* (Washington, D.C.: American Enterprise Institute for Public Policy Research, 1966).

5. The classic account is in E. E. Schattschneider, *Politics, Pressures, and the Tariff* (New York: Prentice-Hall, 1935).

6. "Israeli Schools and Hospitals Seek Funds in Foreign-Aid Bill," *New York Times,* October 4, 1971, p. 10.

7. David Price, *Who Makes the Laws?* (Cambridge Mass.: Schenkman, 1972), p. 29.

8. Robert Griffith, *The Politics of Fear: Joseph R. McCarthy and the Senate* (New York: Hayden, 1970), p. 29.

## 10.2  RICHARD F. FENNO, JR.

# *Home and Washington: Linkage and Representation*

In 1978 Richard F. Fenno, Jr. (b. 1926), an outstanding scholar and an expert on Congress and legislative politics, pubiished *Home Style: House Members in Their Districts* (Little, Brown, 1978), from which the following selection has been excerpted. The book provided new research on the U.S. Congress by observing the political behavior of representatives among their constituents in their home districts instead of focusing on their legislative behavior and policy making in Washington. Fenno's analysis and interpretation of the congressional process of legislative representation, and especially how the perceptions of their constituents by members of the House of Representatives affect their political behavior, have influenced other congressional scholars to focus on this topic in their research and publications.

Fenno recognizes the dual roles and responsibilities of the members of Congress—legislating national policy in the public interest as well as representing the political preferences and special interests of one's district. This reflects the two fundamental institutional functions of Congress—acting as a legislative or lawmaking forum and serving as a representative body. Fenno contends that there is a linkage between the "constituency careers" and "Washington careers" of most members of Congress. "Constituency careers" refer to legislative activities focused on the objective of reelection, while "Washington careers" emphasize legislative performance, recognition, and power. A common expression of the interaction between these legislative roles is the congressional behavior of an issue-oriented congressperson who commits to a policy or legislation perceived to conform to the preferences and interests of constituents.

Fenno received his Ph.D. from Harvard University, and he has taught at Amherst College and Wheaton College. He is currently the Distinguished University Professor at the University of Rochester. Fenno's research has focused on legislative studies and presidential and executive politics. Fenno's publications include *Congressmen in Committees* (Scott, Foresman, 1973) and *When Incumbency Fails: The Senate Career of Mark Andrews* (CQ Press, 1992). He has also published many scholarly articles in political science journals.

**Key Concept:** the linkage between "constituency career" and "Washington career"

$W$e have been able to learn a great deal about House members at home without knowing much about them in Washington. And, it appears that we cannot know all we need to know about House members in Washington unless we do move out beyond the capitol city into the country and into its congressional districts. Washington and home are different milieus, different worlds. But they are not unconnected worlds. The theory and the practice of a representative form of government links them one to the other. Though a congressman be immersed in one, he remains mindful of the other....

# LINKAGE: CONSTITUENCY CAREER AND WASHINGTON CAREER

[We have] noted the interaction between constituency careers and Washington careers. Of all the links between home style and House performance, this is the most apparent. When we speak of constituency careers, we speak primarily of the pursuit of the goal of reelection. When we speak of Washington careers, we speak primarily of the pursuit of goals of influence in the House and the making of good public policy. Thus the intertwining of careers is, at bottom, an intertwining of member goals.

So long as they are in the expansionist stage of their constituency careers, House members will be especially attentive to their home base. They will pursue the goal of reelection with single-minded intensity and will allocate their resources disproportionately to that end.... [F]irst-term members go home more frequently, place a larger proportion of their staff in the district, and more often leave their families at home than do their senior colleagues. Building a reelection constituency at home and providing continuous access to as much of that constituency as possible requires time and energy. Inevitably, these are resources that might otherwise be allocated to efforts in Washington. "The trouble is," said one member near the end of his second term,

> I haven't been a congressman yet. The first two years, I spent all of my time getting myself reelected. That last two years, I spent getting myself a district so that I could get reelected. So I won't be a congressman until next year.

By being "a congressman" he means pursuing goals above and beyond that of reelection (i.e., power in the House and good public policy).

In a House member's first years, the opportunities for gaining inside power and policy influence are limited. Time and energy and staff can be allocated to home without an acute sense of conflict. At rates that vary from congressman to congressman, however, the chances to have some institutional or legislative effect improve. As members stretch to avail themselves of the opportunity, they may begin to experience some allocative strain. It requires time and energy to develop a successful career in Washington just as it does to develop a successful career in the district. Because it may not be possible to allocate these resources to House and home, each to an optimal degree, members may have to make allocative and goal choices.

...The onset of a Washington career is altering [a four-term congress-man's] personal goals and his established home style. He is worried about the costs of the change; but he is willing to accept some loss of reelection support in exchange for his increased influence in Congress.

This dilemma faces every member of Congress. It is built into the twin re-quirements that Congress be a representative and a legislative institution. Some members believe they can achieve reelection at home together with influence or policy in Washington without sacrificing either. During Congressman O's first year as a subcommittee chairman..., I asked him whether his new position would make it more difficult to tend to district matters. He replied,

> If you mean, am I getting Potomac fever, the answer is, no. If you mean, has the change in my official duties here made me a better congressman, the answer is, yes. If you mean has it taken away from my activity in the constituency, the answer is no.

Congressman O... has been going home less; but he has been increasing the number and the activity of his district staff. Although he speaks confidently of his allocative solution, he is not unaware of potential problems. "My staff operation runs by itself. They don't need me. Maybe I should worry about that. You aren't going back and say I'm ripe for the plucking are you? I don't think I am."

# LINKAGE: HOME STYLE AND WASHINGTON STYLE

In probing for linkages between home and Washington, it is natural to ask if there are any connections between home style and Washington behavior. If we mean to ask whether members of Congress do certain things in Washington to shore up constituent support at home, the answer is obviously yes. And what they do is well known and straightforward. They allocate the tasks of their staffs in ways they think helpful in getting reelected. They choose com-mittee assignments they think will bring identification with and benefit to their supportive constituencies. They vote in ways they think will be approved by their supportive constituents. Or, better, they avoid voting in ways they believe will be intensely disapproved by their supportive constituents. They will also vote in ways that help them structure their need to explain back home. There is nothing we can add here to what political scientists already know about such constituency-oriented behavior in Washington.

The question we have to ask is whether the study of home styles can tell us anything we might not otherwise know about behavior in Washington. Are home styles related in any way to Washington styles? It is not an easy question to handle. Political scientists have not produced any consensus as to precisely what might be meant by a "Washington style."[1] Also, we have produced too little Washington-related information in this study to pursue the matter con-structively. Still, the question remains intriguing, if only because from time to time House members talk or act as if the behavior we observed at home is repeated in Washington.

For example, our issue-oriented Congressman *O*, who refuses "to play the groups" at home, also refuses to play them in Washington.

> I met a guy from the postal union [at home]. He said I have them the brush off when they came to Washington. The trouble is they compare me to the congressman in the next district. He wines and dines every little two-bit group that comes down. He spends all his time with them. He doesn't have anything else to do. But I don't have the patience with these guys, or the time. I'm busy over on the floor doing other things.

Stylistic patterns affecting access at home can affect access similarly in Washington. Another congressman commented at home that "I love to campaign at coffee hours with ten or twelve people. I hate standup cocktail parties.... I'm very bad at making small talk with people I don't know. I can't do it." In Washington, he follows the same stylistic predilections—almost.

> Not long ago, I got a letter from the head of the American Legion in my state noting that I hadn't been to their Washington cocktail party for the last two years. I don't go to any of those Washington parties.... But I make two exceptions— groups in which I have personal friends and groups that were with me in 1968 [his first campaign]. Take the Machinists, for example. They were a great help to me when I needed help. I always go to their gatherings.

If access at home carries with it a promise of access in Washington, this is all the more reason why it is so valued by supportive constituents. Our knowledge of home style may, furthermore, help us to locate those constituents most likely to achieve access in Washington.

Another possible linkage might be a relationship between coalition building at home and coalition building inside the House. For example, might not our Congressman *B*, the well-liked local boy who is so suspicious of "outsiders," be handicapped as a coalition builder in Congress by this exclusive view of politics? He was two years on the job, he says, before he began to read *The Washington Post*. More broadly, might not any member who writes off certain constituents as people he "never gets" be limited in his efforts to build coalitions among House colleagues who represent such people? In broader compass still, are some home styles more conducive to the achievement of internal power or good policy than others? Are members with issue-oriented home styles any more likely to provide internal policy leadership than members with other home styles? Such questions are intriguing. But the shortcomings of our home-oriented perspective cannot be overcome sufficiently to answer them.

We shall offer, however, one line of speculation. It is this: Home styles may affect Washington styles in the degree to which home styles produce early commitments to future courses of action in Congress. Some members will act at home, we speculate, to preserve a maximum of maneuvering room for themselves at various points of decision in Washington. Other members will act at home to commit themselves to certain courses of action at various points of decision in Washington. The former remain free to play a variety of parts in the legislative process. The latter are more limited in their range of legislative activity. Both stances are deliberate and, partly at least, a function of their home styles. We are encouraged in these speculations because House members themselves make this distinction between an early and a late commitment to a course of action. And we find traces of evidence in a couple of instances.

Just after his first congressional campaign victory, one individual articulated the first kind of linkage:

> I have an abhorrence of getting myself precommitted. I don't go around looking for chances to commit myself if I can avoid it. Fortunately, my opponent in the campaign didn't force me to get precommitted. He conducted a quiet handshaking campaign, and that's the kind I conduct.... I think you have an obligation to your constituents to make your vote as effective as you can. You want to keep as much bargaining power as you can. If you commit yourself to a group before you know what the situation is, you lose that bargaining power.... Sometimes, [in the state legislature] when I told people what they wanted to hear, I regretted it afterward. When the vote came, the situation had changed and I had to vote against my better judgment or my word.

In the middle of this third term, another House member articulated the second kind of stylistic linkage:

> I don't think the party leadership gets many votes by direct solicitation. I've been up and down the hill with the leadership on that. I tell them that I take my positions on the issues solid and early at home. "If you want to vote, have a legislative platform and stick to it. Take your position early." but they don't do that. When I can take the lead on a party position I feel comfortable with, I do. That makes them feel better toward me.

The first congressman's home style is dominantly person to person; the second congressman's home style is dominantly issue-oriented. Yet both individuals are equally policy-oriented—equally devoted to power and policy goals—in the House. And one may be as influential as the other, for strategies of commitment may be as effective as strategies of maneuver. The difference lies in the freedom to maneuver each normally has throughout the decision-making process. And therein may lie a useful classification of Washington styles.

There were two members whom I traveled with prior to their first election; I went to Washington to talk with them again four weeks into their freshman year. The differences between them provide some support for the stylistic relationships suggested.

One of them had deliberately made legislative style *the* issue against his primary opponent. "Effectiveness—who can get the most done. That's the thing I stress everywhere.... People have to vote on the issues. And the issue is effectiveness." When, during a debate, his opponent said, "I don't mind being called flamboyant and controversial," he countered,

> Do you want someone who does the talk and stirs the pot and then, after the pot is stirred, leaves it? Or do you want someone who gets in there to see what solution can be worked out, what legislative result can be produced?

He spelled out what he meant by an "effective" decision-making style best in another context. As we left the local AFL-CIO endorsement meeting, at which he received their endorsement ("The largest portion of my money has come from organized labor"), he said,

> The state chairman was there and asked if I would be a member of the local welcoming committee for Hubert Humphrey when he comes to the state. I don't want to commit myself. I don't have a [presidential] candidate. But labor loves Hubert Humphrey. Oh, how they love him. . . . I'm going to be at the national convention. I want to be free in making decisions there. Once you commit yourself, people put you in a slot and you're isolated. You lose your freedom to move in the party. I want to keep that freedom.

When I visited him in Washington shortly after his election, he exhibited the same reluctance to commit himself in advance that he had exhibited at home. He was pleased about obtaining a prized committee assignment as a result of some intricate, "effective" planning. Otherwise, his posture was one of avoiding unnecessary conclusions. On his career, he said, "It's all right, but it's nothing I'd want to do for the rest of my life, being a member of the United States House of Representatives." On the Democratic Study Group: "I haven't paid my dues yet. I'm going to a few more of their meetings and see whether it's the kind of group I want to be connected with. Until then, I'm withholding my dues." On the House as an institution: "I'll save my overall impressions till later. I haven't been here long enough, and we haven't gotten into the substance of things yet." These comments seemed perfectly consistent with what I had seen and heard back home—the effort to remain minimally committed to specifics and maximally free for "effective" legislative maneuver.

By the same token, I found the second newcomer much more voluble and much more engaged when I visited him in Washington the same day. Indeed, he ventured a revealing comment on the first member: "A group of us freshmen have decided to meet regularly. [He listed the names, and my other freshman congressman, Paul Kraus, was not among them.] Paul Kraus is very cautious. We've been a lot more active on reform and in the Democratic Study Group than Paul Kraus and those cats." The comment was no surprise, coming as it did from someone who during the election campaign has told his supporters that "The House of Representatives is the least representative part of the government, the one that needs the most changing, the one that changes the slowest and is the hardest to change." He had often spoken of the House reformers as "great guys" and praised "my friends in the Democratic Study Group." During his campaign he had made substantive public policy *the* issue between himself and his general election opponent. And he escalated policy issues at every opportunity. To a group of prospective supporters he had said,

> I can't think of a single issue on which he and I agree. He supports Nixon on the war; he supports Nixon's so-called family assistance plan. He opposes the land use bill. And those are the only positions he has taken so far. Oh, he does support the White House Conference on the Elderly. But I supported it before he did. So there is as complete a difference between us as you can imagine. We have completely different philosophies on what this country ought to be.

When I asked him, in Washington, if he anticipated any difficult voting decisions, he said, "No, people know my position on almost everything."

He was as free with early judgments about the House as his fellow freshman was noncommittal. "Here's a symbol of congressional impotence," he said, pointing to the telephone. "We can talk on the FTS line before 9:00 A.M. and after 5:00 P.M.; between 9:00 A.M. and 5:00 P.M. they shut it off. I'll bet the Secretary of Defense doesn't have to wait till 5:00 P.M. to make his calls. It's ridiculous, absurd." Another time, he said, "I've been reenforced in my belief that the place is unrepresentative. It is. I've heard things said here that don't represent anyone." Complaining, "They may never pass any legislation at the rate they're going," he had thrown himself enthusiastically into what legislative "action" he could find. He had begun, too, to think about the problem of his legislative "effectiveness" and had even made some stylistic adjustments. But it remained a different style from that of his colleagues.

> I wish I knew how the old guys judge you down here. I wonder if I've begun to lose my credibility by standing up in caucus to ask for a vote on every committee chairmanship. I can see where you would tear yourself apart there trying to balance representation of your district against your effectiveness. On the one hand you owe it to your constituents to voice their views; on the other hand you owe it to them to be effective within the institution. So far I've tried by everything I've done to keep from being labeled a screamer. People like Drinan and Bella are totally ineffective down here; yet they are right in expressing their constituents' views. I think it's how you say a thing more than what you say. In the briefing by Kissinger, I was the only freshman to ask a question, and I'm sure the older heads were shocked to hear a freshman ask a question. The Speaker called on me as "the Freshman Representative from _____." I hope I said what I said articulately and carefully and nicely enough so that I didn't offend anyone. But I sure as hell said what I wanted.

It is a Washington style related, we think, to his strongly issue-oriented style at home.

The suggested linkage between home styles and Washington styles depends on the distinction, in Washington, between early commitment and retention of maneuvering room during decision making. If such a distinction can be maintained, then it seems that certain homes styles will be associated with one Washington style more often that with the other. The more issue-oriented a congressman's home style, the more likely is he to commit himself early. And the more he chooses to present himself by talking about policy issues, the more the sheer density of talk will produce early commitments. They may be commitments to introduce legislation, agitate for a given decision in a given forum, vote in a particular fashion, or something else. In proportions that vary from member to member, this talk at home may be pure "position taking"—and thus, in Mayhew's terms, totally devoid of commitment.[2] All we can say, here, is that we are speaking only of that proportion of home talk that does carry some commitment to future activity. We mean to emphasize a commitment to legislative activism, publicly made, with the implied invitation for constituents to watch him in action.

On the other hand, the less issue-oriented a congressman's home style (and this includes person-to-person, constituency service, and community leadership styles) the less likely he is to commit himself to policy positions that will constrain his actions during the legislative process. He will be able to focus on targets of opportunity among policies, take an active or a passive role at one stage or another, work behind the scenes or openly, make his voting decisions early or late, and so on. It is not necessary to adopt extreme views on the distinction between commitment and maneuver. No member is so committed that he has no room for maneuver in Washington; and no member who strives to maintain maneuvering room is totally noncommitted at home.

Further, it must be said, again, that this distinction is *not* one of relative influence inside the House. The distinction may, however, be of some practical moment during the legislative process. To know whether and how strongly any given member has committed himself back home to do something in Washington may be the most important piece of political intelligence one can have about a fellow member in any given legislative struggle. As one member, a House leader, noted, "I never trade votes; I couldn't keep track of them all; I always work on someone through second or third parties in their districts." That is, he regards a commitment made by a member to his strongest supporters back home as the most durable kind of legislative commitment. The ability to classify House members with regard to their tendency to commit early at home (and to whom) or their tendency to remain flexible may represent important political intelligence. In sum, coalition builders in the House may find it helpful to know something about the home styles of House members.

All this is, admittedly, conjectural. And nothing we have said should be taken to diminish the force of our more general proposition that all House members can use their home styles to give themselves a great deal of voting leeway in Washington if they so desire.... [W]e have argued that House members are not tightly constrained in their legislative votes by the necessities of constituent support. So long as members can successfully explain a vote afterward, their constituent support depends—except for one or two issues—more on what they do at home than on what they do in Washington. That is what they believe; and we have described their behavior in that light. Any constraining effect that home style may have on Washington style must be viewed within this set of overarching propositions.

Members with issue-oriented home styles do, we think, come to Washington more constrained by prior commitments than members with other types of home style. These commitments pertain to much more than voting. But even where voting is concerned we should not think of these commitments as so specific or so binding as to force them into casting votes different from ones they would freely cast otherwise. By committing themselves early at home, they have lost some of the voting leeway they might otherwise want. But they will have lost only as much as their constituents will have forced on them. And that, as we have said repeatedly, is not very much. If their constituents have forced anything on them, it is more likely to be a home style that features issue-orientation and a commitment to visible legislative activism. It will not be overly constraining. If it is, the escape into pure position taking is always available.

The main effect we wish to suggest is simply that the distribution and strength of commitments made at home can affect the legislative process in Washington. If home commitments vary according to home styles, then students of the legislative process may find home styles of some relevance. More than this, we would not wish to claim.

# REPRESENTATION: SUMMARY SPECULATION

For students of Congress, the subject of representation comes with the territory. It has not been the focus of this study because we have made no effort to examine either our members' activity in Washington or their constituents' activity at home. Nonetheless, our explorations may have turned up some implications for the family of questions, both descriptive and normative, raised by studies of representation. If our observations can shed any new light on this difficult subject, it will come from having had the vantage point of home, and from having looked at home through the eyes of the representative. What does the representative see when he or she goes home to look at the represented? How does what he or she sees affect his or her representational activity? What can we learn, from this perspective, about the nature, the quality, and the problem of representation in this country?

The member of Congress, we have learned, has a complex, four-circled view of the people he represents. He differentiates among them in terms of their political support for him and, in some cases, their political loyalty to him. If, therefore, we start with the congressman's perception of the people he represents, there is no way that the act of representing can be separated from the act of getting elected. If the congressman cannot win and hold the votes of some people, he cannot represent any people. Further, he cannot represent any people unless he knows, or makes an effort to know, who they are, what they think, and what they want; and it is by campaigning for electoral support among them that he finds out such things. During the expansionist stage of his constituency career, particularly, he probably knows his various constituencies as well as it is possible to know them. It is, indeed, by such campaigning, by going home a great deal, that a congressman develops a complex and discriminating set of perceptions about his constituents. Conversely, only by separating the problem of running for office from the problem of representing while in office could anyone conceive of a constituency as being uncomplicated or undifferentiated or monolithic.[3] As our representatives see it, any such separation is impossible to maintain.

## NOTES

1. The most admirable effort to connect home events (i.e., recruitment) with Washington behavior is Leo Snowiss, "Congressional Recruitment and Representation," *American Political Science Review* 60 (September 1966), pp. 627–39. But his study failed to yield a coherent or reliable classification of performance patterns in Washington. Other attempted classifications of legislative styles (i.e, insider-outsider, trustee-delegate) have not been convincingly related to behavior.

2. David Mayhew, *The Electoral Connection* (New Haven: Yale University Press, 1974). But as Mayhew also notes, when a member "register(s) an elaborate set of pleasing positions, (it is) a course that reduces the chances of vote trading." *Ibid.*, 121.

3. It is the only weakness of Hanna Pitkin's study of representation that she employs a monolithic view of "the constituency" in her analysis. Had she not separated the problem of running for office from the problem of representation, she would have been pulled toward a more differentiated, complex view of the constituency. She understands the complexity but does not incorporate it into her study. Hanna Pitkin, *The Concept of Representation* (Berkeley: University of California Press, 1972).

# 10.3 ROGER H. DAVIDSON
# AND WALTER J. OLESZEK

# *The Two Congresses and the American People*

Roger H. Davidson and Walter J. Oleszek are two of the foremost scholars of the contemporary Congress. Their book *Congress and Its Members,* 6th ed. (Congressional Quarterly Press, 1998), from which the following selection has been excerpted, is considered a classic in legislative studies.

Davidson (b. 1936) received his Ph.D. from Columbia University and is currently a professor of government and politics at the University of Maryland. He has also taught at the University of California, Santa Barbara, and Dartmouth College. Davidson has held several professional legislative positions, including senior specialist of Congressional Research Service and professional staff member of the U.S. House of Representatives. He has authored or edited numerous publications, including *The Role of the Congressman* (Pegasus, 1969) and *The Postreform Congress* (St. Martin's Press, 1992).

Oleszek (b. 1941) received his M.A. from Michigan State University and his Ph.D. from the State University of New York at Albany. He is currently a research specialist at the Library of Congress and a member of the Joint Committee on the Organization of Congress. He has also taught at Colgate University and the University of Maryland. Oleszek's research specialty is legislative politics. He is coauthor, with Roger H. Davidson, of *Congress Against Itself* (Indiana University Press, 1977) and the author of *Congressional Procedure and Policy Process* (Congressional Quarterly, 1978).

The following selection explains how the contemporary Congress works and critically evaluates the congressional reforms of the early 1970s. At the core of Davidson and Oleszek's analysis is the recognition of a profound ambivalent perception by American citizens toward Congress. The authors express the concept of the "two Congresses," which refers to the institutional Congress and the representatives and senators who represent the interests of various constituencies. Although most of the electorate perceive the institutional Congress as incompetent and corrupt, voters view their respective elected officials with the highest esteem. Davidson and Oleszek contend that the workload for both Congresses has greatly increased in recent decades. It has become more difficult for the institutional Congress to develop coherent and comprehensive legislation to resolve serious national problems. Congress as a constituent service-oriented body has also been the recipient of greater intensified demands of voters.

**Key Concept:** the dual character of Congress

$C$itizens' ambivalent feelings toward the popular branch of government bring us . . . to the dual character of Congress. . . . This notion of the two Congresses manifests itself in public perceptions and assessments: citizens look at the Congress in Washington through different lenses from those with which they view their individual senators and representatives.[1] This same dualism appears in media coverage. In fact, the two Congresses are covered by different kinds of reporters working for different kinds of media organizations.

Individual senators and representatives present themselves to their constituents largely on their own terms—through advertising, self-promotion, and uncritical coverage by local or regional news media. Citizens tend to regard their own legislators as agents of personal or localized interests. Legislators are judged on their service to the state or district, their communication with constituents, and their home style—that is, the way they deal with the home folks.

The institutional Congress, by contrast, is covered mainly by the national media—the wire services, radio and television networks, and a few prestigious newspapers. It is viewed by the public as a lawmaking instrument and judged primarily on the basis of citizens' overall attitudes about policies and the state of the nation. Such national concerns typically lead people to conclusions at variance with their evaluations of their own senators and representatives.

## CONGRESS-AS-POLITICIANS . . .

Members of Congress these days are a beleaguered band. Citizens' ambivalence toward politics and politicians is nothing new, but the level of ambivalence and distrust today is alarming, at least by modern standards (that is, since the advent of mass opinion surveys in the late 1930s). The phenomenon is not confined to Capitol Hill or even to the United States. Mounting unrest among voters is reported in nearly every Western democracy.

Despite the pressures, elected representatives cannot yet be classed as an endangered species. The hours are killing, the pay relatively modest, and the psychic rewards fleeting, but diligence and attentive home styles yield dividends at the polls. . . . [I]f voters regard elected officials as a class as rascals, they tend to be more charitable toward their own elected officials. Nor do they seem eager to "throw the rascals out." Since World War II, 92 percent of all incumbent representatives and 78 percent of incumbent senators running for reelection have been returned to office. Even in the anti-incumbent 1990s, fewer members went down to defeat than retired. (Some, to be sure, beat a strategic retreat.) More than four of every five senators and representatives who took the oath of office on January 7, 1997, were returnees from the previous Congress.

This return rate does not mean, as some have suggested, that the membership of the two chambers is stagnant or unresponsive. For one thing, members of Congress scan reelection rates less calmly than do scholars and reporters sitting on the sidelines. They never feel secure. Bent on maintaining their vote margins, members see themselves as "unsafe at any margin."[2] Moreover, high reelection rates do not always reflect low turnover in membership. Voluntary retirements, including those in which members seek other offices, keep turnover brisk.

In addition to the frantic pace and damage to family life, many retirees faulted the decline in comity and erosion of the arts of bargaining and compromise. "We used to have friends on both sides of the aisle," observed Rep. John T. Myers, R-Ind., a fifteen-term member who exited at the close of the 104th Congress. "Today's attitude is that you can't be friends with someone whose opinion is different. And you can't compromise."[3] From retiring senator (now secretary of defense) William S. Cohen, R-Maine, came this assessment:

> We are witnessing a gravitational pull away from center-based politics to the extremes on both the right and left. Those who seek compromise and consensus are depicted with scorn as a "mushy middle" that is weak and unprincipled. By contrast, those who plant their feet in the concrete of ideological absolutism are heralded as heroic defenders of truth, justice, and the American way.[4]

Incivility had gotten so rife in the House that a bipartisan group of lawmakers sponsored a retreat in Hershey, Pennsylvania, in March 1997 for 200 representatives and their families. The objective was to build bipartisan friendships and relationships. The retreat, however, did little to smooth the sharp-edged partisanship that characterizes today's Congress. As one commentator wrote:

> Pressure has been strong within parties to continue grenades-as-usual operations in the House.... The one-minute "attack ads" continue on the House floor at the start of each day's session; House leaders have virtually no bipartisan dealings, formal or otherwise; and there's been no apparent rebound in the public's esteem for lawmakers or interest in their work.[5] ...

### Members' Bonds With Constituents

The visibility that members of Congress enjoy in their states or districts helps explain the support they command from potential voters. A majority of citizens report contacts with their House members by receiving mail from them, reading about them in a newspaper or magazine, or seeing them on television. Incumbents, moreover, lose no opportunities to do favors for constituents—gestures that are remembered or at least appreciated by most recipients.

Another bond between members and voters is forged out of perceived mutual agreement on important issues facing the constituency and the nation.

The recruitment process... yields lawmakers who reflect local views and prejudices. Contacts with voters throughout the campaign and while in office reinforce this convergence of views, as do representational norms adopted by most members. Whatever the source, the result is that voters believe their views are shared by their representatives.

Members and their staffs... devote great attention to generating publicity and local press. Most members employ one or more press aides and regularly use Capitol Hill studios, where audio or video programs or excerpts can be produced for a fraction of their commercial cost. With the advent of low-cost technology to transmit messages by tape or satellite, local media outlets no longer have to rely on network or news service coverage of major events, especially ones with a local angle. What easier way of covering the local story than airing a statement from a senator or representative? "I am never too busy to talk to local TV," said a prominent House member. "Period. Exclamation point."[6] A survey of House press secretaries showed virtually unanimous agreement: "We'd rather get in [the hometown paper] than on the front page of the *New York Times* any day."[7]

Elected officials are at an advantage in impromptu interviews. Local reporters, especially for the electronic media, usually are on general assignment and are ill prepared to question the lawmaker in detail about issues or events. (Sometimes they begin an interview by asking what the lawmaker wants to discuss.) Moreover, local reporters tend to treat national figures with deference and respect. Often their overriding goal is simply to get the legislator on tape or film. For politicians this is an ideal situation: they can express their views in their own words with a minimum of editing and few challenges from reporters.

As a result, individual members of Congress are normally portrayed in a favorable light by the local media, often getting a free ride from reporters eager for a good quote or "news bite." Or they are presented to their constituents through their own press releases, newsletters, targeted mailings, or recorded radio or television appearances. Individual members thus receive a large measure of free, uncritical publicity. Is it little wonder, then, that in their home districts lawmakers have a positive public image?...

## CONGRESS-AS-INSTITUTION

If individual members get respectable marks, people now seem ready to flunk Congress as a whole. The institutional Congress usually ranks well below the respondents' own representatives in public esteem. Citizens' approval of Congress rises or falls with economic conditions, scandals, wars and crises, and waves of satisfaction or cynicism. Support for Congress surged briefly after it handled the Watergate affair in 1974 and again after the Republican takeover twenty years later. But these surges soon subsided.

The public's approval of Congress has often followed approval of presidents. Perhaps people use the more visible presidency as a handle for assessing Congress and the rest of the government. More likely, they form overall impressions of how the government is doing and rate both institutions accordingly.[8]

Thus a surge in Congress's popularity in the mid-1980s occurred because people were buoyed by optimism over the government and its performance; satisfaction with President Ronald Reagan's leadership carried over into optimism and confidence in other parts of the federal government. Similarly, in 1991 euphoria over the Persian Gulf War briefly buoyed public assessments of Congress as well as of President George Bush. On the other hand, President Bill Clinton's positive second-term image did not extend to Capitol Hill.

Although the American public's views of Congress change over time, its expectations of Congress remain relatively demanding. People expect Congress to exert a strong, independent policy-making role. This has been a consistent finding of surveys over a number of years. People want Congress to check the president's initiatives and to examine the president's proposals carefully. They often have expressed support for the notion of divided government: the White House controlled by one party but checked by another party controlling Capitol Hill.

### Media Coverage

The most open and accessible of the branches of government, Congress is covered by a large press corps containing many of the nation's most skillful journalists. (Capitol Hill is, after all, the best news beat in Washington.) But neither reporters nor their editors can convey in the mass media the internal subtleties or the external pressures that shape lawmaking.

The inner circle of the corps includes reporters who work for the major news services, the large radio and television networks, the national news magazines, and a few of the daily newspapers of national repute (including the *New York Times, Washington Post, Los Angeles Times,* and *Wall Street Journal*). Journalists are assigned exclusively to cover Congress or one of the two chambers, or else they handle stories about a specific topic—economics or foreign affairs, for example. With many sources to choose from, they are not dependent on the goodwill of a single senator or representative. Following the canons of investigative journalism, many are on the alert for hints of scandal, wrongdoing, or corruption. Their approach is that of the suspicious adversary on the lookout for stories with good guys and bad guys, winners and losers. Ethical problems, congressional pay and perquisites, campaign war chests, and foreign junkets are frequent targets of their stories. This style of operation is perhaps inevitable, but it reinforces popular negative stereotypes about Congress as an institution.

A recent survey of 331 experienced members of the national news media bears out this picture, though with some instructive exceptions. The journalists were asked to rate the performance of the current Congress, and from their comments a twelve-point "hostility index" toward the institution was constructed. The vast majority of the journalists fell in the middle—with television reporters slightly more critical of Congress than were print, radio, or wire service people. The small number of reporters who covered Capitol Hill full time were significantly more favorable toward the institution. At the other end were hosts of radio talk shows, who were far more hostile toward Congress than were those in any other group. Most radio talk show hosts are not active journalists, although they tend to see themselves as purveyors of information rather than as entertainers.[9] Needless to add, listeners regard Congress every bit as negatively as do the talk show hosts.

### Citizens' Attitudes Toward Congress

Although extensively reported in the media, Congress is not well understood by the average American. Partly to blame are the size and complexity of the institution, not to mention the arcane twists and turns of the legislative process. Indeed, what many citizens find distasteful are the core attributes of lawmaking: controversy (so many contending voices) and messiness (so many committees, so many decision points).

The public's distrust of the institution goes far deeper than unhappiness with specific policies or disgust with scandals, if we are to believe the sobering findings of John R. Hibbing and Elizabeth Theiss-Morse:

> People do not wish to see uncertainty, conflicting opinions, long debate, competing interests, confusion, bargaining, and compromised, imperfect solutions. They want government to do its job quietly and efficiently, sans conflict and sans fuss. In short . . . they often seek a patently unrealistic form of democracy.[10]

In other words, people abhor the very attributes that are the hallmarks of robust representative assemblies such as Congress. As Hibbing and Theiss-Morse observe, Congress "is structured to embody what we dislike about modern democratic government, which is almost everything."[11]

This unfavorable judgment reflects more than outrage at scandals and distrust of politicians. Surveys have uncovered critical views of virtually all public institutions and doubts about the effectiveness of government. "Americans increasingly suspect the worst about their government," according to one nationwide survey.[12] Another survey portrayed voters as feeling remote from Washington politics despite (or perhaps because of) their sense of personal satisfaction and economic confidence. "Politics in Washington doesn't seem to affect me directly," commented an electrician who was interviewed. "It's all too remote. My job and the traffic and the kids swamp out national politics."[13]

## INTO THE THIRD CENTURY

The U.S. Congress is now in its third century. Survival for more than two centuries is no mean feat. Perhaps like Dr. Johnson's dog (noted not for its skill at standing on hind legs but for doing so at all), Congress's longevity is proof enough of its worth. Congress has withstood repeated stress and turbulence including a civil war, political assassinations, domestic scandals, and tenuous foreign involvements. It is sobering to realize that our government charter is far older than most of the world's governments. "Our present Congress was invented before canned food, the first Wright brothers flight, refrigeration, photography, the Bessemer furnace, the typewriter and telephone; before the automobile, radio and TV; before Hiroshima and Auschwitz and computers."[14]

Mere survival, though, is not enough. The U.S. Congress must help America thrive in a world where all countries increasingly face similar or interrelated problems. National borders and the authority of national governments are becoming less potent. In a global economy, "firms have more freedom over where to locate. Activities that require only a screen, a telephone and a modem can be located anywhere. This will make it harder for a country to tax businesses much more heavily than its competitors."[15] ...

Some contend that too much is expected of members of Congress. How can elected generalists render intelligent judgments on the dizzyingly complex problems of governance? "People shouldn't expect those in office to be at the forefront of new developments," observed Rep. Barney Frank, D-Mass. "The best we can do is to be adapters. No one has the intellectual energy to be an elected official and simultaneously break new intellectual ground."[16] ...

Despite the impression of some that Congress is remote and unresponsive, it reacts more than ever to the activities of individuals and groups. A plebiscitary quality has seeped into legislative life. There simply are more direct avenues of communication between constituents and lawmakers. Faxes, e-mail, the Internet, electronic "town halls," radio talk shows, and other vehicles enable citizens to engage in dialogue with their lawmakers. A better educated electorate appears to want more opportunities to sway policy decisions. As one commentator put it:

> The people are becoming the fourth branch of government, alongside the president, the Congress, and the courts. No longer is any major step taken in Washington without first testing the public's opinion; a permanent electrocardiograph seems hooked up to the body politic.[17] ...

Are the two Congresses ultimately compatible? Or are they diverging, each detrimental to the other? Even if the federal government is ultimately downsized (an uncertain prospect), the burden placed on both Congresses will remain heavy by historical standards. Congress-as-Institution is expected to resolve all manner of problems, not only by processing legislation but also by monitoring programs and serving as an all-purpose watchdog. By all outward signs of activity—such as number of committees and subcommittees, hearings, reports, votes, and hours in session—legislators are struggling valiantly to keep abreast of these demands.

At the same moment, Congress-as-Politicians is busier than ever. In part because of the sheer scope of modern government, in part because of constituents' uncertainties about the future, citizens are insisting that senators and representatives communicate with them more often, serve their states or districts materially, play the role of ombudsmen, and adhere to strict standards of personal conduct. Legislators have accepted and profited electorally from these functions, but not without misgivings and not without detriment to their legislative tasks. As former senator and vice president Walter Mondale observed:

> Constituent service can... be a bottomless pit. The danger is that a member of Congress will end up as little more than an ombudsman between citizens and government agencies. As important as this work is, it takes precious time away from Congress's central responsibilities as both a deliberative and a law-making body.[18]

The intensified demands upon the two Congresses could well lie beyond the reach of normal men and women. Reflecting on the multiplicity of presidential duties, Woodrow Wilson once remarked that we might be forced to pick our leaders from among "wise and prudent athletes"—a small class of people.[19] The same can now be said of senators and representatives. And if the job specifications exceed reasonable dimensions, can we expect even our most talented citizens to perform these tasks successfully?

## NOTES

1. Glenn R. Parker and Robert H. Davidson, "Why Do Americans Love Their Congressmen So Much More Than Their Congress?" *Legislative Studies Quarterly* 4 (February 1979): 53–61.

2. Thomas E. Mann, *Unsafe at Any Margin: Interpreting Congressional Elections* (Washington, D.C.: American Enterprise Institute, 1978).

3. Sandy Hume, "Rep. Myers Calls It Quits," *The Hill*, Jan. 10, 1996, 11.

4. William S. Cohen, "Why I Am Leaving," *Washington Post*, Jan. 21, 1996, C7.

5. Richard E. Cohen, "Chaos Still Prevailing over Civility," *National Journal*, July 5, 1997, 1382.

6. Bob Benenson, "Savvy 'Stars' Making Local TV a Potent Tool," *Congressional Quarterly Weekly Report*, July 18, 1987, 1551–1555.

7. Timothy Cook, *Making Laws and Making News: Media Strategies in the U.S. House of Representatives* (Washington, D.C.: Brookings Institution, 1989), 82–83.

8. Glenn R. Parker, "Some Themes in Congressional Unpopularity," *American Journal of Political Science* 21 (February 1977): 93–109; Roger H. Davidson, David M. Kovenock, and Michael K. O'Leary, *Congress in Crisis* (North Scituate, Mass.: Duxbury Press, 1966), 59–62.

9. Kimberly Coursen Parker, "How the Press Views Congress," in *Congress, the Press, and the Public*, ed. Thomas E. Mann and Norman J. Ornstein (Washington, D.C.: Brookings Institution, 1994), 161–166.

10. John R. Hibbing and Elizabeth Theiss-Morse, *Congress as Public Enemy* (Cambridge: Cambridge University Press, 1995), 147.

11. Ibid., 158.

12. Thomas Hargrove and Guido Stempel, "Poll Says Americans Suspect Worst of Their Government," *Washington Times*, July 5, 1997, A2.

13. Dan Baltz and Ceci Connolly, "Voters Feeling Remote from Issues in Capital," *Washington Post*, July 10, 1997, A1.

14. Alvin Toffler, "Congress in the Year 2000," *GAO Review,* Fall 1980, 44.

15. "Disappearing Taxes," *Economist,* May 31, 1997, 21.

16. "Lessons on Opposition," interview with Barney Frank, *Working Papers Magazine,* May–June 1982, 43.

17. Lawrence Grossman, "Beware the Electronic Republic," *USA Today,* Aug. 25, 1995, 13A.

18. U.S. Congress, Joint Committee on the Organization of Congress, *Hearing,* July 1, 1993. S. Hrg. 103–148. 103d Cong., 1st sess. (Washington, D.C.: U.S. Government Printing Office, 1993), 33.

19. Woodrow Wilson, *Constitutional Government in the United States* (New York: Columbia University Press, 1908), 79–80.

# Presidency

### 11.1 CLINTON ROSSITER

# *The Powers of the Presidency*

Clinton Rossiter (1917–1970), an American historian and political scientist, is the author of *The American Presidency* (Harcourt Brace, 1956), from which the following selection has been excerpted. The book focuses on the historical development of the modern presidency and its unique characteristics and powers.

Rossiter's work begins with a political analysis of the enormous and complex tasks, responsibilities, and burdens of the modern presidency. Beginning with Franklin D. Roosevelt, the American presidency has involved expanded powers and duties. Rossiter uses historical case studies to elaborate on the most significant presidential roles, or "hats" that modern presidents wear. He focuses on the formal constitutional responsibilities of the president, including such important functions as chief of state, chief executive, commander in chief, chief diplomat, and chief legislator. Rossiter also elaborates on the president's roles as chief of party, voice of the people, protector of the peace, manager of prosperity, and world leader.

Rossiter received his M.A. and Ph.D. from Princeton University. He was the John L. Senior Professor of American Institutions at Cornell University for several years. He authored several influential books, such as *The Seedtime of the Republic: The Origin of the American Tradition of Political Liberty* (Harcourt, Brace, 1953), for which he won the Bancroft Prize, the

Woodrow Wilson Foundation Award of the American Political Science Association, and the prize of the Institute of Early American History and Culture; *Parties and Politics in America* (Cornell University Press, 1960); and *Conservatism in America* (Vintage Books, 1962), for which he received the Charles Austin Beard Memorial Prize. *The American Presidency* has been translated into 30 languages and has often been used as a standard text in the study of that topic in colleges and universities. Rossiter also served as a consultant to the Ford Foundation and the Rockefeller Foundation.

**Key Concept:** presidential functions

$T$his presentation must begin with a careful accounting of those tasks we call upon the President to perform, for if there is any one thing about him that strikes the eye immediately, it is the staggering burden he bears for all of us. Those who cherish Gilbert and Sullivan will remember Pooh-Bah, the "particularly haughty exclusive person" in *The Mikado* who filled the offices of "First Lord of the Treasury, Lord Chief Justice, Commander-in-Chief, Lord High Admiral, Master of the Buckhounds, Groom of the Back Stairs, Archbishop of Titipu, and Lord Mayor, both acting and elect." We chuckle at the fictitious Pooh-Bah; we can only wonder at the real one that history has made of the American President. He has at least three jobs for every one of Pooh-Bah's, and they are not performed with the flick of a lacquered fan. At the risk of being perhaps too analytical, let me review the functions of the modern President. These, as I interpret them, are the major roles he plays in the sprawling drama of American government.

First, the President is Chief of State. He remains today, as he has always been, the ceremonial head of the government of the United States, and he must take part with real or apparent enthusiasm in a range of activities that would keep him running and posing from sunrise to bedtime if he were not protected by a cold-blooded staff. Some of these activities are solemn or even priestly in nature; others, through no fault of his own, are flirtations with vulgarity. The long catalogue of public duties that the Queen discharges in England, the President of the Republic in France, and the Governor-General in Canada is the President's responsibility in this country, and the catalogue is even longer because he is not a king, or even an agent of one, and is therefore expected to go through some rather undignified paces by a people who think of him as a combination of scoutmaster, Delphic oracle, hero of the silver screen, and father of the multitudes.

As figurehead rather than working head of our government, he greets distinguished visitors from all parts of the world, lays wreaths on the tomb of the Unknown Soldier and before the statue of Lincoln, makes proclamations of thanksgiving and commemoration, bestows medals on flustered pilots, holds state dinners for the diplomatic corps and the Supreme Court, lights the nation's Christmas tree, buys the first poppy from the Veterans of Foreign Wars, gives the first crisp banknote to the Red Cross, throws out the first ball for the Senators (the harmless ones out at Griffith Stadium), rolls the first egg for the

Easter Bunny, and in the course of any month greets a fantastic procession of firemen, athletes, veterans, Boy Scouts, Campfire Girls, boosters, hog callers, exchange students, and heroic school children. The annual United Fund Drive could not possibly get under way without a five-minute telecast from the White House; Sunday is not Sunday if the President and his lady skip church; a public-works project is not public until the President presses a silver key in Washington and explodes a charge of dynamite in Fort Peck or Hanford or the Tennessee Valley. . . .

The President, in short, is the one-man distillation of the American people just as surely as the Queen is of the British people; he is, in President Taft's words, "the personal embodiment and representative of their dignity and majesty." . . .

The second of the President's roles is that of Chief Executive. He reigns, but he also rules; he symbolizes the people, but he also runs their government. "The true test of a good government is its aptitude and tendency to produce a good administration," Hamilton wrote in *The Federalist,* at the same time making clear that it would be the first duty of the proposed President to produce this "good administration." For reasons that I shall touch upon later, the President (and I mean any President, no matter how happily he may wallow in the details of administration) has more trouble playing this role successfully than he does any of the others. It is, in fact, the one major area of presidential activity in which his powers are simply not equal to his responsibilities. Yet the role is an important one, and we cannot savor the fullness of the President's duties unless we recall that he is held primarily and often exclusively accountable for the ethics, loyalty, efficiency, frugality, and responsiveness to the public's wishes of the two and a third million Americans in the national administration.

Both the Constitution and Congress have recognized his authority to supervise the day-to-day activities of the executive branch, strained and restrained though this supervision may often be in practice. From the Constitution, explicitly or implicitly, he receives the twin powers of appointment and removal, as well as the primary duty, which no law or plan or circumstance can ever take away from him, to "take care that the laws be faithfully executed." He alone may appoint, with the advice and consent of the Senate, the several thousand top officials who run the government; he alone may remove, with varying degrees of abruptness, those who are not executing the laws faithfully —or, in the case of all those Secretaries and generals and attorneys directly under his command, not executing them in a manner consistent with his own policies.

It is the power of removal—the "gun behind the door"—that makes it possible for the President to bend his "team" to his will. More to the point, this power is the symbol and final sanction of his position as Chief Executive, and no official in the administration, not even the most nonpartisan chairman of the most independent regulatory commission, is entirely immune to a fatal attack of presidential displeasure. . . .

The President's third major function is one he could not escape if he wished, and several Presidents have wished it mightily. The Constitution designates him specifically as "Commander-in-Chief of the Army and Navy of the United States, and of the militia of the several States when called into the actual service of the United States." In peace and war he is the supreme commander of the armed forces, the living guarantee of the American belief in "the supremacy of the civil over military authority."

In time of peace he raises, trains, supervises, and deploys the forces that Congress is willing to maintain, and he has a great deal to say about the size and make-up of these forces. With the aid of the Secretary of Defense, the Secretaries of the three services, the Joint Chiefs of Staff, and the members of the National Security Council—every one of these men his personal choice—he looks constantly to the state of the nation's defenses. He is never for one day allowed to forget that he will be held accountable by people, Congress, and history for the nation's readiness to meet an enemy assault. . . .

But this, the power of command, is only a fraction of the vast responsibility the modern President draws from the Commander in Chief clause. The framers of the Constitution, to be sure, took a narrow view of the authority they had granted. "It would amount," Hamilton wrote offhandedly in *The Federalist*, "to nothing more than the supreme command and direction of the military and naval forces, as first General and Admiral of the Confederacy." This view of presidential power as something purely military foundered on the hard facts of the first of our modern wars. Faced by an overriding necessity for harsh, even dictatorial action, Lincoln used the Commander in Chief clause, at first gingerly, in the end boldly, to justify an unprecedented series of measures that cut deeply into the accepted liberties of the people and the routine pattern of government. Wilson added another cubit to the stature of the wartime Presidency by demanding that Congress give him those powers over the economy about which there was any constitutional doubt, and Franklin Roosevelt, who had read about Lincoln and lived with Wilson, carried the wartime Presidency to breath-taking heights of authority over the American economy and social order. The creation and staffing of a whole array of emergency boards and offices, the seizure and operation of more than sixty strike-bound or strike-threatened plants and industries, and the forced evacuation of 70,000 American citizens of Japanese descent from the West Coast are three startling and prophetic examples of what a President can do as Commander in Chief to stiffen the home front in support of the fighting forces. It is important to recall that Congress came to Roosevelt's aid in each of these series of actions by passing laws empowering him to do what he had done already or by fixing penalties for violating the orders of his subordinates. Congress, too, likes to win wars, and Congressmen are more likely to needle the President for inactivity and timidity than to accuse him of acting too swiftly and arbitrarily.

Now that total war, which ignores the old line between battlefield and home front, has been compounded by the absolute weapon, which mocks every rule we have ever tried to honor, we may expect the President to be nothing short of a "constitutional dictator" in the event of war. The next wartime President, who may well be our last, will have the right, of which Lincoln spoke with feeling, to take "any measure which may best subdue the enemy," and he alone will be the judge of what is "best" for the survival of the republic. We have placed a shocking amount of military power in the President's keeping, but where else, we may ask, could it possibly have been placed?

Next, the President is Chief Diplomat. Although authority in the field of foreign relations is shared constitutionally among three organs—President, Congress, and, for two special purposes, the Senate—his position is paramount, if not indeed dominant. In 1799 John Marshall, no particular friend of executive power, spoke of the President as "the sole organ of the nation in its external relations, and its sole representative with foreign nations." In 1936 Justice Sutherland, no particular friend of executive power and even less of Franklin D. Roosevelt, put the Court's stamp of approval on "the very delicate, plenary and exclusive power of the President as the sole organ of the government in the field of international relations." ...

The field of foreign relations can be conveniently if somewhat inexactly divided into two sectors: the formulation of policy and the conduct of affairs. The first of these is a joint undertaking in which the President proposes, Congress disposes, and the wishes of the people prevail in the end. The President's leadership is usually vindicated. Our most ancient and honored policy is significantly known as the *Monroe* Doctrine; our leading policies of recent years have been the *Truman* Doctrine and the *Eisenhower* Doctrine. From Washington's Proclamation of Neutrality in 1793 to Eisenhower's decision to stand fast in Berlin in 1959, the President has repeatedly committed the nation to decisive attitudes and actions abroad, more than once to war itself. Occasionally Congress has compelled him to abandon a policy already put forward, as it did in the case of Grant's plans for Santo Domingo, or has forced distasteful policies upon him, as it did upon Madison in 1812 and McKinley in 1898. Nevertheless, a stubborn President is hard to budge, a crusading President hard to thwart. The diplomatic lives of the two Roosevelts are proof enough of these assertions. Mr. Truman was not exaggerating much when he told an informal gathering of the Jewish War Veterans in 1948: "I make American foreign policy." ...

The President's duties are not all purely executive in nature. He is also intimately associated, by Constitution and custom, with the legislative process, and we may therefore consider him to be the Chief Legislator. Congress has a wealth of strong and talented men, but the complexity of the problems they are asked to solve by a people who assume that all problems are solvable has made *external* leadership a requisite of effective operation. The President alone is in a political, constitutional, and practical position to provide such leadership, and he is therefore expected, within the limits of constitutional and political propriety, to guide Congress in much of its lawmaking activity. Indeed, since Congress is no longer organized to guide itself, not even under such tough-minded leaders as Senator Johnson and Speaker Rayburn, the refusal or inability of the President to point out the way results in weak or, at best, stalemated government.

Success in the delicate area of executive-legislative relations depends on several variables: the political complexion of President and Congress, the state of the Union and of the world around us, the vigor and tact of the President's leadership, and the mood of Congress, which is generally friendly near the beginning of a President's term and rebellious near the end. Yet even the President whose announced policy is to "restore our hallowed system of the separation of powers" and leave Congress strictly alone (Coolidge is a capital example, one not likely to be repeated) must exercise his constitutional option to veto or not to veto about a thousand times each session, must discourse once a year on the state of the Union and occasionally recommend "such measures as he shall judge necessary and expedient," must present the annual budget, and must make some effort to realize at least the less controversial promises in his party's platform. "After all," Mr. Eisenhower told a press conference in 1959, "the Constitution puts the President right square into the legislative business." In the hands of a Wilson or a Roosevelt, even at times in the hands of an Eisenhower, the Presidency becomes a sort of prime ministership or "third House of Congress," and the chief concern of the President is to push for the enactment of his own or his party's legislative desires.

Upon many of our most celebrated laws the presidential imprint is clearly stamped. Each of these was drafted in the President's offices, introduced and supported by his friends, defended in committee by his aides, voted through by a party over which every form of discipline and persuasion was exerted, and then made law by his signature....

Even the President who lacks a congressional majority must go through the motions of leadership. The Republicans in the Eightieth Congress always waited politely for Mr. Truman's proposals on labor, taxes, inflation, civil rights, and education, however scant the regard they intended to pay them. The Democrats, if we may believe the protests of Speaker Rayburn and Senator Johnson, were impatient to hear President Eisenhower's proposals and to feel the lash of his leadership. In any case, the chief responsibility for bridging the constitutional gulf between executive and legislature now rests irrevocably with the President. His tasks as leader of Congress are difficult and delicate, yet he must bend to them steadily or be judged a failure. The President who will not give his best thoughts to guiding Congress, more so the President who is temperamentally or politically unfitted to "get along with Congress," is now rightly considered a national liability.

Chief of State, Chief Executive, Commander in Chief, Chief Diplomat, Chief Legislator—these functions make up the strictly constitutional burden of the President. As Mr. Truman himself allowed in several of his folksy sermons on the Presidency, they form an aggregate of power that would have made Caesar or Genghis Khan or Napoleon bite his nails with envy. Yet even these are not the whole weight of presidential responsibility. I count at least five additional functions that have been piled on top of the original load.

The first of these is the President's role as Chief of Party, one that he has played by popular demand and to a mixed reception ever since the administration of Thomas Jefferson. However sincere Washington's abhorrence of "factions" may have been, his own administration and policies spawned our first two parties, and their arrival upon the scene altered the character of the

Presidency radically. No matter how fondly or how often we may long for a President who is above the heat of political strife, we must acknowledge resolutely his right and duty to be the leader of his party. He is at once the least political and most political of all heads of government.

The value of this function has been attested by all our first-rate Presidents. Jackson, Lincoln, Wilson, and the two Roosevelts were especially skillful party leaders. By playing the politician with unashamed zest the first of these gave his epic administration a unique sense of cohesion, the second rallied doubting Republican leaders and their followings to the cause of the Union, and the other three achieved genuine triumphs as catalysts of congressional action....

Yet [the President] is, at the same time if not in the same breath, the Voice of the People, the leading formulator and expounder of public opinion in the United States. While he acts as political leader of some, he serves as moral spokesman for all....

The President is the American people's one authentic trumpet, and he has no higher duty than to give a clear and certain sound. "Words at great moments of history are deeds," Clement Attlee said of Winston Churchill on the day the latter stepped down in 1945. The strong and imaginative President can make with his own words the kind of history that Churchill made in 1940 and 1941. When the events of 1933 are all but forgotten, we shall still recall Roosevelt's words, "The only thing we have to fear is fear itself."

In the memorable case of *In re Neagle* (1890), which still makes good reading for those who like a touch of horse opera in their constitutional law, Justice Samuel Miller spoke with a feeling of the "peace of the United States"—a happy condition, it would appear, of domestic tranquillity and national prosperity that is often broken by violent men and forces and just as often restored by the President. Perhaps the least known of his functions is the mandate he holds from the Constitution and the laws, but even more positively from the people of the United States, to act as Protector of the Peace. The emergencies that can disturb the peace of the United States seem to grow thicker and more vexing every year, and hardly a week now goes by that the President is not called upon to take forceful steps in behalf of a section or city or group or enterprise that has been hit hard and suddenly by disaster. Generally, it is for state and local authorities to deal with social and natural calamities, but in the face of a riot in Detroit or floods in New England or a tornado in Missouri or a railroad strike in Chicago or a panic in Wall Street, the people turn almost instinctively to the White House and its occupant for aid and comfort....

There is at least one area of American life, the economy, in which the people of this country are no longer content to let disaster fall upon them unopposed. They now expect their government, under the direct leadership of the President, to prevent a depression or panic and not simply to wait until one has developed before putting it to rout. Thus the President has a new function, which is still taking shape, that of Manager of Prosperity....

In order to grasp the full import of the last of the President's roles, we must take him as Chief Diplomat, Commander in Chief, and Chief of State, then thrust him onto a far wider stage, there to perform before a much more numerous and more critical audience. For the modern President is, whether we or our friends abroad like it or not, marked out for duty as a World Leader. The President has a much larger constituency than the American electorate: his words and deeds in behalf of our own survival as a free nation have a direct bearing upon the freedom and stability of at least several score other countries. . . .

Having engaged in this piecemeal analysis of the Presidency, I hasten to fit the pieces back together into a seamless unity. For that, after all, is what the Presidency is, and I hope this exercise in political taxonomy has not obscured the paramount fact that it is a single office filled by a single man. I feel something like a professor of nutritional science who has just ticked off the ingredients of a wonderful stew. The members of the audience may be clear in their minds about the items in the pot, but they have not the slightest notion of what the final product looks like or tastes like or will feel like in their stomachs. The Presidency, too, is a wonderful stew whose unique flavor cannot be accounted for simply by making a list of its ingredients. It is a whole greater than and different from the sum of its parts, an office whose power and prestige are something more than the arithmetical total of all its functions. The President is not one kind of official during one part of the day, another kind during another part—administrator in the morning, legislator at lunch, king in the afternoon, commander before dinner, and politician at odd moments that come his weary way. He is all these things all the time, and any one of his functions feeds upon and into all the others. He is a more exalted Chief of State because he is also Voice of the People, a more forceful Chief Diplomat because he commands the armed forces personally, a more effective Chief Legislator because the political system forces him to be Chief of Party, a more artful Manager of Prosperity because he is Chief Executive.

# Presidential Power and the Modern Presidents

Richard E. Neustadt (b. 1919) served as personal adviser to American presidents Harry S. Truman, John F. Kennedy, and Lyndon B. Johnson. In 1960 Neustadt published a classic book on the American presidency entitled *Presidential Power: The Politics of Leadership* (John Wiley & Sons, 1960). This book had a direct impact on the decision making of President Kennedy during his administration. The latest revised edition of this insightful work on presidential skills and styles is entitled *Presidential Power and the Modern Presidents: The Politics of Leadership from Roosevelt to Reagan* (Free Press, 1990). In this book, from which the following selection is taken, Neustadt evaluates the policies and presidential leadership skills of Kennedy, Johnson, Richard Nixon, Jimmy Carter, and Ronald Reagan. This work is considered an excellent guidebook to presidential decision making and power for both presidents and students of government.

In *Presidential Power and the Modern Presidents,* Neustadt uses historical case studies of presidential decision making to support his central thesis about the limitations of presidential power. Although modern presidents have elaborate formal or constitutional powers, such comprehensive authority does not automatically guarantee presidential power or successful executive leadership. Neustadt argues that a president's influence and success depend upon his professional reputation and prestige, which is related to his negotiating skills and ability to bargain with bureaucrats and legislators. According to Neustadt, a president's power is primarily based upon his ability to persuade.

Neustadt received his M.A. and Ph.D. from Harvard University. He is the Douglas Dillon Professor of Government Emeritus in the John F. Kennedy School of Government at Harvard University. He has also taught at Cornell University, Columbia University, and Princeton University, and he has served as adviser and professional consultant to presidents and various governmental officials and agencies. He is the author of *The Presidency at Mid-Century* (Bobbs-Merrill, 1956) and coauthor, with Ernest R. May, of *Thinking in Time: The Uses of History for Decision-Makers* (Free Press, 1986).

**Key Concept:** the presidential power of persuasion

*I*n the early summer of 1952, before the heat of the campaign, President Truman used to contemplate the problems of the general-become-President should Eisenhower win the forthcoming election. "He'll sit here," Truman would remark (tapping his desk for emphasis), "and he'll say, 'Do this! Do that!' *And nothing will happen*. Poor Ike—it won't be a bit like the Army. He'll find it very frustrating."

Eisenhower evidently found it so. "In the face of the continuing dissidence and disunity, the President sometimes simply exploded with exasperation," wrote Robert Donovan in comment on the early months of Eisenhower's first term. "What was the use, he demanded to know, of his trying to lead the Republican Party...."[1] And this reaction was not limited to early months alone, or to his party only. "The President still feels," an Eisenhower aide remarked to me in 1958, "that when he's decided something, that *ought* to be the end of it... and when it bounces back undone or done wrong, he tends to react with shocked surprise."

Truman knew whereof he spoke. With "resignation" in the place of "shocked surprise," the aide's description would have fitted Truman. The former senator may have been less shocked than the former general, but he was no less subjected to that painful and repetitive experience: "Do this, do that, and nothing will happen." Long before he came to talk of Eisenhower he had put his own experience in other words: "I sit here all day trying to persuade people to do things they ought to have sense enough to do without my persuading them.... That's all the powers of the President amount to."

In these words of a President, spoken on the job, one finds the essence of the problem now before us: "powers" are no guarantee of power; clerkship is no guarantee of leadership. The President of the United States has an extraordinary range of formal powers, of authority in statute law and in the Constitution. Here is testimony that despite his "powers" he does not obtain results by giving orders—or not, at any rate, merely by giving orders. He also has extraordinary status, ex officio, according to the customs of our government and politics. Here is testimony that despite his status he does not get action without argument. Presidential power is the power to persuade....

The limits on command suggest the structure of our government. The Constitutional Convention of 1787 is supposed to have created a government of "separated powers." It did nothing of the sort. Rather, it created a government of separated institutions *sharing* powers. "I am part of the legislative process," Eisenhower often said in 1959 as a reminder of his veto. Congress, the dispenser of authority and funds, is no less part of the administrative process. Federalism adds another set of separated institutions. The Bill of Rights adds others. Many public purposes can only be achieved by voluntary acts of private institutions; the press, for one, in Douglass Cater's phrase, is a "fourth branch of government." And with the coming of alliances abroad, the separate institutions of a London, or a Bonn, share in the making of American public policy.

The separateness of institutions and the sharing of authority prescribe the terms on which a President persuades. When one man shares authority with

*Richard E. Neustadt*

another, but does not gain or lose his job upon the other's whim, his willingness to act upon the urging of the other turns on whether he conceives the action right for him. The essence of a President's persuasive task is to convince such men that what the White House wants of them is what they ought to do for their sake and on their authority. (Sex matters not at all; for *man* read *woman*.)

Persuasive power, thus defined, amounts to more than charm or reasoned argument. These have their uses for a President, but these are not the whole of his resources. For the individuals he would induce to do what he wants done on their own responsibility will need or fear some acts by him on his responsibility. If they share his authority, he has some share in theirs. Presidential "powers" may be inconclusive when a President commands, but always remain relevant as he persuades. The status and authority inherent in his office reinforce his logic and his charm.

Status adds something to persuasiveness; authority adds still more. When Truman urged wage changes on his secretary of commerce while the latter was administering the steel mills, he and Secretary Sawyer were not just two men reasoning with one another. Had they been so, Sawyer probably would never have agreed to act. Truman's status gave him special claims to Sawyer's loyalty or at least attention. In Walter Bagehot's charming phrase "no man can *argue* on his knees." Although there is no kneeling in this country, few men—and exceedingly few cabinet officers—are immune to the impulse to say "yes" to the President of the United States. It grows harder to say "no" when they are seated in his Oval Office at the White House, or in his study on the second floor, where almost tangibly he partakes of the aura of his physical surroundings. In Sawyer's case, moreover, the President possessed formal authority to intervene in many matters of concern to the secretary of commerce. These matters ranged from jurisdictional disputes among the defense agencies to legislation pending before Congress and, ultimately, to the tenure of the secretary, himself. There is nothing in the record to suggest that Truman voiced specific threats when they negotiated over wage increases. But given his formal powers and their relevance to Sawyer's other interests, it is safe to assume that Truman's very advocacy of wage action conveyed an implicit threat.

A President's authority and status give him great advantages in dealing with the men he would persuade. Each "power" is a vantage point for him in the degree that other men have use for his authority. From the veto to appointments, from publicity to budgeting, and so down a long list, the White House now controls the most encompassing array of vantage points in the American political system. With hardly an exception, those who share in governing this country are aware that at some time, in some degree, the doing of *their* jobs, the furthering of *their* ambitions, may depend upon the President of the United States. Their need for presidential action, or their fear of it, is bound to be recurrent if not actually continuous. Their need or fear is his advantage.

A President's advantages are greater than mere listing of his "powers" might suggest. Those with whom he deals must deal with him until the last day of his term. Because they have continuing relationships with him, his future, while it lasts, supports his present influence. Even though there is no need or fear of him today, what he could do tomorrow may supply today's advantage. Continuing relationships may convert any "power," any aspect of his status, into vantage points in almost any case. When he induces other people to do what he wants done, a President can trade on their dependence now and later.

The President's advantages are checked by the advantages of others. Continuing relationships will pull in both directions. These are relationships of mutual dependence. A President depends upon the persons whom he would persuade; he has to reckon with his need or fear of them. They too will possess status, or authority, or both, else they would be of little use to him. Their vantage points confront his own; their power tempers his.

Persuasion is a two-way street. Sawyer, it will be recalled, did not respond at once to Truman's plan for wage increases at the steel mills. On the contrary, the secretary hesitated and delayed and only acquiesced when he was satisfied that publicly he would not bear the onus of decision. Sawyer had some points of vantage all his own from which to resist presidential pressure. If he had to reckon with coercive implications in the President's "situations of strength," so had Truman to be mindful of the implications underlying Sawyer's place as a department head, as steel administrator, and as a cabinet spokesman for business. Loyalty is reciprocal. Having taken on a dirty job in the steel crisis, Sawyer had strong claims to loyal support. Besides, he had authority to do some things that the White House could ill afford. Emulating Wilson, he might have resigned in a huff (the removal power also works two ways). Or, emulating Ellis Arnall, he might have declined to sign necessary orders. Or he might have let it be known publicly that he deplored what he was told to do and protested its doing. By following any of these courses Sawyer almost surely would have strengthened the position of management, weakened the position of the White House, and embittered the union. But the whole purpose of a wage increase was to enhance White House persuasiveness in urging settlement upon union and companies alike. Although Sawyer's status and authority did not give him the power to prevent an increase outright, they gave him capability to undermine its purpose. If his authority over wage rates had been vested by a statute, not by revocable presidential order, his power of prevention might have been complete. So Harold Ickes demonstrated in the famous case of helium sales to Germany before the Second World War.[2]

The power to persuade is the power to bargain. Status and authority yield bargaining advantages. But in a government of "separated institutions sharing powers," they yield them to all sides. With the array of vantage points at his disposal, a President may be far more persuasive than his logic or his charm could make him. But outcomes are not guaranteed by his advantages. There remain the counter pressures those whom he would influence can bring to bear on him from vantage points at their disposal. Command has limited utility; persuasion becomes give-and-take. It is well that the White House holds the vantage points it does. In such a business any President may need them all— and more....

The essence of a President's persuasive task, with congressmen and everybody else, is to induce them to believe that what he wants of them is what their own appraisal of their own responsibilities requires them to do in their interest, not his. Because men may differ in their views on public policy, because differences in outlook stem from differences in duty—duty to one's office, one's constituents, oneself—that task is bound to be more like collective bargaining than like a reasoned argument among philosopher kings. Overtly or implicitly, hard bargaining has characterized all illustrations offered up to now. This is the reason why: Persuasion deals in the coin of self-interest with men who have some freedom to reject what they find counterfeit. . . .

A President's persuasiveness with others in the government depends on something more than his advantages for bargaining. The men he would persuade must be convinced in their own minds that he has skill and will enough to *use* his advantages. Their judgment of him is a factor in his influence with them. . . .

The men who share in governing this country are inveterate observers of a President. They have the doing of whatever he wants done. They are the objects of his personal persuasion. They also are the most attentive members of his audience. These doers comprise what in spirit, not geography, might well be termed the "Washington community." This community cuts across the President's constituencies. Members of Congress and his Administration, governors of states, military commanders in the field, leading politicians in both parties, representatives of private organizations, newsmen of assorted types and sizes, foreign diplomats (and principals abroad)—all these are "Washingtonians" no matter what their physical location. In most respects the Washington community is far from homogeneous. In one respect it is tightly knit indeed: By definition all its members are compelled to watch the President for reasons not of pleasure but vocation. They need him in their business just as he needs them. Their own work thus requires that they keep an eye on him. Because they watch him closely his persuasiveness with them turns quite as much on their informed appraisals as on his presumed advantages.

In influencing Washingtonians, the most important law at a President's disposal is the "law of anticipated reactions," propounded years ago by Carl J. Friedrich.[3] The individuals who share in governing do what they think they must. A President's effect on them is heightened or diminished by their thoughts about his probable reaction to their doing. They base their expectations on what they can see of him. And they are watching all the time. Looking at themselves, at him, at the immediate event, and toward the future, they may think that what he might do in theory, he would not dare to do in fact. So MacArthur evidently thought before he was dismissed. They may think that the President has tied his hands behind his back, as Faubus thought, apparently, before and after Newport. They may conclude with Arnall that the President has more to lose than they do, should he not support them. Or they may conclude, as Sawyer evidently did, that they risk more than he does if they do not support him. A Marshall and a Vandenberg may decide that the President can be relied upon to put his powers and his status at their service. A Charles E. Wilson, after Key West, may decide the opposite. . . .

What other men expect of him becomes a cardinal factor in the President's own power to persuade. When people in the government consider their relationships with him it does them little good to scan the Constitution or remind themselves that Presidents possess potential vantage points in excess of enumerated powers. Their problem is never what abstract Presidents might do in theory but what an actual incumbent will try in fact. They must anticipate, as best they can, his ability and will to make use of the bargaining advantages he has. Out of what others think of him emerge his opportunities for influence with them. If he would maximize his prospects for effectiveness, he must concern himself with what they think. To formulate his power problem in these terms is to illuminate the job of being President. . . .

A President who values power need not be concerned with every flaw in his day-by-day performance, but he has every reason for concern with the residual impressions of tenacity and skill accumulating in the minds of Washingtonians-at-large. His bargaining advantages in seeking what he wants are heightened or diminished by what others think of him. Their thoughts are shaped by what they see. They do not see alone, they see together. What they think of him is likely to be much affected by the things they see alike. His look in "everybody's" eyes becomes strategically important for his influence. Reputation, of itself, does not persuade, but it can make persuasion easier, or harder, or impossible.

Ideally, any President who valued personal power would start his term with vivid demonstrations of tenacity and skill in every sphere, thereby establishing a reputation sure to stand the shocks of daily disarray until he was prepared to demonstrate again. This is no more than Franklin Roosevelt did in his first term. It is the ideal formula for others. Unfortunately, FDR's successors have not held the combination of advantages that helped him make his first-term demonstration: the public memory of his predecessor, the crisis of the Great Depression, the easy escape from foreign affairs, the eagerness of intellectuals, the patronage for partisans, the breadth of his experience in government (unmatched in this century save by the other Roosevelt). Nor is there anything to indicate that while midcentury conditions last, a future President is likely to hold comparable advantages. Emergencies in policy with politics as usual can hardly favor an effective use of Roosevelt's formula.

A contemporary President may have to settle for a reputation short of the ideal. If so, what then should be his object? It should be to induce as much uncertainty as possible about the consequences of ignoring what he wants. If he cannot make men think him bound to win, his need is to keep them from thinking they can cross him without risk, or that they can be sure what risks they run. At the same time (no mean feat) he needs to keep them from fearing lest he leave them in the lurch if they support him. To maximize uncertainties in future opposition, to minimize the insecurities of possible support, and to avoid the opposite effect in either case—these together form a goal for any midcentury President who seeks a reputation that will serve his personal power.

*Chapter 11*
*The Presidency*

1. Robert J. Donovan, *Eisenhower: The Inside Story* (New York: Harper, 1956), p. 151.

2. As secretary of the interior in 1939, Harold Ickes refused to approve the sale of helium to Germany despite the insistence of the State Department and the urging of President Roosevelt. Without the Secretary's approval, such sales were forbidden by statute. See *The Secret Diaries of Harold L. Ickes* (New York: Simon & Schuster, 1954), vol. 2, especially pp. 391–93, 396–99.

3. Carl J. Friedrich, "Public Policy and the Nature of Administrative Responsibility," *Public Policy*, vol. 1 (Cambridge: Harvard University Press, 1940), pp. 3–24.

## 11.3 THOMAS E. CRONIN AND MICHAEL A. GENOVESE

# *"If Men Were Angels...":*
# *Presidential Leadership and Accountability*

Thomas E. Cronin (b. 1940) and Michael A. Genovese are the authors of *The Paradoxes of the American Presidency* (Oxford University Press, 1998), from which the following selection has been excerpted. This book is considered a classic presidential study and has already had a profound impact upon the analysis of contemporary presidential scholars. The authors use historical case studies in their examination of the complexities of the institution of the American presidency, particularly the paradoxical nature of American public opinion, which has led to contradictory interpretations and expectations of presidential powers, roles, and responsibilities. The American public demands both strong dynamic leadership and passive leadership that conforms to public opinion; an ideological party leader and a pragmatic, compromising, bipartisan, consensus-building negotiator; and a president who is an innovator and decisive but one who rigidly conforms to precedent. In *The Paradoxes of the American Presidency,* Cronin and Genovese focus on the complex contemporary issue of presidential accountability, which they maintain implies such disparate criteria as responsiveness to public opinion, responsibility for executive actions and decisions, decision making guided by the public good, and the communication of actions to the public to enable it to assess presidential performance. At the core of this investigation is the assertion that accountability is a critical democratic principle signifying that government officials are answerable for their behavior.

*The Paradoxes of the American Presidency* is critical to the contemporary literature on presidential accountability in that the authors articulate sustained theoretical analysis of impeachment as the absolute check on abuses of executive authority and of the necessity for occasional independent counsels. Cronin and Genovese articulate political rather than formal constitutional measures (e.g., a single six-year presidential term) to promote presidential integrity and accountability. The authors' recommendations for increasing presidential accountability and thereby reducing arbitrary leadership include establishing a responsible party system, empowering American

255

political parties, and encouraging political parties to become more disciplined, cohesive, and ideological. In addition to sustained public oversight, Cronin and Genovese also suggest that congressional authority should be strengthened to scrutinize presidential behavior.

Cronin received his M.A. and Ph.D. from Stanford University. He is currently the president of Whitman College. As a presidential scholar, Cronin has been a prolific author, coauthor, and editor of numerous books, including *The Presidency Reappraised* (Praeger, 1977),*Rethinking the Presidency* (Little, Brown, 1982), and *Direct Democracy: The Politics of Initiative, Referendum, and Recall* (Harvard University Press, 1989). He is also a frequent contributor to various newspapers and political journals, including *Politics, Commonweal, Society, Public Administration Review, New York Times Magazine,* and *The Washington Monthly.* In addition to his academic background, he has extensive practical experience as a U.S. Senate aide, a White House aide, a delegate at the Democratic National Conventions of 1980, 1984, and 1988, a Democratic candidate for the U.S. Congress, and a consultant to congressional committees. It is from this rich background that he has articulated significant insights in his works on the presidency.

Genovese received his Ph.D. from the University of Southern California. He is currently a professor of political science and director of the Institute for Leadership Studies at Loyola Marymount University. As a scholar on the presidency, he has authored or edited numerous publications, including *The Nixon Presidency: Power and Politics in Turbulent Times* (Greenwood Press, 1990), *The Presidency in an Age of Limits* (Greenwood Press, 1993), *Women as National Leaders* (Sage Publications, 1993), and *The Presidential Dilemma: Leadership in the American System* (HarperCollins, 1995). He is also a prolific author of scholarly articles and reviews, and his work has appeared in such journals as *Presidential Studies Quarterly, The American Political Science Review, Congress and the Presidency, Governance, Political Science Quarterly, Western Political Quarterly, The Journal of Politics,* and the *International Journal on World Peace.*

**Key Concept:** presidential accountability

# HOLDING PRESIDENTS TO ACCOUNT

... Some part of us wants a larger-than-life, two-gun, charismatic Mount Rushmore leader. Harrison Ford in the film *Air Force One* (1997) vivified this yearning. Still, there is the remarkably enduring antigovernment, antileadership, chronic-complainer syndrome. We want strong, gutsy leadership to operate on alternate days with a "national city manager." We want presidents to have a wealth of power to solve our problems, yet not so much they can do lasting damage.

Accountability implies not only responsiveness to majority desires and answerability for actions but also taking the people and their views into account. It also implies a performance guided by integrity and character. Accountability implies as well that important decisions could be explained to the people to allow them to appraise how well a president is handling the responsibility of the office.

To whom is accountability owed? No president, it would seem, can be more than partially accountable to the people, for each president will listen to some people and some points of view more than to others. If we have learned anything in recent years, however, it is that the doctrine of presidential infallibility has been rejected. Arbitrary rule by powerful executives has always been rejected here. But what should be done when there are sharp differences between experts or when expert opinion differs sharply from the preponderance of public opinion? How much accountability, and what kind, is desirable? Is it not possible that the quest for ultimate accountability will result in a presidency without the prerogatives and independent discretion necessary for creative leadership?

The modern presidency, in fact, may be unaccountable because it is too strong and independent in certain areas and too weak and dependent in others. One of the perplexing circumstances characterizing the modern presidency is that considerable restraints sometimes exist where restraints are least desirable and inadequate restraints are available where they are needed. Also, presidential strength is no guarantee that a president will be responsive or answerable. Indeed, significant dependent strength may encourage low answerability when it suits a president's short-term personal power goals.

# THE PRESIDENCY AND DEMOCRATIC THEORY

How do you grant yet control power? Can leaders be empowered yet also democratized?

These are classic questions our framers faced and these have been central to debates in democratic political theory. Leadership implies power, accountability implies limits. Contradictions aside, accountability is a fundamental piece of the democratic puzzle. In essence it denotes that public officials are answerable for their actions. But to whom? Within what limits? Through what means?

There are essentially three types of accountability: *ultimate accountability* (which the United States has via the impeachment process), *periodic accountability* (provided for by general elections and occasional landmark Supreme Court decisions), and *daily accountability* (somewhat contained in the separation of power).[1] James Madison believed elections provided the "primary check on government" and that the separation of powers ("ambition will be made to counteract ambition") plus "auxiliary precautions" should take care of the rest.[2]

There *are* times when presidents abuse power or behave corruptly. But even in the two notable bouts with presidential abuses, Watergate and the Iran-Contra scandal, the president was stopped by the countervailing forces of a free press, an independent Congress, an independent judiciary, and a (late to be sure) aroused public.

We may hold presidents accountable, but can they be held responsible? That is, can they muster enough power to govern? One means to improve accountability and also empower leadership is to strengthen the party system in America. Our parties are, at least by European standards, relatively weak, undisciplined, and nonideological. A stronger party system could organize and mobilize citizens and government, diminish the fragmentation of the separation of powers, and mitigate against the atomization of our citizenry. If the parties were more disciplined and programmatic, the government's ability to push through its programs would doubtless be enhanced.

A more responsible party system would also ground presidents in a more consensus-oriented style of leadership, and thereby diminish the independent, unconnected brand of leadership so often attempted by recent presidents. A more robust party system can help join the president and Congress together in a more cooperative relationship.[3] . . .

A president's leeway for achievement can be determined by the degree to which consensus or conflict exists among elite interest groups within a particular arena of public policy. If the policy elite of a given profession or industry share wide agreement on a particular issue, it is very difficult for a president to effect an opposing point of view. Occasional exceptions such as Medicare, automobile safety devices, and antipollution legislation are not persuasive, because the profession or industry in question seldom lost much and the costs for such programs were in most cases passed on in some way to the consumer or taxpayer. If, however, cleavage or confusion occurs over substantive or procedural matters, a president has some independent influence; although even then, the scope and type of his influence will be shaped by the character of the conflict among these elite. Thus, Johnson's effort to create model cities as demonstrations of how social and physical planning could produce decent and livable cities soon was heavily influenced by pressures from home builders, developers, real-estate associations, big-city mayors, and other strategically positioned interests. Likewise, despite widespread public support for rapid progress on the environmental front, Carter's environmental protection recommendations soon became influenced by the views of the automobile manufacturers as well as by the unions potentially affected by stringent standards and too rapid implementation. More recently, President Clinton's efforts at health care reform met with fierce opposition from insurance companies and medical care providers who felt threatened by the proposed reforms. They were able to mobilize the public and Congress and prevented Clinton's proposals from being enacted into law. Sometimes a consensus among policy elites may be the product of presidential commitment, but the reverse is more likely to be the case.

Prior commitments to special interests inhibit planning, brake a president's capacity to focus on new problems, and help to exhaust his political credit. Despite high expectations, presidents may find themselves merely a strategically situated broker for their own party, able only in a limited way to affect existing patterns of grants or subsidies.

Every grant program generates concrete benefits to a particular group, and possessiveness characterizes nearly every group that has participated in the growth of federal aid programs since the New Deal. According to the doctrine of interest groups, the unorganized are left out of most policymaking equations.

In fact, seldom does an interest group emerge that has as its aim the promotion of the public benefit, a program that would benefit everybody. At the same time, the standards of justice and respect for law deteriorate amid informal, frankly feudal negotiations among those stronger interests who can adjust the laws to their own advantage and profit.

In the end, all three branches of government and the bureaucracy listen more attentively and usually yield to the ideas from those segments of society able to represent themselves, able to shape the character of those branches, and able to supply precisely that information and argumentation needed to make the system move. So it is that the many well-heeled interests continue to enjoy a special advantage in any contest with a president who is a genuine progressive....

# THE SIX-YEAR NONRENEWABLE TERM NONSENSE

One of the more curious remedies persistently suggested in discussions of reforming the presidency is the idea of a single six-year presidential term. This is certainly not a new idea, having been originally proposed in Congress as early as 1826. It has been reintroduced more than 150 times since then and has won backing from at least ten presidents, including Johnson, Nixon, and Carter. This reform could only be achieved by amending our Constitution....

Arguing that we must liberate the presidency from "unnecessary political burdens," Senator Mike Mansfield said in 1971 that it is intolerable that a president "is compelled to devote his time, energy and talents to what can be termed only as purely political tasks.... A president facing reelection faces...a host of demands that range from attending the needs of political office holders, office seekers, financial backers and all the rest to riding herd on the day-to-day developments within the pedestrian partisan arena."[4] Others also feel that the country's chief executives should be more businesslike and that reducing their reelection activities would ensure more time and energy for substantive planning and systematic program implementation. Some hope, moreover, that the six-year term would enable a president to overcome both a deference to special interests and the timidity that results from having to keep an eye on the forthcoming election.

In short, the case in favor of the single six-year term is based on several expectations, namely, that it would:

- reduce the role of politics in the White House
- liberate a president from the worries and indignities of a reelection effort
- allow more time to concentrate on policy planning and program implementation
- liberate a president from the pressures of special-interest groups and party-line politics, allowing him to exercise greater independence of judgment and nonpartisan leadership

- eliminate the advantages of incumbency from presidential elections
- allow a president to make decisions free from the temptation of political expediency
- enforce the common-sense idea that a period of six years is enough even for the most robust individual

Despite a few attractive features, the six-year term would cause more problems than it would solve. The required reelection after four years is one of the most democratic aspects of the presidency. It affords an opportunity for assessment. It enhances the likelihood that a president will carefully weigh the effects of whatever he or she does on his reelection chances. At the core of our system is the belief that our president should have to worry about reelection and be subject to all the same vicissitudes of politics as other elected officials. Moreover, a political party should retain the threat of dumping a president as a check on the incumbent and the office, especially on a president who refuses to honor his or her party's pledges. . . .

The proposed divorce between the presidency and politics presupposes a significantly different kind of political system from that of the United States, which is glued together largely by ambiguity, compromise, and the extensive sharing of powers. In light of the requisites of democracy, the presidency must be a highly political office and the president an expert practitioner of the art of politics. Quite simply, there is no other way for presidents to negotiate favorable coalitions within the country, Congress, and the executive branch and to gather the authority needed to translate ideas into accomplishments. A president who remains aloof from politics, campaigns, and partisan alliances does so at the risk of becoming the prisoner of events, special interests, or his own whims.

The very means for bringing a president in touch with reality is the process of political debate and political bargaining, with all of the necessary uncertainty, changes of course, arguments, and listening to other points of view. What makes domestic politics so distasteful to presidents, that it is full of groups to persuade and committees to inform, is precisely its virtue; indeed, it is the major hope for maintaining an open presidency, one neither bound by its own sources of information nor aloof to the point that it will no longer listen.

By calling the president "more presidential" whenever a president ignores partisan politics, citizens encourage that president to even greater isolation. By turning up their noses at politics in the White House and urging the president to get on with the real business of guiding the nation, they also help to establish the two important conditions for secrecy and duplicity, with which the nation has become so familiar. First, with all the apparatus and technology for secret statesmanship at hand, presidents can more easily call on aides when something needs fixing than persuade the public or Congress to their point of view. Second, because presidents will look unpresidential if they participate in normal party politics, their aides must go through grotesque contortions to prove that their boss has never thought about anything except being president of all the people. The tactic of secrecy, so tempting to those who have it within their grasp, amounts to insulating the president from the normal checks and balances of the political system. New bait will be needed to lure presidents out of this comfortable sanctuary and into the morass of open politics, for the present enticements are small.

One way to prevent future abuses of presidential power, as others have noted, is to make the White House more open; and one way to do that, as has not been suggested so often, is to begin regarding a president as a politician once again. *Politics,* in the best sense of that term, is the art of making decisions in the context of debate, dialogue, and open two-way conversations, the art of making the difficult and desirable possible. This kind of politics at the White House should not be diminished. Indeed, as pointed out above, it is highly desirable that presidents be great practitioners of the craft of politics. They, as well as Congress and our parties, would profit from more politics, not less.

Most of the effective presidents have been highly political. They knew how to stretch the limited resources of the office, and they loved politics and enjoyed the responsibilities of party leadership. The nation has been well served by sensitive politicians disciplined by the general thrust of partisan and public thinking. Many of the least political presidents were the least successful and seemingly the least suited temperamentally to the rigors of the office. The best have been those who listened to people, who responded to majority as well as to intense minority sentiment, who saw that political parties are often the most important vehicle for communicating voter preferences to those in public office, and who were attentive to the diversity and intensity of public attitudes even as they attempted to educate and to influence the direction of opinion. . . .

# THE ULTIMATE CHECK: IMPEACHMENT AND REMOVAL

Impeachment is obviously one of the most potent checks against the abuse of executive power, yet over the nation's history it has been the least used check. For practical purposes, it is a political action, phrased in legal terminology, against an official of the federal government. The Constitution deals with the subject of impeachment and conviction in six places, but the scope of the power is outlined in Article II, Section 4.

> The President, Vice President and all civil officers of the United States, shall be removed from Office on Impeachment for, and Conviction of, Treason, Bribery, or other high Crimes and Misdemeanors.

In the impeachment process, the House of Representatives acts as the prosecutor and the Senate serves as judge and jury. Any member of the House may initiate impeachment proceedings by introducing a resolution to that effect in the House. The House Judiciary Committee may conduct hearings and investigations. The committee then decides either in favor of or against an impeachment verdict and sends its conclusions on to the full house. A 50-percent vote in the House is needed to impeach. Select members of the House, if an impeachment is enacted, would then try the case before the U.S. Senate. In the Senate a two-thirds vote of those members present is needed for conviction and removal.

Only thirteen national officials have been impeached by the House since 1789. Of these, eleven were tried in the Senate. Four were convicted, six were acquitted, and one resigned before the Senate took action. In the two remaining cases, the charges were dismissed after the person had been forced to resign national office. Nine of these cases involved federal judges, one involved a senator, one a secretary of war, and one a president, Andrew Johnson, who was overwhelmingly impeached by the House in February 1868 but missed conviction in the Senate by one vote (35–19) in May of that same year.

The impeachment and removal of a president has been a much misunderstood and an obviously cumbersome means of accountability. Its use is fraught with emotion and hazardous side effects, and it necessarily remains a device to be used only as a last resort.

One of President Nixon's involuntary contributions to our understanding of presidential politics is that he provided the occasion for clarifying the character and usage of the impeachment and removal power, for the most significant controversial constitutional question about impeachment had been what were the appropriate grounds for this action. *Treason* and *bribery* are clear legal terms and cause no problem. It was the phrase *other high Crimes and Misdemeanors* that raised so many hard-to-answer questions....

Some analysts, especially lawyers defending the potentially impeached, have argued that a person can be impeached and removed from office only on criminal charges or on offenses that would be indictable in the criminal court. The weight of most recent scholarship, however, Nixon's defense to the contrary notwithstanding, supports the construction of "high crimes and misdemeanors" as not limited to offenses under ordinary criminal law.[5]

One possible view is that an impeachable offense is whatever a majority of the House say it is. The extreme opposite view, or the Nixon defense view, holds that impeachment should be voted only on proof of serious, indictable crimes. In the celebrated Richard Nixon impeachment proceedings, the House Judiciary Committee adopted a middle stance, one that is likely to have a controlling, if not legal, influence on future impeachment efforts. The Judiciary Committee in 1974 held that violation of a criminal statute is not a prerequisite for impeachment as long as the offense is a serious one. Committee members were well aware that an impeachable offense should not be taken to mean anything around which political expediency might organize a majority in the House and two-thirds in the Senate. In effect, the majority of the House Judiciary Committee believed that a gross breach of trust or serious abuse of power was necessary before passage of an impeachment resolution....

Only a handful of the more than one hundred Watergate-related reform bills ever made it through Congress. One of the more controversial ones that did was a provision that would establish, under certain circumstances, a temporary special prosecutor to investigate and prosecute executive branch conflict-of-interest allegations. Later legislators would rightly substitute the name *independent counsels* for the more biased term *special prosecutors.*

Watergate demonstrated that the executive branch could not investigate itself lest there be the appearance—if not the reality—of a conflict of interest. After considerable debate Congress passed the Special Prosecutor Act in 1978. This law allowed the attorney general to appoint a special investigator under certain circumstances.

Under this legislation it is up to the attorney general to determine whether a case of conflict of interest is valid enough to warrant further investigation and prosecution. This would apply in the cases of about one hundred top executive office and Justice Department posts and top officers of a presidential election campaign. The statute mandates the appointment by a designated panel of three federal judges of an independent counsel whenever charges of a violation of federal criminal law arise in connection with these top officials.

Did the Congress overreact in creating the special prosecutor law? No. Presidents, like all executives, set the moral tone for their administrations, give clues as to acceptable and unacceptable behavior, establish norms and limits. Presidents demonstrate by words and deeds the kind of behavior that will be tolerated and the standards applicable to the entire administration. Independent counsels, while perhaps overused in recent years, do serve a useful purpose when employed in appropriate circumstances.

If politics is, or appears to be, scandal ridden; if self-interest and not pursuit of the public interest appears to be the chief motivating force in politics, then it should not surprise us that the general public sees "politics" as a dirty word. But this may undermine democracy and the respect for the rule of law, as well as drive people out of the political process. Thus, it is vital to the health of constitutional democracy that corruption be exposed and the wrongdoers punished.

In the history of the presidency, the administrations considered most corrupt are the Grant, Harding, and Nixon presidencies.[6] The Reagan and Clinton administrations, sadly, have also had major ethical and criminal problems. Ulysses S. Grant, inexperienced in the world of politics, was taken advantage of by avaricious associates. Likewise, Warren G. Harding's lax management style allowed greedy underlings to take advantage of him.

The Nixon administration was markedly different from the Grant and Harding presidencies in that here the president was an active "co-conspirator" in the crimes of Watergate.[7] And during the Reagan years, several types of corruption were exposed, some of which were linked directly to the president. With both what was referred to as the "sleaze factor," in which over two hundred White House officials were accused of criminal behavior[8] (among them

263

Richard Allen, the president's first national security adviser; Labor Secretary Raymond Donovan, who was indicted but not convicted; Rita Lavalle of the EPA; Attorney General Ed Meese; aide Michael Deaver; and White House political director Lyn Nofzinger) and the Iran-Contra scandal, the Reagan administration faced an unprecedented number of accusations of wrongdoing.

Charges of wrongdoing have hounded President Clinton. In January of 1992, then candidate Clinton faced accusations of sexual misconduct, and shortly after he was elected, charges of shady financial dealings surfaced in the Whitewater affair. When aide Vince Foster committed suicide, charges that the Clintons had a hand in the death were leveled. And charges of fund-raising improprieties stemming from Clinton's 1996 reelection bid hounded him in his second term.

Several independent counsels were appointed to investigate Clinton and his associates. Kenneth Starr, appointed to investigate Whitewater-related accusations, sparked controversy for his public association with anti-Clinton organizations, and for the lengthy and expensive investigation against the president. Clinton's prepresidential as well as presidential behavior certainly provided a lot for investigators.[9]

There were seventeen independent counsel investigations between 1978 and 1998. The process has not worked perfectly, and indeed for a two-year period from 1992 to 1994 the law was allowed to lapse.

Critics have argued that some independent counsels have politicized their investigations and that in some cases, such as the Iran-Contra affair and in the more recent Whitewater and campaign financing investigations, the investigations have gone on for too long.

Some critics think too that the independent counsels are too independent. But this independence is necessary if the process is to have integrity....

What is now called the *Independent Counsel Act* will always be controversial. Republicans complained bitterly when Iran-Contra and other Reagan-era scandals were investigated. Democrats complained almost as loudly as investigations of the Clinton administration dragged on. But the independent counsel process is essential to keeping presidents and other cabinet-level executive officials accountable....

# THE NECESSITY FOR POLITICS AND HEALTHY POLITICAL PARTIES

...The simplistic notion that returning to the drawing boards and coming up with a new charter or a new constitution will provide the needed solutions is rejected. A new constitutional convention is not needed. Solving major policy problems and keeping presidents honest and responsible are more likely to be accomplished by *political* than any additional *constitutional* means. No single institutional innovation we have ever heard of could guarantee a commitment to truth, compassion, and justice. Formal constitutional provisions to guard against presidential isolation, such as the institutionalization of government-sponsored votes of confidence or a lengthened presidential term, are not sensible ways to increase accountability....

Political controls, however, do need to be sharpened and strengthened to ensure a continual public and congressional scrutiny of presidential activity. Openness and candor often have been lacking. Presidents and their aides sometimes supply disappointingly little information to the press, to Congress, or to the public on matters of executive agreements, vetoes, executive orders, complex arms sales, and how they raise campaign contributions. In the seemingly endless attempt to accentuate the positive, White House spin controllers too often have distorted news and thereby aggravated difficulties in credibility by claiming too much credit for fortuitous events or for policy initiatives that may or may not achieve sustained or desirable ends and by projecting the appearance of boldness, usually at the expense of candid discussions of the complexity of problems, the modesty of proposed solutions, and the realities of who must pay and how much.

A free society must mean a society based explicitly on free competition, most particularly competition in ideas and opinions, and by frank discussions of alternative national purposes and goals. Elected leaders and a vigorous press must ceaselessly attack ignorance, apathy, and mindless nationalism—the classic enemies of democracy. The citizen must resist sentimental and rhetorical patriotism that espouses everything as a matter for top priority but in practice eschews the tough political programs that must be begun and implemented. Needed is a far more thoughtful way of looking at the presidency, leadership, and citizen responsibilities.

Also, Congress, the press, and the public must use all existing political controls as a means to inspire as well as to check presidents. Citizens must insist that presidents lend their voice and energies to those who are not represented by well-heeled lobbyists. Strengthening the have-not sectors of society and giving a fair hearing to minorities will always remain major presidential responsibilities and an essential part of the legitimacy of the modern presidency.

We may want to change the presidency, yet *we* must change also. We must make the presidency work, but we must also strengthen Congress, modify public expectations and demands, and strengthen the party system. The interconnectedness of the American system—not the reform of one branch, but the reform of the American governmental system—should be the goal.

## NOTES

1. Theodore C. Sorensen, *Watchmen in the Night* (Cambridge, Mass.: MIT Press, 1975).

2. James Madison, *The Federalist Papers,* No. 51. (Modern Library, 1937).

3. Sidney M. Milkis, *The President and the Parties* (New York: Oxford University Press, 1993).

4. Mike Mansfield, *Statement in Support of Senate Joint Resolution 77,* before the Subcommittee on Constitutional Amendments of the U.S. Senate, Committee on the Judiciary,

October 8, 1971, processed. For his extended views and those of several other witnesses, see U.S. Congress, Senate, Committee on the Judiciary, Subcommittee on Constitutional Amendments, *Single Six-Year Term for President*, 92nd Congress, 1st Session, 1972, p. 32.

5. John R. Labovitz, *Presidential Impeachment* (New Haven, Conn.: Yale University Press, 1978). See also Charles Black, *Impeachment: A Handbook* (New Haven, Conn.: Yale University Press, 1974); Raoul Berger, *Impeachment: The Constitutional Problems* (Cambridge, Mass.: Harvard University Press, 1973); and Stanley I. Kutler, *The Wars of Watergate* (New York: Knopf, 1990).

6. Michael A. Genovese, "Presidential Corruption," paper presented at the annual meeting of the American Political Science Association, New York, September, 1994. Some would add President Clinton's problems with Whitewater to this list.

7. Michael A. Genovese, *The Nixon Presidency: Power and Politics in Turbulent Times* (Westport, Conn.: Greenwood Press, 1990).

8. Shelley Ross, *Fall From Grace* (New York: Ballantine Books, 1988), p. 269.

9. See, for example, James B. Stewart's provocative analysis in *Blood Sport: The President and His Adversaries* (New York: Simon & Schuster, 1996).

# CHAPTER 12 The Bureaucracy

## 12.1 HUGH HECLO

# *Political Executives: A Government of Strangers*

Hugh Heclo has been recognized by students and scholars of public administration and public policy as an expert on the federal bureaucracy. The following selection is excerpted from Heclo's *A Government of Strangers: Executive Politics in Washington* (Brookings Institution, 1977), what many political scientists consider to be one of the most significant contributions to the study of the Washington bureaucracy and the recruitment and appointment of political executives. In the book, Heclo focuses on how high-ranking professional bureaucrats attempt to maintain administrative stability and how political appointees attempt to dominate and manipulate the administrative bureaucracy. In addition, he analyzes how government careerists, or professional administrators, attempt to resist the efforts of political appointees to consolidate power within their respective departments or agencies. This book has shifted the theoretical focus of administrative behavior to emphasize the relations of political appointees with bureaucrats and the president.

Heclo depicts the political executives or political appointees as members of the social economic elite of American society. He claims that, in contrast to many private organizations, high-ranking public officials and administrators in the executive branch of the national government are less familiar and less informed about their working environment than administrative subordinates.

Heclo is the Clarence J. Robinson Professor of Public Affairs at George Mason University. He has also taught at Yale University (where he received his Ph.D.), Essex, and the Massachusetts Institute of Technology, and he has been a research associate with the Brookings Institution in Washington, D.C. Heclo has been a staff assistant on domestic policy in the Office of the Vice President of the United States and a consultant to the Department of Health and Social Security for the British government. His research has focused on American government and politics, public policy, social welfare, the presidency, and comparative politics.

**Key Concept:** political characteristics of executive branch appointees

$T$ o speak of political appointees in Washington is obviously to embrace a wide variety of people and situations. Political appointments cover everything from the temporary file clerk recouping a campaign obligation to the cabinet secretary heading a department organization larger than many state governments or the national administrations of some foreign countries....

# THE POLITICAL EXECUTIVE SYSTEM

From the outset political executives share one broad feature: all hold an ambivalent leadership position in what might loosely be termed the American "system" of public executives. To appreciate the peculiarity of their political situation, one must return to the basic rationale for having a number of non-elected political appointees in the executive branch in the first place. According to the Founding Fathers' design, power for the legislative functions of government was spread among the various representatives from states and congressional districts; for the executive function, power was deliberately unified in one elected chief executive. A single president to nominate and supervise the principal officers of the executive branch would promote the unity and vigor of executive operations, while requiring the Senate's consent to make appointments final would safeguard against any presidential abuse of the appointment power and would stabilize administration.[1] Theorists of party government later elaborated on what some of the Founders only hinted at—that competition in the electoral marketplace would result in choices between alternative political teams and policies.

The idea of a single chief executive entering office to promote his measures through a band of loyal political supporters in the executive branch is an easily understood model. It fits well with the media's desire to focus on the central presidential personality, and the notion of undertaking public service at the call of the President attracts many new political appointees to Washington. Astute scholars have pointed out that in reality the President's formal power as the single chief executive is often illusory, that even within his own executive branch he must persuade others and calculate his power stakes rather than

cudgel his minions. This revisionist view, however, has not altered the customary concentration on the President and, like the standard constitutional or party
government models, it relegates the bulk of political executives to a secondary,
derivative role in the executive branch. . . .

# CHARACTERISTICS OF POLITICAL EXECUTIVES

Although reliable information about political executives' behavior is lacking, a
surfeit of data exists concerning their biographical characteristics. These data
add up to a description of a statistical elite—statistical because there is little evidence of a self-conscious group seeking agreed upon goals and screening out
other entrants; elite because political appointees in the federal government are
consistently drawn from the most socially and economically advantaged portions of the population. With a degree of certainty rare in social science, political
executives can be predicted to be disproportionately white, male, urban, affluent, middle-aged, well educated at prestige schools, and pursuers of high-status
white-collar careers. They are unlikely to be female, nonwhite, wage-earning,
from a small town, or possessors of average educational and social credentials.[2]

### Work Experience

These socioeconomic data, however, reveal little about the kind of experience political executives gain on the job. For this type of information, re-
searchers have examined job tenure and mobility in hopes of describing the
government executives' opportunities to learn about their working environ-
ments. Such information does not entirely support several commonly held assumptions about the characteristics of political appointees. One is that the top
political layers are filled with newcomers to government—politically imported
outsiders credited by defenders with introducing a fresh view of government
operations and labeled by detractors as ignorant intruders. Another common
view (and one of the chief justifications for the extensive use of political appointments in government) is that those in the top strata resemble the Founding
Fathers, in that they are "in-and-outers," that is, people who periodically interrupt their private careers to move in and out of the public service. Qualifying, if
not entirely dispelling, each of these assumptions leaves behind a more realistic
picture of the public careers of political executives. . . .

It is worth emphasizing the general point evident in such data: unlike the
situation in most private organizations, in the U.S. executive branch those in
the top positions of formal authority are likely to be substantially less familiar with their working environment than both their civil service and political
subordinates. . . .

These statistics . . . should not summon up images of a top government
layer peopled with men of public affairs who, like modern counterparts of
Cincinnatus or George Washington, repeatedly exchange private lives for public offices. While prominent examples of such men do exist (Nelson Rockefeller,

Clark Clifford, Averell Harriman, etc.), true in-and-out careers are much less common than usually thought. Such careers would presumably show a periodic interchange of public service and private employment, possibly with several appointments in different administrations. In fact, these characteristics are uncommon....

In sum, political appointees are generally people who will move in and sometimes up. They will cope as best they can and move out without returning. The few top executives with continual government experience may be extraordinarily valuable, but as a former civil servant said, "What most people don't realize is that an in-and-outer usually ends up staying an outer." The conventional image of Washington in-and-outers erroneously suggests a political team of utility players, when what actually exists is a one-time sequence of pinch hitters.

### Birds of Passage

The single most obvious characteristic of Washington's political appointees is their transience. While most take up their appointments with somewhat more government experience and have a more terminal government career than is usually assumed, political executives are not likely to be in any one position for very long. The standard figure quoted is that the average undersecretary or assistant secretary remains in his job for about twenty-two months. More detailed breakdowns show this average to contain a large number of very short tenures; about half the top political executives can expect to stay in their jobs less than two years....

Much more important than the experience or inexperience of political appointees as individuals is their transience as a group. Cabinet secretaries may bring with them a cadre of personal acquaintances to fill some of their subordinate political positions, but in general public executives will be strangers with only a fleeting chance to learn how to work together. This characteristic is worth examining in a little more detail.

One of the most persistent themes in comments from political executives of all recent administrations is the absence of teamwork characterizing the layers of appointees. This absence of unifying ties is foreordained, given the fractionalized, changing, and job-specific sets of forces that make up the selection process. But it is not only methods of selection that put mutually reinforcing loyalties at a premium. Rapid turnover intensifies all the other problems of political teamwork.

In many ways what matters most is not so much an individual's job tenure as the duration of his executive relationships. Those in superior positions need to assess the capacities of their subordinates; subordinates need to learn what is expected of them. Political appointees at the same hierarchical level need to learn each other's strengths, weaknesses, priorities, and ways of communicating. Normally the opportunity to develop these working relationships is even shorter than the time span for learning a particular job....

*Hugh Heclo*

The unstable teams within departments are positively collegial when compared with the attenuated relations of political appointees across departments. At least within departments there may be the shared need to protect and promote a common set of agency programs. Weighed against this territorial imperative, political appointees elsewhere can seem like alien tribes.

Few political appointees are likely to be united by bonds of party loyalty, the academics' favorite prescription for overcoming political incoherence in Washington. Though they may be in broad agreement with the President's general approach, political executives usually will not have been active members of his party and only a small minority will have struggled together against common opponents in electoral campaigns. Civil servants are identifying a fundamental characteristic of executive leadership in Washington when they report that they have worked for many political appointees but rarely for a politician.[3] Most would probably agree with the assistant secretary who said, "As far as I can tell, in this town a political appointee is simply someone whose career isn't in this department."

None of this inexperience necessarily means a lack of partisanship in "nonpolitical" political appointees. Quite the opposite. Many of those eventually known as the most partisan of Nixon's appointees came from backgrounds with a minimum of party-political experience. "I came to Washington with absolutely no party or political background," one of them said. "I had a naive idea of managing as in private enterprise but quickly learned political factors are all pervasive."

The record of the Nixon White House demonstrated in a number of cases how those least politically experienced can be susceptible to developing more extreme personal partisanship than those accustomed to regular political interaction and its inevitable compromises. Often the zealousness of the new convert to Washington politics can make effective political teamwork that much more difficult. One official summed up his experience in four administrations by observing: "Inexperienced people tend to lack the political instinct. . . . Sometimes the political instinct means the best politics is no politics. And it knows where that's true, it's not pure partisanship."

Lacking any larger political forces to help unify political executives, the lines of mutual interdependence normally run vertically down the departments and their loosely related programs—not horizontally across the layers of political leadership in various departments. Insofar as top political executives need each other (as opposed to needing the President's support or endorsement) the needs are temporary and issue-specific, not enduring. Even at the height of public criticism concerning the placement of Nixon loyalists in the departments, many of those placed recognized the lack of any workable horizontal contacts. As one appointee said: "For all the talk about teams, I have no contact that amounts to anything with other appointees outside the department. The few lunches we have aren't of much use for getting business done. There is no strong mechanism for getting political appointees together. As a group there's no trust."

It would be a mistake, however, to conclude that political executives are averse to creating alliances. At any given moment, informal communications and networks do exist throughout the political levels and across the departments in Washington. But as participants and issues change frequently, so do the nature and location of these relationships. Some political appointees will have enough common objectives and mutual knowledge to create fairly close informal groups. "There are me and six other assistant secretaries from other departments," said one such man. "We've got some management techniques we want to move on." A year later two of these executives were left in government. Another appointee was trying to draw his counterparts into monthly meetings but recognized "the problem is how to get continuity and institutionalize this sort of thing to keep it going." A year later, he too was gone and his group largely dismantled.

Equally revealing of the flux confronting any outsider is the fact that the last man quoted was like many resigning political appointees. He did not depart for reasons bearing any relation to the substance of what he was doing in government but because his own political patrons were leaving. While resignation for reasons of conscience or policy are relatively rare,[4] the chancy circumstances that create political executives in the first place can just as easily lead to their departure. Political executives and their particular sets of relationships with each other not only fade, but fade fortuitously. Even a close observer of these political comings and goings is likely to pick up confusing signals about whether an executive personnel change is a case of tactics, accident, or grand political strategy....

Yet if there were to be such a serious effort at decisionmaking by enduring teams of political leaders across the top of departments, the U.S. presidency would look far different than it does today or ever has. In such a system cabinet secretaries would need each other as a group more than they would need their departmental identifications and more than they would need any individual member, including the President. Presidents may be advised that they need more collegial help and reactivated cabinets, and they may with good reason even take such advice, at least for a while. But barring any profound institutional and structural changes, no modern president can be expected to be like a foreign prime minister, merely the first among equals. He needs the particular colleagues in his cabinet too little; his colleagues need him too much and each other too little for that to happen. No public executive short of the President has a vested interest in coordinating political leadership in the executive branch as a whole. Political appointees out in the departments and agencies can expect to remain in their twilight zone.

Because the executive branch has a single head, its political leadership is inherently noncollegial—except for a sharing of some executive powers with Congress. That is the way the Founders designed it. That is the way it functions. But "single" does not mean unitary. The political executives' very lack of co-equality—no one is the President's peer—means that their successes are likely to be expropriated by the President, their failures left behind in the departments with little effect on the appointees' real vocations outside government. Since there is only one chief executive but many sources of political support and inspiration, top political appointees do not necessarily hang separately if they fail to hang together. *E unibus plurum.*

# A SUMMARY AND LOOK FORWARD

Any commitment to democratic values necessarily means accepting a measure of instability in the top governing levels. Democratic elections are, after all, "a political invention to assure uncertainty of leadership, in what are deemed to be optimum amounts and periods of time."[5] But to the inherent electoral changes, the American executive political system adds a considerably greater range of nonelectoral uncertainty to political leadership. This system produces top executives who are both expendable over time and in a relatively weak, uncertain position at any one time.

The number of political executives is small vis-à-vis the bureaucracy but large and fragmented in relation to any notion of a trim top-management structure. To the normal confusions of pluralistic institutions and powers in Washington, the selection process contributes its own complexities. White House personnel efforts have rarely been effectively organized. Political forces intervene from many quarters, and their interests in political appointments often bear little relation to presidential needs or to qualifications required for effective performance by public executives. White House efforts at political recruitment can be effective, but the organizational requirements are difficult to master. A White House operation that veers too far in the direction of centralized control can easily become self-defeating by overlooking the need for political executives to balance their responsiveness to the President with their usefulness to the departments....

Weaknesses among political executives lead inevitably to White House complaints about their "going native" in the bureaucracy. The image is apt. To a large extent the particular agencies and bureaus *are* the native villages of executive politics. Even the most presidentially minded political executive will discover that his own agency provides the one relatively secure reference point amid all the other uncertainties of Washington. In their own agencies, appointees usually have at least some knowledge of each other and a common identity with particular programs. Outside the agency it is more like life in the big city among large numbers of anonymous people who have unknown lineages. Any common kinship in the political party or a shared political vocation is improbable, and in the background are always the suspicions of the President's "true" family of supporters in the White House. Political appointees in the larger Washington environment may deal frequently with each other, but these are likely to be the kind of ad hoc, instrumental relations of the city, where people interact without truly knowing each other.

Yet the political appointee's situation is not so simple that he can act as if he is surrounded by a random collection of strangers outside the confines of his agency village. Everywhere extensive networks of village folk in the bureaucracy, Congress, and lobby organizations share experiences, problems, and readings on people and events. An appointee may or may not be in touch with people in these networks, but they are certain to be in touch with each other independently of him. In sociological terms his networks are thin, transient, and single-stranded; theirs are dense, multiple, and enduring. Among public executives themselves there is little need to worry about any joint action to enforce community norms, because there is no community. In dealing with outside villagers who know each other, however, appointees can find that reprisals for any misdeeds are extraordinarily oblique and powerful. The political executive system may be a government of strangers, but its members cannot act as if everyone else is.

Now one can begin to see the real challenge to the political executives' statecraft in Washington. They must be able to move in two worlds—the tight, ingrown village life of the bureaucratic community and the open, disjointed world of political strangers. A public executive in Washington needs the social sensitivity of a villager and the political toughness of a city streetfighter. It is an increasingly unlikely combination. Despite all the resources devoted to more topside staff, new management initiatives, more elaborate analytic techniques, and so on, there remain few—probably fewer than ever—places where political executives can look for reliable political support in any efforts at leadership in the bureaucracy. Political appointees in Washington are substantially on their own and vulnerable to bureaucratic power.

# NOTES

1. For the political appointment process and the decision against a plural executive, see Arthur Taylor Prescott, *Drafting the Federal Constitution* (Louisiana State University Press, 1941), pp. 544–646; and Alexander Hamilton, James Madison, and John Jay, *The Federalist*, Max Beloff, ed. (Oxford: Basil Blackwell, 1948), nos. 70, 72, and 76. There is some question about how far the Founders actually intended the President to function alone or with the cabinet and Senate as a semicollegial group.

2. See David T. Stanley, Dean E. Mann, and Jameson W. Doig, *Men Who Govern* (Brookings Institution, 1967), pp. 9–36; and Thomas R. Dye and John W. Pickering, "Governmental and Corporate Elites," *Journal of Politics*, vol. 37 (1974), pp. 913–15.

3. Although data are not entirely comparable, certainly less than half the political executives in all recent administrations had any record of political party activity, if by that is meant experience as campaign or party officials, convention delegates, elected officials, or political candidates or their staff members. See Stanley, Mann, and Doig, *Men Who Govern*, table E-1, p. 132; and Dean E. Mann, *The Assistant Secretaries* (Brookings Institution, 1965), table A-9, p. 295.

4. See Edward Weisband and Thomas Franck, *Resignation and Protest* (Penguin, 1976), especially pp. 121–63 and fig. 1, app. B, p. 201.

5. Dwight Waldo, *Perspectives on Administration* (University of Alabama Press, 1956), p. 14.

## 12.2 JAMES Q. WILSON

# *Bureaucracy and the Public Interest*

James Q. Wilson (b. 1931), a scholar of public administration, regulatory politics, and the federal bureaucracy, published an article entitled "The Rise of the Bureaucratic State" in the Fall 1975 issue of *The Public Interest.* This essay became a landmark in the contemporary scholarly study of administrative behavior. In it, Wilson linked the historical development and expansion of the national government and the executive branch in particular with the evolutionary enlargement of the federal bureaucracy. He emphasized the fundamental risks posed to democratic government in the United States by the concentration of power among unelected bureaucratic appointees in relatively unaccountable executive departments in the modern bureaucratic state.

This essay served as an intellectual precedent to Wilson's contemporary study of the federal bureaucracy and public administration entitled *Bureaucracy: What Government Agencies Do and Why They Do It* (Basic Books, 1989), from which the following selection is taken. The book investigates the inevitable weaknesses and problems of American bureaucracy and offers a theoretical explanation of the restrictions placed upon public agencies. In particular, Wilson analyzes differences in standards of efficiency and performance between the public sector and the private sector. Wilson sees governmental agencies as less productive than private corporations primarily because of the excess restrictions placed on public institutions. The sources of many of the problems confronted by the federal bureaucracy are the American constitutional principles of separation of powers, federalism, governmental accountability, and accessibility to diverse popular interests and preferences. Many public administration and policy scholars have adopted Wilson's constructive criteria to evaluate the effectiveness of governmental agencies.

Wilson received his M.A. and Ph.D. from the University of Chicago, and he taught at Harvard University as the Henry Lee Shattuck Professor of Government. Wilson is currently the James Collins Professor of Management and Public Policy at the University of California, Los Angeles. He has also served on numerous national commissions concerned with public policy. Wilson's research and publications have focused on such diverse fields as criminal justice, public administration, organization behavior, and public policy.

**Key Concept:** suggested reforms of the federal bureaucracy

# A FEW MODEST SUGGESTIONS THAT
# MAY MAKE A SMALL DIFFERENCE

To do better we have to deregulate the government.[1] If deregulation of a market makes sense because it liberates the entrepreneurial energies of its members, then it is possible that deregulating the public sector also may help energize it. The difference, of course, is that both the price system and the profit motive provide a discipline in markets that is absent in non-markets. Whether any useful substitutes for this discipline can be found for public-sector workers is not clear, though I will offer some suggestions. But even if we cannot expect the same results from deregulation in the two sectors we can agree at a minimum that detailed regulation, even of public employees, rarely is compatible with energy, pride in workmanship, and the exercise of initiative. The best evidence for this proposition, if any is needed, is that most people do not like working in an environment in which every action is second-guessed, every initiative viewed with suspicion, and every controversial decision denounced as malfeasance.

James Colvard, for many years a senior civilian manager in the navy, suggests that the government needs to emulate methods that work in the better parts of the private sector: "a bias toward action, small staffs, and a high level of delegation which is based on trust."[2] A panel of the National Academy of Public Administration (NAPA), consisting of sixteen senior government executives holding the rank of assistant secretary, issued a report making the same point:

> Over many years, government has become entwined in elaborate management control systems and the accretion of progressively more detailed administrative procedures. This development has not produced superior management. Instead, it has produced managerial overburden.... Procedures overwhelm substance. Organizations become discredited, along with their employees.... The critical elements of leadership in management appear to wither in the face of a preoccupation with process. The tools are endlessly "perfected"; the manager who is expected to use these tools believes himself to be ignored.... Management systems are not management.... The attitude of those who design and administer the rules... must be reoriented from a "control mentality" to one of "how can I help get the mission of this agency accomplished."[3]

But how can government "delegate" and "trust" and still maintain accountability? If it is a mistake to foster an ethos that encourages every bureaucrat to "go by the book," is it not an equally serious problem to allow zealots to engage in "mission madness," charging off to implement their private versions of some ambiguous public goal? (Steven Emerson has written a useful account of mission madness in some highly secret military intelligence and covert-action agencies.[4]) Given everything we know about the bureaucratic desire for autonomy and the political rewards of rule making, is there any reason to suppose that anybody will find it in his or her interest to abandon the "control mentality" and adopt the "mission accomplishment" mentality?

Possibly not. But it may be worth thinking about what a modestly deregulated government might look like. It might look as it once did, when some of the better federal agencies were created. At the time the Corps of Engineers, the Forest Service, and the FBI were founded much of the federal government was awash in political patronage, petty cabals, and episodic corruption. Organizing an elite service in those days may have been easier than doing so today, when the problems are less patronage and corruption than they are officiousness and complexity. But the keys to organizational success have not changed. The agencies were started by strong leaders who were able to command personal loyalty, define and instill a clear and powerful sense of mission, attract talented workers who believed they were joining something special, and make exacting demands on subordinates.

Today there is not much chance to create a new agency; almost every agency one can imagine already has been created. Even so, the lessons one learns from changing agencies confirm what can be inferred from studying their founding.

First: Executives should understand the culture of their organizations—that is, what their subordinates believe constitute the core tasks of the agency—and the strengths and limitations of that culture. If members widely share and warmly endorse that culture the agency has a sense of mission. This permits the executive to economize on scarce incentives (people want to do certain tasks even when there are no special rewards for doing it); to state general objectives confident that subordinates will understand the appropriate ways of achieving them; and to delegate responsibility knowing that lower-level decisions probably will conform to higher-level expectations.

A good executive realizes that workers can make subtle, precise, and realistic judgments, but only if those judgments refer to a related, coherent set of behaviors. People cannot easily keep in mind many quite different things or strike reasonable balances among competing tasks. People want to know what is expected of them; they do not want to be told, in answer to this question, that "on the one hand this, but on the other hand that." . . .

These advantages of infusing an agency with a sense of mission are purchased at a price. An agency with a strong mission will give perfunctory attention, if any at all, to tasks that are not central to that mission. Diplomats in the State Department will have little interest in embassy security; intelligence officers in the CIA will not worry as much as they should about counterintelligence; narcotics agents in the DEA will minimize the importance of improper prescriptions written by physicians; power engineers in the TVA will not think as hard about environmental protection or conservation as about maximizing the efficiency of generating units; fighter pilots in the USAF will look at air transport as a homely stepchild; and navy admirals who earned their flag serving on aircraft carriers will not press zealously to expand the role of minesweepers. . . .

Second: Negotiate with one's political superiors to get some agreement as to which are the *essential* constraints that must be observed by your agency and which the marginal constraints. This, frankly, may be impossible. The decentralization of authority in Congress (and in some state legislatures) and the unreliability of most expressions of presidential or gubernatorial backing are such that in most cases you will discover, by experience if not by precept, that all constraints are essential all of the time. But perhaps with effort some maneuvering room may be won. A few agencies obtained the right to use more flexible, less cumbersome personnel systems modeled on the China Lake experiment, and Congress has the power to broaden those opportunities. Perhaps some enlightened member of Congress will be able to get statutory authority for the equivalent of China Lake with respect to procurement regulations. An executive is well advised to spend time showing that member how to do it.

Third: Match the distribution of authority and the control over resources to the tasks your organization is performing. In general, authority should be placed at the lowest level at which all essential elements of information are available. Bureaucracies will differ greatly in what level that may be. At one extreme are agencies such as the Internal Revenue Service or maximum-security prisons, in which uniformity of treatment and precision of control are so important as to make it necessary for there to be exacting, centrally determined rules for most tasks. At the other extreme are public schools, police departments, and armies, organizations in which operational uncertainties are so great that discretion must be given to (or if not given will be taken by) lower-level workers.

A good place in which to think through these matters is the area of weapons procurement. The overcentralization of design control is one of the many criticisms of such procurement on which all commentators seem agreed. Buying a new aircraft may be likened to remodeling one's home: You never know how much it will cost until you are done; you quickly find out that changing your mind midway through the work costs a lot of money; and you soon realize that decisions have to be made by people on the spot who can look at the pipes, wires, and joists. The Pentagon procures aircraft as if none of its members had ever built or remodeled a house. It does so because both it and its legislative superiors refuse to allow authority to flow down to the point where decisions rationally can be made. . . .

Fourth: Judge organizations by results. This book has made it clear that what constitutes a valued result in government usually is a matter of dispute. But even when fairly clear performance standards exist, legislatures and executives often ignore them with unhappy results. William E. Turcotte compared how two state governments oversaw their state liquor monopolies. The state that applied clear standards to its liquor bureaucrats produced significantly more profit and lower administrative costs than did the state with unclear or conflicting standards.[5]

Even when results are hard to assess more can be done than is often the case. If someone set out to evaluate the output of a private school, hospital, or security service, he or she would have at least as much trouble as would someone trying to measure the output of a public school, hospital, or police department. Governments are not the only institutions with ambiguous products. . . .

The fifth and final bit of advice flows directly from the limits on judging agencies by their results. All organizations seek the stability and comfort that comes from relying on standard operating procedures—"SOPs." When results are unknown or equivocal, bureaus will have no incentive to alter those SOPs so as better to achieve their goals, only an incentive to modify them to conform to externally imposed constraints. The SOPs will represent an internally defined equilibrium that reconciles the situational imperatives, professional norms, bureaucratic ideologies, peer-group expectations, and (if present) leadership demands unique to that agency. The only way to minimize the adverse effect of allowing human affairs to be managed by organizations driven by their autonomous SOPs is to keep the number, size, and authority of such organizations as small as possible. If none of the four preceding bits of advice work, the reader must confront the realization that there are no solutions for the bureaucracy problem that are not also "solutions" to the government problem. More precisely: All complex organizations display bureaucratic problems of confusion, red tape, and the avoidance of responsibility. Those problems are much greater in government bureaucracies because government itself is the institutionalization of confusion (arising out of the need to moderate competing demands); of red tape (arising out of the need to satisfy demands that cannot be moderated); and of avoided responsibility (arising out of the desire to retain power by minimizing criticism).

In short, you can have less bureaucracy only if you have less government. Many, if not most, of the difficulties we experience in dealing with government agencies arise from the agencies being part of a fragmented and open political system. If an agency is to have a sense of mission, if constraints are to be minimized, if authority is to be decentralized, if officials are to be judged on the basis of the outputs they produce rather than the inputs they consume, then legislators, judges, and lobbyists will have to act against their own interests. They will have to say "no" to influential constituents, forgo the opportunity to expand their own influence, and take seriously the task of judging the organizational feasibility as well as the political popularity of a proposed new program. It is hard to imagine this happening, partly because politicians and judges have no incentive to make it happen and partly because there are certain tasks a democratic government must undertake even if they cannot be performed efficiently. The greatest mistake citizens can make when they complain of "the bureaucracy" is to suppose that their frustrations arise simply out of management problems; they do not—they arise out of governance problems.

## BUREAUCRACY AND THE AMERICAN REGIME

The central feature of the American constitutional system—the separation of powers—exacerbates many of these problems. The governments of the United States were not designed to be efficient or powerful, but to be tolerable and malleable. Those who devised these arrangements always assumed that the federal government would exercise few and limited powers. As long as that assumption was correct (which it was for a century and a half) the quality of public administration was not a serious problem except in the minds of those reformers (Woodrow Wilson was probably the first) who desired to rationalize government in order to rationalize society. The founders knew that the separation of powers would make it so difficult to start a new program or to create a new agency that it was hardly necessary to think about how those agencies would be administered. As a result, the Constitution is virtually silent on what kind of administration we should have. At least until the Civil War thrust the problem on us, scarcely anyone in the country would have known what you were talking about if you spoke of the "problem of administration." . . .

Today, the United States at every level has big and active governments. Some people worry that a constitutional system well-designed to preserve liberty when governments were small is poorly designed to implement policy now that governments are large. The contrast between how the United States and the nations of Western Europe manage environmental and industrial regulation . . . is illuminating: Here the separation of powers insures, if not causes, clumsy and adversarial regulation; there the unification of powers permits, if not causes, smooth and consensual regulation.

I am not convinced that the choice is that simple, however. It would take another book to judge the advantages and disadvantages of the separation of powers. The balance sheet on both sides of the ledger would contain many more entries than those that derive from a discussion of public administration. But even confining our attention to administration, there is more to be said for the American system than many of its critics admit.

America has a paradoxical bureaucracy unlike that found in almost any other advanced nation. The paradox is the existence in one set of institutions of two qualities ordinarily quite separate: the multiplication of rules and the opportunity for access. We have a system laden with rules; elsewhere that is a sure sign that the bureaucracy is aloof from the people, distant from their concerns, and preoccupied with the power and privileges of the bureaucrats—an elaborate, grinding machine that can crush the spirit of any who dare oppose it. We also have a system suffused with participation: advisory boards, citizen groups, neighborhood councils, congressional investigators, crusading journalists, and lawyers serving writs; elsewhere this popular involvement would be taken as evidence that the administrative system is no system at all, but a bungling, jerry-built contraption wallowing in inefficiency and shot through with corruption and favoritism.

That these two traits, rules and openness, could coexist would have astonished Max Weber and continues to astonish (or elude) many contemporary students of the subject. Public bureaucracy in this country is neither as rational and predictable as Weber hoped nor as crushing and mechanistic as he feared. It is rule-bound without being overpowering, participatory without being corrupt. This paradox exists partly because of the character and mores of the American people: They are too informal, spontaneous, and other-directed to be either neutral arbiters or passionless Gradgrinds. And partly it exists because of the nature of the regime: Our constitutional system, and above all the exceptional power enjoyed by the legislative branch, makes it impossible for us to have anything like a government by appointed experts but easy for individual citizens to obtain redress from the abuses of power. Anyone who wishes it otherwise would have to produce a wholly different regime, and curing the mischiefs of bureaucracy seems an inadequate reason for that. Parliamentary regimes that supply more consistent direction to their bureaucracies also supply more bureaucracy to their citizens. The fragmented American regime may produce chaotic government, but the coherent European regimes produce bigger governments.

1. I first saw this phrase in an essay by Constance Horner, then director of the federal Office of Personnel Management: "Beyond Mr. Gradgrind: The Case for Deregulating the Public Sector," *Policy Review* 44 (Spring 1988): 34–38. It also appears in Gary C. Bryner, *Bureaucratic Discretion* (New York: Pergamon Press, 1987), 215.

2. James Colvard, "Procurement: What Price Mistrust?" *Government Executive* (March 1985): 21.

3. NAPA, *Revitalizing Federal Management: Managers and Their Overburdened Systems* (Washington, D.C.: National Academy of Public Administration, November 1983), vii, viii, 8.

4. Steven Emerson, *Secret Warriors* (New York: G. P. Putnam's Sons, 1988).

5. William E. Turcotte, "Control Systems, Performance, and Satisfaction in Two State Agencies," *Administrative Science Quarterly* 19 (1974): 60–73.

## CHAPTER 13

# The Judiciary

### 13.1   JOHN MARSHALL

# *Marbury v. Madison*

In the 1803 landmark decision *Marbury v. Madison* (1 Cranch 137), from which the following selection is taken, the U.S. Supreme Court articulated an opinion that is considered by American political scientists and constitutional legal scholars to be one of the most significant decisions of the Court. The judgment of the Court established judicial review, which refers to the power of the Court to declare congressional and presidential acts invalid because they are unconstitutional. This was the first case in which the U.S. Supreme Court explicitly found unconstitutional a particular act of Congress. This decision enabled the Court to become a very powerful judiciary body.

The election of 1800 was a disastrous defeat for President John Adams and the Federalists. In 1801, at the very end of his administration, Adams and his Federalist colleagues attempted to immediately implement Federalist political objectives and judicial principles. The Judiciary Act of 1801 limited the size of the Supreme Court to five justices, established several new circuit courts consisting of 16 new judgeships, and released the Supreme Court justices from circuit court duties. Subsequently, the Federalist Congress passed legislation authorizing Adams to appoint an unlimited number of justices of the peace on five-year terms for the District of Columbia. In the final days of his administration, Adams attempted to appoint all of these new judicial vacancies with supportive Federalists. Although these "midnight appointments" were signed and sealed prior to Thomas Jefferson's occupation of the office, in the confusion of the transition of administrations several commissions were not delivered.

William Marbury's appointment as justice of the peace for the District of Columbia was among four commissions that had not been delivered when Jefferson took office. Marbury petitioned the U.S. Supreme Court to issue a *writ of mandamus* (an order issued by a court to require the performance of an act) compelling Madison to deliver him his commission.

Chief Justice John Marshall delivered the unanimous opinion of the Court. He contended that the provision of the Judiciary Act of 1789 granting the Court authority to issue the *writ of mandamus* was unconstitutional. Furthermore, Marshall declared that the Court had lacked jurisdiction to decide the case, although Marbury deserved his commission.

**Key Concept:** the Supreme Court's power of judicial review

$M$r. Chief Justice **Marshall** delivered the opinion of the Court, saying in part:

In the order in which the court has viewed this subject, the following questions have been considered and decided.

1st. Has the applicant a right to the commission he demands? [The Court finds that he has.]

2d. If he has a right, and that right has been violated, do the laws of his country afford him a remedy? [The Court finds that they do.]

3d. If they do afford him a remedy, is it a mandamus issuing from this court?...

This, then, is a plain case for a mandamus, either to deliver the commission, or a copy of it from the record; and it only remains to be inquired,

Whether it can issue from this court.

The act to establish the judicial courts of the United States authorizes the Supreme Court "to issue writs of mandamus in cases warranted by the principles and usages of law, to any courts appointed, or persons holding office, under the authority of the United States."

The Secretary of State, being a person holding an office under the authority of the United States, is precisely within the letter of description, and if this court is not authorized to issue a writ of mandamus to such an officer, it must be because the law is unconstitutional, and therefore absolutely incapable of conferring the authority, and assigning the duties which its words purport to confer and assign.

The constitution vests the whole judicial power of the United States in one Supreme Court, and such inferior courts as congress shall, from time to time, ordain and establish....

In the distribution of this power it is declared that "the Supreme Court shall have original jurisdiction in all cases affecting ambassadors, other public ministers and consuls, and those in which a state shall be a party. In all other cases, the Supreme Court shall have appellate jurisdiction."...

If it had been intended to leave it in the discretion of the legislature to apportion the judicial power between the supreme and inferior courts according to the will of that body, it would certainly have been useless to have proceeded further than to have defined the judicial power, and the tribunals in which it should be vested....

The question, whether an act, repugnant to the constitution, can become the law of the land, is a question deeply interesting to the United States; but, happily, not of an intricacy proportioned to its interest. It seems only necessary to recognize certain principles, supposed to have been long and well established, to decide it.

That the people have an original right to establish, for their future government, such principles, as, in their opinion, shall most conduce to their own happiness is the basis on which the whole American fabric has been erected. The exercise of this original right is a very great exertion; nor can it, nor ought it, to be frequently repeated. The principles, therefore, so established, are deemed fundamental. And as the authority from which they proceed is supreme, and can seldom act, they are designed to be permanent.

This original and supreme will organizes the government, and assigns to different departments their respective powers. It may either stop here, or establish certain limits not to be transcended by those departments.

The government of the United States is of the latter description. The powers of the legislature are defined and limited; and that those limits may not be mistaken, or forgotten, the constitution is written. To what purpose are powers limited, and to what purpose is that limitation committed to writing, if these limits may, at any time, be passed by those intended to be restrained? The distinction between a government with limited and unlimited powers is abolished, if those limits do not confine the persons on whom they are imposed, and if acts prohibited and acts allowed, are of equal obligation. It is a proposition too plain to be contested, that the constitution controls any legislative act repugnant to it; or, that the legislature may alter the constitution by an ordinary act.

Between these alternatives there is no middle ground. The constitution is either a superior paramount law, unchangeable by ordinary means, or it is on a level with ordinary legislative acts, and, like other acts, is alterable when the legislature shall please to alter it.

If the former part of the alternative be true, then a legislative act contrary to the constitution is not law: if the latter part be true, then written constitutions are absurd attempts, on the part of the people, to limit a power in its own nature illimitable.

Certainly all those who have framed written constitutions contemplate them as forming the fundamental and paramount law of the nation, and, consequently, the theory of every such government must be, that an act of the Legislature, repugnant to the constitution, is void.

This theory is essentially attached to a written constitution, and, is consequently, to be considered, by this court, as one of the fundamental principles of our society. It is not therefore to be lost sight of in the further consideration of this subject.

If an act of the Legislature, repugnant to the constitution, is void, does it, notwithstanding its invalidity, bind the courts, and oblige them to give it effect? Or, in other words, though it be not law, does it constitute a rule as operative as if it was a law? This would be to overthrow in fact what was established in theory; and would seem, at first view, an absurdity too gross to be insisted on. It shall, however, receive a more attentive consideration.

It is emphatically the province and duty of the judicial department to say what the law is. Those who apply the rule to particular cases, must of necessity expound and interpret that rule. If two laws conflict with each other, the courts must decide on the operation of each.

So if a law be in opposition to the constitution; if both the law and the constitution apply to a particular case, so that the court must either decide that case conformably to the law, disregarding the constitution; or conformably to the constitution, disregarding the law; the court must determine which of these conflicting rules governs the case. This is of the very essence of judicial duty.

If, then, the courts are to regard the constitution, and the constitution is superior to any ordinary act of the Legislature, the constitution, and not such ordinary act, must govern the case to which they both apply.

Those then who controvert the principle that the constitution is to be considered, in court, as a paramount law, are reduced to the necessity of maintaining that courts must close their eyes on the constitution, and see only the law.

This doctrine would subvert the very foundation of all written constitutions. It would declare that an act which, according to the principles and theory of our government, is entirely void, is yet, in practice, completely obligatory. It would declare that if the legislature shall do what is expressly forbidden, such act, notwithstanding the express prohibition, is in reality effectual. It would be giving to the legislature a practical and real omnipotence, with the same breath which professes to restrict their powers within narrow limits. It is prescribing limits, and declaring that those limits may be passed at pleasure.

That it thus reduces to nothing what we have deemed the greatest improvement on political institutions, a written constitution, would of itself be sufficient, in America, where written constitutions have been viewed with so much reverence, for rejecting the construction. But the peculiar expressions of the constitution of the United States furnish additional arguments in favor of its rejection.

The judicial power of the United States is extended to all cases arising under the constitution.

Could it be the intention of those who gave this power, to say that in using it the constitution should not be looked into? That a case arising under the constitution should be decided without examining the instrument under which it arises?

This is too extravagant to be maintained.

In some cases, then, the constitution must be looked into by the judges. And if they can open it at all, what part of it are they forbidden to read or to obey?

There are many other parts of the constitution which serve to illustrate this subject.

It is declared that "no tax or duty shall be laid on articles exported from any State." Suppose a duty on the export of cotton, of tobacco, or of flour; and a suit instituted to recover it. Ought judgment to be rendered in such a case? Ought the judges to close their eyes on the constitution, and only see the law?

The constitution declares "that no bill of attainder or ex post facto law shall be passed."

If, however, such a bill should be passed, and a person should be prosecuted under it; must the court condemn to death those victims whom the constitution endeavors to preserve?

"No person," says the constitution, "shall be convicted of treason unless on the testimony of two witnesses to the same overt act, or on confession in open court."

Here the language of the constitution is addressed especially to the courts. It prescribes, directly for them, a rule of evidence not to be departed from. If the legislature should change that rule, and declare one witness, or a confession out of court, sufficient for conviction, must the constitutional principle yield to the legislative act?

From these, and many other selections which might be made, it is apparent, that the framers of the constitution contemplated that instrument as a rule for the government of courts, as well as of the legislature....

Why does a judge swear to discharge his duties agreeably to the constitution of the United States, if that constitution forms no rule for his government? if it is closed upon him, and cannot be inspected by him?

If such be the real state of things, this is worse than solemn mockery. To prescribe, or to take this oath, becomes equally a crime.

It is also not entirely unworthy of observation, that in declaring what shall be the supreme law of the land, the constitution itself is first mentioned; and not the laws of the United States generally, but those only which shall be made in pursuance of the constitution, have that rank.

Thus, the particular phraseology of the constitution of the United States confirms and strengthens the principle, supposed to be essential to all written constitutions, that a law repugnant to the constitution is void; and that courts, as well as other departments, are bound by that instrument.

The rule must be discharged.

## 13.2 LAURENCE H. TRIBE

# The Myth of the Strict Constructionist: Our Incomplete Constitution

Laurence H. Tribe is a prominent judicial and constitutional scholar whose reputation has been achieved by the publication of such books as *Abortion: The Clash of Absolutes* (W. W. Norton, 1990) and, coauthored with Michael C. Dorf, *On Reading the Constitution* (Harvard University Press, 1991).

The following selection is taken from Tribe's *God Save This Honorable Court: How the Choice of Supreme Court Justices Shapes Our History* (Random House, 1985). This classic in constitutional thought has contributed to the contemporary debate and literature on judicial politics. It has helped to shift the theoretical focus of constitutional research to the connection between judicial philosophy and judicial behavior. In the following selection, Tribe investigates the multiple partisan, ideological, and philosophical factors that affect the selection process for U.S. Supreme Court justices. The philosophy of strict constructionism, or judicial restraint, and the philosophy of judicial activism are the two antithetical approaches to judicial review that Tribe studies. The school of constitutional interpretation that is referred to as strict constructionism is exclusively guided by a literal interpretation of the text of the Constitution. Tribe rejects this judicial approach. The school of constitutional interpretation that is referred to as judicial activism is guided by the principles of a broad interpretation of the text of the Constitution and the Supreme Court's obligation to express a policy agenda (e.g., desegregation, school prayer, and abortion). Tribe is a strong proponent of this judicial approach.

Tribe received his J.D. from Harvard University, where he is currently the Ralph S. Tyler, Jr., Professor of Constitutional Law. Tribe has received numerous prestigious academic awards for his legal scholarship. He is also a prominent attorney, and he has been ranked as one of America's 10 best legal scholars. As a practitioner of constitutional law, Tribe has achieved numerous Supreme Court victories and has often been an expert witness before Congress.

**Key Concept:** the constitutional doctrine of strict constructionism

287

*S*ome would argue that one Justice or two would not make that much difference—and that even the many 5–4 splits would gradually disappear—if the Supreme Court were staffed, as they believe it should be, with men and women who understand that constitutional adjudication is simply the job of correctly reading the Constitution. If the Justices interpret our great charter in a straightforward manner—if they pay close attention to its words and avoid twisting or stretching their meanings—there will be few occasions for controversies that can be manipulated by well-chosen appointments. All that the President and the Senate need do is stop appointing "activist" judges who impose their own philosophies upon the document they are sworn to uphold, and appoint instead properly "restrained" jurists who know, and will not exceed, a judge's proper place. So the argument goes. It is simple, appealing, and plainly wrong.

## STRICT CONSTRUCTIONISM EXPLAINED

In 1717 Bishop Benjamin Hoadly told the King of England that, in his opinion, "whoever hath an absolute authority to interpret any written laws is truly the Lawgiver to all intents and purposes, and not the person who first wrote them." Thus began a controversy that has continued unabated for the last two hundred and fifty years. Not everyone has agreed that the power of judicial review gives the Supreme Court wide discretion in reading the law. Justice Joseph Story argued in 1833 that the Court must give to the constitutional text only its ordinary and natural meaning: "Constitutions are instruments of a practical nature, founded on the common business of human life, adapted to common wants, designed for common use and fitted for common understanding." A century later Justice Owen Roberts described the Supreme Court's task in an even more limited and mechanical way: "to lay the article of the Constitution which is involved beside the statute which is challenged and to decide whether the latter squares with the former."

This approach to judicial review is usually known as strict constructionism, and its guiding principle is exclusive attention to the constitutional text. The Supreme Court's Justices must take the Constitution as they find it, and not make things up as they go along. Even if the Justices are appalled by the results this method produces, or believe that the Constitution's literal commands are severely out of step with the times, it is not their job to rewrite it. That prerogative belongs to the Congress and the President—and ultimately to the people, who retain the power to *amend* the Constitution. The watchword of strict constructionism is "restraint." The continuing popularity of this approach to constitutional interpretation is revealed by the fact that President Nixon announced a policy of appointing only strict constructionists to the Supreme Court; the same "judicial philosophy" appears to be a sine qua non for nomination under President Reagan as well.

The central flaw of strict constructionism is that words are inherently indeterminate—they can often be given more than one plausible meaning. If simply *reading* the Constitution the "right" way were all the Justices of the Supreme Court had to do, the only qualification for the job would be literacy, and the only tool a dictionary. But the meanings of the Constitution's words are especially difficult to pin down. Many of its most precise commands are relatively trivial—such as the requirement that the President be thirty-five years old—while nearly all of its most important phrases are deliberate models of ambiguity. Just what does the Fourth Amendment prohibit as an "unreasonable search"? What exactly is the "speech" whose freedom the government may not "abridge"? What is it that we gain by being guaranteed the "equal protection of the laws"? And what, in heaven's name, is "due process"? Such vague phrases not only invite but *compel* the Supreme Court to put meaning *into* the Constitution, not just to take it out. Judicial construction inevitably entails a major element of judicial creation.

This is not to say that the Court is free to take the position of Humpty Dumpty, that "a word means just what I choose it to mean—neither more not less." The Justices may not follow a policy of "anything goes" so long as it helps put an end to what they personally consider to be injustice. But the constitutional text is not enough—we need to search for, and explain our selection of, the *principles behind* the words.

Consider the First Amendment to the Constitution. Beyond dispute, it prohibits the Congress from dictating official religious beliefs, censoring newspapers, or punishing criticism of the government. The words of the First Amendment—which command that "Congress shall make no law respecting an establishment of religion, or prohibiting the free exercise thereof; or abridging the freedom of speech, or of the press"—could be read no other way. Yet not one word in the entire Constitution says that the *President* cannot do those things, even though such a notion seems unthinkable. What are we to make of this omission? A resort to the Constitution's text and *only* its text for an answer is a shortcut to a dead end. We must ask *why* the Congress is prohibited from violating our rights but the President is not. Is the President to be considered less of a threat to our liberty? Even if such a thought might have been plausible in 1791, when the First Amendment was ratified, it is certainly not plausible today: the modern American President is the repository of perhaps the world's greatest concentration of power; and that power is growing. We must look deeper than the surface of the Constitution's words.

The principle that animates the Bill of Rights, including the First Amendment, is that there are certain freedoms that are fundamental in determining the kind of society we wish to be. These freedoms must be protected from political compromise, and even democratically elected governments must fully respect them. In light of this principle, it is perfectly sensible to see the shield of the First Amendment as a bulwark of freedom against presidential as well as congressional acts. Indeed, it would be indefensible *not* to. . . .

Chief Justice [John] Marshall once wrote that we must remember that "it is a *Constitution* we are expounding." It is the grand charter of a democratic republic, the philosophical creed of a free people, and it was written in broad, even majestic language because it was written to evolve. The statesmen who wrote the Constitution meant the American experiment to endure without having to be reinvented with an endless series of explicit amendments to its basic blueprint. There is a message in the common adage "Ours is a Constitution of limited powers." The Tenth Amendment makes that maxim a reminder that the federal government in particular may exercise only the powers ceded to it by the people in the Constitution. Perhaps even more important, the Ninth Amendment expressly states that even the Bill of Rights itself is not to be understood as an exhaustive list of individual liberties. The Ninth Amendment thereby invites us, and our judges, to expand on the panoply of freedoms that are uniquely our heritage. Thus the Constitution tells us, both implicitly and explicitly, that what it does *not* say must also be interpreted, understood, and applied.

# A RELATED FALLACY: THE INTENT OF THE FRAMERS

Another school of constitutional interpretation takes as its lodestar the intent of the authors of the Constitution. The task of the Supreme Court, when confronted by ambiguous or open-ended language, is simply to divine what the Framers and the authors of the amendments had in mind. This method employs historical research in addition to textual analysis. One obvious problem with asking "what they meant" is that we must first determine who "they" are. In the case of the Bill of Rights, do we defer to the intentions of the men—yes, it was men only—who drafted it and saw it as an essential safeguard against encroachment on fundamental freedoms, or to the intentions of those among them who saw the Bill of Rights as unnecessary and unwise, but acceded to its passage because otherwise some states might never have ratified the Constitution? And how should we understand the purpose of the Slave Trade Clause of Article I of the Constitution, which prohibits Congress from restricting the importation of slaves until 1808? Did the Framers mean by this provision that when they said, in the Declaration of Independence, "all men are created equal," they really meant "all *white* men"? Was this, too, merely a bargaining chip, a concession to the slaveholding states to entice them into the Union? Or did the Founding Fathers mean to give the South a two-decade period in which to phase out slavery before Congress did it for them? And how was this clause understood by the Southern legislators who ratified the Constitution?

The nagging doubt prompted by inquiries like these is that no collective body—be it the Congress or the Constitutional Convention or the aggregate of state legislatures—can really be said to have a *single*, ascertainable "purpose" or "intent." And even if such a mythical beast could be captured and examined, how relevant would it be to us today? Should the peculiar opinions held, and the particular applications envisioned, by men who have been dead for two centuries *always* trump contemporary insights into what the living Constitution means and ought to mean? Should we permit others to rule us from the grave not only through solemn enactments democratically ratified, but through hidden beliefs and premises perhaps deliberately left unstated? ...

## ABDICATING RESPONSIBILITY
## FOR TOUGH CHOICES

The most serious flaw in both slavish adherence to the constitutional text and the inevitably inconclusive inquiry into the intent of those who wrote it is not just that these methods of judicial reasoning ask the wrong questions, but that they abdicate responsibility for the choices that constitutional courts *necessarily* make. The Supreme Court just cannot avoid the painful duty of exercising judgment so as to give concrete meaning to the fluid Constitution, because the constitutional rules and precepts that it is charged with administering lack that certainty which permits anything resembling automatic application. Strict constructionism in all of its variants is thus built on a conceit—which through the years has become a full-blown myth—that the Supreme Court does not *make* law, but *finds* law ready-made by others. In this mythology, the Justices do not really render their own opinions in deciding cases, for they are the mere mouthpieces of oracles beyond themselves; just as God spake by the prophets, so the Constitution speaketh by Supreme Court Justices. Even those who say they know it's not so—who claim, when wishing to sound sophisticated, that they realize some measure of choice is unavoidable—fall back on the myth when they criticize "activist" judicial decisions without specifying just *why* a particular "activist" interpretation strikes them as wrong.

Thus the members of the Court themselves occasionally duck responsibility for their substantive decisions about what the Constitution should be taken to mean by shoving the blame—or the credit—onto the document's supposedly plain words or onto the supposedly evident intentions of the people who penned those words two hundred years ago. When Chief Justice [Roger B.] Taney declared that blacks were an "inferior class of beings" that could "justly and lawfully be reduced to slavery for the white man's benefit," he claimed that this was not *his* opinion but a conclusion dictated by the language of the Constitution and the obvious intent of the men who wrote it.

But disclaimers that "the Constitution made me do it" are rarely more persuasive than those that blame the devil. When Justice [Hugo] Black refused in 1967 to agree with the majority of the Court in *Katz v. United States* that the Fourth Amendment restricts the government's power to put a tap on your telephone line, it was not because *he* thought that electronic eavesdropping was acceptable, but because the plain language of the Fourth Amendment prohibits only "unreasonable *searches*," not unreasonable *wiretaps*. Naturally, such electronic invasions of privacy were not anticipated by men who knew neither telephones nor tape recorders. Such are the unwholesome fruits of what is sometimes called strict constructionism. Indeed, as the wiretap example suggests, a Constitution frozen in eighteenth-century ice would soon become obsolete; as the centuries pass, and technology changes basic patterns of life, that kind of Constitution would melt into meaningless words signifying nothing. ...

It may be that the most subtle danger of nearsighted examination of the Constitution's text or of its authors' intentions is that, by making extremely difficult choices seem easy, such examination stops the judicial inquiry just when it becomes clear that more questions should be asked. Those crucial questions ask both *how* particular legal issues should be resolved and *who* should be trusted to resolve them. The allure of strict constructionism and of those who claim to practice it—their ability to make complicated issues sound simple and tough decisions easy—is precisely what should make us suspicious of it. For it threatens to put us to sleep at the very moments when we must be most alert to the choices that are in fact being made about the Constitution and its impact on our daily lives—choices whose shape is necessarily prefigured by the sorts of men and women we permit our Presidents to place on our nation's highest court.

# PART SEVEN

# *Dimensions of Public Policy*

# On the Internet . . .

## Sites appropriate to Part Seven

This page of the Office of Management and Budget features the budget of the U.S. government for fiscal year 2000, budgets for prior years, and a citizen's guide to the federal budget.

```
http://www.access.gpo.gov/su_docs/budget/
    index.html
```

Since the end of the cold war, analysts around the world have been struggling to reorient their thinking on the meaning of security in the new international environment. The Project on World Security (PWS), an initiative of the Rockefeller Brothers Fund, is an effort to develop a comprehensive and integrative framework for discussing security at the end of the twentieth century.

```
http://www.rbf.org/pws/
```

This site of the American Foreign Policy Council (AFPC) links to AFPC bulletins, issues, programs, resources, and more.

```
http://afpc.org
```

The Office of the Historian, Bureau of Public Affairs, is headed by William Z. Slany. The Historian's Office publishes the official documentary history of U.S. foreign policy and provides historical research and advice for the Department of State. This site includes a timeline of diplomatic history, Department of State records, and the office's *Foreign Relations* series.

```
http://www.state.gov/www/about_state/
    history/
```

# CHAPTER 14 Domestic Public Policy Making

## 14.1 AARON WILDAVSKY

# *Budgeting as Conflicting Promises*

Over the past three decades, Aaron Wildavsky (1930–1993) has been considered one of the most influential scholars on American domestic public policy making. His book *The Politics of the Budgetary Process* (Little, Brown, 1964) established Wildavsky's reputation as a leading expert on the complexities of the budgetary process. In *The New Politics of the Budgetary Process* (Scott, Foresman, 1988), from which the following selection is taken, Wildavsky investigates the multiple procedures and stages of contemporary federal budgetary decision making.

Wildavsky's central argument is that current federal budgetary decision making essentially involves complex political operations designed to allocate limited financial resources. Budgetary practices are directly impacted by distinct political preferences and public policy priorities. For example, various interest groups attempt to influence and pressure congressional budget and appropriations committees to protect and promote their desired programs. Wildavsky focuses on the particular aspects and stages of the president's budgetary relationship with Congress. In the following selection, Wildavsky critically evaluates the complexities of the annual congressional process of appropriating funds for federal agencies.

Wildavsky earned his Ph.D. from Yale University. He had a distinguished career as a professor of political science and public policy at the University of California, Berkeley, for 30 years, where he was chairman of the political science department and founding dean of the Graduate School of Public Policy. Wildavsky was honored with a Fulbright grant and a Guggenheim Fellowship. Wildavsky was also president of the American Political Science Association and is considered one of the most respected and influential American political scientists of this century. He published more than 30 books.

**Key Concept:** the political process of allocating scarce financial resources

*J*ust as it is made up of many policies, the budget also has many meanings according to one's institutional position in the government. To the ordinary citizen, budgeting is both mysterious and simple. It is so hard to understand that its complexity may be ignored in resorting to a simple test of virtue: Can the government balance its books or not? Is it in control of itself? For a federal agency —and for the state, local, and semiprivate organizations largely funded by the federal government—the budget is the irrigation system that provides the water without which an agency and its products would parch and wither. Interest groups may see the many steps of budgeting as opportunities or obstacles and budgeting institutions as allies or enemies. Some parts—an appropriations or authorizing subcommittee—may be "captured," but there are too many centers of decision to capture them all. If interest groups can simply try to get more for their favored programs, their strategies may be straightforward; if the budgetary process is arranged so that desires of various groups conflict—more for one of them means less for others—it is harder for each group to figure out what to do.

For the budget and appropriations committees, budgeting is their purpose and their power; their members must work to preserve that power. Since budgeting often encroaches on the turf of authorizing committees, they may view the budgetary process as a threat and an intrusion. For congressmen with strong issue preferences that have been stymied by the relevant authorizing committees (committees whose domain is to recommend programs and activities for congressional approval), budgetary action may provide power. The budget resolutions, appropriations, and occasional debt-ceiling increases are trains that must run, and there may not be time to kick off the stowaways. Appropriations especially become targets of opportunity for "riders"—opposition to abortion and military aid to Central American forces, for example. Budget resolutions provide chances for votes on issues that might not otherwise reach the floor (e.g., public works funding or increases in veterans' benefits). For partisans, particularly leaders, of the Democratic and Republican parties, the totals for big programs in the budget resolutions measure their party's influence on the course of American government; short of the actual organization of the two houses (election of the speaker, committee assignments), no other action is potentially of as great moment to the party leadership. The battle of the budget is the test of generalship. The ability of the parties to stay together in the final encounter (apart from the vote to organize the houses along partisan lines) is now their ultimate test of cohesion. . . .

The complexity of the federal budgetary process—the large numbers of wide-ranging, yet uncertain consequences—reveals that the purposes of budgets are as varied as the purposes of the people who make them. One budget may be designed to coordinate diverse activities so that they complement one another in the achievement of common goals. Another budget may be put together primarily to discipline subordinate officials within a government agency by reducing amounts for their salaries and pet projects. And a third budget may be directed essentially to mobilizing the support of clientele groups who benefit by the services the agency provides. Nothing is gained, therefore, by insisting that a budget is only one of these things when it might be any or all of them or many other kinds of things as well.[1] ...

*Aaron Wildavsky*

Taken as a whole, the federal budget is a representation in monetary terms of governmental activity. If politics is regarded in part as conflict over whose preferences shall prevail in the determination of national policy, then the budget records the outcomes of this struggle. If one asks, "Who gets what the government has to give?" then the answers for a moment in time are recorded in the budget. If one looks at politics as a process by which the government mobilizes resources to meet pressing problems, then the budget is a focus of these efforts.

The size and shape of the budget is a matter of serious contention in our political life. Presidents, political parties, administrators, congressmen, interest groups, and interested citizens vie with one another to have their preferences recorded in the budget. The victories and defeats, the compromises and the bargains, the realms of agreement and the spheres of conflict in regard to the role of national government in our society all appear in the budget. In the most integral sense, budgeting—that is, attempts to allocate scarce financial resources through political processes in order to realize disparate visions of the good life—lies at the heart of the political process. That there are visions of the good life enables people to make commitments to one another through the budget; that these visions conflict means that not all such promises can be kept. ...

## APPROPRIATIONS: THE POWER OF CONGRESS AND POWER WITHIN CONGRESS

Americans have long feared oppression by the political executive. Congressmen have long seen themselves as the bulwark against such oppression. The public, judging from opinion polls, trusts Congress no more than the presidency; but congressmen still see themselves in a protective role. Their major weapon is the "power of the purse"—the fact that, as the Constitution states, "No money shall be drawn from the Treasury, but in consequence of Appropriations made by law." The power of the purse is, then, a legislative power in that no money may be spent without the granting of budget authority by Congress.

The process of annually appropriating funds for federal agencies is intended to enforce dependence upon Congress of those agencies' officers. Unless an agency justifies itself each year, it risks losing funding. If the agency behaves in ways that upset Congress, it has an annual opportunity to bring the agency into line through threats or actual changes in appropriations. The agency does not have the advantage of delay, as it would if Congress needed to legislate a change because funding was permanent or multiyear unless otherwise altered. Unlike entitlement funding, annual appropriations mean that delay will cause funding to run out and the agency's activities to cease. Appropriations acts are privileged in floor consideration because congressmen do not ordinarily want maneuvering or logjams to shut down programs.

The House Appropriations Committee, being larger in number but with fewer duties (and therefore more specialized), has always paid more attention to detail than has its Senate counterpart. Not all details are incorporated into the annual act or report, but intensive review enables members and staff of the appropriate House subcommittee to judge whether an agency is using the money as Congress intended, or as its members intend, rather than in the political interests of the current administration or the desires of administrators....

All congressmen care about the relation of spending to taxing, and so do voters; congressmen fear the consequences, both for their own reelection and for the institution, if they continually spend more than they can raise. For that reason the appropriations committees were constituted with extensive powers. Congressmen on authorizing committees delegated to congressmen on appropriations committees the power (subject to floor votes) to limit spending. Thus the appropriations committees are in an inherently adversarial relation with the rest of Congress. They are protected by confidence in their discretion; when they are believed to have overstepped their bounds, they might lose their power (as happened in both House and Senate in the last quarter of the nineteenth century). The late nineteenth century experience, however, was not deemed a success, and since 1921 the appropriations committees have been among the more powerful in Congress.

Budgetary policy is determined by both authorizing and appropriating legislation. Louis Fisher has described the standard model of the relationship:

> As a general principle, authorizing committees are responsible for recommending programs and activities to be approved by Congress. The committees establish program objectives and frequently set dollar ceilings on the amounts that can be appropriated. Once this authorization stage is complete, the Appropriations Committees recommend the actual level of "budget authority," allowing federal agencies to enter into obligations. This, of course, is an idealized model. Actual congressional operation is substantially different.[2]

And it is different because appropriations now fund substantially less than half the budget.

The old authorizing–appropriating dichotomy no longer works so neatly. The old relationship does not apply mostly because presidents and Congresses have wanted to spend more by guaranteeing payments to individuals. Appropriations acts are so complicated, moreover, that the appropriations subcommittees develop substantial independence from the parent committee, thus limiting the potential to trade off spending among the activities funded by the acts. The authorizing committees, unsurprisingly, sometimes resist and try to reverse appropriations committee action on the floor. Almost always this is done to increase spending.

The boundaries between authorizing and appropriating decisions are hard to maintain in practice. A decision not to fund an activity, or to fund it under certain conditions (e.g., abortions allowed only in case of rape or serious threat to the life of the mother), looks much like a policy decision. Unfortunately, the many possibilities for undermining appropriations and authorizations exacerbate power struggles among committees. They also create incentives to complicate appropriations legislation with floor amendments ("riders" that the authorizing committees would disapprove); appropriations, which must pass, thus may be held hostage....

# THE PRESIDENT IS BOTH RIVAL OF AND PARTNER OF CONGRESS

The president has the first and last moves in the budget process. He can both check and use Congress, and it can both check and use him.

The last move is the veto—a bludgeon where a scalpel might be more apt. Rarely will a president dislike more than a small part of an appropriations bill, the bulk of which funds relatively uncontroversial and long-standing activities. Therefore, the veto of an appropriation act becomes part of a game of chicken; neither the president nor the act's supporters in Congress want to be blamed for shutting down federal activities in a dispute over details. The president—if only because members of his own party do not want to see him lose—usually can find enough support in at least one house to sustain the veto. He also holds the high ground in a public mudslinging contest with Congress: The president commands more media attention; as the only nationally elected official, he can claim to represent the national interest better than any set of congressional leaders; and Congress is less popular with voters than even the most unpopular president. For these reasons the president is likely to win a veto battle, with Congress having to pass a new bill that suits the chief executive.

Yet the relationship has its own dynamic. Congressmen do not like a pattern of vetoes and may unite to defend their institutional power against a president who overdoes it. Presidents do not like to lose, especially because losses reduce the White House's credibility. Anticipated reaction—the side that expects to lose giving in—is the usual rule. When the president fails to heed the signals, as with the Women's, Infants, and Children's program, he can ask for less and end up having to spend more.... In essence, both president and Congress have good reason to avoid a public veto fight, in which one or the other may be embarrassed, programs that each values be hurt, and much time be wasted. The veto, therefore, gives the president a loud voice in the bargaining over spending and tax legislation; its threat is more important than its use.

The Constitution, through the veto, gave the president a voice in bargaining; Congress gave him the right to set many of the terms. The Budget and Accounting Act of 1921 created the Bureau of the Budget. The Bureau, in a couple of steps, became the Office of Management and Budget (OMB), located in the Executive Office of the president. OMB prepares, and the president submits to Congress, a budget for each fiscal year. (Each fiscal year runs from October 1 of the previous calendar year to September 30 of the same numbered calendar year; thus fiscal 1986 began October 1, 1985, and ended September 30, 1986.) The president's budget is submitted at the beginning of the congressional session at which appropriations for that fiscal year must be made (e.g., January of 1985 for fiscal 1986).

The president's budget is a combination of proposals for legislation and predictions of events. It suggests amounts of budget authority for various line items (e.g., salaries and expenses) for each agency, which will be considered by the appropriations committees. The president's budget estimates outlays both from last year's actual spending and from the combination of old and new budget authority. It predicts the performance of the economy and, from that, the revenues and expenditures that will be produced by current tax and entitlement law....

In preparing his budget, the president faces the problem of matching preferences over programs with preferences about overall spending, taxing, and borrowing. In the past, since agencies limited their spending bids, the first step was to ask them what they needed or wanted. Budget examiners at OMB analyzed detailed agency submissions, searching for the best places to make cuts, if needed. Their judgments were based both on rules of thumb (cut new elements or reduce ineffective programs) and on a sense of the administration's attitude toward each program. While OMB was examining, the president's economic advisors—the Secretary of the Treasury, Chairman of the Council of Economic Advisors, Director of OMB, and others—prepared estimates of economic performance and arguments in support of particular tax and spending levels. But that was then. Nowadays, with presidential preferences starting out at much lower totals, the OMB sends out advice on the level of permissible spending. Sometimes this advice includes "give backs," i.e., previously allowed funds that must be returned. This is not to say that the OMB previously existed only as a passive repository of departmental requests. The OMB did provide spending guidelines in the past, but the extent and focus of this involvement has changed dramatically....

However the president defines his problem, his budget is issued with great fanfare. The budget documents include detailed justifications of his choices. Agency heads are expected to argue for the president's proposals even if they had requested larger funds.

The obvious questions are: Why did Congress establish this procedure? How much effect does it have on what Congress does? The main advantage to Congress is that this procedure gives the president primary responsibility for proposing cuts. The president can impose his priorities on the executive branch in a way that is impossible for any part of Congress, since the executive is in principle (and, in part, in fact) a hierarchy; Congress is anything but. A president can create a package that the noncentralized appropriations committees would have a hard time doing. Congressmen can then respond to his package of programs, changing it where it differs too much from their own priorities or where constituency pressures are great, and letting the president take the blame for other decisions.

Often the price of power is blame; this gives both president and congressmen reason to duck responsibility in budget politics. The process was once flexible enough for congressmen to act if they felt it necessary. They could beat up on agencies in hearings, showing these agencies did not deserve increases. They could ask leading questions at appropriation hearings, enabling agency heads to establish for the record why higher spending might be justified. They could pick and choose among presidential requests, raising popular ones (the National Institutes of Health) and cutting unpopular ones (foreign aid). By cutting here and increasing there, appropriations committees could expand some programs while staying below the president's total. Congressmen who disliked the committees' actions could blame them or fight for changes on the floor.

## NOTES

1. A good discussion of the nature and variety of budgets may be found throughout Jesse Burkhead's *Government Budgeting* (New York: Wiley, 1956). See also the illuminating comments in Frederick C. Mosher, *Program Budgeting: Theory and Practice, with Particular Reference to the U.S. Department of the Army* (Chicago: Public Administration Service, 1954), pp. 1–18.

2. Louis Fisher, "The Authorization–Appropriation Process in Congress: Formal Rules and Informal Practices," *Catholic University Law Review,* Vol. 29, No. 5 (1979), pp. 52–105.

## 14.2  HAYNES JOHNSON AND DAVID S. BRODER

# *Lessons: Lost Opportunities*

Haynes Johnson (b. 1931) and David S. Broder (b. 1921) have collaborated as news journalists and correspondents for over 30 years. The following selection is an excerpt from their book *The System: The American Way of Politics at the Breaking Point* (Little, Brown, 1996), a contemporary classic on President William Jefferson Clinton's initiative to provide universal health insurance for Americans and the subsequent political struggle between supporters and adversaries of this plan. Filling a gap in the contemporary literature on this subject, the authors analyze the most significant problems of current American health care in the context of the critical behavior and roles performed by the president, the Congress, the political parties, the lobbyists, the press, and other key decision makers of the U.S. political system. These two distinguished journalists use their insider's position to conduct interviews of key political players (e.g., President Clinton, Hillary Rodham Clinton, the congressional leadership, and powerful lobbyists) who were directly involved in the design, advocacy, and rejection of a very controversial comprehensive public policy and social reform.

In the following selection, Johnson and Broder depict the failure of health care reform in the Clinton administration—which occurred without any roll call vote in the Democratic Congress and which was immediately followed by the Republicans' regaining control of Congress in 1994, after a 40-year absence—as one of the most significant lost political opportunities of the twentieth century. The authors contend that there were multiple contributing factors that caused the collapse of President Clinton's health care reform legislation, including the sustained and intense efforts by the Republican congressional leadership to regain control of Congress and promote a revolutionary conservative political agenda (i.e., the "Contract With America") in conjunction with the strongly mobilized, greatly financed, and sophisticated lobbying effort of many special interest groups. Johnson and Broder acknowledge that one of the most egregious failures of the Clinton administration in its attempt to promote comprehensive reform legislation was its inability to understand the limitations on the president's power due to electoral results (i.e., Clinton did not gain majority support, as he won 43 percent of the popular vote). Beyond focusing on the specific stages of the failed health care legislation, the authors analyze the fundamental problem of private interests' increasing power to influence and manipulate the political process and public policy and the political system's inability to promote the public interest.

Johnson received his M.S. in American history from the University of Wisconsin. He has been a reporter, columnist, and national correspondent for the *Washington Star* and the *Washington Post,* and he was the Ferris Professor of Journalism at Princeton University. He is a frequent news commentator on such national television programs as *Today, Washington Week in Review,* and *The NewsHour With Jim Lehrer.* Among his numerous honors and awards is the Pulitzer Prize in national reporting in 1966 for outstanding national coverage of the civil rights demonstrations in Selma, Alabama.

Broder received his M.A. in political science from the University of Chicago. He has been a reporter and national political correspondent for the *Congressional Quarterly, Washington Star, New York Times,* and *Washington Post,* and he was a fellow of the Institute of Politics at Harvard University, a Poynter fellow at Yale University and Indiana University, and a fellow of the Institute of Policy Science and Public Affairs at Duke University. He is a frequent news commentator for CNN, NBC's *Meet the Press, The NewsHour With Jim Lehrer,* and PBS's *Washington Week in Review.* Broder received the Pulitzer Prize in journalism in 1973 and the National Society of Newspaper Columnists Lifetime Achievement Award in 1997.

**Key Concept:** The American political system's failure to achieve comprehensive health care reform

*I*n one of our early interviews, Secretary of Health and Human Services Donna Shalala described the battle launched by President Bill Clinton and his wife, Hillary Rodham Clinton, as one for "the last great social policy of this century." Enumerating the programs passed during the previous decades, she said. "This is the last piece, the country focusing on improving the quality of life for its people at the turn of the century."

She was correct in those judgments, but the battle represented much more than an attempt to forge a major policy. It became a fundamental test of the clashing elements in The System. As Shalala pointed out in that interview, for the first time in a dozen years one party had been entrusted by the voters with control of the executive and legislative branches of government. "If this Democratic Party doesn't move to cover people who get up in the morning and go to work in minimum-wage jobs," she said, "then it's not only lost its soul, it's lost its political coalition for the future."

When she spoke, she and others in the Clinton administration were optimistic. But in the end, the Democratic Congress adjourned without even a roll call on reform, and the Clinton White House barely addressed its demise—an outcome that no one, including its most determined opponents, thought possible when the fight began. As Shalala feared, the Democratic coalition collapsed in the historic midterm election of 1994: a widely recognized public need went unfulfilled; Republicans ended forty years of Democratic control of Congress and initiated the great struggle over the role and purpose of the federal government that will continue through the 1996 presidential election and beyond. Thus the story of the life and death of health reform shines a harsh light on the way The System—and the men and women in it—succeeds or fails. As Paul Starr, the Princeton scholar and author who played a major part in designing the Clinton health care reform, ruefully said later, "The collapse of health care reform in the first two years of the Clinton administration will go down as one of the great lost political opportunities in American history. It is a story of compromises that never happened, of deals that were never closed, of Republicans, moderate Democrats, and key interest groups that backpedaled from proposals they themselves had earlier co-sponsored or endorsed. It is also a story of strategic miscalculations on the part of the President and those of us who advised him."

He also accurately said, "The Republicans enjoyed a double triumph, killing reform and then watching jurors find the President guilty. It was the political equivalent of the perfect crime."

It is easy in retrospect to say that this kind of fundamental change was too much for The System to resolve. But another ambitious proposal, the tax reform bill of 1986, was enacted in a divided government, and there were many moments when different decisions could have produced a different result. As we have seen, the lessons of that earlier tax reform battle and the 1989 fiasco with Medicare catastrophic health insurance were either ignored or forgotten. They are instructive not only for our story, but also for future attempts to achieve major reform on controversial issues. . . .

It is our view, as well, that in this great test The System failed the people it was designed to serve. The goal of providing affordable quality health care for all—more substantially addressed, if not fully achieved, by every other advanced industrial country in the world—is farther from realization in the United States in 1996 than it was at the beginning of the decade. When the debate began, a broad public bipartisan consensus had developed on the need for fundamental reform, although not on the best policy to pursue or on the solutions people were ready to support. The battle was fought amid the most favorable conditions in this century. Paul Starr's epitaph is correct: The loss of this battle will be recorded as one of the great lost opportunities in American history.

How great a failure this turned out to be became clear over the next year. Many of the problems that prompted the Clinton initiative remain, and one of them, the number of uninsured Americans, grows steadily larger. Medical inflation continues. Public health services for the poorest Americans rapidly erode, and older Americans in need of health care find themselves threatened with higher costs for reduced services. States, counties, and cities, which face sharply reduced federal support, search in vain for local tax dollars to maintain basic services. Major public hospitals close. The already great chasm separating America's haves from its have-nots continues to widen. At the end of 1995, a year after the Clinton effort crashed, the triumphant Republican majorities in Congress struggled with the same runaway costs of the largest federal health programs, Medicare and Medicaid, that led Clinton to try to reform them. The increasingly fractious battle between the Democratic President and the Republican Congress over the federal budget that resulted in the longest shutdown of the federal government in history exposes the greater struggle that health care symbolizes: over two conflicting visions of the role of American government and the values of the society at century's end.

The failure of The System on health care reform might not loom so large if other great challenges facing the society were being met. They are not. Personal safety, economic opportunity, international peace, and health care are the four great security questions by which the American people judge the quality of their lives. On all but one of these, international peace, the last quarter of the twentieth century has witnessed the failure of The System to meet the legitimate expectations of the people it is supposed to be serving.

...Increasingly embittered debates over such intensely divisive issues as Vietnam and Watergate have added to the feeling that confrontation, not consensus, drives The System. More and more Americans now view both Democrats and Republicans as intent on tearing down opponents rather than building up the country. Energy policy fails to ensure conservation of natural resources or sufficient protection of the environment. Tax policy produces bewildering complexities. Crime policy involves more posturing than policing. In the most glaring failure, government has been unable to put its fiscal house in order. Annual deficits on a previously unimaginable scale accumulate; future generations are burdened with a geometrically rising national debt that threatens their personal prospects and the American future.

It was in this context that the battle between the President and the Congress over health reform was waged. Difficult and complex as that battle proved to be, restoring a sense of personal safety and fostering economic security are far more daunting. The twin scourges of crime and drugs are fed by powerful sociological forces that include the breakdown of the family structure and the disappearance, in many neighborhoods, of adult males capable of imposing discipline and establishing role models for a generation of alienated and increasingly violent teenagers. The Information Age transforms the entire marketplace from one with primary dependence on the creation and distribution of tangible goods to one relying mainly on the generation and transmission of data. In a time when billions of dollars of currency and investment whiz around the world in fractions of a second of microchip activity, debates about tariffs and trade seem antique. Clearly, education and training are even more important keys to individual prosperity than in the past. Yet Americans entering the workplace face a formidable new problem: No one knows how many and what kind of jobs there will be and where they will be located. There are no easy solutions; most of the problems are structural, having developed over decades. They present long-term challenges to a System, and a society, fixated on the immediate moment.

In contrast to these immensely complex challenges, the goal of providing access to quality health care for everyone was not an impossible dream. No doubt the credibility of the Clintons would have been enhanced had they admitted from the beginning that hard choices were involved—and acknowledged, too, that some people would have to pay a price in dollars, convenience, or freedom of choice for a new system that enabled everyone, not just the 85 percent with insurance, to receive care. There were reasons to be skeptical of Ira Magaziner's belief that waste in the existing health care system was so great that fine-tuning could produce sufficient savings to finance universal care, but no one seriously challenged his assertion about its enormous inefficiencies. Short-changing such preventive measures as immunization has resulted in millions of people seeking expensive, unreimbursed care in hospital emergency rooms for conditions that could—and should—be treated for more cheaply and humanely at earlier stages of the illness. The administrative costs of competing insurance companies could—and should—be cut significantly by some mechanism, whether termed a purchasing cooperative or an alliance, that draws small groups or individuals into larger blocks of health care consumers. Real competition could—and should—limit medical inflation even more than private business was beginning to experience when the Clintons began their effort. Even if one rejects the government-financed single-payer plan, which the Congressional Budget Office says would provide health insurance for everyone at lower overall total cost, room clearly existed for reforms that made practical economic and social sense.

Failure to achieve any of those possible changes was a failure of The System and every one of its parts: the presidency, the Congress, the political parties, the interest groups, and the press.

We cannot render a tougher judgment on Bill Clinton and his administration than the one he pronounced on himself: "I set the Congress up for failure." The errors of judgment, of omission and execution, that he and First Lady Hillary Clinton and their associates made were critical. While they deserve great credit for tackling a problem that Presidents had found reasons to postpone for six decades or more, and for placing it at the center of national debate and consciousness, they cannot avoid blame for the ultimate failure. Though many factors contributed to that end, we agree with Paul Starr's retrospective judgment: The lesson for the next time in health care reform is faster, smaller. "We made the error of trying to do too much, took too long, and ended up achieving nothing." Even worse, Starr said, is the ultimate irony that appears to be coming true a year after the end of the Clinton attempt; a movement that began with liberal proposals to control costs and expand coverage has produced conservative legislation that raises costs and reduces coverage.

Of all the mistakes, the greatest was the failure to recognize the limits on the President's authority imposed by the election returns. Conventional wisdom holds that you do not build bold agendas on small majorities, and Bill Clinton had no majority at all. He won with 43 percent of the popular vote, while his party lost ten seats in the House and just held its own in the Senate. Clinton limped into Washington, trailing the popular vote district by district of almost every member of Congress and with few longtime political alliances on which to draw. Moreover, health care reform was not the only item on his agenda or, to a majority of his advisers, the most important. During his presidential transition discussions in Little Rock, the highest priority, understandably and inevitably, was placed on dealing with the soaring budget deficit he had inherited. By reducing the deficit, he hoped to stimulate the economic growth he had promised in the campaign. . . .

Despite all the warning signals, the Clintons marched ahead, fortified by a belief that the rightness of their cause and the hard work they were prepared to expend on it would overcome all obstacles. They did not. Indeed, the Clintons compounded their problems by the structure they themselves designed.

The decision to create the special White House task force headed by Hillary Rodham Clinton and Ira Magaziner was a major mistake. Magaziner did a thorough job of devising a plan that was internally consistent and that addressed as many of the complex problems as any public policy could. The First Lady was an eloquent, tireless, and, for the most part, effective advocate for the cause. But the consequences of the President's decision to entrust the task to them were overwhelmingly negative. Having Hillary at the head of the task force inhibited the political debate within the administration. The secrecy under which it operated alienated not only important congressional leaders but others in the administration whose support was critical for its success. These people, in significant instances, resorted to the classic Washington tactic of making their objections public by leaking damaging (and often inaccurate) information to a press corps thoroughly frustrated by the curtain of silence erected by Hillary Clinton and Ira Magaziner. Leaks that plagued the project reflected an extraordinary lack of discipline and cohesion in the heart of the government. These repeated and destructive leaks exposed a larger problem: Despite the obvious importance both the President and the First Lady attached to health care reform, it remained something of an orphan within their administration. The White House staff for domestic policy, budget, politics, and lobbying, to say nothing of aides at Treasury, Health and Human Services, and other departments, were never fully committed to a project from which they felt excluded. The task force joke about living on "Planet Ira" contained a hard truth: Many in the White House said of the reform group, "They're so smart. Let them figure out how to pass it." That attitude was echoed, and amplified, on Capitol Hill.

All these were political mistakes, and the ultimate responsibility for them goes to the man in charge, who, as we have seen, was more than ready to take the blame. We've already explored two of these errors: first, the mismatch between the scale of reform and the political capital available to achieve it; second, the decision to place responsibility for devising the plan on a small group within the White House in a way that made their officials with expertise feel circumvented and that cast doubt on the President's claim to policy flexibility. A third set of errors involves the Congress.

The White House never resolved the contradiction between a House strategy based on the Democratic Left and a Senate strategy aimed at achieving consensus on a bill by winning moderates of both parties. Even within the Senate, the chairmen of the two committees, each believing he had White House backing, operated under very different assumptions about what served the President's interests. And there was another problem: Few on Capitol Hill could claim any expertise on the subject; fewer were even vaguely familiar with the program he chose to support, and many of them disagreed with Clinton's version as they examined it....

Americans have learned, from bitter experience, not to take their Presidents at their word. The phrase "credibility gap" entered the language with Lyndon

Johnson and Vietnam: the phenomenon it described grew with every successive President. From Watergate to "read my lips," Americans have been disillusioned again and again and again. Whitewater, and a host of lesser stories, shattered Clinton's credibility—and Hillary's as well—during the time health care was on the national agenda. Trust was destroyed. In the end, Hillary was literally driven offstage by near-fanatical opponents, and the President was forced to participate in a political charade when he supposedly removed his name from the health care bill. . . .

Another fateful decision Clinton made early in his presidency was to rely heavily on the advice and judgment of the Democratic congressional leaders to pass his program. As we have noted, Clinton ran against Washington and constantly pressed Magaziner and others to get beyond "conventional Washington thinking" on the substance of his health care program.

But at a dinner in Little Rock, during his transition period, Clinton listened attentively as Vice President Gore, Speaker Foley, House Majority Leader Gephardt, and Senate Majority Leader Mitchell begged him not to repeat the "error" Jimmy Carter had made by holding himself aloof from the congressional Democrats. Let us be your foot soldiers, they said. Gephardt and Mitchell were particularly forceful in warning that Carter's legislative program had been crippled by the early divorce between him and the congressional Democrats. This miscalculation left him vulnerable to a serious renomination challenge from an esteemed legislator, Senator Edward M. Kennedy, and ultimately led to his defeat by Reagan.

No matter how narrow Clinton's victory, no matter how slim the congressional majorities, the leaders assured the new President that the congressional Democrats would deliver for him—if he gave them a chance. Gephardt said many Democrats like himself, who were newcomers when Carter became President, had learned their lesson: Failure to back your President opens the White House door to the Republicans. They would not make that mistake again, Gephardt said. But, please, Mr. President, he added, once you've given us our marching orders, let us carry them out *our* way.

Clinton cannot be seriously faulted for listening to them, even though none of them had been a close ally in helping him win the nomination or the election. They were the veterans. They knew The System. It hardly made sense to begin his term by refusing to agree to cooperate with his own party leaders, especially given the hostile signals from the Republicans. . . .

In the 1980s, facing Republican Presidents, Democrats in Congress realized that they might have gone too far in democratizing their institution and began to strengthen their leadership. They gave the Speaker and the two majority leaders more say in committee assignments; they beefed up their policy and communications staffs; occasionally they even disciplined a notable defector, like Phil Gramm, by removing him from an influential committee. But these steps did not alter the basic fact that when the health care battle began, the centrifugal forces of personal ambition and predilection were far more powerful in both houses of Congress than the cohesive forces of party loyalty.

Forming a unified, disciplined political front was nearly impossible in that Congress. Because the Clintons' health care reform would touch the jurisdictions of at least five major committees of the House and Senate in major ways, and an additional eight or nine in peripheral ways, some thought was given to creation of an ad hoc supercommittee in each chamber that could move the bill promptly to the floor. As we have seen, the First Lady ardently sought this approach. Gephardt, Foley, and Mitchell immediately rejected the idea; the members of the committees with jurisdiction would never yield that much power to a select group appointed by the leaders.

And, as we have also seen, the obstacles in the multicommittee approach proved to be so formidable that the leaders were unable to get a measure to the point of being voted up or down in either the House or the Senate. Responsibility was hopelessly, destructively, fragmented. . . .

The health care battle exposed as clearly as any recent legislative effort the infirmities that had developed in Congress under the long period of Democratic control. Clinton was not to blame for them; he was their victim. And when he had to sit and watch, in August of 1994, as the very leaders he had trusted to deliver for him squabbled for weeks over petty, parochial jurisdictional questions while health care reform went down the tubes, he must have wondered whether he had made a mistake in trying to move this broken system.

The fight also exposed the weakness of the Democratic Party—and led directly to its further dismemberment in the election of 1994. What Donna Shalala told us was the simple truth: Bringing health insurance within reach of every American family was the final piece of the Social Security system the Democrats had begun assembling under Franklin Roosevelt. It represented the single most important unfulfilled commitment of that party to its working-class and middle-class base. The very rich and the very poor had health care coverage. So did the elderly. The millions of ordinary working Americans without coverage were the people for whom the Democrats supposedly stood.

The most stunning fact about this entire effort is that when the Democrats controlled both houses of Congress and had in the White House in Bill and Hillary Clinton the two most knowledgeable and committed advocates of universal health care coverage in history, they failed over two years even to bring the measure to a vote.

This failure spoke to weaknesses in both the presidency and in Congress. But it screamed to the world that the Democratic Party, the oldest and arguably most successful political institution in the free world, had lost its core, lost its heart, lost its soul. . . .

The political strategy the Republicans employed to demolish the Clinton plan was brilliant in its boldness. If Ira Magaziner thought the administration could "make complexity our alley," the Republican pollsters quickly discovered that the specter of a Big Government health care bureaucracy was their most powerful weapon. They took only a few weeks to recover from the initial favorable wave of stories about the President's speech and Hillary Clinton's round of appearances at congressional committees before they launched a series of ever-stronger attacks on "government health care." . . .

Republicans were far from alone in playing narrow politics. Dozens of interest groups that the Democrats had counted on also demonstrated how parochial they could be; how fixated on their own agendas, how heedless of the necessity to compromise to achieve a larger goal. At every stage of the story, many of them—from the giant American Association of Retired Persons to the tiny Foundation for Hospice and Home Care—declined to say flat out, "Help pass the Clinton plan."

Not that the White House was always skillful in negotiating with these interest groups. But administration ineptitude did not justify their holding back their vital support. Talking with their lobbyists and directors after the battle, we heard repeatedly, "We always assumed we would get something through Congress. We just wanted to get the best deal we could." But this was a classic case where the perfect became the enemy of the good—and of the attainable. Thus, these groups must ultimately share the blame for the fact that the country got nothing.

In the end, this battle revealed something even more significant about the interest groups that were so determined to defeat the Clinton reform. On the evidence of this struggle, they have so far outgrown the conceptions and definitions of past interest-group operations that it is necessary to rethink the way The System works.

For many decades, we have known that the schoolbook model of representative democracy obscures the reality. We remember the disillusioned reaction of the dedicated young White House Delivery Room volunteer who, when invited to speak to his hometown high school students about the lessons he had learned about our democracy, would not tell them how The System *really* works for fear it would make them even more cynical. One of those lessons is that the majority does not always—or automatically—prevail. Our system of government is littered with constitutional and political roadblocks that make it hard for huge policy changes like health care reform to be enacted quickly. We agree, up to a point, with those who point this out and who conclude that The System operated exactly as it is supposed to in the health care battle: Where no strong consensus exists, major change should wait.

But that argument ignores a deeper truth about the critical role that public opinion plays in The System. In many respects, the story of the life and death of health care reform is the story of how to manufacture and manipulate public opinion. A fundamental question that emerges from this story is, Why did the anticipated, and needed, great public debate about what kind of health care Americans want never occur? And why did the initially favorable American public become so frightened by the President's reform?

The answer is that "public opinion" was largely an artifact of the groups that mobilized to defeat reform. They created opinion with their grassroots and media efforts. Then they invoked that public opinion to convince, or provide a rationale for, the members of Congress who for reasons of self-interest wanted to vote no.

*Haynes Johnson and David S. Broder*

One of the most striking aspects of this battle is that, from beginning to end, 70 percent or more of those polled said they agreed with two fundamental propositions underlying the Clinton plan; that all American families should have health insurance and that all employers should contribute to paying for their workers' premiums.

Seventy percent-plus agreement on anything is most rare in American politics. It suggests a strong climate for change. Yet when we asked pollsters and lobbyists working to defeat the Clinton plan why these public attitudes did not represent a clear public mandate for reform, the answer we got went like this: "Of course, people want employers to pay for their health insurance. Why wouldn't they? But if you ask a follow-up question, 'Do you want the government to require business to pay for health insurance if it means lower wages and fewer jobs?' the number of those supporting reform turns around."

The interest groups opposing Clinton successfully persuaded much of the public that his plan would mean not only lower wages and fewer jobs but less freedom to choose a doctor, a hospital, or an insurer. It would mean more bureaucracy and lower-quality care. They spread this largely false message relentlessly in a campaign that cost literally hundreds of millions of dollars and involved the use of every technique developed for the modern high-tech election campaign.

## 15.1 SAMUEL P. HUNTINGTON

# *The Erosion of American National Interests*

Samuel P. Huntington (b. 1927) is considered one of the most productive and influential contemporary scholars of American foreign policy and international relations. As a prolific author of major, innovative, scholarly publications on American foreign policy and global politics, his works are often cited and referred to by political scientists and foreign policy decision makers. Huntington's article "The Erosion of American National Interests," *Foreign Affairs* (September/October 1997), from which the following selection is taken, is a landmark interpretative analysis of American foreign policy because it has promoted the contemporary scholarly study of American national interests.

Huntington is currently the Albert J. Weatherhead III University Professor at Harvard University, where he has taught for many years. He is also director of the John M. Olin Institute for Strategic Studies at Harvard University and chairman of the Harvard Academy for International and Area Studies. His expertise on foreign policy has enabled him to influence foreign policy decions through his membership in various important advisory organizations, including the National Security Council, in which he was director of security planning for the Carter administration; the Social Science Research Council; the Institute of Strategic Studies; and the Council on Foreign Relations. He has been awarded numerous fellowships, including a Guggenheim Fellowship. He was the founder and coeditor of the journal

*Foreign Policy* and president of the American Political Science Association. Huntington's many publications include *Political Order in Changing Societies* (Yale University Press, 1969), *The Soldier and the State: The Theory and Politics of Civil-Military Relations* (Belknap Press, 1981), *American Politics: The Promise of Disharmony* (Harvard University Press, 1983), *American Military Strategy* (University of California, 1986), *The Third Wave: Democratization in the Late Twentieth Century* (University of Oklahoma Press, 1993), and *The Clash of Civilizations and the Remaking of World Order* (Simon & Schuster, 1996).

The following selection is a critical analysis of the current confusion in precisely identifying American national interests in the post–cold war period. This article has filled a critical intellectual gap in the contemporary literature on American foreign policy and strategic defense planning because it has promoted serious reexamination of the specific sources responsible for the formulation of American national interests. Huntington argues that erosion of a coherent understanding of American national identity has been accelerated by the demise of the cold war and by complex social, cultural, and demographic transformations in American society. This has resulted in a confused awareness of American national interests. Huntington's classic essay is a unique contribution to the study of American foreign policy in that he attempts to demonstrate that such policy and American national interests have shifted from legitimate broad global concerns to highly parochial commercial and ethnic objectives. In addition to promoting the commercial or economic interests of particular American businesses, contemporary American foreign policy has also been shaped by dominant transnational or nonnational ethnic interests.

In lieu of an American foreign policy of particularism oriented toward the fulfillment of specific commercial and ethnic interests, Huntington advocates a renewal of commitment by Americans to central, identifiable national interests. Instead of an abstract foreign policy based upon idealistic goals, a comprehensive strategy, or moralistic visions, Huntington prescribes a reconceptualization of American foreign policy guided by the pragmatic principle and realistic objective of a national interest of national restraint, which would have the broad support of the American people. According to Huntington, this would reduce American commitments in the global arena in conjunction with a planned reduction of American resources promoting narrow commercial and ethnic objectives.

**Key Concept:** the replacement of American national interests by narrow commercial and ethnic interests

# THE DISINTEGRATION OF IDENTITY

The years since the end of the Cold War have seen intense, wide-ranging, and confused debates about American national interests. Much of this confusion stems from the complexity of the post-Cold War world. The new environment has been variously interpreted as involving the end of history, bipolar conflict between rich and poor countries, movement back to a future of traditional power politics, the proliferation of ethnic conflict verging on anarchy, the clash of civilizations, and conflicting trends toward integration and fragmentation. The new world is all these things, and hence there is good reason for uncertainty about American interests in it. Yet that is not the only source of confusion. Efforts to define national interest presuppose agreement on the nature of the country whose interests are to be defined. National interest derives from national identity. We have to know who we are before we can know what our interests are.

Historically, American identity has had two primary components: culture and creed. The first has been the values and institutions of the original settlers, who were Northern European, primarily British, and Christian, primarily Protestant. This culture included most importantly the English language and traditions concerning relations between church and state and the place of the individual in society. Over the course of three centuries, black people were slowly and only partially assimilated into this culture. Immigrants from western, southern, and eastern Europe were more fully assimilated, and the original culture evolved and was modified but not fundamentally altered as a result. In *The Next American Nation*, Michael Lind captures the broad outlines of this evolution when he argues that American culture developed through three phases: Anglo-America (1789–1861), Euro-America (1857–1957), and Multicultural America (1972–present). The cultural definition of national identity assumes that while the culture may change, it has a basic continuity.

The second component of American identity has been a set of universal ideas and principles articulated in the founding documents by American leaders: liberty, equality, democracy, constitutionalism, liberalism, limited government, private enterprise. These constitute what Gunnar Myrdal termed the American Creed, and the popular consensus on them has been commented on by foreign observers from Crevecoeur and Tocqueville down to the present. This identity was neatly summed up by Richard Hofstadter: "It has been our fate as a nation not to have ideologies but to be one."

These dual sources of identity are, of course, closely related. The creed was a product of the culture. Now, however, the end of the Cold War and social, intellectual, and demographic changes in American society have brought into question the validity and relevance of both traditional components of American identity. Without a sure sense of national identity, Americans have become unable to define their national interests, and as a result subnational commercial interests and transnational and nonnational ethnic interests have come to dominate foreign policy.

## LOSS OF THE OTHER

The most profound question concerning the American role in the post-Cold War world was improbably posed by Rabbit Angstrom, the harried central character of John Updike's novels: "Without the cold war, what's the point of being an

American?" If being an American means being committed to the principles of liberty, democracy, individualism, and private property, and if there is no evil empire out there threatening those principles, what indeed does it mean to be an American, and what becomes of American national interests?

From the start, Americans have constructed their creedal identity in contrast to an undesirable "other." America's opponents are always defined as liberty's opponents. At the time of independence, Americans could not distinguish themselves culturally from Britain; hence they had to do so politically. Britain embodied tyranny, aristocracy, oppression; America, democracy, equality, republicanism. Until the end of the nineteenth century, the United States defined itself in opposition to Europe. Europe was the past: backward, unfree, unequal, characterized by feudalism, monarchy, and imperialism. The United States, in contrast, was the future: progressive, free, equal, republican. In the twentieth century, the United States emerged on the world scene and increasingly saw itself not as the antithesis of Europe but rather as the leader of European-American civilization against upstart challengers to that civilization, imperial and then Nazi Germany.

After World War II the United States defined itself as the leader of the democratic free world against the Soviet Union and world communism. During the Cold War the United States pursued many foreign policy goals, but its one overriding national purpose was to contain and defeat communism. When other goals and interests clashed with this purpose, they were usually subordinated to it. For 40 years virtually all the great American initiatives in foreign policy, as well as many in domestic policy, were justified by this overriding priority: the Greek-Turkish aid program, the Marshall Plan, NATO, the Korean War, nuclear weapons and strategic missiles, foreign aid, intelligence operations, reduction of trade barriers, the space program, the Alliance for Progress, military alliances with Japan and Korea, support for Israel, overseas military deployments, an unprecedentedly large military establishment, the Vietnam War, the openings to China, support for the Afghan mujahideen and other anticommunist insurgencies. If there is no Cold War, the rationale for major programs and initiatives like these disappears.

As the Cold War wound down in the late 1980s, Gorbachev's adviser Georgiy Arbatov commented: "We are doing something really terrible to you—we are depriving you of an enemy." Psychologists generally agree that individuals and groups define their identity by differentiating themselves from and placing themselves in opposition to others.[1] While wars at times may have a divisive effect on society, a common enemy can often help to promote identity and cohesion among people. The weakening or absence of a common enemy can do just the reverse. Abraham Lincoln commented on this effect in his Lyceum speech in 1837 when he argued that the American Revolution and its aftermath had directed enmity outward: "The jealousy, envy, avarice incident to our nature, and so common to a state of peace, prosperity, and conscious strength, were for a time in a great measure smothered and rendered inactive, while the deep-rooted principles of hate, and the powerful motive of revenge, instead of being turned against each other, were directed exclusively against the British nation." Hence, he said, "the basest principles of our nature" were either dormant or "the active agents in the advancement of the noblest of causes—that of establishing and maintaining civil and religious liberty." But he warned, "this state of feeling must fade, is fading, has faded, with the circumstances that produced it." He spoke, of course, as the nation was starting to disintegrate. As the heritage of World War II and the Cold War fades, America may be faced with a comparable dynamic.

The Cold War fostered a common identity between American people and government. Its end is likely to weaken or at least alter that identity. One possible consequence is the rising opposition to the federal government, which is, after all, the principal institutional manifestation of American national identity and unity. Would nationalist fanatics bomb federal buildings and attack federal agents if the federal government was still defending the country against a serious foreign threat? Would the militia movement be as strong as it is today? In the past, comparable bombing attacks were usually the work of foreigners who saw the United States as their enemy, and the first response of many people to the Oklahoma City bombing was to assume that it was the work of a "new enemy," Muslim terrorists. That response could reflect a psychological need to believe that such an act must have been carried out by an external enemy. Ironically, the bombing may have been in part the result of the absence of such an enemy. . . .

# IN SEARCH OF NATIONAL INTERESTS

A national interest is a public good of concern to all or most Americans; a vital national interest is one which they are willing to expend blood and treasure to defend. National interests usually combine security and material concerns, on the one hand, and moral and ethical concerns, on the other. Military action against Saddam Hussein was seen as a vital national interest because he threatened reliable and inexpensive access to Persian Gulf oil and because he was a rapacious dictator who had blatantly invaded and annexed another country. During the Cold War the Soviet Union and communism were perceived as threats to both American security and American values; a happy coincidence existed between the demands of power politics and the demands of morality. Hence broad public support buttressed government efforts to defeat communism and thus, in Walter Lippmann's terms, to maintain a balance between capabilities and commitments. That balance was often tenuous and arguably got skewed in the 1970s. With the end of the Cold War, however, the danger of a "Lippmann gap" vanished, and instead the United States appears to have a Lippmann surplus. Now the need is not to find the power to serve American purposes but rather to find purposes for the use of American power.

This need has led the American foreign policy establishment to search frantically for new purposes that would justify a continuing U.S. role in world affairs comparable to that in the Cold War. The Commission on America's National Interests put the problem this way in 1996: "After four decades of unusual single-mindedness in containing Soviet Communist expansion, we have seen five years of ad hoc fits and starts. If it continues, this drift will threaten our values, our fortunes, and indeed our lives."[2]

The commission identified five vital national interests: prevent attacks on the United States with weapons of mass destruction, prevent the emergence of hostile hegemons in Europe or Asia and of hostile powers on U.S. borders or in control of the seas, prevent the collapse of the global systems for trade, financial markets, energy supplies, and the environment, and ensure the survival of U.S. allies.

What, however, are the threats to these interests? Nuclear terrorism against the United States could be a near-term threat, and the emergence of China as an East Asian hegemon could be a longer-term one. Apart from these, however, it is hard to see any major looming challenges to the commission's vital interests. New threats will undoubtedly arise, but given the scarcity of current ones, campaigns to arouse interest in foreign affairs and support for major foreign policy initiatives now fall on deaf ears. The administration's call for the "enlargement" of democracy does not resonate with the public and is belied by the administration's own actions. Arguments from neoconservatives for big increases in defense spending have the same air of unreality that arguments for the abolition of nuclear weapons had during the Cold War.

The argument is frequently made that American "leadership" is needed to deal with world problems. Often it is. The call for leadership, however, begs the question of leadership to do what, and rests on the assumption that the world's problems are America's problems. Often they are not. The fact that things are going wrong in many places in the world is unfortunate, but it does not mean that the United States has either an interest in or the responsibility for correcting them. The National Interests Commission said that presidential leadership is necessary to create a consensus on national interests. In some measure, however, a consensus already exists that American national interests do not warrant extensive American involvement in most problems in most of the world. The foreign policy establishment is asking the president to make a case for a cause that simply will not sell. The most striking feature of the search for national interests has been its failure to generate purposes that command anything remotely resembling broad support and to which people are willing to commit significant resources.

# COMMERCIALISM AND ETHNICITY

The lack of national interests that command widespread support does not imply a return to isolationism. America remains involved in the world, but its involvement is now directed at commercial and ethnic interests rather than national interests. Economic and ethnic particularism define the current American role in the world. The institutions and capabilities—political, military, economic, intelligence—created to serve a grand national purpose in the Cold War are now being suborned and redirected to serve narrow subnational, transnational, and even nonnational purposes. Increasingly people are arguing that these are precisely the interests foreign policy should serve.

The Clinton administration has given priority to "commercial diplomacy," making the promotion of American exports a primary foreign policy objective.

It has been successful in wringing access to some foreign markets for American products. Commercial achievements have become a primary criterion for judging the performance of American ambassadors. President Clinton may well be spending more time promoting American sales abroad than doing anything else in foreign affairs. If so, that would be a dramatic sign of the redirection of American foreign policy. In case after case, country after country, the dictates of commercialism have prevailed over other purposes including human rights, democracy, alliance relationships, maintaining the balance of power, technology export controls, and other strategic and political considerations described by one administration official as "stratocrap and globaloney."[3] "Many in the administration, Congress, and the broader foreign policy community," a former senior official in the Clinton Commerce Department argued in these pages, "still believe that commercial policy is a tool of foreign policy, when it should more often be the other way around—the United States should use all its foreign policy levers to achieve commercial goals." The funds devoted to promoting commercial goals should be greatly increased; the personnel working on these goals should be upgraded and professionalized; the agencies concerned with export promotion need to be strengthened and recognized. Landing the contract is the name of the game in foreign policy.

Or at least it is the name of one game. The other game is the promotion of ethnic interests. While economic interests are usually subnational, ethnic interests are generally transnational or nonnational. The promotion of particular businesses and industries may not involve a broad public good, as does a general reduction in trade barriers, but it does promote the interests of some Americans. Ethnic groups promote the interests of people and entities outside the United States. Boeing has an interest in aircraft sales and the Polish-American Congress in help for Poland, but the former benefits residents of Seattle, the latter residents of Eastern Europe.

The growing role of ethnic groups in shaping American foreign policy is reinforced by the waves of recent immigration and by the arguments for diversity and multiculturalism. In addition, the greater wealth of ethnic communities and the dramatic improvements in communications and transportation now make it much easier for ethnic groups to remain in touch with their home countries. As a result, these groups are being transformed from cultural communities within the boundaries of a state into diasporas that transcend these boundaries. State-based diasporas, that is, trans-state cultural communities that control at least one state, are increasingly important and increasingly identify with the interests of their homeland. "Full assimilation into their host societies," a leading expert, Gabriel Sheffer, has observed in *Survival,* "has become unfashionable among both established and incipient state-based diasporas . . . many diasporal communities neither confront overwhelming pressure to assimilate nor feel any marked advantage in assimilating into their host societies or even obtaining citizenship there." Since the United States is the premier immigrant country in the world, it is most affected by the shifts from assimilation to diversity and from ethnic group to diaspora.

During the Cold War, immigrants and refugees from communist countries usually vigorously opposed, for political and ideological reasons, the governments of their home countries and actively supported American anticommunist policies against them. Now, diasporas in the United States support their home governments. Products of the Cold War, Cuban-Americans ardently support U.S. anti-Castro policies. Chinese-Americans, in contrast, overwhelmingly pressure the United States to adopt favorable policies toward China. Culture has supplanted ideology in shaping attitudes in diaspora populations.

Diasporas provide many benefits to their home countries. Economically prosperous diasporas furnish major financial support to the homeland, Jewish-Americans, for instance, contributing up to $1 billion a year to Israel. Armenian-Americans send enough to earn Armenia the sobriquet of "the Israel of the Caucasus." Diasporas supply expertise, military recruits, and on occasion political leadership to the homeland. They often pressure their home governments to adopt more nationalist and assertive policies towards neighboring countries. Recent cases in the United States show that they can be a source of spies used to gather information for their homeland governments.

Most important, diasporas can influence the actions and policies of their host country and co-opt its resources and influence to serve the interests of their homeland. Ethnic groups have played active roles in politics throughout American history. Now, ethnic diaspora groups proliferate, are more active, and have greater self-consciousness, legitimacy, and political clout. In recent years, diasporas have had a major impact on American policy towards Greece and Turkey, the Caucasus, the recognition of Macedonia, support for Croatia, sanctions against South Africa, aid for black Africa, intervention in Haiti, NATO expansion, sanctions against Cuba, the controversy in Northern Ireland, and the relations between Israel and its neighbors. Diaspora-based policies may at times coincide with broader national interests, as could arguably be the case with NATO expansion, but they are also often pursued at the expense of broader interests and American relations with long-standing allies. Overall, as James R. Schlesinger observed in a 1997 lecture at the Center for Strategic and International Studies, the United States has "less of a foreign policy in a traditional sense of a great power than we have the stapling together of a series of goals put forth by domestic constituency groups...The result is that American foreign policy is incoherent. It is scarcely what one would expect from the leading world power."

Schlesinger had to recognize, however, that multiculturalism and heightened ethnic consciousness have caused many political leaders to believe this is "the *appropriate* way to make foreign policy." In the scholarly community some argue that diasporas can help promote American values in their home countries and hence "the participation of ethnic diasporas in shaping U.S. foreign policy is a truly positive phenomenon."[4] The validity of diaspora interests was a central theme at a May 1996 conference on "Defining the National Interest: Minorities and U.S. Foreign Policy in the 21st Century." Conference participants attacked the Cold War definition of national interest and what was described as "the traditional policy community's apparent animosity toward the very idea of minority involvement in international affairs." Conferees explored "the experiences of Jewish-Americans and Cuban-Americans and sought to extract lessons from the way these two groups succeeded in influencing foreign policy while others failed." The sponsorship of this conference by the New York Council on Foreign Relations, once the capstone institution of the foreign policy establishment, was the ultimate symbol of the triumph of diaspora interests over national interests in American foreign policy.

The displacement of national interests by commercial and ethnic interests reflects the domesticization of foreign policy. Domestic politics and interests have always inevitably and appropriately influenced foreign policy. Now, however, previous assumptions that the foreign and domestic policymaking processes differ from each other for important reasons no longer hold. For an understanding of American foreign policy it is necessary to study not the interests of the American state in a world of competing states but rather the play of economic and ethnic interests in American domestic politics. At least in recent years, the latter has been a superb predictor of foreign policy stands. Foreign policy, in the sense of actions consciously designed to promote the interests of the United States as a collective entity in relation to similar collective entities, is slowly but steadily disappearing.

# THE PUSH AND PULL OF AMERICAN POWER

A decade after the end of the Cold War, a paradox exists with respect to American power. On the one hand, the United States is the only superpower in the world. It has the largest economy and the highest levels of prosperity. Its political and economic principles are increasingly endorsed throughout the world. It spends more on defense than all the other major powers combined and has the only military force capable of acting effectively in almost every part of the world. It is far ahead of any other country in technology and appears certain to retain that lead in the foreseeable future. American popular culture and consumer products have swept the world, permeating the most distant and resistant societies. American economic, ideological, military, technological, and cultural primacy, in short, is overwhelming.

American influence, on the other hand, falls far short of that. Countries large and small, rich and poor, friendly and antagonistic, democratic and authoritarian, all seem able to resist the blandishments and threats of American policymakers. On issues of protectionism, sanctions, intervention, human rights, proliferation of weapons of mass destruction, peacekeeping, and others, officials of foreign governments listen politely to American demands and entreaties, perhaps express general agreement with the ideas advanced, and then quietly go their own way. This tendency "to follow their own counsels," Jonathan Clarke observed in *Foreign Policy* in 1996, "includes both great and small nations...."

American foreign policy is becoming a foreign policy of particularism increasingly devoted to the promotion abroad of highly specific commercial and ethnic interests. The institutions, resources, and influence generated to serve national interests in the Cold War are being redirected to serve these interests. These developments may have been furthered by the almost exclusive concern of the Clinton administration with domestic politics, but their roots lie in broader changes in the external and internal context of the United States and changing conceptions of American national identity.

The likelihood that these contextual factors will shift in the near future seems remote. Conceivably China could become a new enemy. Certainly, important groups in China think of the United States as *their* new enemy. A China threat sufficient to generate a new sense of national identity and purpose in the United States, however, is not imminent, and how serious that threat is judged to be will depend on the extent to which the Americans view Chinese hegemony in East Asia as damaging to American interests. Reviving a stronger sense of national identity would also require countering the cults of diversity and multiculturalism within the United States. It would probably involve limiting immigration along the lines proposed by the Jordan Commission and developing new public and private Americanization programs to counter the factors enhancing diaspora loyalties and to promote the assimilation of immigrants. These developments may well occur, but given the extent to which, in Nathan Glazer's phrase, "we are all multiculturalists now," it will be a while before the recent denationalizing trends are reversed.

The replacement of particularism would require the American public to become committed to new national interests that would take priority over and lead to the subordination of commercial and ethnic concerns. At present, as polls show, majorities of the American public are unwilling to support the commitment of significant resources to the defense of American allies, the protection of small nations against aggression, the promotion of human rights and democracy, or economic and social development in the Third World.[5] As a result the articulation of these and other broad goals by administration officials produces little follow-through, and with rare exceptions the calls of establishment figures for American leadership generate no effective action. Unable to deliver on its broad promises, American foreign policy becomes one of rhetoric and retreat, with the active energies of the administration concentrated on the advancement of particularistic concerns. Foreign governments have learned not to take seriously administration statements of its general policy goals and to take very seriously administration actions devoted to commercial and ethnic interests.

The alternative to particularism is thus not promulgation of a "grand design," "coherent strategy," or "foreign policy vision." It is a policy of restraint and reconstitution aimed at limiting the diversion of American resources to the service of particularistic subnational, transnational, and nonnational interests. The national interest is national restraint, and that appears to be the only national interest the American people are willing to support at this time in their history. Hence, instead of formulating unrealistic schemes for grand endeavors abroad, foreign policy elites might well devote their energies to designing plans for lowering American involvement in the world in ways that will safeguard possible future national interests.

At some point in the future, the combination of security threat and moral challenge will require Americans once again to commit major resources to the defense of national interests. The *de novo* mobilization of those resources from a low base, experience suggests, is likely to be easier than the redirection of resources that have been committed to entrenched particularistic interests. A more restrained role now could facilitate America's assumption of a more positive role in the future when the time comes for it to renew its national identity and to pursue national purposes for which Americans are willing to pledge their lives, their fortunes, and their national honor.

## NOTES

1. See Vamik D. Volkan, *The Need to Have Enemies and Allies: From Clinical Practice to International Relationships,* Northvale, NJ: Aronson, 1994, and Jonathan Mercer, "Anarchy and Identity," *International Organizations,* Spring 1996, pp. 237–68.

2. *America's National Interests, A Report from the Commission on America's National Interests,* Cambridge: Center for Science and International Affairs, John F. Kennedy School of Government, Harvard University, 1996, p. 1.

3. Lawrence F. Kaplan, "The Selling of American Foreign Policy," *The Weekly Standard,* April 23, 1997, pp. 19–22.

4. Yossi Shain, "Multicultural Foreign Policy," *Foreign Policy,* Fall 1995, p. 87.

5. See John E. Reilly, ed., *American Public Opinion and U.S. Foreign Policy 1994,* Chicago: Chicago Council on Foreign Relations, 1995, and Arthur M. Schlesinger, Jr., "Back to the Womb? Isolationism's Renewed Threat," *Foreign Affairs,* July/August 1995, pp. 2–8.

## 15.2 STANLEY HOFFMANN

# *The Crisis of Liberal Internationalism*

Stanley Hoffmann (b. 1928) is a contemporary scholar of global politics, particularly European politics, French culture and politics, international law, international organizations, and American foreign policy. He received his M.A. from Harvard University and his LL.D. from the University of Paris. He is the Douglas Dillon Professor of the Civilization of France and chairman of the Center for European Studies at Harvard University, where he has taught for over 40 years. Hoffmann has received numerous prestigious honors and awards, including the Carnegie Prize in International Organization and the Prix Alphonse Bentinck. The scholarly insights articulated in his numerous writings, particularly in international relations, European politics, and American foreign policy, have made him one of the most frequently cited authors in these areas of study. His numerous publications include *France Seventeen Eighty-Nine to Nineteen Hundred* (Viking Penguin, 1986); *Janus and Minerva: Essays in the Theory and Practice of International Politics* (Westview, 1987); *The New European Community: Decisionmaking and Institutional Change* (Westview, 1991), coedited with Robert O. Keohane; *International Relations: The Long Road to Theory* (Irvington, 1993); and *The European Sisyphus: Essays on Europe, 1964–1994* (Westview, 1995). Hoffmann is a frequent contributor to international and comparative scholarly journals, including *Foreign Policy, Foreign Affairs, Daedalus,* and the *New York Review of Books.*

 The following selection is an excerpt from "The Crisis of Liberal Internationalism," *Foreign Policy* (Spring 1995), Hoffmann's classic study of the declining influence of the ideology of liberal democratic internationalism in the contemporary global context. Liberal democratic internationalism, or Wilsonianism, is the twentieth-century foreign policy approach that prescribes that the United States should design its foreign policy decisions according to idealistic moral criteria, universal ethical principles, and abstract philosophical ideals, such as the promotion of democracy, global human rights, and free trade. Hoffmann contends that American hegemony was responsible for promoting this perspective, particularly in its containment of totalitarianism and Soviet communism and its opposition to colonialism and imperialism. He also argues that there has been a recent erosion of consensus by the American people and political leadership for a U.S. policy of liberal internationalism due to perceived extensive human and financial costs. Instead, many Americans have argued for a return to the traditional realistic approach to global relations, which recommends that the United States design its foreign policy objectives to conform to its perception of its concrete, nonideological national interests. Hoffmann also contends that liberal democratic internationalism is itself responsible to some degree for its failures in the contemporary global arena.

Hoffmann says that the contemporary threat to the implementation of the liberal internationalist vision of global stability and cooperation consists of global social and political anomie and chaos. This is a world characterized by disintegrating states due to such complex factors as the collapse of the Soviet Union, pervasive conflicts, and civil wars among rival ethnic, religious, and political factions. It is in this context of disintegrating states that Hoffmann examines the four critical norms that are responsible for much of the confusion over the liberal agenda: sovereignty, self-government or democracy, national self-determination, and human rights. In this classic essay, which should have a profound impact upon contemporary foreign policy scholars and leaders, Hoffmann calls for a serious reformulation of liberal internationalism. A concept of human rights that would entail limitations on the principles of sovereignty and self-determination would be the cornerstone of his prescription for a reinvigorated liberal vision of the world.

**Key Concept:** the decline and reformulation of liberal internationalism

$C$ommunism is dead, but is the other great postwar ideology, liberal internationalism, also dying? A recent book by political scientist Tony Smith as well as several speeches by National Security Adviser Anthony Lake have reminded Americans that "liberal democratic internationalism, or Wilsonianism, has been the most important and distinctive contribution of the United States to the international history of the twentieth century," as Smith states it. Lake, presenting the Clinton administration's foreign policy as a pragmatic Wilsonianism, has explained that it aims at expanding democracy and free trade, at defending democracy from its foes, at quarantining repressive and pariah states, and at protecting and promoting human rights.

After two years, however, pragmatism is more visible than Wilsonianism. In a speech at Harvard, Lake stated that the promotion of democracy and the defense of human rights would entail the use of force only if, among other qualifications, there were clearly defined American interests. He also suggested that the spread of liberalism was not *ipso facto* an American interest: an inadvertent but remarkable concession to traditional realism. As in the Carter years, the different elements of the liberal agenda are again in competition with one another —human rights versus the expansion of free trade, as one example. Whether the liberal agenda should be carried out by multilateral means or, in case of need, by the United States alone, has again become a source of confusion and grief, as in Bosnia. Meanwhile, the nation's enthusiasm for bearing the human and financial costs of carrying out a policy of liberal internationalism has waned. Whereas containment had provided a reasonably clear rationale for policy and a lever for mobilizing public support, neo-Wilsonianism seems a guideline made of rubber and has left the American public deeply ambivalent.

This is not new. As Tony Smith establishes in *America's Mission,* the golden ages of liberal democratic internationalism were the periods that followed the two world wars, and, to some extent, the 1980s, when the Cold War was being "won" by the West and the "third wave" of democratization occurred. This is not a coincidence; it suggests that in order to understand the current difficulties of liberalism on the world stage there is a need to go far beyond the all too familiar and depressing litany of what is wrong with Bill Clinton's foreign policy. An examination of the plight of liberal internationalism must shift to the flaws and limitations of liberalism itself. . . .

But liberalism's embrace of national self-determination raised more questions than it answered. There was, once more, the dilemma of intervention for the emancipation of oppressed nationalities. In addition, there were formidable new question marks. Nationalities do not come in neat packages. One could conceive abstractly of a world of distinct liberal states, but a world of separate nation-states would leave vast areas of confusion: minorities in existing nation-states, plus the vexing problem of what is the "self" that is entitled to self-determination (what, in other words, distinguishes a group that deserves to become a nation-state from one that does not). There were also questions of whether self-determination was necessarily synonymous with sovereignty, and whether a world of independent sovereign nation-states would find harmony as easily as the world of states envisaged by seventeenth- and eighteenth-century liberals—precisely because of the conflicts that were likely to result from the problems of minorities and of who can claim to form a nation.

Second, the national cause might be separate from the liberal one: There could be authoritarian versions of nationalism, definitions of the nation in terms of "blood and earth," not consent—conceptions that make of the individual a pure product of his national community, and not the master of his civic fate. Non-liberal nationalisms thus could give new strength and relevance to authoritarian doctrines and might derail the philosophy of historical progress that predicted the gradual triumph of liberal government over tyranny. The replacement, on the illiberal Right, of divine right (or the power of tradition) with the needs and demands of the nation was to give a formidable new lease on life to ideas previously associated with obsolescent aristocracies, a reactionary Church, or frivolous courts.

Third, liberalism's embrace of nationalism introduced into liberalism a philosophical incongruity. The appeal of liberalism had been an appeal to reason—the reason embodied in John Locke's Natural Law, Kant's idea of a Good Will rooted in human reason, and the rationalism of utilitarian calculations of pleasure and pain. Nationalism has much more to do with will than with reason; its connections are with Rousseau's General Will, which is exclusively that of the separate community, and with Jacobinism. If the legitimacy of power is derived not merely from rational consent to a system of checks and balances and to a careful separation between a public sphere and a domain of individual liberty, but also from the existence of a common national will, are there not serious risks that such a will, however democratic, could overrun the restraints on power and remove the barrier that protects individuals? Nationalism, in other words, reopened the inherent tension between liberalism and democracy that had broken out in the French Revolution, and thus threatened both the liberal program at home and the cosmopolitan vision abroad—by creating new sources of intense conflict between states with different conceptions of the nation and overlapping nationalities, and by weakening the two transnational pillars of the liberal international order: a transnational economy and world public opinion.

## LIBERAL INTERNATIONALISM AND REALPOLITIK

With such blind spots and contradictions, how could liberal internationalism nevertheless have been as successful as it has been at times, particularly in the period that followed the Second World War? A part of the answer is undoubtedly provided by American hegemony in the vast areas in which the United States was able and willing to exert its influence after the calamitous insulation of the interwar period. It is already paradoxical enough that the progress of liberal vision, in the creation of a transnational economy as well as in the development of cooperation among liberal states, should depend so much on the preponderance of power in one state, and on its willingness to provide others with a variety of public goods. After all, the kind of liberal internationalism achieved through hegemony raises questions both about what happens "after hegemony," and about the fairness of the order thus established. But one has to go deeper and examine both why the "hegemon" acted as decisively as it did and why others were willing to accept some of the costs.

The reason is another paradox. Liberal internationalism, a vision of harmony that remained rather vague about how to reach nirvana, has been best at performing what might be called negative tasks. In the economic realm, this was, of course, exactly what the doctrines of laissez-faire demanded. Liberalism has—under the impulse of a hegemon for which self-interest and liberal conviction converged—succeeded in removing a vast number of barriers to trade and communication, and thus in establishing that transnational economic society that liberalism itself called for. The same result was achieved within the European Community, where many of the powers given up by the states have gone not to the new central institutions, but to the market. And there, progress resulted not from the hegemony of one power, but from a consensus among liberal regimes. In the political realm, however, liberalism, in order to reach its conception of peace, had to give priority to battle. Liberal internationalism has both fueled and supported the revolt against colonialism and imperialism, thus carrying forward Wilson's call that "no nation should seek to extend its polity over any other nation or people." Liberal internationalism has spoken up against violations of human rights, especially in the last 20 years. Above all, it waged a protracted cold war against Soviet totalitarianism in order to "contain" it, in the expectation, formulated in 1946–47 by George Kennan, that the Soviet system would eventually succumb to its internal flaws.

Thus the prelude to liberal harmony had to be a skillful exercise in limited war—limited both because of the liberal aversion to war and because of nuclear weapons. But it was the force of the totalitarian challenge that resolved the ambivalence of liberalism toward international activism and neutralized, for a long while, its noninterventionist potential. Even many of the "positive" missions accomplished by liberal internationalism after 1945—the democratization of Germany and Japan, the establishment of the European Community, the integration of the world capitalist economy—were undertaken or advanced as essential parts of the battle against the Soviet totalitarian threat. It was a remarkable fusion of realpolitik and liberal internationalism. But that fusion was not without strains. Some were over priorities: Was the containment of Soviet influence or of communism's expansion so overriding a goal that it left little space for the nurturing of liberal democracy in, say, Greece in 1967–74, in the Shah's Iran, or in Central American and Caribbean countries? Was the Soviet version of communism so dangerous that it became necessary to court and accommodate Moscow's communist rivals—especially in China—and to close one's eyes to the crimes committed by them against human rights? What should one do when anti-imperialism struck at interests America's main allies deemed essential (Suez), or when there was a dramatic confluence of communism and anti-imperialism (Vietnam)?

There was also a problem of means: Did not the battle against communism entail a risk of using distinctly "illiberal" methods, particularly in the realm of subversion or in so-called revolutionary wars like Vietnam? And there was one issue whose importance was barely realized in the momentous sweep of decolonization: The support the United States and liberals in Europe provided to the revolts against colonialism put the demand for self-determination (that is, against alien rule) ahead of any concern for self-government (that is, liberal democracy). These revolts resulted in the establishment of states within the borders arbitrarily drawn by the imperial powers, and amounted to a grant of self-determination not to nations, but often to heterogeneous collections of peoples living within these borders. . . .

## LIBERALISM'S MODERN PREDICAMENT

Basically, the plight of the liberal vision results from the fallacy of believing that all good things can come together. They rarely do, and many that were expected to be good have turned out rotten. More specifically, the liberal vision was focused on one particular enemy: the Moloch of power, wherever found, either arbitrary and excessive at home or imperial and militaristic abroad. Insofar as abuse of power is a hardy perennial, liberalism remains an indispensable source of inspiration and value. But there is another enemy in today's world: not the violence that results from the clash of mighty powers or from the imposition of the power of the strong on the weak, but the violence that results from chaos from below. The world today is threatened by the disintegration of power—by anomie, which denotes the absence of norms but can also refer to the collision of norms.

The Wilsonian edifice, its Rooseveltian version of 1945, the Bush coat of fresh paint of 1990, all were undertaken to deal with a world of interstate conflicts. All three assumed that the nature of the regime is a key determinant of state behavior: that liberal nation-states do not fight each other. It is difficult to provide decisive evidence for such a hypothesis, however, and neo-realists believe that the anarchic "structure" of international relations imposes the same kind of behavior on all states. But even if that hypothesis is true, wars among states are only one of the perils of the post–Cold War international system. What is now at stake is the very nature of the state. The "Westphalian" system that has inspired all theories of international relations presupposed well-determined states, clashing or cooperating. Both realism and liberalism shared that assumption; Marxism rejected it, but only because of its belief that the "logic" of state behavior was merely an expression of the logic, and contradictions, of capitalism—that states were, so to speak, puppets manipulated by the global economic system. Liberalism—or the U.N. Charter—finds it difficult to cope with a variety of phenomena: the disintegration of the Soviet Union and Yugoslavia; ethnic conflicts in the successor states; civil wars among rival ethnic, religious, or political factions in countries long ravaged by the Cold War (such as Cambodia or Afghanistan) or in much of Africa; the failure of many post-colonial states, especially in Africa but also in parts of Asia, to become nation-states; and the attempts by Islamic or Hindu fundamentalists to replace a secular with a religious and thus highly exclusionary definition of the state. To arrive at a world of liberal polities, there must be a clear idea of the state. If the world consists of disintegrating states, then the cooperative processes and institutions that are supposed to fuel harmony under the banner of liberal internationalism are easily overwhelmed by millions of refugees who flee massacres and disasters and seek asylum in liberal states, or call for protection whenever they cannot escape.

Liberal internationalism thus faces a predicament. First, it needs a set of clear principles to set goals. Yet, in two crucial respects all it finds is a cacophony of principles governing two issues that are anything but new: what to do about violations of human rights by tyrannical regimes—in places such as Haiti, Burma, or China—and how to react to the imposition of alien rule on reluctant peoples—such as the Kurds of Iraq (or Turkey), the Tibetans of China, the East Timorese of Indonesia. On both issues the old split about whether or not to intervene is a deep as ever. On balance, however, the noninterventionist impulse is strengthened by the disappearance of the Soviet threat and rationalized with the argument that the propagation of political liberalism will ultimately result from the spread of global economic liberalism. Thus, paradoxically, the principle of state sovereignty (which is not particularly liberal, since many states are not based on consent) is often given precedence over the liberal norms of self-government and of national self-determination. The old argument for nonintervention was that intervention even for liberal causes would multiply violent conflicts, whereas liberalism's aim was to dampen them. A new argument is that in a world where chaos is now a major peril, intervention even for good liberal causes may only create more chaos.

It is precisely in the realm of chaos I described above—the realm of disintegrating states—that the clash of norms is the most evident and paralyzing: Sovereignty (as a principle of order and, still, a barrier against aggressive or imperial designs), self-government or democracy, national self-determination (with all its ambiguities and flaws), and human rights (which are not devoid of ambiguities of their own, as debates over the priority of political over economic and social rights, and over the rights of individuals vs. the rights of peoples and groups indicate) are four norms in conflict and a source of complete liberal disarray. Human rights—the major strand of non-utilitarian liberalism—often cannot be protected without infringing upon another state's sovereignty, or without circumscribing the potential for a "tyranny of the majority" entailed by national self-determination and by Jacobin versions of democracy. The trouble-making potential of self-determination, both for interstate order and for human rights, is not so obvious that many liberals want to curb it or even get rid of it, yet the demand for its simply cannot be ignored, and denying its legitimacy would rarely be a recipe for order of democracy. Inconsistency is the result of this confusion: the international "community" has recognized Croatia, Bosnia, and Eritrea, but not Biafra, Chechnya, or the right of the Kurds and Tibetans to states of their own.

In a search for a thread that would allow them to set priorities and a strategy, liberal statesman receive little help from liberal philosophers. In his recent lectures, titled "The Law of Peoples," John Rawls fails to discuss the meaning of "peoples." Cosmopolitan liberals such as Martha Nussbaum, who stress the moral arbitrariness of borders (between states or between nations), step outside the limits of traditional liberalism (which saw the universal values of its creed realized in and through a world of states, not a world state). They also go far beyond what the moral traffic will bear. Communitarian liberals such as Michael Walzer are torn between the cosmopolitan and interventionist implications of their liberalism—when "domestic brutality, civil war, political tyranny, ethnic or religious persecution" become intolerable—and the noninterventionist and relativist implications of their communitarianism. What is needed, and still missing, is a complex and sophisticated rethinking of liberal internationalism; its Ariadne's thread would be human rights (including the right to participate in one's government, and the right to be part of, but not a slave to, national community). It would curtail sovereignty—so that the powers entailed by it could be shared at home and pooled abroad—and it would limit self-determination so that minorities everywhere could have a genuine choice between assimilation and protection of their distinctiveness, and so that the desire for self-rule need not take the form of full state sovereignty in every instance.

## INTERVENTION AND THE USE OF FORCE

Liberal internationalism is also in disarray over methods for defending or promoting its vision. Among liberals today, two sets of alternatives intersect. On the one hand, there is an argument over intervention. Some remain sufficiently suspicious of outside interventions (whether unilateral or collective) to prefer not stepping beyond humanitarian operations whose aim is to protect the victims of natural or manmade disasters. Others fear that the politics of band-aids will only allow the do-gooders to feel good, and leave unaltered the deeper causes of the disasters: murderous gangs and armies, as in Liberia, Somalia, and Rwanda; ethnic absolutists, like Serbs or Bosnian Serbs; tyrants such as Saddam Hussein, and so on. The logic of that viewpoint leads, of course, to far deeper foreign involvements, indeed to protectorates or trusteeships (Cambodia being one current example).

The other great division is over the use of force. Traditionally, liberalism has tried to limit legitimate force to self-defense and collective defense against aggression. But the scope of state chaos, as well as the murderousness of some contemporary tyrannies, has led many liberals to endorse in principle the idea of an outside resort to force whenever domestic chaos threatens the peace and security of other states (for instance through the mass flight of refugees) or whenever domestic chaos or tyrannical government results in massive violations of human rights, such as ethnic cleansing and genocide. Other liberals are doubly dubious about the resort to force because of a traditional tendency to look at it as an instrument of last resort only, and because of a conviction that many of these uses of force could only lead to quagmires and entrapments. Both sides often agree on the dispatching of U.N. peacekeepers, but when it comes to having these troops actually *use force* (except in self-defense), or to having "peace-builders" with missions far more extensive than peacekeepers, disagreement reappears. The Bosnia fiasco has been the result of all these cleavages. Bosnia has been the victim of the imbalanced compromise between those who gave priority to the restoration of peace, however unfair the solution may be, and those who gave priority to the suppression of what they saw as a double assault on liberal values: Serb aggression and ethnic cleansing.

A final predicament concerns not norms or methods, but agents. Who should be the secular arm of liberal action? Great powers (global or regional) claiming to act as enforcers of community norms inspire suspicion, even if, as in the case of India's intervention in Bangladesh, the ratio of self-interest to common good was clearly tilted toward the latter. There is a second problem with hegemonic enforcers: What happens when they choose not to act, failing to realize that the spread of chaos or the triumph of tyranny are antithetical to their interests as great powers? What has happened in the Clinton years, and may happen even more in the second, "Republican" half of the Clinton era, is ominous. Deprived of the relatively clear and widely shared goals that had pushed America to the fore of what was propagandistically called the free world, Washington has been left with Anthony Lake's laundry list of worthy goals, but appears incapable of turning them into a coherent strategy. The administration, sensing the reluctance of its public and Congress to have America play the role of world policeman, and marked by memories of Vietnam, suggested that if vital interests were not at stake, force would be used only multilaterally. But the story has been one of a double retreat: from military intervention (except in Haiti, where force was coupled with a very limited or ambivalent mandate) and from multilateralism—except when the latter made inaction or minimal action "legitimate," as in Bosnia. Unilateralism has become a way to appease anti-internationalists (a loose collection of realists and of American nationalists) and to justify doing very little.

The alternative to great powers as enforcers would be international organizations, but the lesson of recent years is that the United Nations tends to act effectively only when great powers provide the necessary leadership. When the powers are divided or predominantly reluctant, operations become fiascoes, as has been the case in Somalia and Bosnia, or too little and too late, as in Rwanda (largely because of American pressure to keep the intervention small in size and scope). The United Nations—like traditional liberalism—was designed for a world of interstate conflicts: Many of the tasks it has had thrust on it since 1991 therefore exceed its capacities. As an institution it suffers from the contradiction between a liberal vision that makes harmony depend on the right kind of state (liberal-national) on the one hand, and an international system that requires a heavy dose of international regimes and organizations aimed at overcoming the drawbacks of state sovereignty on the other. The fact that the U.N. has been provided neither with the enforcement institutions Chapter VII of the U.N. Charter had foreseen for collective security nor with a permanent force capable of preventive action or of peace-building in domestic crises has resulted both in calamitous conflicts of loyalty for the contingents that states placed at the U.N.'s disposal and in massive inefficiencies. It would be unfair to accuse liberals of having neglected international agencies, but the literature on regimes has focused much more on norms and institutions at the crossroads of interstate economic cooperation and the transnational world economy than on norms and institutions that deal with what I have called the domain of chaos. Liberals have also paid a lot of attention to agencies for the international protection of human rights. But the gap between liberal theory and practice on human rights is wide indeed. It is explained by the existence of so many states with skeletons in their closets and no desire to do more than pass resolutions on subjects as thorny as minority rights, political freedoms, the rights of migrants and refugees, and international criminal justice.

## THE RISE OF TRANSNATIONAL SOCIETY

So far, we have analyzed the plight of liberalism in the world of states. What about the other side of its vision for the planet: transnational society, constraining the capacity of states for evil? Insofar as world public opinion is concerned, Wilson's hopes have not been realized for many reasons. First, when one looks only at the public opinion of open and liberal societies, as expressed in their media, one finds a reflection of the diversity of ideological and religious positions, as over population issues. One also finds the diversity of national perspectives, such as the frequent American reluctance to look at economic and social rights as genuine claims. Second, this is still a world half free and half not. A large number of authoritarian regimes still control the formation and expression of public opinion. They succeed, especially in discussions of human rights issues, in hiding their abuses behind arguments for relativism and the defense of local customs and norms. A variety of economic issues has also put up road blocks on the way to Wilson's vision. In dealing with the problems of distributive justice associated with the allocation of wealth and resources among and within states, and with the intra- and intergenerational choices in environmental policies, liberalism has traditionally been rather silent. When it has raised its voice, it has been torn between its pure laissez-faire types who favor efficiency over equity, defend the status quo, and maintain their faith in the "trickle down" effects of growth on the one hand, and on the other more socially troubled or New

Dealish types who are eager to find safety nets for the poor, to orient free enterprise toward "sustainable human development," and to entrust international agencies with some redistributive functions and resources. As a result, on issues of singular importance for the vast majority of humankind, "world public opinion" has not been a cohesive force orienting governments. It has been divided—often along the lines of the rich vs. the poor, with significant elements in each camp crossing over and adopting the arguments of the other. And it has fluctuated over time. This is not to deny the importance of nongovernmental organizations in many areas and their capacity to graduate from "world public opinion" to "transnational actors." But one must face the limits as well.

The formation of global transnational economy constitutes a triumph of the liberal vision that first appeared in the eighteenth century (when philosophers saw private interests cutting across borders as potential tamers of clashing state passions), but it also provides evidence of the fact that fulfillment of the vision has mounting costs and unexpected consequences. Liberalism has always been a somewhat delicate coalition of two different perspectives on human nature. One of them emphasizes selfishness, defines interests in material terms, and celebrates the (general) benefits from individual greed. The other touts the moral aptitudes of human beings, focuses on rights and duties, and emphasizes both moral self-fulfillment and civic virtues. Many liberal philosophers—particularly the utilitarians—have tried to make the two strands converge. Much of the admiration Alexis de Tocqueville had for America came from his belief that here they had indeed been merged. Many of his doubts about liberal democracy's future came from his fears about the possible victory of greed and individual self-interest. It should not be surprising that in the drive to create a global economy through the dismantling of state barriers, concerns for human rights, democracy, or self-determination have often been submerged or twisted according to the highly debatable assumption that free economies must "ultimately" lead to free polities as well. The assumption may turn out to be correct, but it is fair to say that the jury is still out.

The new transnational economy has not merely, and beneficially, constrained the power of states. It has not only deprived them of much of their capacity to build command economies that ignore the signals given by markets and produce colossal inefficiencies. It has, alas, also deprived them of some of their ability to perform necessary tasks, to carry out basic functions liberalism never intended to remove from them. The free flow of drugs and the free circulation of crime have accompanied the formation of a global world economy. Governments find it difficult to restore against such "bad goods" the controls they have removed to facilitate the flow of the good ones. Moreover, the ability of governments to define their own monetary policies and to orient investments, employment, and growth has been seriously curtailed by the very size and weight of the transnational economy. The case of the European Monetary System and of its two huge crises in the summers of 1992 and 1993, when private capital movements played havoc with the exchange rates set up by the European Community and overwhelmed the efforts of central banks, is an extreme but important example of what is happening. The liberals of past centuries had thought primarily in terms of trade. We are now moving toward an integrated world market of trade, production, and distribution. The new world economy is made of national and multinational corporations operating across borders, and of millions of individual bond holders, shareholders, and holders of savings accounts in search of maximal and quick profits across borders. That has two effects, also unforeseen by liberal internationalism, and both contribute to the prevalence of chaos. One is the creation of a huge zone of irresponsibility: The global economy is literally out of control, not subject to the rules of accountability and principles of legitimacy that apply to relations between individuals and the state. States hesitate to impose their own rules unilaterally, out of fear of inefficiency and self-damage. Thus liberalism, successful in reducing the state's power, has created a formidable anonymous new power. It affects both states and individuals, but is treated as if it were merely an extension of the individual's sphere of protected freedoms. What is desperately needed is a theory that acknowledges the public aspects and effects of such private activities across borders and establishes a kind of common government for those activities—just as within civil societies liberalism aimed at setting up legitimate central institutions in order to rule out the flaws of a "state of nature." ...

Liberal internationalism has never been very good at specifying what liberal state interests were, beyond physical security and survival, and whether setting up an international system of liberal states was a vital interest, and not merely a legitimate aspiration, of liberal states. It has not been good at confronting the illiberal aspects of nationalism and the destructive potential of national self-determination. It has not paid enough attention to the contradiction between a cosmopolitan but uncontrolled world economy and a world of sovereign albeit cooperating states. Nor has it heeded the need for strong common institutions capable both of coping with whatever states cannot accomplish by themselves and of regulating what may soon be seen as a transnational Frankenstein monster.

Marxism is discredited. Realism promises only the perpetuation of the same old game and is no better equipped to face the politics of chaos than is liberalism. Liberalism remains the only comprehensive and hopeful vision of world affairs, but it needs to be thoroughly reconstructed—and that task has not proceeded very far, either in its domestic or its international dimensions.

# ACKNOWLEDGMENTS

1.1    From John Locke, *Two Treatises of Government* (1690). Notes omitted.

1.2    From Alexis de Tocqueville, *Democracy in America* (1835). Notes omitted.

1.3    From Robert N. Bellah, Richard Madsen, William M. Sullivan, Ann Swidler, and Steven M. Tipton, *Habits of the Heart: Individualism and Commitment in American Life* (University of California Press, 1985). Copyright © 1985 by the Regents of the University of California. Reprinted by permission. Notes omitted.

1.4    From Amitai Etzioni, *Rights and the Common Good: The Communitarian Perspective* (St. Martin's Press, 1995). Copyright © 1995 by St. Martin's Press, Inc. Reprinted by permission of Bedford/St. Martin's Press, Inc.

2.1    From James Madison, *Federalist*, Nos. 47, 48, and 51 (1788).

2.2    From Charles A. Beard, *An Economic Interpretation of the Constitution of the United States* (Macmillan, 1935). Copyright © 1935 by Macmillan Publishing Company; copyright renewed 1963 by William Beard and Miriam Beard Vagts. Reprinted by permission of Simon & Schuster. Some notes omitted.

2.3    From Gordon S. Wood, "The Intellectual Origins of the American Constitution," *National Forum: The Phi Kappa Phi Journal*, vol. 64, no. 4 (Fall 1984). Copyright © 1984 by Gordon S. Wood. Reprinted by permission of the publishers.

3.1    From *McCulloch v. Maryland*, 4 Wheaton 316; 4 L. Ed. 579 (1819).

3.2    From Samuel H. Beer, "Federalism, Nationalism, and Democracy in America," *American Political Science Review* (March 1978). Copyright © 1978 by The American Political Science Association. Reprinted by permission. Notes and references omitted.

3.3    From Daniel J. Elazar, "Opening the Third Century of American Federalism: Issues and Prospects," *The Annals of the American Academy of Political and Social Science*, vol. 509 (May 1990), pp. 12, 14–18, 20–21. Copyright © 1990 by The American Academy of Political and Social Science. Reprinted by permission of Sage Publications, Inc. Some notes omitted.

3.4    From Alice M. Rivlin, *Reviving the American Dream: The Economy, the States and the Federal Government* (Brookings Institution, 1992). Copyright © 1992 by The Brookings Institution. Reprinted by permission. Some notes omitted.

4.1    From John Stuart Mill, *On Liberty* (1859). Notes omitted.

4.2    From *Gideon v. Wainwright*, 372 U.S. 335; 83 S. Ct. 792; 9 L. Ed. 2d 799 (1963).

4.3    From *Lee v. Weisman*, 112 S. Ct. 2649 (1992).

4.4    From *Roe v. Wade*, 410 U.S. 113; 93 S. Ct. 705; 35 L. Ed. 2d 147 (1973). Notes omitted.

5.1    From Richard Kluger, *Simple Justice: The History of* Brown v. Board of Education *and Black America's Struggle for Equality* (Alfred A. Knopf, 1987). Copyright © 1975 by Richard Kluger. Reprinted by permission of Alfred A. Knopf, Inc.

5.2    From Jane J. Mansbridge, *Why We Lost the ERA* (University of Chicago Press, 1986). Copyright © 1986 by The University of Chicago. Reprinted by permission. Some notes omitted.

5.3    From *Korematsu v. United States*, 323 U.S. 214; 65 S. Ct. 193; 89 L. Ed. 194 (1944).

6.1    From James Madison, *Federalist*, No. 10 (1788)

6.2   From Burdett A. Loomis and Allan J. Cigler, "The Changing Nature of Interest Group Politics," in Allan J. Cigler and Burdett A. Loomis, eds., *Interest Group Politics,* 5th ed. (CQ Press, 1998). Copyright © 1998 by Congressional Quarterly, Inc. Reprinted by permission.

7.1   From Larry Sabato, "New Campaign Techniques and the American Party System," in Vernon Bogdanor, ed., *Parties and Democracy in Britain and America* (Praeger, 1984). Copyright © 1984 by Larry Sabato. Reprinted by permission of Greenwood Publishing, Inc., Westport, CT. Some notes omitted.

7.2   From James L. Sundquist, "Strengthening the National Parties," in A. James Reichley, ed., *Elections American Style* (Brookings Institution, 1987). Copyright © 1987 by The Brookings Institution. Reprinted by permission. Some notes omitted.

8.1   From V. O. Key, Jr., *The Responsible Electorate: Rationality in Presidential Voting, 1936-1960* (Harvard University Press, 1966). Copyright © 1966 by the President and Fellows of Harvard College. Reprinted by permission. Some notes omitted.

8.2   From Walter Dean Burnham, *Critical Elections and the Mainsprings of American Politics* (W. W. Norton, 1970). Copyright © 1970 by W. W. Norton & Company, Inc. Reprinted by permission. Some notes omitted.

8.3   From W. Lance Bennett, *The Governing Crisis: Media, Money, and Marketing in American Elections* (St. Martin's Press, 1992). Copyright © 1992 by St. Martin's Press, Inc. Reprinted by permission of Bedford/St. Martin's Press, Inc. Some notes omitted.

9.1   From Michael Parenti, *Inventing Reality: The Politics of the Mass Media* (St. Martin's Press, 1986). Copyright © 1986 by St. Martin's Press, Inc. Reprinted by permission of Bedford/St. Martin's Press, Inc. Some notes omitted.

9.2   From Kathleen Hall Jamieson and Karlyn Kohrs Campbell, *The Interplay of Influence: News, Advertising, Politics, and the Mass Media,* 3rd ed. (Wadsworth, 1992). Copyright © 1992 by Wadsworth, Inc. Reprinted by permission.

10.1  From David R. Mayhew, *Congress: The Electoral Connection* (Yale University Press, 1974). Copyright © 1974 by Yale University. Reprinted by permission. Some notes omitted.

10.2  From Richard F. Fenno, Jr., *Home Style: House Members in Their Districts* (Little, Brown, 1978). Copyright © 1978 by Little, Brown & Company. Reprinted by permission of Addison-Wesley Educational Publishers, Inc.

10.3  From Roger H. Davidson and Walter J. Oleszek, *Congress and Its Members,* 6th ed. (CQ Press, 1998). Copyright © 1998 by Congressional Quarterly, Inc. Reprinted by permission.

11.1  From Clinton Rossiter, *The American Presidency* (Harcourt, Brace, 1956). Copyright © 1956 by Clinton Rossiter; renewed 1988 by Mary Crane Rossiter, Winston G. Rossiter, David G. Rossiter, and Caleb S. Rossiter. Reprinted by permission of Harcourt, Brace & Company.

11.2  From Richard E. Neustadt, *Presidential Power and the Modern Presidents: The Politics of Leadership from Roosevelt to Reagan* (Free Press, 1990). Copyright © 1990 by Richard E. Neustadt. Reprinted by permission of The Free Press, a division of Simon & Schuster.

11.3  From Thomas E. Cronin and Michael A. Genovese, *The Paradoxes of the American Presidency* (Oxford University Press, 1998). Copyright © 1998 by Oxford University Press, Inc. Reprinted by permission.

**336**

*Acknowledgments*

12.1  From Hugh Heclo, *A Government of Strangers: Executive Politics in Washington* (Brookings Institution, 1977). Copyright © 1977 by The Brookings Institution. Reprinted by permission. Some notes omitted.

12.2  From James Q. Wilson, *Bureaucracy: What Government Agencies Do and Why They Do It* (Basic Books, 1989). Copyright © 1989 by Basic Books, a division of Harper-Collins Publishers, Inc. Reprinted by permission of Basic Books, a member of Perseus Books, L.L.C.

13.1  From *Marbury v. Madison*, 1 Cranch 137 (1803).

13.2  From Laurence H. Tribe, *God Save This Honorable Court: How the Choice of Supreme Court Justices Shapes Our History* (Random House, 1985). Copyright © 1985 by Laurence H. Tribe. Reprinted by permission of Random House, Inc.

14.1  From Aaron Wildavsky, *The New Politics of the Budgetary Process* (Scott, Foresman, 1988). Copyright © 1988 by Aaron Wildavsky. Reprinted by permission of Addison-Wesley Educational Publishers, Inc.

14.2  From Haynes Johnson and David S. Broder, *The System: The American Way of Politics at the Breaking Point* (Little, Brown, 1996). Copyright © 1996 by Haynes Johnson and David S. Broder. Reprinted by permission of Little, Brown & Company.

15.1  From Samuel P. Huntington, "The Erosion of American National Interests," *Foreign Affairs*, vol. 76, no. 5 (September/October 1997). Copyright © 1997 by The Council on Foreign Relations, Inc. Reprinted by permission of *Foreign Affairs*.

15.2  From Stanley Hoffmann, "The Crisis of Liberal Internationalism," *Foreign Policy*, no. 98 (Spring 1995). Copyright © 1995 by The Carnegie Endowment for International Peace. Reprinted by permission of *Foreign Policy*.

# Index

337